Dr. Gerard M. Verschuuren

130 Excel Simulations in Action

130 Excel Simulations to Model Gambling, Statistics, Monte Carlo Analysis, Science, Business, and Finance

Simulations in Action - 130 Excel Simulations
© 2018 Gerard M. Verschuuren
All rights reserved. No part of this book may be reproduced or transmitted in any form or by any means, electronic or mechanical, including photocopying, recording, or by any information or storage retrieval system without permission from the publisher.
Every effort has been made to make this book as complete and accurate as possible, but no warranty or fitness is implied. The information is provided on an "as is" basis.

The authors and the publisher shall have neither liability nor responsibility to any person or entity with respect to any loss or damages arising from the information contained in this book.

Author: Dr. Gerard M. Verschuuren

Cover Design: Shannon Travise

Layout: Bill Jelen

Printed in USA

ISBN 978-1978429871

I. TABLE OF CONTENTS

I.	TABLE OF CONTENTS	4
II.	INSTRUCTIONS	7
I.	GAMBLING	2
	Chapter 1: The Die Is Cast	2
	Chapter 2: Casting Six Dice	4
	Chapter 3: Roulette Machine	6
	Chapter 4: An X-O Game	8
	Chapter 5: A Slot Machine	10
	Chapter 6: Gamblers' Ruin	12
	Chapter 7: Lottery Numbers	14
	Chapter 8: Win or Lose?	16
	Chapter 9: A Letter Game (1)	18
	Chapter 10: A Letter Game (2)	20
	Chapter 11: A Game Board	22
	Chapter 12: A Gambling Strategy	24
	Chapter 13: A Three-Way Circuit	26
	Chapter 14: Flocking Behavior	28
II.	STATISTICS	30
	Chapter 15: Samples	30
	Chapter 16: A Normal Distribution	32
	Chapter 17: The Perfect Bell Curve	34
	Chapter 18: Types of Distributions	36
	Chapter 19: Peaks	38
	Chapter 20: Standard Error	40
	Chapter 21: Confidence Margins	42
	Chapter 22: Confidence Intervals	44
	Chapter 23: Power Curves	46
	Chapter 24: Sampling Sizes	48
	Chapter 25: Polling Errors	50
	Chapter 26: Flipping a Fair Coin?	52
	Chapter 27: Simulation of Sick Cases	54
	Chapter 28: Bean Machine Simulation	56
	Chapter 29: Correlated Distributions	58
	Chapter 30: Transforming a LogNormal Distribution	60
	Chapter 31: Bootstrapping	62
	Chapter 32: Outlier Detection	64
	Chapter 33: Chi-Squared Test	66
	Chapter 34: Unbiased Sampling	68
	Chapter 35: Sorted Random Sampling	70
	Chapter 36: Sorted Random Dates	72
III.	MONTE CARLO SIMULATIONS	74
	Chapter 37: The Law of Large Numbers	74
	Chapter 38: Random Walk	76
	Chapter 39: Brownian Motion	78
	Chapter 40: Ehrenfest Urn	80
	Chapter 41: A Data Table with Memory	82
	Chapter 42: Juror Selection in Court	84
	Chapter 43: Running Project Costs	86

	Chapter 44: Forecasting Profits	88
	Chapter 45: Uncertainty in Sales	90
	Chapter 46: Exchange Rate Fluctuations	92
	Chapter 47: Monte Carlo Stock Values	94
	Chapter 48: Monte Carlo Retirement	96
	Chapter 49: Monte Carlo and Pi	98
	Chapter 50: Integration Simulated	100
	Chapter 51: Two Monte Carlo Integrations	102
IV.	**GENETICS**	**104**
	Chapter 52: Shuffling Chromosomes	104
	Chapter 53: Sex Determination	106
	Chapter 54: Mendelian Laws	108
	Chapter 55: The Hardy-Weinberg Law	110
	Chapter 56: Genetic Drift	112
	Chapter 57: Two Selective Forces	114
	Chapter 58: Balanced Polymorphism	116
	Chapter 59: Differential Fitness	118
	Chapter 60: Random Mating	120
	Chapter 61: Molecular Clock	122
	Chapter 62: DNA Sequencing	124
V.	**SCIENCE**	**126**
	Chapter 63: Matrix Elimination	126
	Chapter 64: Interpolation	128
	Chapter 65: Extrapolation	130
	Chapter 66: Boltzmann Equation for Sigmoidal Curves	132
	Chapter 67: Rounding in Excel	134
	Chapter 68: Simple Decay Simulation	136
	Chapter 69: Radioactive Decay	138
	Chapter 70: Michaelis-Menten Equation	140
	Chapter 71: Chemical Equilibria	142
	Chapter 72: Spectrum Simulation	144
	Chapter 73: Oscillations	146
	Chapter 74: Ballistic Trajectories	148
	Chapter 75: Logistic Bacterial Growth	150
	Chapter 76: Predator-Prey Cycle	152
	Chapter 77: The Course of an Epidemic	154
	Chapter 78: Taking Medication	156
	Chapter 79: A Hawk-Dove Game	158
	Chapter 80: A Population Pyramid	160
	Chapter 81: False Positives	162
VI.	**BUSINESS**	**164**
	Chapter 82: Cycle Percentiles	164
	Chapter 83: Profit Estimates	166
	Chapter 84: Production Costs	168
	Chapter 85: Profit Changes	170
	Chapter 86: A Filtering Table	172
	Chapter 87: Risk Analysis	174
	Chapter 88: Scenarios	176
	Chapter 89: Market Growth	178
	Chapter 90: Target Analysis	180
	Chapter 91: Fiscal Year	182
	Chapter 92: Resource Allocation	184
	Chapter 93: A Traffic Situation	186
	Chapter 94: Quality Control	188
	Chapter 95: Logistics	190

  Chapter 96: Customer Flow 192
  Chapter 97: Project Delays 194

VII. FINANCE **196**
  Chapter 98: Smoothing Data 196
  Chapter 99: Investing Optimized 198
  Chapter 100: Return on Investment (ROI) 200
  Chapter 101: Fluctuating APR 202
  Chapter 102: Loan Payments 204
  Chapter 103: Buy or Sell Stock? 206
  Chapter 104: S&P500 Performance 208
  Chapter 105: Stock Market Analysis 210
  Chapter 106: Employee Stock Options 212
  Chapter 107: Stock Volatility 214
  Chapter 108: Net Present Value 216
  Chapter 109: Asian Options 218
  Chapter 110: Black-Scholes Model 220
  Chapter 111: Value at Risk (VaR) 222
  Chapter 112: Historical Value at Risk 224
  Chapter 113: Combined Value at Risk 226
  Chapter 114: Stock Price Movements 228

VIII. MISCELLANEA **230**
  Chapter 115: Numbering Records 230
  Chapter 116: Cracking a Password 232
  Chapter 117: Area Code Finder 234
  Chapter 118: Data Management 236
  Chapter 119: Chart Snapshots 238
  Chapter 120: Sizing Bins for Frequencies 240
  Chapter 121: Chart Markers 242
  Chapter 122: Scrolling Charts 244
  Chapter 123: Graph Manipulation 246
  Chapter 124: Creating Gradients 248
  Chapter 125: Summarizing in Steps 250
  Chapter 126: A Monthly Calendar 252
  Chapter 127: Comparison of Values 254
  Chapter 128: Letter Permutations 256
  Chapter 129: Metric Conversion 258
  Chapter 130: Probability of Beliefs 260

IX. APPENDIX **262**
  Sheet Navigation 262
  Locking Cell References 263
  Nested Functions 265
  Data Tables 267
  Simulation Controls 268
  Monte Carlo Simulations 269

X. INDEX **271**
  About the Author 275

II. Instructions

I assume that you are already familiar with many Excel features, including graphs or charts. In this book, I will only explain in more detail those features that are very helpful when you do what-if-analysis with simulations. For more basic features of Excel, I refer you to some learning tools that you can find on **www.mrexcel.com/microsoft-office-visual-learning.html**.

This book tells you how to create simulations exclusively with Excel functions and formulas, without using VBA. So this book is not about Visual Basic (VBA) or how to use VBA for simulations. To learn how to make simulations with VBA, I recommend my other book on simulations: **http://genesispc.com/tocsimulations100VBA.htm**.

If you want more information as to how to use Excel for scientific purposes, I would recommend the following book: **http://genesispc.com/tocscience2013book.htm**.

Finally a more general note. You may want to start with the **Appendix** section at the end of this book to become more familiar with some special Excel features that we use in this book for our simulations.

All simulations in this book are supported by files that you can download from the link that is mentioned on the last page of this book.

I. GAMBLING

Chapter 1: The Die Is Cast

What the simulation does

   We start with a very simple case of simulation—casting a die. In cell A1 is a formula that generates a random number between 1 and 6. According to that outcome, the colored die shows the appropriate number of eyes at their proper locations. Each time the random number changes, the die adjusts accordingly.

What you need to know

   Cell A1 has a formula that uses a volatile function called RAND. On each recalculation, this function generates a new random number between 0 and 1. Because we want numbers between 1 and 6, we need to multiply by 6, round the number down by using the INT function, and then add 1 to the end result. More in general: =INT((high-low+1)*RAND()+low).

   Users of Excel 2007 and later can also use the "easier" function RANDBETWEEN which has two arguments: one for the lower limit (in this case 1) and one for the upper limit (in this case 6). I decided not to use that function, because in pre-2007 Excel versions this function was only available through the *Analysis Toolpak*.

   To generate a new random number, you either hit the key *F9*[1] or the combination of the *Shift* key and the *F9* key. The *F9* key alone would recalculate all sheets in a file, which may take lots of calculating time. The combination *Shift F9* recalculates only the current sheet.

---

[1] On a Mac: *Fn 9*.

Finally, we need to regulate which eyes should pop up for each new random number. This is done inside some of the die cells by using the IF function. This function is a "decision maker," which determines whether a specific eye should be on or off.

What you need to do

1. Type in cell A1: =INT (RAND ()*6) + 1. In this case, the function RAND is "nested" inside the function INT (INT eliminates decimals). Nested functions are very common in Excel (for more information, see Appendix).
2. Type in B3: =IF (A1>1,0,""). The two double quotes in the last argument return an empty string, showing up as nothing.
3. Type in D3: =IF (A1>3,0,"").
4. Type in B5: =IF (A1=6,0,"").
5. Type in D5: =IF (A1=6,0,"").
6. Type in B7: =IF (A1>3,0,"").
7. Type in D7: =IF (A1>1,0,"").
8. Type in C5: =IF (OR(A1=1,A1=3,A1=5),0,""). In this case, the function OR is nested inside IF. The function OR returns "true" if any of the enclosed arguments is "true."

If you want to see all formulas at once, hit *Ctrl ~* (the tilde can be found below the *Esc* key). This shortcut toggles the sheet, back and forth, between value-view and formula-view.

	A	B	C	D	E
1	3				
2					
3		0			
4					
5			0		
6					
7				0	
8					

Chapter 2: Casting Six Dice

What the simulation does

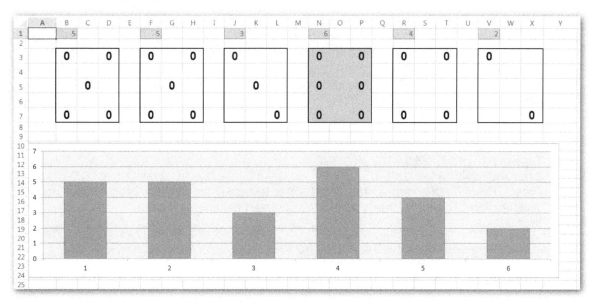

This time we have six different dice. Each die "listens" to a random number above it. The settings for each die are similar to what we did in the previous chapter. The number of eyes for each die is plotted in a column chart below the dice.

A die that shows six eyes gets marked with a color. When there are at least 2 dice in a row with six eyes, all dice get marked at the same time.

What you need to know

There is not much new on this sheet. The main difference is that we need 6 different cells with a RAND function in order to control the six die displays. Each die has the same structure as the one used in Chapter 1.

In addition, we use conditional formatting to change colors of the dice when they show six eyes, or contain at least two dice with six eyes.

What you need to do

1. Make sure all six dice are set up as was done in Chapter 1, but now each die is connected to the random cell just above it.
2. Select range B3:D7 first, then Home | Conditional Format | Formula: =$B$1=6.
3. Do something similar for the other five dice.
4. Finally select B3:X7 (that is, all six dice) and format them conditionally: =COUNTIF($B$1:$V$1,6)>=2.

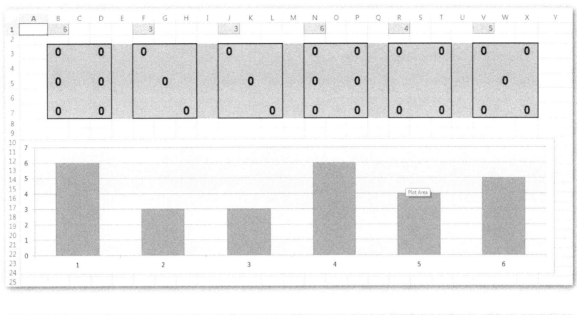

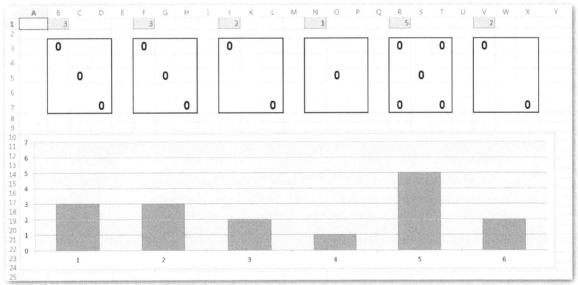

Chapter 3: Roulette Machine

What the simulation does

	A	B	C	D	E	F
1		1 (odd) or 2 (even)		Score:	0	
2	3	1			1	
3	7	1			2	
4	17	1			3	
5	1	1			4	
6	7	1			3	
7	12	1			2	
8	12					
9						
10						
11						
12						

Column A simulates a roulette with 1,000 random numbers between 1 and 36. In column B, you type 1 if you expect the next number to be odd—otherwise 2 for even.

Column E keeps the score: it adds 1, when your prediction was correct—otherwise it subtracts 1. Once you are finished, you can just empty your predictions in B2:B1001—and start all over (you may need *F9*, though).

What you need to know

Most people believe that if they keep consistently betting "odd," the ball will most certainly land on an odd number sometime soon. This is called "the law of averages or large numbers" which says, the longer you wait for a certain random event, the more likely it becomes.

Do not believe it! Try it out in this "real life" simulation and find out how the casino makes money on people who think that way. You may initially gain but eventually you'll lose.

What you need to do

1. Column A has 1,000 random numbers. They were once generated and then changed into values. You will not see all of them because 999 of them are hidden through conditional formatting.
2. Cell E2 has this formula: =IF (MOD(A2,2)=B2,E1+1,E1-1). Copy the formula down to E1001. The MOD function divides a number by 2 and returns the remainder. The remainder is either 0 or 1 here. If what the user had predicted in column B is correct, the score goes up by 1—otherwise down by 1.
3. Select range A3:A1001 and apply the following conditional formatting formula: =$B2="". Notice that B is locked but 2 is not (see Appendix on this issue). Format the entire range to a white font—which means you will not see this number if the cell in the next column of the previous row is still empty, but it will show its value once that cell has been filled with either 1 (odd) or 2 (even).
4. Validate range B2:B1001 with this custom formula: =OR ($B2=1,$B2=2). So the cell accepts only 1s or 2s.
5. Now you can make your predictions for every next roulette outcome—either 1 or 2. You may have to hit *F9* each time if the file has been set to manual calculation (or change that).
6. To start all over, just clear the colored cells in column B (and again you may have to manually recalculate the sheet).
7. Notice how easily you can lose by going for the "law of averages or large numbers" by repeating constantly 1 for "odd" or 2 for "even."

	A	B	C	D	E	F
1		1 (odd) or 2 (even)		Score:	0	
2	3	1			1	
3	7	1			2	
4	17	1			3	
5	1	1			4	
6	7	1			5	
7	12	1			4	
8	12	1			3	
9	35	1			4	
10	30	1			3	
11	23					
12						
13						

Chapter 4: An X-O Game

What the simulation does

	A	B	C	D	E	F	G
1	O	X	X	O	O		
2	O	X	O	X	X		
3	X	O	X	X	X		
4	O	X	X	O	X		
5	O	X	O	X	X		
6						no winner	
7							

This is a game with two players who "choose" either X or O randomly. They win when a row or column has the same entries, and the margin displays who won that particular row or column. If no one wins, cell F6 displays "no winner."

This is not a sophisticated game, for that would require Visual Basic code, which is beyond the scope of this book. As a result, the players X and O do not interact with each other, the game does not progress step by step, and there can be more than 1 winner. Sorry for these imperfections.

What you need to know

Since the upcoming formulas often have a reference to the very cell they are in—which causes a so-called "circular reference"—we need to turn iteration on and set it to 1: File | Options | Formulas | ☑ Enable iterative calculation | Maximum iterations 1.

	A	B	C	D	E	F
1	O	O	O	O	X	
2	O	O	X	O	X	
3	X	O	X	O	X	
4	X	X	X	O	O	
5	O	O	X	O	O	
6				O won		
7						

What you need to do

1. Set iteration to 1.
2. Select A1:E5, starting in A1, and insert the following formula: =IF(A1=0,IF(RAND()>0.5,"X","O"),A1).
3. Accept this formula with *Ctrl Enter*. The *Ctrl* key makes sure this formula goes into all the selected cells (see Appendix).
4. Place in F1: =IF(OR(COUNTIF(A1:E1,"X")=5,COUNTIF(A1:E1,"O")=5),E1 & " won","").
5. Copy this formula downwards to F5.
6. Place in A6: =IF(OR(COUNTIF(A1:A5,"X")=5,COUNTIF(A1:A5,"O")=5),A5 & " won","").
7. Copy this formula to the right, up to E6.
8. Place in F6: =IF(AND(COUNTBLANK(F1:F5)=5,COUNTBLANK(A6:E6)=5),"no winner","").
9. To run the game again, you must select A1:E5, click inside the formula bar, and hit *Ctrl Enter*.
10. Keep repeating these actions until you become bored.

	A	B	C	D	E	F	G
1	O	O	O	O	O	O won	
2	O	X	O	X	O		
3	O	O	X	X	X		
4	O	O	O	O	X		
5	O	X	O	X	X		
6	O won						
7							

Formula bar: =IF(A1=0,IF(RAND()>0.5,"X","O"),A1)

Chapter 5: A Slot Machine

What the simulation does

	A	B	C	D	E	F	G	H	I	J	K	L	M	N	O
1		run			0					cumulative					
2		7			1	2	-2	-2		-2			run 1	-0.20	
3					2	0	2	0		2			run 2	-0.40	
4	rerun through B2				3	1	0	2		3			run 3	-0.05	
5	20->false->1				4	-2	1	0		-1			run 4	0.70	
6	set iteration to 1				5	1	0	-1		0			run 5	0.15	
7					6	1	2	2		5			run 6	0.30	
8					7	0	-1	-1		-2			run 7	0.60	
9					8	1	-2	0		-1					
10					9	2	-2	2		2					
11					10	2	2	2		6					
12					11	2	-1	2		3					
13					12	-1	0	1		0					
14					13	-1	1	2		2					
15					14	2	-1	0		1					
16					15	-2	-2	0		-4					
17					16	-2	-2	0		-4					
18					17	2	-1	-2		-1					
19					18	2	1	-1		2					
20					19	-1	2	-2		-1					
21					20	1	0	1		2					

This simulation generates 20 runs for each game (columns F:H). Each run creates 3 random integer numbers between -2 and +2, and then calculates the cumulative total in column J. In columns M:N, we keep track of the average score of each run. After 20 runs, we start all over again with run 1 for game 1.

What you need to know

The tables E2:H21 and M2:N21 automatically expand with a new row after hitting *F9*. Once we reach the last row, the process starts all over again. Holding the *F9* key, makes you run through the game quite quickly.

To make all of this possible, we need nested IF functions, plus the ROW function (see Appendix for nested functions). Instead of RANDBETWEEN(-2,2), we could also use RAND here: -2+INT(RAND()*5). Take your pick.

Because most of these IF functions regulate the outcome in their very own cell, we need to avoid circular references by making sure iterations are ON, set to 1 iteration.

What you need to do

1. Turn iterations ON, set to 1 iteration.
2. Place in cell B2: =IF(B2=20,B2=1,B2+1).
3. Place in range E2:E21: =IF(ROW(A1)<=$B$2,ROW(A1),"").
4. Place in the next 3 columns (F2:H21): =IF($E2="","",IF(F2="",-2+INT(RAND()*5),F2)).
5. Place in cell J2:J21: =SUM(F2:H2).
6. Place in cell M2:M21: =IF(ROW(A1)>$B$2,"",IF(ROW(A1)=$B$2,"run "&$B$2,M2)).
7. Place the following nested formula in N2:N21, starting in N2: =IF(ROW(A1)>$B$2,"",IF(ROW(A1)=$B$2,AVERAGE($J$2:$J$21),N2)).
8. To run the game hit *F9*. You can do so repeatedly, or just hold *F9* down.
9. At the end of each run, cell B2 changes from 20 back to 1 while going through a brief FALSE position.

	A	B	C	D	E	F	G	H	I	J	K	L	M	N	O
1		run			0					cumulative					
2		20			1	-2	2	-1		-1			run 1	0.40	
3					2	0	2	0		2			run 2	0.60	
4	rerun through B2				3	-1	2	-2		-1			run 3	-0.25	
5	20->false->1				4	2	0	-2		0			run 4	-0.45	
6	set iteration to 1				5	0	-1	-1		-2			run 5	-0.60	
7					6	2	1	-1		2			run 6	-0.30	
8					7	1	1	2		4			run 7	0.65	
9					8	0	1	-1		0			run 8	-0.45	
10					9	-2	-1	0		-3			run 9	0.45	
11					10	-2	2	-1		-1			run 10	0.35	
12					11	-1	-2	-2		-5			run 11	-0.10	
13					12	-1	2	2		3			run 12	0.05	
14					13	1	0	-1		0			run 13	0.00	
15					14	-2	0	0		-2			run 14	0.35	
16					15	2	2	-1		3			run 15	0.50	
17					16	1	0	2		3			run 16	-0.25	
18					17	0	0	0		0			run 17	0.00	
19					18	-1	0	-2		-3			run 18	-0.90	
20					19	-2	1	0		-1			run 19	0.55	
21					20	-2	2	1		1			run 20	-0.05	

Chapter 6: Gamblers' Ruin

What the simulation does

	A	B	C	D	E	F	G	H	I
1	0			average	min	max	SD	final	
2	1			0.2	-7	10	5.152	-5	
3	2			-2.3	-11	3	3.404	-9	
4	3			0.7	-4	8	2.477	-1	
5	4			6.4	0	13	2.958	1	
6	5			4.1	-3	14	4.419	7	
7	6			5.9	0	12	2.544	1	
8	7			0.9	-5	6	2.712	3	
9	8			-2.0	-6	2	1.943	-1	
10	9			-0.5	-10	5	3.636	-9	
11	10			6.4	-2	12	2.620	7	
12	9			1.9	-3	12	3.287	11	
13	8			-2.2	-8	2	2.212	-3	
14	7			8.9	0	14	3.507	9	
15	6			-1.4	-9	4	2.886	-9	
16	5			5.8	-1	13	3.204	11	
17	4			0.7	-6	5	2.442	-1	
18	3			-7.2	-17	5	7.100	-15	
19	4			7.0	0	13	3.257	7	
20	5			12.7	-2	22	7.308	19	
21	6			-4.6	-19	5	6.827	-17	
22	5			-9.6	-17	0	4.250	-11	
23	6								
24	5						below	11	
25	4						above	10	
26	5								

This sheet simulates what may happen to people who are addicted to gambling. The player has 100 chances (in column A) to go for odd or even. We simulate a 50% probability for either choice. If the choice was correct, the count in column A goes up by 1, otherwise down by 1.

Next we simulate that this addicted player repeats the game for some twenty more times. For each game, we calculate average, minimum, maximum, standard deviation, and the final score (in column H). At the end, we calculate how often the player had a positive final score, and how often a negative one. This looks like much more work than it actually is…

What you need to know

In column A, we use the RAND function for each individual choice the player makes. Then we simulate doing this 20 more times in the right table. To do the latter, we use Excel's *Data Table* tool (see more details in Appendix). I consider this an ideal tool for *what-if* analysis.

How does it work? Usually *Data Table*s have one or more formulas in the first row—which would be cells D2:H2 in our case. Based on those formulas, a *Data Table* typically uses a row

Simulations in Action   GAMBLING

input of variables and a column input of variables to recalculate the formulas placed at its origin. It does so by filling the table cells with a formula that has the following syntax: =TABLE (row-input, col-input).

In this case we use a what-if table merely to trick Excel into simulating 20 (or many more) iterations of column A. We do so by not placing a formula at the origin, by just leaving the row-input argument empty, and having the col-input argument refer to an empty cell somewhere outside the table. Notice how the *Data Table* runs 20 x 100 choices each time you hit the *F9* key.

What you need to do

1. Place in cell A2: =IF(RAND()>0.5,A1+1,A1-1).
2. Copy this formula down for 100 rows.
3. Place in cell D2: =AVERAGE(A:A). Do something similar with MAX (in E2), MIN (in F2), and STDEV (in G2).
4. Place in cell H2 a reference to the last cell in column A: =A100.
5. Now select C2:H22 (yes, the empty cell C2, not D2).
6. Start the table: Data | What-If Analysis | *Data Table*.
7. Set the row input to nothing and the column input to an empty cell outside the table (say, J2).
8. This automatically places the following formula in the range D2:H22 (yes, D2 this time): {=TABLE (,J2)}. Do not type this formula or the braces—both kick in automatically.
9. The number of negative scores in H24: =COUNTIF ($H$2:$H$22,"<0").
10. The number of positive scores in H25: =COUNTIF ($H$2:$H$22,">0").
11. Select H2:H22: Home | Conditional Formatting | Data Bars (the last option not in pre-2007).

C	D	E	F	G	H
	average	min	max	SD	final
	0.8	-5	8	3.207	5
	3.6	-3	11	3.749	3
	-1.0	-8	8	3.581	-3
	3.3	-1	7	1.978	-1
	12.5	0	23	5.839	21
	7.4	-1	14	4.310	7
	-3.7	-9	3	2.891	-1
	-4.3	-14	5	4.938	1
	0.5	-9	8	4.029	-9
	-4.2	-8	0	1.445	-5
	5.9	-2	11	3.334	3
	-3.3	-9	0	2.555	-7
	9.5	-2	18	4.794	13
	-4.8	-10	3	2.908	1
	1.2	-4	7	2.783	-1
	-3.0	-13	4	4.257	-13
	10.8	0	18	5.000	13
	-2.1	-10	7	3.501	7
	8.5	-1	15	3.374	9
	2.5	-5	7	2.739	3
	1.3	-5	7	2.529	3
				below	8
				above	13

Chapter 7: Lottery Numbers

What the simulation does

	A	B	C	D
1	winning number		winning number	
2	552		552	
3				
4	buying ticket		buying ticket	
5	910		552	
6				
7	wins after n tickets		wins after n tickets	
8	1319		1066	
9				
10				

In this simulation, the cells A2 and C2 display what the winning 3-digit number is. Each time we run this simulation, Excel creates a new 3-digit *random* number in cells A5 and C5, until the buying ticket equals the winning number. In the meantime, it keeps track in cells A8 and C8 of the number of tickets that were bought so far.

What you need to know

Because we use formulas with circular reference, we need to turn iteration on.

Each random 3-digit number can be generated by *INT(RAND() * 1000)* or by using the newer function RANDBETWEEN. The *INT* function always rounds down to the nearest integer (0 – 9).

To show 1- or 2-digit numbers as 3-digit numbers, we need to format them as 001, 002, 010, 099, 111, etc.

When the number of the buying ticket matches the winning number, the cell changes color.

In this Excel file, we used the same number in cells A1 and C1 so as to show how different the number of tickets can be (A8 and C8) before we get a match, because there is randomness involved (see the opposite page).

Simulations in Action — GAMBLING

	A	B	C	D
1	winning number		winning number	
2	552		552	
3				
4	buying ticket		buying ticket	
5	552		552	
6				
7	wins after n tickets		wins after n tickets	
8	2064		1066	
9				
10				

What you need to do

1. Set iteration to 1.
2. Put a 3-digit validation range on cells A1 and C1: Data | Validation | Whole Number | Between 1 and 999.
3. To show those numbers in 3-digit format: R-click on cell | Format cells | Number | Custom | 000.
4. Place in cell A5:C5: =IF(A2=A5,A5,RANDBETWEEN(1,999)).
5. Place in cell A8:C8: =IF(A5=A2,A8,A8+1). Use conditional formatting on cells A5 and C5: Home | Conditional formatting | New Rule | Use formula | Set the fill color. In cell A5: =$A$5=$A$2. In cell C5: =$C$5=$C$2.
6. Once you have reached the target after holding or hitting *F9* repeatedly, you can start all over by selecting A5 and C5 separately, click in the formula bar, and hit *Ctrl Enter*. Do something similar for A8 and C8. Now you can start all over again.

	A	B	C	D
1	winning number		winning number	
2	552		552	
3				
4	buying ticket		buying ticket	
5	=IF(A2=A5,A5,RANDBETWEEN(1,999))		=IF(C2=C5,C5,RANDBETWEEN(1,999))	
6				
7	wins after n tickets		wins after n tickets	
8	=IF(A5=A2,A8,A8+1)		=IF(C5=C2,C8,C8+1)	
9				
10				

Chapter 8: Win or Lose?

What the simulation does

	A	B	C	D	E	F	G
1	START?	yes	/7/2017 6:56	total		score so far	
2			$0.07	$0.07		($1.77)	
3			($0.76)	($0.70)			
4			$0.59	($0.11)			
5			($0.79)	($0.90)			
6			$0.65	($0.25)			
7			($0.39)	($0.65)			
8			($0.27)	($0.92)			
9			($0.84)	($1.75)			
10			($0.92)	($2.67)			
11			$0.89	($1.78)			
12			($0.66)	($2.44)			
13			$0.83	($1.62)			
14			($0.54)	($2.16)			
15			($0.20)	($2.36)			
16			($0.49)	($2.85)			
17			$0.56	($2.29)			
18			$0.63	($1.66)			
19			$0.62	($1.03)			
20			($0.97)	($2.01)			
21			($0.27)	($2.28)			
22			$0.27	($2.01)			
23			($0.71)	($2.73)			
24			$0.66	($2.06)			
25			$0.29	($1.77)			
26							
27							

When the user sets cell B1 to "yes," Excel puts the current date and time in cell C1 and then begins consecutively entering new amounts of money between -2 and +2 dollars in the cells of column C, down to row 140.

In column D, the sheet calculates the total score after each new amount of money. In cell F2, it keeps track of the total amount the gambler has earned or lost so far.

When hitting *F9* doesn't change the total score anymore, the gambler has reached the last of 140 trials. By changing B1 to "no," the gambler can start all over again after setting B1 back to "yes." Now hitting *F9* begins adding new entries. There may be some delay, though.

What you need to know

The NOW function returns the serial number of the current date and time, whereas the TODAY function only returns the current date. (For dates, see also Chapter 126.)

The ROW function returns the row number of the cell it happens to be in—so ROW() in A10 would return 10. If you provide a cell reference as an argument, it returns the row number of that specific cell reference—so ROW(B25) in cell A10 (or in cell B1) would always return 25.

Two other new functions are COUNT and INDEX.

The COUNT function counts cells with a value in them.

The function INDEX is a more sophisticated version of VLOOKUP. It looks in a table at a certain row position and a certain column position. It uses this syntax: INDEX(table, row#, col#). Whereas VLOOKUP works only with column numbers, INDEX also uses row numbers, which is very important when we want to look at a record that is located X or Y rows above another record. In this case, we use COUNT to find the last cell with a value in it, and we ignore the column position, since there is only one column used here.

What you need to do

1. Put validation in cell B1: Data | Validation | Allow: List | Source: yes,no.
2. Place in cell C1: =IF(B1="no","",IF(C1="",NOW(),C1)).
3. Place in cells C2:C104: =IF(NOW()>$C$1+ROW()/50000, IF(C2="",1-2*RAND(),C2),"").
4. Place in cells D2:D104: =IF(C2="","",SUM($C$2:C2)). This is a combination of an absolute ("locked") and a relative ("unlocked") cell reference. (See Appendix for more information.)
5. Place in cell F2: =INDEX(D2:D140,COUNT(D2:D140)).
6. After you set B1 to "no," columns C and D display #VALUE!.
7. After you set B1 to "yes," hit *F9* to fill C1, and then keep hitting *F9* to add new entries, but there may be some delay depending on processing speed.

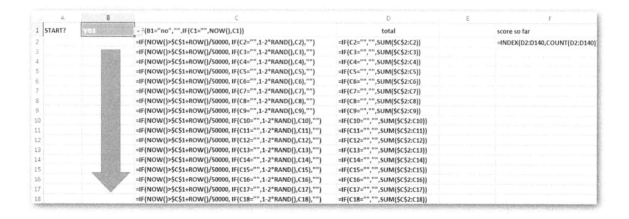

Chapter 9: A Letter Game (1)

What the simulation does

	A	B	C	D	E	F	G	H	I	J	K	L	M	N	O	P	Q
1	2-letters		X	A	Q	F	U	G	P	V	S	P			A	3	
2	NO		B	F	C	G	Y	U	M	Z	T	R			B	4	
3			W	G	G	R	B	N	U	N	D	F			C	3	
4			U	G	E	U	E	Z	B	D	Y	D			D	7	
5			I	A	W	K	H	J	Y	F	Z	Q			E	4	
6			Y	J	F	Z	K	S	J	I	B	U			F	6	
7			N	D	N	Q	A	T	O	D	V	N			G	5	
8			Y	N	D	S	P	S	Z	P	S	Q			H	1	
9			E	S	F	E	L	N	D	U	C	J			I	2	
10			Z	O	N	M	N	O	N	J	O	C			J	5	
11															K	2	
12															L	1	

On a "board" of 10 by 10, random letters appear each time we hit *F9*. If the word "NO"—or any other 2-letter word (see cell A2)—appears horizontally, the first letter (N) gets marked (see above); later we willl also mark the second letter (O), as shown on the opposite page.

In addition, column P keeps track of how often each letter was used, creating a uniform distribution, more or less equally distributed.

What you need to know

All capital characters have a so-called *asci* number between 65 and 90. There is a function called CHAR which returns the character that comes with a certain asci number. The capital letters A-Z run from asci numbers 65 to 90. (To find out what the asci number of a certain key is, you could use the function CODE; for instance, CODE("A") would give you the number 65; so CHAR(65) would return "A.")

Now we should be able to generate random numbers, and thus random capitals, between 65 and 90 by using either RANDBETWEEN(65,90).

As said before, there are various ways of replacing RANDBETWEEN with RAND. One is: ROUND(RAND()*(90-65)+65,0). Another one is: =INT((high-low+1)*RAND()+low). Or for a random integer between 0 and 3: =INT(RAND()*4). Or for a random integer between 1 and 4: =1+INT(RAND()*4). The function INT always rounds a number down to the nearest integer. RAND runs from 0 to 0.9999.

We use the ROW function again. ROW(A65) in cell O1 would return 65, but when copied downward to O2, it becomes A66 and would return 66, which is the asci number for letter B.

What you need to do

1. Put validation in cell A2: Data | Validation | Text length between 2 and 2. (Of course, you can increase the text length, but that may take much more time to get a match on the board.)
2. Place in C1:L10: =CHAR(RANDBETWEEN(65,90)).
3. Select C1:L10 and enforce conditional formatting: Home | Conditional formatting | New rule | Formula: =(C1&D1)=$A$2 | Choose a fill color.
4. This only highlights the 1st letter (in our case "N"). If you want also the 2nd letter highlighted, add a second condition: =(B1&C1)=$A$2.
5. Select O1:O26, starting in O1, and fill with: =CHAR(ROW(A65)).
6. Select P1:P26, starting with P1, and fill with: =COUNTIF($C$1:$L$10,O1).
7. Each time you hit *F9*, the letter board gets populated with new random letters. If the word "NO" is found in any row, the "N" will be marked in color. Sometimes, by mere chance, you may find more than 1 case of "NO" (see below).
8. Column P counts how often each letter appeared on the board.

	A	B	C	D	E	F	G	H	I	J	K	L	M	N	O	P
1	2-letters		H	F	A	Z	P	S	X	Z	T	T			A	5
2	NO		D	K	D	Q	C	Z	G	E	K	A			B	4
3			I	Z	U	W	E	P	S	A	Z	E			C	6
4			I	I	Y	O	G	K	C	S	B	Y			D	4
5			O	S	R	I	C	T	R	C	H	M			E	4
6			W	U	S	G	D	Z	H	Z	V	K			F	1
7			W	H	V	A	Q	N	S	C	Z	N			G	4
8			C	E	X	Z	O	D	B	Z	J	U			H	4
9			A	X	R	X	Y	B	U	J	Q	R			I	4
10			J	B	N	O	W	N	O	G	Q	Z			J	3
11															K	4
12															L	0
13															M	1
14															N	4
15															O	5
16															P	2
17															Q	4
18															R	4
19															S	6
20															T	3

Chapter 10: A Letter Game (2)

What the simulation does

	A	B	C	D	E	F	G	H	I	J	K	L	M	N	O	P	Q	R	S	T
1	2-letters		R	N	N	E	N	O	A	D	L	S		0	A	4			6	
2	NO		N	J	V	T	H	Q	N	E	O	K		4	B	3			4	
3			C	N	O	V	S	N	O	C	S	I		7	C	2			2	
4			N	A	F	P	S	E	W	A	G	R		9	D	3			2	
5			W	O	B	B	E	S	T	S	O	B		12	E	5			6	
6			F	O	H	V	A	O	O	L	N	N		17	F	2			4	
7			F	O	O	N	O	Z	F	O	O	O		19	G	2			2	
8			O	G	N	N	R	A	N	O	Z	V		21	H	3			2	
9			N	J	W	O	D	E	N	B	V	K		24	I	4			1	
10			R	A	E	N	V	N	J	S	N	T		28	J	2			3	
11														30	K	1			2	
12														31	L	2			2	
13														33	M	3			0	
14														36	N	20	N + O are heavily		19	
15														56	O	20	weighted		18	
16														76	P	3			1	
17														79	Q	1			1	
18														80	R	5			4	
19														85	S	4			7	
20														89	T	3			3	
21														92	U	2			0	
22														94	V	3			6	
23														97	W	2			3	
24														99	X	1			0	
25														100	Y	1			0	
26														101	Z	1			2	

This simulation is almost identical to the previous one, except for one big difference. The letters in our alphabet do not occur with equal frequencies. In regular English text, the E's and I's occur much more frequently than the X's and Z's, for instance.

We can simulate this by giving each letter a specific weight in column P. The letters with a higher weight—in our case, the N's and O's—have a higher chance of being chosen. So the letter board will usually show many more cases of "NO." And column S shows the real occurrences of each letter on the board.

What you need to know

New in this simulation is also the presence of column N. It calculates the cumulative chances for each character to be chosen. So cell N2 (!) has this formula: =SUM(P1:$P$1), which will change in the next cell down into =SUM(P2:$P$1). This is a combination of an absolute ("locked") and a relative ("unlocked") cell reference. (See Appendix for more information.)

Now VLOOKUP can find a random number between 0 and 102 in column N, and then return the corresponding letter from column O. So the number 3, for instance, would find the letter A in column O. VLOOKUP always searches vertically, from top to bottom, in the first column of a table and then finds a corresponding value in a column to the right, specified by a number. If there is no exact match, VLOOKUP always looks for the previous value in an ascending order. That's why there is an extra row after the letter Z.

GAMBLING

	A	B	C	D	E	F	G	H	I	J	K	L	M	N	O	P	Q	R	S
1	2-letter		=VLOOKUP(RANDBETWEEN(0,101),$N$1:$O$26, 2,TRUE)	=VL	=VL	=VL	=VL	=VL	=VL	=VL	=VL	=VL		0	=CHAR(ROW(B65))	4			=COUNTIF($C$1:$L$10,O1)
2	NO		=VLOOKUP(RANDBETWEEN(0,101),$N$1:$O$26, 2,TRUE)	=VL	=VL	=VL	=VL	=VL	=VL	=VL	=VL	=VL		=SUM(P1:$P$1)	=CHAR(ROW(B66))	3			=COUNTIF($C$1:$L$10,O2)
3			=VLOOKUP(RANDBETWEEN(0,101),$N$1:$O$26, 2,TRUE)	=VL	=VL	=VL	=VL	=VL	=VL	=VL	=VL	=VL		=SUM(P$1:$P2)	=CHAR(ROW(B67))	2			=COUNTIF($C$1:$L$10,O3)
4			=VLOOKUP(RANDBETWEEN(0,101),$N$1:$O$26, 2,TRUE)	=VL	=VL	=VL	=VL	=VL	=VL	=VL	=VL	=VL		=SUM(P$1:$P3)	=CHAR(ROW(B68))	3			=COUNTIF($C$1:$L$10,O4)
5			=VLOOKUP(RANDBETWEEN(0,101),$N$1:$O$26, 2,TRUE)	=VL	=VL	=VL	=VL	=VL	=VL	=VL	=VL	=VL		=SUM(P$1:$P4)	=CHAR(ROW(B69))	5			=COUNTIF($C$1:$L$10,O5)
6			=VLOOKUP(RANDBETWEEN(0,101),$N$1:$O$26, 2,TRUE)	=VL	=VL	=VL	=VL	=VL	=VL	=VL	=VL	=VL		=SUM(P$1:$P5)	=CHAR(ROW(B70))	2			=COUNTIF($C$1:$L$10,O6)
7			=VLOOKUP(RANDBETWEEN(0,101),$N$1:$O$26, 2,TRUE)	=VL	=VL	=VL	=VL	=VL	=VL	=VL	=VL	=VL		=SUM(P$1:$P6)	=CHAR(ROW(B71))	2			=COUNTIF($C$1:$L$10,O7)
8			=VLOOKUP(RANDBETWEEN(0,101),$N$1:$O$26, 2,TRUE)	=VL	=VL	=VL	=VL	=VL	=VL	=VL	=VL	=VL		=SUM(P$1:$P7)	=CHAR(ROW(B72))	3			=COUNTIF($C$1:$L$10,O8)
9			=VLOOKUP(RANDBETWEEN(0,101),$N$1:$O$26, 2,TRUE)	=VL	=VL	=VL	=VL	=VL	=VL	=VL	=VL	=VL		=SUM(P$1:$P8)	=CHAR(ROW(B73))	4			=COUNTIF($C$1:$L$10,O9)
10			=VLOOKUP(RANDBETWEEN(0,101),$N$1:$O$26, 2,TRUE)	=VL	=VL	=VL	=VL	=VL	=VL	=VL	=VL	=VL		=SUM(P$1:$P9)	=CHAR(ROW(B74))	2			=COUNTIF($C$1:$L$10,O10)
11														=SUM(P$1:$P10)	=CHAR(ROW(B75))	1			=COUNTIF($C$1:$L$10,O11)
12														=SUM(P$1:$P11)	=CHAR(ROW(B76))	2			=COUNTIF($C$1:$L$10,O12)
13														=SUM(P$1:$P12)	=CHAR(ROW(B77))	3			=COUNTIF($C$1:$L$10,O13)
14														=SUM(P$1:$P13)	=CHAR(ROW(B78))	20	N + O		=COUNTIF($C$1:$L$10,O14)
15														=SUM(P$1:$P14)	=CHAR(ROW(B79))	20	are		=COUNTIF($C$1:$L$10,O15)
16														=SUM(P$1:$P15)	=CHAR(ROW(B80))	3			=COUNTIF($C$1:$L$10,O16)

What you need to do

1. Put validation in cell A2: Data | Validation | Text length between 2 and 2. (Of course, you can increase the text length, but that may take much more time to get a match on the board.)
2. Place in cell N1: 0.
3. Place in cells N2:N27 (to include last entry): =SUM(P1:$P$1). This is a combination of an absolute ("locked") and a relative ("unlocked") cell reference. (See Appendix for more information.)
4. Place in cells C1:L10: =VLOOKUP(RANDBETWEEN(0,102),$N$1:$O$27,2).
5. Place in cells S1:S26: =COUNTIF($C$1:$L$10,O1).
6. Select cells C1:L10 and enforce conditional formatting: Home | Conditional formatting | New rule | Formula: =(C1&D1)=$A$2 | Choose a fill color.
7. Each time you hit *F9*, notice how the letter board usually shows several cases of "NO."
8. Notice also how column S remains close to column P.

	A	B	C	D	E	F	G	H	I	J	K	L	M	N	O	P	Q	R	S	T
1	2-letters		B	O	N	B	O	G	X	U	V	O		0	A	4			5	
2	NO		N	J	L	O	X	H	H	F	H	J		4	B	3			4	
3			N	O	F	O	W	R	O	P	N	I		7	C	2			0	
4			D	H	N	P	O	Y	R	B	V	P		9	D	3			2	
5			P	I	B	N	V	O	P	N	O	T		12	E	5			2	
6			I	I	Q	O	R	N	A	P	T	I		17	F	2			3	
7			A	N	F	N	N	N	N	H	E	S		19	G	2			1	
8			O	Z	N	D	S	N	O	A	T	U		21	H	3			5	
9			N	P	O	W	M	W	N	N	W	N		24	I	4			5	
10			N	L	O	T	E	A	R	A	S	O		28	J	2			2	
11														30	K	1			0	
12														31	L	2			2	
13														33	M	3			1	
14														36	N	20	N + O are heavily		20	
15														56	O	20	weighted		16	
16														76	P	3			7	
17														79	Q	1			1	
18														80	R	5			4	
19														85	S	4			3	
20														89	T	3			4	
21														92	U	2			2	
22														94	V	3			3	
23														97	W	2			4	
24														99	X	1			2	
25														100	Y	1			1	
26														101	Z	1			1	

Chapter 11: A Game Board

What the simulation does

	A	B	C	D	E	F	G	H	I	J	K	L	M	N
1	X	X	X	X	X					X		5	row	
2	X				X		X			X		4	column	
3	X	X	X	X		X				X				
4		X	X						X			46	X's	
5		X		X	X					X		982	trials	
6		X	X						X	X				
7	X					X								
8	X		X			X			X	X				
9		X	X	X				X		X				
10		X	X	X	X	X	X			X				
11														

This simulation randomly chooses a row (L1) and column (L2), and then places on the game board an X at their intersection. It keeps doing this until all 100 positions have been filled, and in the meantime it keeps track in M5 of the number of trials needed to reach this point.

What you need to know

To keep track of the number of trials, we need a formula in cell L5 that refers to itself. So we need to set iterations to 1. The number of trials is obviously determined by randomness.

To find the intersection of a specific row and a specific column, we need the AND function. This function has at least 2 arguments—in this case the row position (L1) and the column position (L2).

When the game board is completely filled, its background color changes.

	A	B	C	D	E	F	G	H	I	J	K	L	M	N
1	X	X	X	X	X	X	X	X	X	X		7	row	
2	X	X	X	X	X	X	X	X	X	X		10	column	
3	X	X	X	X	X	X	X	X	X	X				
4	X	X	X	X	X	X	X	X	X	X		100	X's	
5	X	X	X	X	X	X	X	X	X	X		584	trials	
6	X	X	X	X	X	X	X	X	X	X				
7	X	X	X	X	X	X	X	X	X	X				
8	X	X	X	X	X	X	X	X	X	X				
9	X	X	X	X	X	X	X	X	X	X				
10	X	X	X	X	X	X	X	X	X	X				
11														

What you need to do

1. Set iteration to 1.
2. Place in cell L1: =RANDBETWEEN(1,10).
3. Place in cell L2: =RANDBETWEEN(1,10).
4. Place in cell L4: =COUNTIF(A1:J10,"X").
5. Place in cell L5: =L5+1.
6. Select A1:J10, starting in A1: =IF(AND(ROW()=$L$1,COLUMN()=$L$2),"X",IF(A1=0,"",A1)).
7. Apply conditional formatting to range A1:J10: Home | Conditional formatting | New rule | Formula: =$L$4>=100 | Choose a fill color.
8. Hitting or holding *F9* fills the game board gradually with X's, until L4 = 100 and the background color of the game board changes. In the beginning the board fills much quicker than when we get closer to 100 X's.
9. To start from scratch again, select A1:J10, click in the formula bar, and hit *Ctrl Enter*.
10. Do something similar for cell L5 to set the counter back to 1. The number of trials is always one cycle behind, because we reset this range after cleaning the game board.

	A	B	C	D	E	F	G	H	I	J	K	L	M
1												4	row
2									X			3	column
3													
4			X									2	X's
5												1	trials
6													
7													
8													
9													
10													

Chapter 12: A Gambling Strategy

What the simulation does

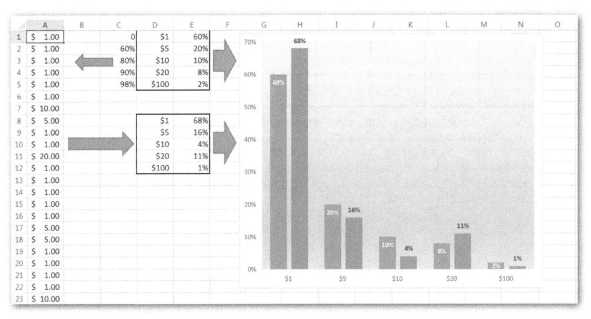

Let's pretend you are a persistent, but very systematic, gambler. You decide ahead of time how to spend your different kinds of banknotes, which is specified in range D1:E5. Of each pair of columns in the column chart, the *left* one displays these settings as well.

Then we let Excel determine one hundred times, in column A, when and which kind of banknotes to use and in which order. This is a random process, but within the margins set in D1:E5. The results are shown in the *right* column of each pair in the chart.

Although the process is random, it follows a discrete distribution which comes always very close to what you would expect as can be seen in range D8:E12.

What you need to know

In order to let column A determine which banknote to choose, we call the function RAND to create a random percentage between 0 and 1 (0% and 100%). Then the function VLOOKUP uses this percentage to find the corresponding type of banknote.

However, VLOOKUP always searches *vertically*, from top to bottom, in the *first* column of a table and then finds a corresponding value in a column to the right, specified by a *number*. So we need a lookup column before D1:D5 in order to determine the type of banknote to use. Besides, VLOOKUP looks for the previous value in an *ascending* order, so it would find $1 for all percentages between 0% and 60%, $5 between 60% and 80%, and $100 for percentages greater than or equal to 98%.

To make this happen, we need cumulative totals in the first column shown above, starting at 0%. The third column is now redundant, but is still needed for the chart to the right in order to show the expected frequencies—versus the randomly generated frequencies.

In order to calculate frequencies, we need the function FREQUENCY. This is a so-called *array* function. The function FREQUENCY returns an array of multiple answers based on a set of "bins." In this case, the bins are in column D. The function "reads" the bins as follows: 2 covers all cases up to and including 2, 3 covers all cases >2 and <=3, etc. To make this function work, you need to select all the cells that are going to hold the frequency values all at once, before you use the array function. Once the array function has been implemented with *Ctrl Shift Enter*[2], you will see the formula in the formula bar surrounded by braces—like this: {=FREQUENCY(...,...)}. Do not type the braces; they come automatically with *Ctrl Shift Enter*.

What you need to do

1. Place in cell C1 the number 0 (or 0%).
2. Place in cell C2: =SUM($E$1:E1). This is a combination of an absolute ("locked") and a relative ("unlocked") cell reference. (See Appendix for more information.)
3. Copy this formula down to C5. This creates cumulative totals.
4. Place in cell A1: =VLOOKUP (RAND(),$C$1:$D$5,2). Copy this formula down to cell A100. This formula does the random work in accordance with a frequency table (C1:D5), where it finds the corresponding type of banknote in column 2 (specified by the last argument in the function).
5. In order to calculate the actual frequencies for the various banknotes, we use the array function FREQUENCY in cells E8:E12: =FREQUENCY(A1:A100,D8:D12)/100. Make sure you select E8:E12 at once ahead of time, place the formula, and then accept this formula with *Ctrl Shift* Enter.

Each time you hit *F9*, column A updates, as do the right columns in the chart. Notice how close you stay to your preset expectations—but "results may vary," as the saying goes.

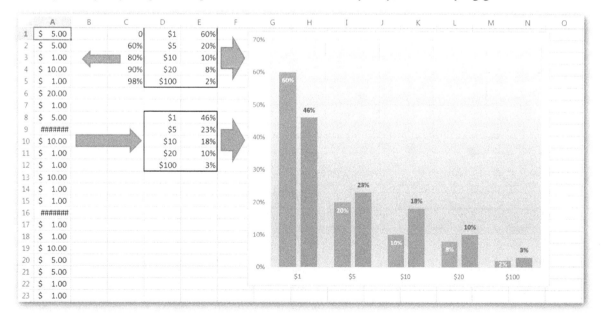

---

[2] On a Mac: *Command + Return* (or: ^ ↑ *Return*).

Chapter 13: A Three-Way Circuit

What the simulation does

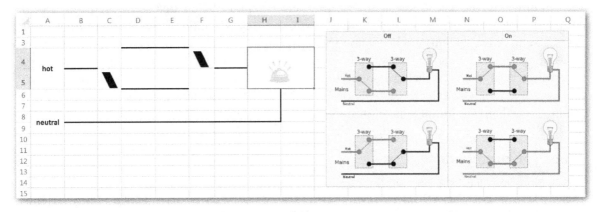

This sheet has a simulation of a three-way circuit, which is, for example, used when a light is regulated by two light switches. Either switch can turn the light on or off, but the connections have to be in a certain way, as explained in the diagrams to the right.

The position of the switches in column C and F is regulated randomly by either showing the switch with a black font or hiding it with a white font.

The icon in cells H4:J5 (merged) "lights up" when the switches have the proper position.

What you need to know

The "secret" of this simulation is located in cells C2 and F2 which are hidden in row 2.

The rest is done with conditional formatting.

To regulate whether the icon "lights up," we need a combination of an OR plus an AND function. OR returns true when either one or two arguments are true. AND returns true only when both arguments are true. (For nested functions see Appendix.)

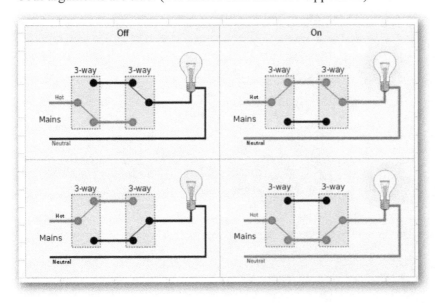

This is ON:

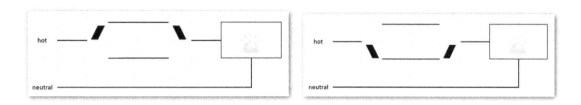

This is OFF:

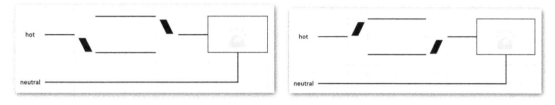

What you need to do

1. Place in cell C2: =IF(RAND()>0.5,"on","off").
2. Place in cell F2: =IF(RAND()>0.5,"on","off")
3. Hide row 2 by R-clicking on row 2 in the left margin and then selecting Hide.
4. In cell C4 conditional formatting: =$C$2="off" (set to white font).
5. In cell C5 conditional formatting: =$C$2="on" (set to white font).
6. In cell F4 conditional formatting: =$F$2="off" (set to white font).
7. In cell F5 conditional formatting: =$F$2="on" (set to white font).
8. In cells H4:J5 (merged), we place more sophisticated conditional formatting: =OR(AND($C$2="on",$F$2="on"),AND($C$2="off",$F$2="off")). Change the font color.
9. Hit *F9* to test all settings.

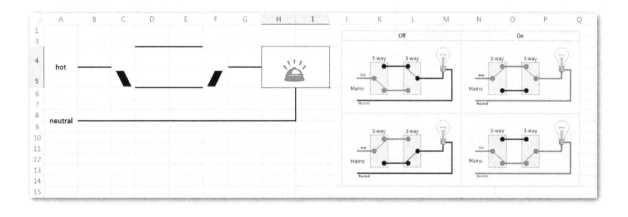

Chapter 14: Flocking Behavior

What the simulation does

	B	C	D	E	F	G	H	I	J	K	L	M	N	O	P	Q
1												chance	direction	count	majority	preference
2	↗	↘	↘	↖	↘	↘	↖	↘	↖	↗		0%	↖	31	-	
3	↗	↗	↗	↖	↗	↗	↙	↘	↗	↙		25%	↗	27	-	
4	↘	↘	↗	↖	↘	↘	↖	↖	↖	↘		50%	↘	22	-	
5	↗	↘	↖	↙	↗	↙	↗	↘	↙	↘		75%	↙	29	-	
6	↘	↗	↖	↙	↖	↖	↖	↗	↖	↘						
7	↖	↗	↖	↙	↘	↗	↗	↘	↘	↘						
8	↖	↖	↙	↙	↖	↙	↖	↖	↖	↗						
9	↗	↘	↖	↙	↙	↖	↘	↘	↖	↗						
10	↖	↖	↘	↖	↖	↙	↘	↘	↙	↗						
11	↖	↗	↙	↗	↗	↖	↖	↘	↗	↗						
12																

Flocking behaviorr is the behavior exhibited when a group of birds, called a flock, are foraging or in flight. There are clear parallels with the shoaling behavior of fish, the swarming behavior of insects, and herd behavior of land animals. It is considered the emergence of collective behavior arising from simple rules that are followed by individuals and does not involve any central coordination.

Scientists have demonstrated a similar behavior in humans. In their studies, people exhibited the behavioral pattern of a "flock": If a certain percentage of the flock changes direction, the others follow suit. In experiments, when one person was designated as a "predator" and everyone else was supposed to avoid him or her, the human flock behaved very much like a school of fish.

What you need to know

	B	C	D	E	F	G	H	I	J	K	L	M	N	O	P	Q
1												chance	direction	count	majority	preference
2	↘	↘	↘	↘	↘	↘	↘	↘	↘	↘		0%	↖	7	-	
3	↘	↘	↘	↘	↘	↘	↘	↘	↘	↘		25%	↗	8	-	
4	↘	↘	↘	↘	↘	↘	↘	↘	↘	↘		50%	↘	89	+	↘
5	↘	↘	↘	↘	↘	↘	↘	↘	↘	↘		75%	↙	1	-	
6	↘	↘	↘	↘	↘	↘	↘	↘	↘	↘						
7	↘	↘	↘	↘	↘	↘	↘	↘	↘	↘						
8	↘	↘	↘	↘	↘	↘	↘	↘	↘	↘						
9	↘	↘	↘	↘	↘	↘	↘	↘	↘	↘						
10	↘	↘	↘	↘	↘	↘	↘	↘	↘	↘						
11	↘	↘	↘	↘	↘	↘	↘	↘	↘	↘						
12																

We assume that all animals (100 in B2:K11) start randomly in one of four different directions (M2:N5). Once animals with a certain direction happen to gain a certain percentage (say, 35%), all the other animals follow suit.

In the range B2:K11 we place a VLOOKUP function that finds in M2:M5 a random number between 0 and 1, and then returns the corresponding direction arrow in column N. Once column O registers a count over 35, all cells in B2:K11 display that arrow, and the count becomes 100. In other words, the flock has "decided" in which direction to fly or to swim

Another new function is OFFSET. It returns an offset range of cells and has 5 arguments: OFFSET(start,row-offset,col-offset,#rows,#cols). The 1st argument determines where to start the range (e.g. P2). The 2nd argument controls the number of rows up (-) or down (+). The 3rd argument is the number of columns to the left or right (-2 in our case). The 4th and 5th arguments are optional and specify the numbers of rows (height) and the number of columns (width); left empty, the height and width are assumed to be the same as for the starting cell (in our case P2).

What you need to do

1. Make sure iteration is ON and set for only 1 iteration.
2. Place in cell O2:O5: =COUNTIF($B$2:$K$11,N2).
3. Place in cell P2:P5: =IF(O2>=35,"+","-").
4. Place in cell Q2:Q5: =IF(P2="+",OFFSET(P2,,-2),"").
5. The formula for range B2:K11 is a very long-winding one, so I split it in pieces to make it easier for you to understand better what the formula really does:
   =IF(COUNTIF($O$2:$O$5,100),
   VLOOKUP(RAND(),$M$2:$N$5,2),
   IF(COUNTIF($B$2:$K$11,$N$2)>=35,$N$2,
   IF(COUNTIF($B$2:$K$11,$N$3)>=35,$N$3,
   IF(COUNTIF($B$2:$K$11,$N$4)>=35,$N$4,
   IF(COUNTIF($B$2:$K$11,$N$5)>=35,$N$5,
   VLOOKUP(RAND(),$M$2:$N$5,2))))))
6. Because iterations have to be limited to one, the system sometimes lags one step behind when pressing the key *F9*.

M	N	O	P	Q
chance	direction	count	majority	preference
0	↖	=COUNTIF($B$2:$K$11,N2)	=IF(O2>=35,"+","-")	=IF(P2="+",OFFSET(P2,,-2),"")
0.25	↗	=COUNTIF($B$2:$K$11,N3)	=IF(O3>=35,"+","-")	=IF(P3="+",OFFSET(P3,,-2),"")
0.5	↘	=COUNTIF($B$2:$K$11,N4)	=IF(O4>=35,"+","-")	=IF(P4="+",OFFSET(P4,,-2),"")
0.75	↙	=COUNTIF($B$2:$K$11,N5)	=IF(O5>=35,"+","-")	=IF(P5="+",OFFSET(P5,,-2),"")

II. STATISTICS

Chapter 15: Samples

What the simulation does

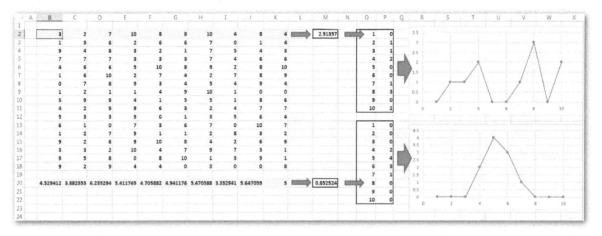

Each cell in the range B2:K18 holds a random number between 0 and 10. Columns O and P hold two frequency tables. The top one calculates frequencies for the 1st row (row 2 on the sheet), which are the values for a sample of 10 cases. The bottom one calculates frequencies for row 20, which holds the averages of each column based on a sample of 17x10=170 cases.

It is to be expected that the frequency curve for the large sample with 170 cases comes close to a normal distribution, whereas the curve for the small sample of 10 cases does not. At the end of this chapter is another outcome of the simulation. Notice how the top curve can be very different, whereas the bottom one stays rather close to a normal distribution.

What you need to know

As explained in Chapter 12, the FREQUENCY function is a so-called array function. That means in Excel, you have to select multiple cells at once (e.g. P2:P11) and accept the formula with *Ctrl Shift Enter* (on a Mac: Command + Return).

$$\sqrt{\frac{\sum(x-\bar{x})^2}{(n-1)}}$$

$$\sqrt{\frac{\sum(x-\bar{x})^2}{n}}$$

In column M, we calculate the standard deviation—which is a measure of how widely values are dispersed from their mean or average ($\bar{x}$). This can be done with the function STDEV. In Excel there are two versions: STDEV.S (called STDEV in older Excel versions), which is for samples, or STDEV.P (called STDEVP in older Excel versions) for the entire population. The difference is a matter of dividing by *n* for the population, or by *n-1* for a sample, where *n* stands for the sample size. For very large sample sizes, STDEV.S and STDEV.P return approximately equal values. If your data represents a sample of the population, then compute the standard deviation using STDEV.S.

Simulations in Action — STATISTICS

What you need to do

1. Select range B2:K18, starting in B2, and insert: =INT(RAND()*11).
2. Select range B20:K20, starting in B20, and insert: =AVERAGE(B2:B18).
3. Place in M2: =STDEV.S(B2:K2).
4. Place in M20: =STDEV.S(B20:K20). Even here we are not dealing with the entire population, but only a larger sample.
5. Select P2:P11 at once: =FREQUENCY(B2:K2,O2:O11), and accept with *Ctrl Shift Enter*.
6. Select P13:P22 at once: =FREQUENCY(B20:K20,O13:O22), and accept with *Ctrl Shift Enter*.
7. The top graph is linked to to top frequency table (for 1 sample).
8. The bottom graph is linked to to bottom frequency table (for an average of 10 samples).

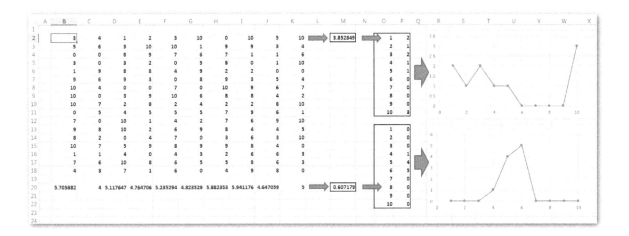

Chapter 16: A Normal Distribution

What the simulation does

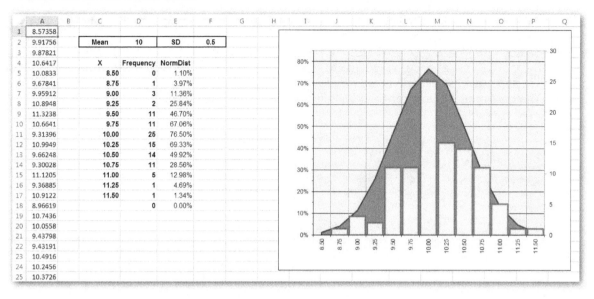

In this simulation, column A shows 100 random numbers, normally distributed, with a mean as shown in D2 and a standard deviation as shown in F2. Column C holds the bins we want to use for the values in column A. Column D calculates the frequencies for each bin, and column E displays what the corresponding normal distribution values would be.

Each time the user hits *F9*, the values in column A will be recalculated, which updates columns D and E.

In the chart, the background area chart is based on the columns C and E, whereas the column chart in front of the area chart uses data in the columns C and D. Since there is randomness involved, results may vary between succesive runs.

What you need to know

The key function in this simulation is NORMINV (or NORM.INV, if available). It calculates in column A the inverse of the normal cumulative distribution for the specified mean ($\bar{x}$) in D2 and the standard deviation (SD) in F2. It has 3 arguments: NORM.INV(probability,mean,SD). By using RAND for the first argument, we can simulate values according to a specific mean and SD.

The function NORMDIST in E returns the normal distribution for the specified mean in D2 and SD in F2. It has 4 arguments: NORMDIST(x,mean,SD,cumulative). If the argument cumulative is set to TRUE, then NORMDIST returns the *cumulative* distribution function.

We use the function FREQUENCY again. This time we also use an extra feature of this function. When you make its range one cell longer than its bins, this extra cell (D18) acts like a "garbage can"—it holds any values beyond the last bin. If the value of the bottom cell is not 0, then we must have overlooked a value higher than the last bin (11.50 in this case).

The column chart may seem shifted a bit to the right. That's because the frequency bins represent the "top" of the bin, and not its average.

What you need to do

1. Place in A1:A100: =NORM.INV(RAND(),$D$2,$F$2).
2. Select D5:D18 at once and insert: =FREQUENCY(A:A,C5:C17). Accept this formula for the entire selected range with *Ctrl Shift Enter*.
3. Place in E5:E18: =NORM.DIST(C5,AVERAGE(A:A),STDEV(A:A),FALSE).
4. Hit *F9* repeatedly to see random variations in the simulation. As to be expected, results may, and will, vary!

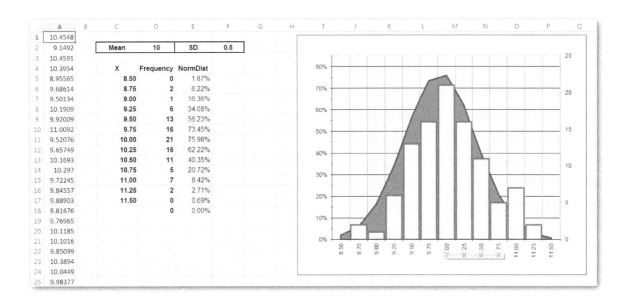

Chapter 17: The Perfect Bell Curve

What the simulation does

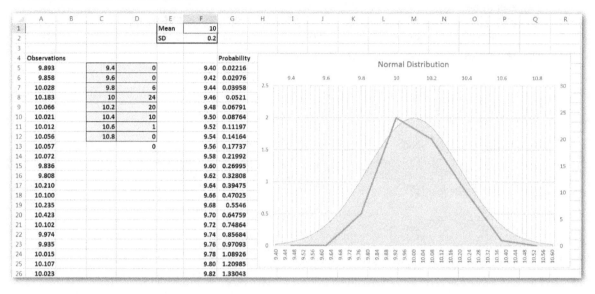

If you ever want or need the shape of a perfect "bell curve," use this simulation.

The bell curve is based on the columns F and G. This curve is rather "stable." The other curve reflects a series of 60 observations in column A, which are normally distributed according to the mean in cell F1 and the SD in cell F2. As to be expected, this curve shows some fluctuations.

What you need to know

To create a nice bell curve, we need a range running from 3x SD to the left of the mean to 3x SD to the right of the mean with some 60 steps. Formulas make that happen.

The observations in column A are done with NORM.INV again (see previous simulations). Next we calculate their frequencies in D5:D13 according to bins in C5:C12. These frequencies are plotted in front of the bell curve.

Because the two curves work with different scales, we also need a secondary X-axis and Y-axis in the chart. We won't go into all the details since that is not specific for this book.

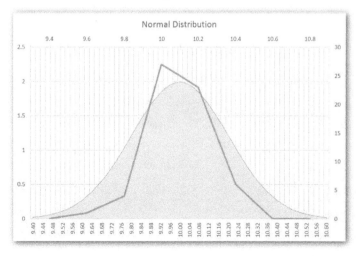

What you need to do

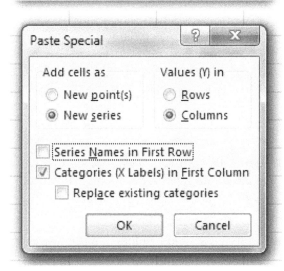

1. Place in cell F5: =$F$1-$F$2*3.
2. Place in cell F6: =F5+(6*$F$2)/60. Copy this formula downwards to cell F65. This adds 6x SD for 60 more rows
3. Place in range G5:G65: =NORM.DIST(F5,$F$1,$F$2,FALSE).
4. Create the bell curve based on these two columns.
5. Place in range A5:A65: =NORM.INV(RAND(),$F$1,$F$2).
6. Place in cells C5:D13 the formulas shown to the left.
7. Now we need to add the data of this frequency table to the chart. Here are the best steps:
    a. Copy C5:D12.
    b. Click inside the chart and use Paste Special with the settings shown to the left.
    c. R-click the peak chart: Change Chart Type | Give the 2nd chart a Line type | Click on its secondary axis icon.
    d. To create also a secondary X-axis: Go to the Design tab on top.
    e. Next: Add Chart Element (top left) | Axes | Secondary Horizontal.

Chapter 18: Types of Distributions

What the simulation does

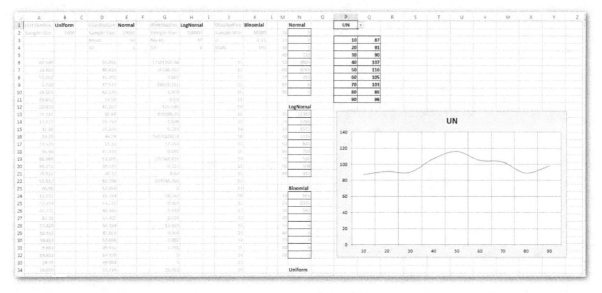

A *normal* distribution is just one type of distribution. Other ones are a *uniform* distribution, a *lognormal* distribution, and a *binomial* distribution. All these four types are randomly similated on this sheet in the columns A, D, G, and J. The frequency distributions for each distribution type are calculated in column N. The uniform distribution is shown in the picture above.

In cell P1, the user can select which one of the four types should be plotted in the line chart. The key *F9* will then simulate the chosen distribution again and again. Depending on the sample size in row 2 (running from 1,000 to 100,000), the resulting curve will be more or less stable.

All of this is done with a frequency table in P3:Q11, which is populated with one of the four frequency tables from column N, depending on what the user has selected in cell P1. And the chart is hooked up to the frequency table of range P3:Q11.

What you need to know

The functions to simulate a certain type of distribution are well covered in Excel:

RAND creates uniform distributions (column A).

NORM.INV creates normal distributions (column D).

LOGNORM.INV creates lognormal distributions (column G).

BINOM.INV creates binormal distributions (column J).

What you need to do

1. Place in cells A6:A100005: =IF(ROW(A1)<=$B$2,ROUND(RAND()*100,3),"").
2. Place in cells D6:D100005 the following heavily nested NORM.INV formula: =IF(ROW(D1)<=$E$2,ROUND(NORM.INV(RAND(),$E$3,$E$4),3),"").
3. Place in cells G6:G100005 the following heavily nested LOGNORM.INV formula: =IF(ROW(D1)<=$H$2,ROUND(LOGNORM.INV(RAND(),$H$4,$H$3),3),"")
4. Place in cells J6:J100005 the following heavily nested BINOM.INV formula: =IF(ROW(D1)<=$K$2,BINOM.INV($K$4,$K$3,RAND()),"").
5. Place in cells N2:N10: =FREQUENCY(D:D,$M$2:$M$10). The sum of all frequencies matches E2 (sample size).
6. Place in cells N13:N21: =FREQUENCY(D:D,$M$2:$M$10). The sum is much smaller than the sample size in H2, because the curve has a much longer tail to the right.
7. Place in cells N24:N32: =FREQUENCY(J:J,M24:M32). The sum reflects K2 (sample size).
8. Place in cells N35:N43: =FREQUENCY(A:A,M35:M43). The bins do not cover all values.
9. Put in cell P1 Data Validation: Data | Data Validation | List | Source: UN,ND,LN,BI.
10. Place in cell Q3:Q11: =IF($P$1="ND",N2,IF($P$1="LN",N13,IF($P$1="BI",N24,N35))).
11. The line chart is connected to this last frequency table.
12. You can change cell P1 and vary the sample sizes from 1,000 to 100,000.

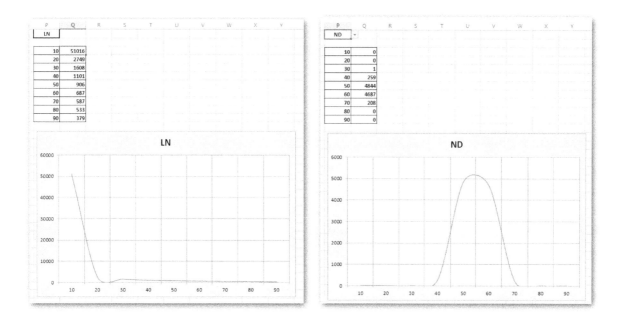

Chapter 19: Peaks

What the simulation does

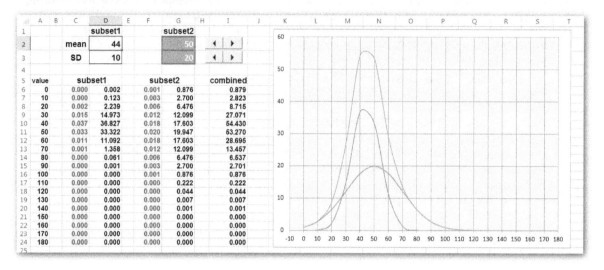

In this simulation we are dealing with a sample (values in column I) that is composed of two sub-samples (values in columns D and G). As long as the two sub-samples have the same mean, even with different standard deviations, the entire sample may look nicely symmetrical. But when the mean of one sub-sample is different, the symmetrical curve may easily lose its symmetry and may even become *bi-modal* (see facing page).

The sheet simulates this by using two controls (see Appendix) that change the mean and SD of subset2. Below is shown the situation when the mean of subset 2 changes from 50 to 70.

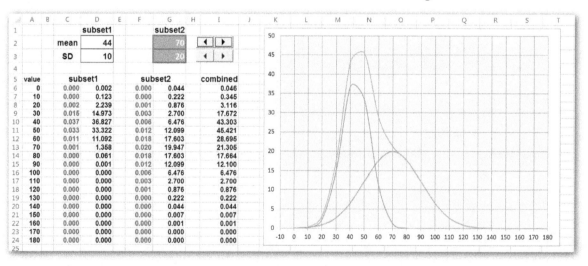

What you need to know

The symmetry of a curve is an important condition for many statistical tests such as the Students *t*-test (see Chapter 22) and the analysis-of-variance test (ANOVA). A normal distribution is typically symmetrical, but an asymmetrical distribution is called "skewed." Positive skewness indicates a distribution with an asymmetric tail extending toward higher values (to the right of the mean). Negative skewness indicates a distribution with an asymmetric tail extending toward lower values (to the left of the mean). Although there are techniques to "normalize" skewed data sets, that issue is beyond the scope of this book.

What you need to do

1. Place two spinbutton controls next to cells G2 and G3 (see Appendix).
2. The first one: Min 40 | Max 100 | SmallChange 10 | LinkedCell G2.
3. The second one: Min 14 | Max 20 | SmallChange 2 | LinkedCell G3.
4. Place in cells C6:C24: =NORMDIST (A6,$D$2,$D$3,FALSE).
5. Place in cells D6:D24: =C6*1000.
6. Place in cells F6:F24: =NORMDIST (A6,$G$2,$G$3,FALSE).
7. Place in cells G6:G24): =F6*1000.
8. Place in cells I6:I24): =D6+G6. This represents the value for the total population based on its two subgroups.
9. The figure below simulates what happens to the curve of the total population when the mean of a subpopulation changes to 100 (in cell G2) and then becomes bi-modal.
10. Be aware: Since the main population does no longer have a normal distribution, standard statistical techniques for significance, etc., may no longer be valid.

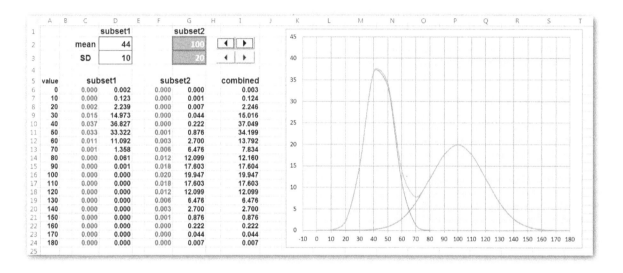

Chapter 20: Standard Error

What the simulation does

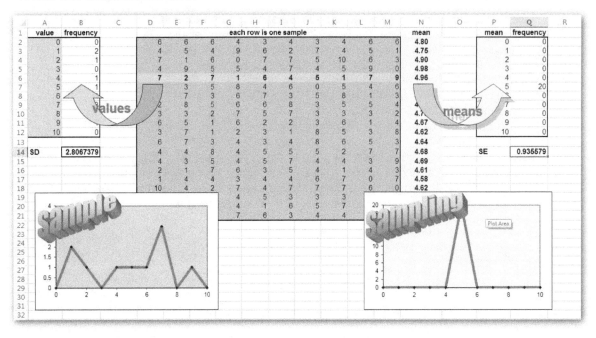

The center part of this simulation shows 20 rows of 10 random numbers between 0 and 10. However, the frequency tables on both sides differ from each other. The left one calculates frequencies for one specific sample—in this case, the sample of 10 cases in row 6. The right one calculates frequencies for the means of all 20 samples.

Notice how the graph to the right displays a curve that usually comes close to a normal distribution, whereas the one to the left does not at all. The difference is crucial: The left one shows a *sample* distribution, but the right one a *sampling* distribution

What you need to know

In science, we usually deal with a single sample of a very limited size, whereas statistics wants to deal with situations where the samples are much larger.

In order to say something statistically significant about a *sample* distribution (to the left), we need a way to assess what the *sampling* distribution (to the right) would be like.

Two important measures for a sample distribution are the average (or mean) and the standard deviation (or SD). Most of the times, all we have on hand are the mean and standard deviation as found in the *sample* (to the left). So, to get a *sampling* distribution, we have to obtain an *estimate* of the SD of the means based on the SD of the observations.

We do so by calculating the standard error (SE), also called the relative SD. The formula for the SE is as follows: $=SD/\sqrt{n}$ or $=SD/\sqrt{(n-1)}$. There is a battle of "n versus n-1." Some divide by the square root of n, others by the square root of n-1. Why? They call the first one "biased," as it is always off, in the long term, by a very small amount from its target value, so they "tweak" it by subtracting 1. Take your pick; in this book we go for $\sqrt{n-1}$.

As you can gather from this formula, SE decreases when the sample size increases—and, of course, when SD decreases. Notice the difference between SD (in B14) and SE (in Q14).

In normal distributions, deviations from the mean are expressed in SE-units, typically ranging from -3 x SE to +3 x SE. Significance testing is often done with ±1.96 x SE.

What you need to do

1. Range D2:M21: =INT(NORM.INV(RAND(),5,2)).
2. Range B2:B12: =FREQUENCY (D6:M6,A2:A12).
3. Range Q2:Q12: =FREQUENCY (N2:N21,P2:P12).
4. Cell B14: =STDEV.S (D6:M6). There is also a function STDEV.P, which is appropriate when dealing with the entire population, instead of one of its samples.
5. Cell Q14: =B14/SQRT (10-1). This calculates the sampling SE based on the sample SD divided by the square root of n-1 cases.
6. Hit *F9* to see new simulations. The left graph may vary wildly, but the right one remains more or less stable, staying close to a normal distribution (see below).

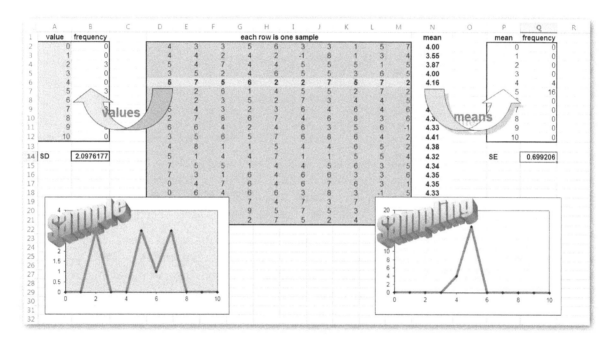

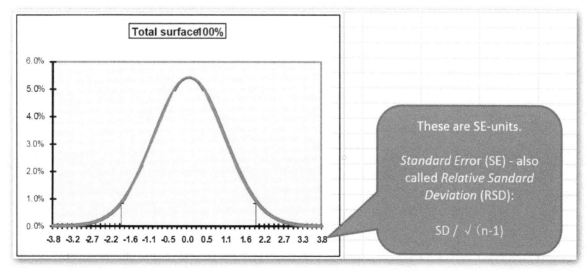

These are SE-units.

*Standard Erro*r (SE) - also called *Relative Sandard Deviation* (RSD):

SD / √ (n-1)

Chapter 21: Confidence Margins

What the simulation does

	A	B	C	D	E	F	G	H	I	J	K	L	M
1	Mean	4.5								-3.0	0.1%	3.30	
2	SD	0.4								-2.7	0.3%	3.42	
3	Size	35								-2.4	0.8%	3.54	
4	2-tailed error level	5%		row	6	4.25 to 4.75	4.25			-2.1	1.8%	3.66	
5	Confidence margin	0.13		column	1		4.75			-1.8	3.6%	3.78	
6										-1.5	6.7%	3.90	
7	95% conf. margin	4.37 to 4.63	30	35	40	45	50	Size		-1.2	11.5%	4.02	
8		0.2	4.43 to 4.57	4.43 to 4.57	4.44 to 4.56	4.44 to 4.56	4.44 to 4.56			-0.9	18.4%	4.14	
9		0.3	4.39 to 4.61	4.40 to 4.60	4.41 to 4.59	4.41 to 4.59	4.42 to 4.58			-0.6	27.4%	4.26	
10		0.4	4.36 to 4.64	4.37 to 4.63	4.38 to 4.62	4.38 to 4.62	4.39 to 4.61			-0.3	38.2%	4.38	
11		0.5	4.32 to 4.68	4.33 to 4.67	4.35 to 4.65	4.35 to 4.65	4.36 to 4.64			0.0	50.0%	4.50	
12		0.6	4.29 to 4.71	4.30 to 4.70	4.31 to 4.69	4.32 to 4.68	4.33 to 4.67			0.3	61.8%	4.62	
13		0.7	4.25 to 4.75	4.27 to 4.73	4.28 to 4.72	4.30 to 4.70	4.31 to 4.69			0.6	72.6%	4.74	
14		0.8	4.21 to 4.79	4.23 to 4.77	4.25 to 4.75	4.27 to 4.73	4.28 to 4.72			0.9	81.6%	4.86	
15		0.9	4.18 to 4.82	4.20 to 4.80	4.22 to 4.78	4.24 to 4.76	4.25 to 4.75			1.2	88.5%	4.98	
16		1.0	4.14 to 4.86	4.17 to 4.83	4.19 to 4.81	4.21 to 4.79	4.22 to 4.78			1.5	93.3%	5.10	
17		SD								1.8	96.4%	5.22	
18										2.1	98.2%	5.34	
19										2.4	99.2%	5.46	
20										2.7	99.7%	5.58	
21										3.0	99.9%	5.70	
22													

This simulation calculates the confidence margin based on data collected through a sample (B1:B3). These figures can be manually changed. We assume a 5% 2-tailed error level. Based on this information, the sheet calculates a 95% chance that the values in the real population or in a new sample taken from that population lie between the two values shown in cell B7.

Using a *Data Table*, we repeat this calculation for different sample sizes (30-50) and for different SDs (0.2 to 1.0). Then we have the simulation select a cell in the Data Table through a random row number (E4) and a random column number (E5). The Data Table highlights one or more cells that correspond to cell F4. In columns J:L we highlight the range between the two confidence intervals.

What you need to know

The function CONFIDENCE in Excel returns the confidence interval for a population mean, using a normal distribution. Its syntax is: CONFIDENCE(alpha,standard_dev,size).

It works best for sample sizes over 32 (which is the case here). Cell B5 uses the CONFIDENCE function. In this case, it has the following arguments: the alpha error (in this case 5% error chance in B4, so 95% confidence), the SD (which CONFIDENCE transforms automatically into SE-units), and the size of the sample. It returns the margin on both sides of the mean, if we accept a 5% error chance.

In this case we used a 2-tailed error level of 5% (2.5% for each tail), which equates to a 95% confidence level. This means we have a 95% confidence that the vales we found in this sample lie actually between the two values mentioned in the origin cell of the *Data Table* (which equates to the mean *plus* the confidence margin and the mean *minus* the confidence margin). Notice how confidence margins depend heavily on sample size (in the top row of the table) and standard deviation (in the left column of the table).

In column K we use the function NORMSDIST (or NORM.S.DIST). It returns the standard normal cumulative distribution function, with a mean of 0 (zero) and a standard deviation of 1. The function has one argument: the distance from the mean in SE units. In column L, we "inverse" the probabilities from column K back to "real" values with NORM.INV.

What you need to do

1. Place in cell B5: =CONFIDENCE(B4,B2,B3).
2. Place in cell B7: =TEXT(B1-B5,"0.00") & " to " & TEXT(B1+B5,"0.00").
3. Select range B7:G16 and implement a *Data Table* (see Appendix) with a row input of B3 and a column input of B4: =TABLE(B3,B2).
4. Place in cell E4: =RANDBETWEEN(1,9).
5. Place in cell E5: =RANDBETWEEN(1,5).
6. Place in cell F4: =INDEX(C8:G16,E4,E5).
7. Place in cell G4: =VALUE(LEFT(F4,4)).
8. Place in cell G5: =VALUE(RIGHT(F4,4)).
9. Select range C8:G16 and implement conditional formatting: =C8=$F$4.
10. Place in cells J1:J21 the SEs that run from -3 to +3.
11. Place in cells K1:K21: =NORM.S.DIST(J1).
12. Place in cells L1:L21: =NORM.INV(K1,$B$1,$B$2).
13. Select range J1:L21 and implement conditional formatting with a formula and a fill color of your choice: =AND($L1>=$G$4,$L1<=$G$5).
14. Hitting F9 selects a different cell in the table and a new range in J:L.
15. You can also manually change the cells B1:B3.

	A	B	C	D	E	F	G	H	I	J	K	L	M
1	Mean	4.5								-3.0	0.1%	3.30	
2	SD	0.4								-2.7	0.3%	3.42	
3	Size	35								-2.4	0.8%	3.54	
4	2-tailed error level	5%		row	3	4.36 to 4.64	4.36			-2.1	1.8%	3.66	
5	Confidence margin	0.13		column	1		4.64			-1.8	3.6%	3.78	
6										-1.5	6.7%	3.90	
7	95% conf. margin	4.37 to 4.63	30	35	40	45	50	Size		-1.2	11.5%	4.02	
8			0.2	4.43 to 4.57	4.43 to 4.57	4.44 to 4.56	4.44 to 4.56	4.44 to 4.56		-0.9	18.4%	4.14	
9			0.3	4.39 to 4.61	4.40 to 4.60	4.41 to 4.59	4.41 to 4.59	4.42 to 4.58		-0.6	27.4%	4.26	
10			0.4	4.36 to 4.64	4.37 to 4.63	4.38 to 4.62	4.38 to 4.62	4.39 to 4.61		-0.3	38.2%	4.38	
11			0.5	4.32 to 4.68	4.33 to 4.67	4.35 to 4.65	4.35 to 4.65	4.36 to 4.64		0.0	50.0%	4.50	
12			0.6	4.29 to 4.71	4.30 to 4.70	4.31 to 4.69	4.32 to 4.68	4.33 to 4.67		0.3	61.8%	4.62	
13			0.7	4.25 to 4.75	4.27 to 4.73	4.28 to 4.72	4.30 to 4.70	4.31 to 4.69		0.6	72.6%	4.74	
14			0.8	4.21 to 4.79	4.23 to 4.77	4.25 to 4.75	4.27 to 4.73	4.28 to 4.72		0.9	81.6%	4.86	
15			0.9	4.18 to 4.82	4.20 to 4.80	4.22 to 4.78	4.24 to 4.76	4.25 to 4.75		1.2	88.5%	4.98	
16			1.0	4.14 to 4.86	4.17 to 4.83	4.19 to 4.81	4.21 to 4.79	4.22 to 4.78		1.5	93.3%	5.10	
17		SD								1.8	96.4%	5.22	
18										2.1	98.2%	5.34	
19										2.4	99.2%	5.46	
20										2.7	99.7%	5.58	
21										3.0	99.9%	5.70	
22													

Chapter 22: Confidence Intervals

What the simulation does

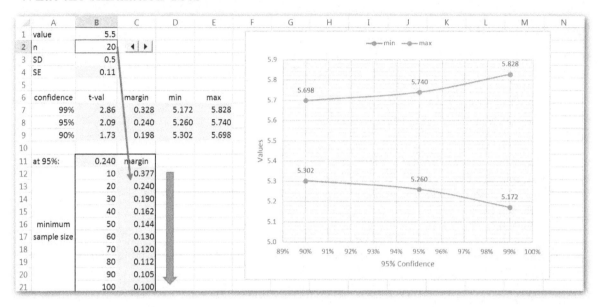

For samples with a size below 32, the function CONFIDENCE is no longer reliable. Instead we should use the Student's t-Test, which covers all sample sizes, even below 32.

In this simulation we calculate the minimum and maximum values (columns D and E) that we can accept with a 95% confidence for sample sizes ranging from 10 to 100. The minimum value is the mean *minus* the margin; the maximum value is the mean *plus* the margin. Notice how the margin decreases when the sample size increases (cells B11:D21).

The chart is based on the minimum and maximum values in columns D and E for three different confidence levels (99%, 95%, and 90%). A level of 95% is usually standard. The chart obviously changes when we change the sample size in B2 by using a spinbutton control.

What you need to know

Keep in mind that t-values are SE units. (SE is explained in Chapter 20). To calculate SE in B4 use: SD/SQRT(n-1).

To calculate the t-value at a certain confidence level, we use the function T.INV.2T. It returns the two-tailed inverse of the Student's t-distribution with the following syntax: T.INV.2T(probability,deg_freedom). Because T.INV.2T uses two tails, you must look for the t-value that comes with the 5% area outside the confidence area of 95%. Had you used the one-tailed version, T.INV, based on 2.5%, you would have gotten the same result, but this time negative.

The *t*-distribution can be used for any sample *size*. It does so by using *degrees of freedom*— which is the sample size minus 1 ($df = n - 1$). When the sample size increases, the *t*-curve becomes steeper, and high *t*-values become more unlikely. To put it differently, the x-axis of *t*-values extends farther to the right when the samples become smaller.

What you need to do

1. Place a spinbutton next to cell B2: Min 10 | Max 100 | SmallChange 5 | LinkedCell B2.
2. Place in cell B4: =B3/SQRT(B2-1). SE is explained in Chapter 20.
3. Place in cells B7:B9: =T.INV.2T(1-A7,$B$2-1).
4. Place in cells C7:C9: =B7*$B$4.
5. Place in cells D7:D9: =$B$1-$B7*$B$4.
6. Place in cells E7:E9: =$B$1+$B7*$B$4.
7. Place in cell B11: =C8.
8. Select range B11: C21 and implement a *Data Table* with a row input of D11 and a column input of B2: =TABLE(D11,B2).
9. The chart displays the min and max values for 3 levels of confidence.
10. Notice that the two curves get closer and closer when the sample size increases.

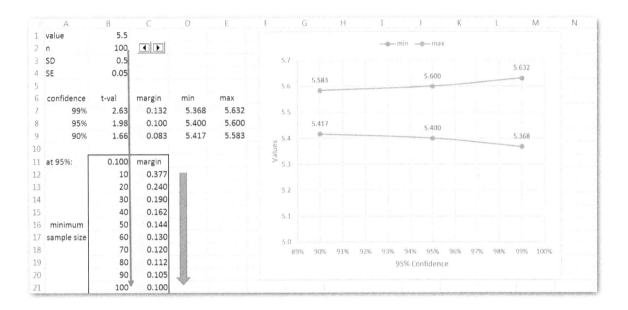

Chapter 23: Power Curves

What the simulation does

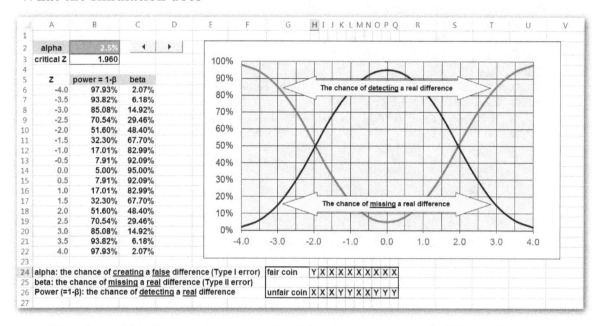

This simulation allows you to change the alpha error in B2 with a spinbutton in order to see how this affects the beta curve and the power curve. To do so, cell B3 calculates a *z*-value, which represents the number of SE-units around the mean in a normal distribution. All *z*-values are SE-units. So the critical *z*-value, or number of SE-units, is 1.96 (B3) for an error chance of 2.5% on one end and 2.5% on the other end of the curve—which gives us a confidence of 95%.

What you need to know

Here is some statistical terminology. *Alpha* stands for the chance of creating a false difference (Type I error). *Beta* represents the chance of missing a real difference (Type II error). Power (=1-β) stands for the chance of detecting a real difference. The up-curve represents *beta*, the down-curve is the *power* curve.

Let's use the analogy of a coin test (see also Chapter 26). A Type I error represents the situation where the coin was actually fair, but your data led you to conclude it was not, just by mere chance (H24:Q24). To reduce this chance, we can lower *alpha*. A Type II error represents the situation where the coin was actually unfair, but your data did not provide enough evidence to catch it, just by chance (H26:Q26). To lower this chance we must raise the sample size.

In cell B3, the function NORM.S.INV or NORMSINV (notice the S in the center) returns a *z*-value for a specific probability as shown in B2. The *z*-value is -1.96 at the 2.5% end (left of the mean); it is +1.96 at the 97.5% end (right of the mean).

Something similar holds for NORM.S.DIST. It returns the probability for a specific *z*-value. Remember *z*-values are SE-units.

What you need to do

1. Place a spinbutton next to B2 (see Appendix): Min 10 | Max 100 | SmallChange 5 | LinkedCell C2 (not B2). Cell B2 has the following formula: =C2/1000.
2. Place in cell B3: =ABS (NORMSINV (B2)). The ABS function eliminates the minus sign for z-values left of the mean.
3. Place in cells C6:C22): =(NORMSDIST ($A6+B$3)-NORMSDIST($A6-B$3)).
4. Place in cells B6:B22): =1-C6.
5. Place in cells H24:Q24: =IF(RAND()>0.5,"X","Y").
6. Place in cells H26:Q26: =IF(RAND()>0.3,"X","Y").
7. Changing alpha to 5% or 10% should have quite an impact; see below how the curves changed.

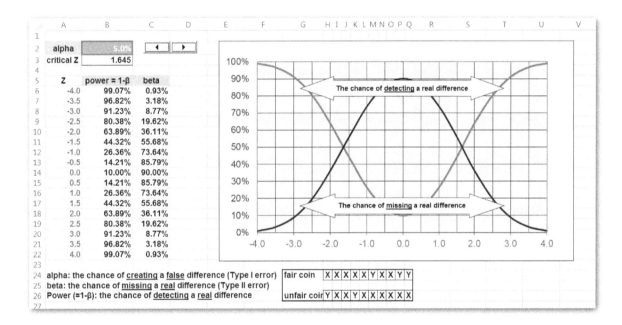

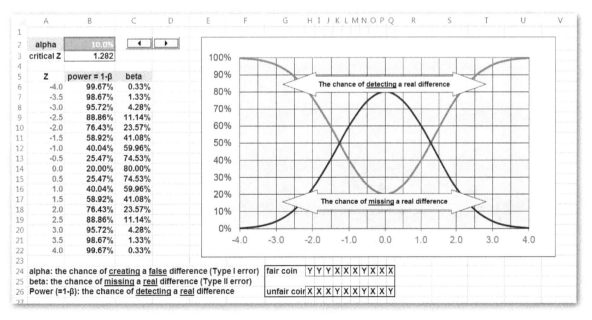

Chapter 24: Sampling Sizes

What the simulation does

	A	B	C	D	E	F	G	H	I	J	K
1	Mean	40									
2	SD	10	◄ ►	10-15			larger margin of error (relative to mean)				
3	Margin	4	◄ ►	1-5							
4									margin/mean		
5	SD/mean	0.25			24		0.025	0.050	0.075	0.100	0.125
6	margin/mean	0.1									
7					0.250		384	96	43	24	15
8	Min. sample size	24			0.275		465	116	52	29	19
9					0.300		553	138	61	35	22
10				larger SD (relative to mean)	0.325		649	162	72	41	26
11					0.350	SD/mean	753	188	84	47	30
12					0.375		864	216	96	54	35
13					0.400		983	246	109	61	39
14					0.425		1110	278	123	69	44
15					0.450		1245	311	138	78	50
16					0.475		1387	347	154	87	55
17					0.500		1537	384	171	96	61
18					0.525		1694	424	188	106	68

The basic question behind this simulation is: How large should the sample be in order to discover a certain significant difference? Based on an error margin of 4 (B3), and given a certain mean (B1) and a certain SD (B2) the answer is: a sample of at least 24 cases (B8).

Based on the formula shown below, the table in the middle was constructed with two dimensions—a vertical dimension for different ratios of SD/mean and a horizontal one for different ratios of margin/mean.

Changing one or more cells in range B1:B3, calculates a new minimum sample size and highlights that value in the table. Two spinbutton controls help us to do so.

What you need to know

The formula that allows us to calculate the minimum sample size is shown in the figure below. It uses the ratio of SD/mean and the ratio of margin/mean. This formula is used in cell B8 and E8.

$$n = \left(\frac{1.96}{margin/\mu}\right)^2 \left(\frac{SD}{\mu}\right)^2$$

What you need to do

1. Place a spinbutton next to cell B2: Min 10 | Max 15 | SmallChange 1 | LinkedCell B2.
2. Place a spinbutton next to cell B3: Min 1 | Max 5 | SmallChange 1 | LinkedCell B3.
3. Cell B8: =((1.96/B6)^2)*(B5^2). The value 1.96 is based on 95% confidence.
4. Cell E5: =B8.
5. Place in range E5:K18 a *Data Table* with B6 for row input and B5 for column input. Be aware that column F and row 6 in the table do have TABLE formulas, but they are not functional and can be hidden with a white font.
6. There is conditional formatting for range $E$7:$E$18: =AND ($B$5>$E6,$B$5<=$E7). This highlights the chosen SD/mean value.
7. There is conditional formatting for range $G$5:$K$5: =AND ($B$6>F$5,$B$6<=G$5). This highlights the chosen margin/mean value.
8. Select the cell range $G$7:$K$18 and apply conditional formatting by using as formula with 2 nested AND functions: =AND(AND($B$5>$E6,$B$5<=$E7),AND($B$6>F$5,$B$6<=G$5)). This highlights the minimum sample size.
9. Change any of the cells B1:B3 and watch the results. A smaller error margin and a larger SD (in relation to the mean) would require a much larger sample size (see below).

	A	B	C	D	E	F	G	H	I	J	K
1	Mean	40									
2	SD	15		10-15			larger margin of error (relative to mean)				
3	Margin	1		1-5							
4									margin/mean		
5	SD/mean	0.375			864		0.025	0.050	0.075	0.100	0.125
6	margin/mean	0.025									
7					0.250		384	96	43	24	15
8	Min. sample size	864			0.275		465	116	52	29	19
9					0.300		553	138	61	35	22
10					0.325		649	162	72	41	26
11					0.350	SD/mean	753	188	84	47	30
12					0.375		864	216	96	54	35
13					0.400		983	246	109	61	39
14					0.425		1110	278	123	69	44
15					0.450		1245	311	138	78	50
16					0.475		1387	347	154	87	55
17					0.500		1537	384	171	96	61
18					0.525		1694	424	188	106	68

Chapter 25: Polling Errors

What the simulation does

	A	B	C	D	E	F
1		Calculate Margin of Error (ME)				
2	Sample Size (n)	1000				
3	Proportion (p)	79%				
4						
5	confidence	z-value	SE	ME		
6	99.0%	2.33	0.013	3.0%		
7	97.5%	1.96	0.013	2.5%		
8	95.0%	1.64	0.013	2.1%		
9						
10						
11		Calculate Minimum Sample Size (n)				
12	Proportion (p)	79%				
13	Margin (ME)	2.5%				
14						
15	confidence	z-value	(ME/z)^2)	p*(1-p)	n	
16	99.0%	2.33	0.000115	0.1659	1437	
17	97.5%	1.96	0.000163	0.1659	1020	
18	95.0%	1.64	0.000231	0.1659	718	
19						

This simulation calculates what the margin of error is when pollsters use surveys. It all depends on the size of the polling sample. The size can be regulated in cell B2 with a scrollbar control. For instance, when 79% of the people in a sample of 1000 is for or against something, then the margin of error (ME) is as shown in D6:D8 for three different confidence levels (A5:A8).

What this means is this: A poll having a margin of error of 2.5% means that if you ran that poll 100 times—asking a different sample of people each time—the overall percentage of people who responded the same way would remain within ±2.5% of your original result in at least 95 of those 100 repeated polls.

When using the scrollbar control, notice that smaller samples lead to larger error margins.

The second half of the simulation does the opposite. It determines how large the sample should be if we want to reach a specific error of margin. When using the spinbutton control for ME, notice the obvious—that smaller error margins require larger samples.

If you notice small discrepancies between cells B2 and E17, you should realize that cell B13 has a rounded value, whereas cell D7 does not.

What you need to know

$$ME = z\sqrt{\left(\frac{p(1-p)}{n}\right)}$$

The formula to calculate the margin of error is shown to the left, where *p* is the sample proportion in favor of something and *(1-p)* the sample proportion of those who are not in favor of that issue.

The formula uses z-values (see Chapter 23). When using a z-value in the formula for the margin of error for a sample proportion, ensure two conditions: (#1) $n*p$ is at least 10 and (#2) $n*(1-p)$ is at least 10.

ME = z * SE.

SE = SQRT((p * (1-p)) / n)

What you need to do

1. Place a scrollbar control next to cell B1: Min 500 | Max 1000 | SmallChange 100 | LargeChange 100 | LinkedCell B1.
2. Place a spinbutton control next to cell B13: Min 20 | Max 50 | SmallChange 5 | LinkedCell C13 (not B13!).
3. Place in cell B13: =C13/1000.
4. Place in cells B6:B8: =NORM.S.INV(A6).
5. Place in cells C6:C8: =SQRT($B$3*(1-$B$3)/$B$2).
6. Place in cells D6:D8: =B6*C6.
7. Place in cells B16:B18: =NORM.S.INV(A16).
8. Place in cells C16:C18: =($B$13/B16)^2 — which is (ME/z)^2.
9. Place in cells D16:D18: =$B$12*(1-$B$12) — which is p*(1-p).
10. Place in cells E16:E16: =D16/C16.

	A	B	C	D	E	F
1		Calculate Margin of Error (ME)				
2	Sample Size (n)	500				
3	Proportion (p)	79%				
4						
5	confidence	z-value	SE	ME		
6	99.0%	2.33	0.018	4.2%		
7	97.5%	1.96	0.018	3.6%		
8	95.0%	1.64	0.018	3.0%		
9						
10						
11		Calculate Minimum Sample Size (n)				
12	Proportion (p)	79%				
13	Margin (ME)	3.5%				
14						
15	confidence	z-value	(ME/z)^2	p*(1-p)	n	
16	99.0%	2.33	0.000226	0.1659	733	
17	97.5%	1.96	0.000319	0.1659	520	
18	95.0%	1.64	0.000453	0.1659	366	
19						

Chapter 26: Flipping a Fair Coin?

What the simulation does

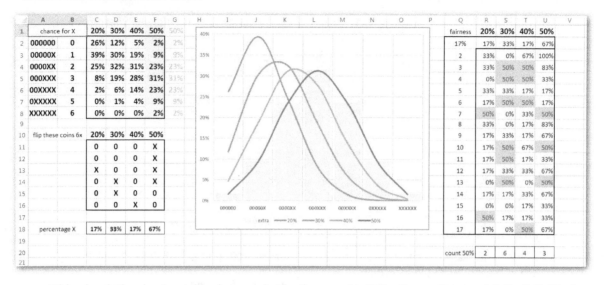

This simulation is about flipping a coin six times, calculating how often we hit "tails" (0) six times, five times, and so on (column A). The most likely outcome is 3x "heads" (X) and 3x "tails" (0)—actually 31% of all cases (cell F5). The center curve in the graph is a "bell-shaped" curve that represents this situation. Going more to the left or to the right under the bell-shaped curve, the chances decrease dramatically, but they will never become something like 0.000000000000.

Events with random outcomes have the property that no particular outcome is known in advance. However, in the aggregate, the outcomes occur with a specific frequency. When we flip a "fair" coin, we do not know how it will land, but if we flip the coin millions of times, we know that it will land heads up (X) very close to 50% of the time—unless...

Unless... the coin is not "fair" and has a "preference" for lower X percentages (columns C:E and the other curves in the graph). To determine whether a coin is fair or not, we would need to flip a coin millions of times.

We tried to simulate this somehow by using a *Data Table*—however, with only a moderate amount of rows. So we only simulated some 100 coin tosses (6x17). In the situation shown above, we would probably declare the fair coin unfair (column U). They call this a *Type I error*—a false alarm. And we probably would declare the unfair coins (in columns S and T) fair—which would be a *Type II error* (more on this in Chapter 23). It is clear we need many more flips for a reliable verdict. That's where Monte Carlo simulations would come in (see III: Chapters 37-51).

What you need to know

The bell-shaped curve is very common in statistics. It is also called a "normal distribution." In order to create this curve for a binary situation—such as yes/no, correct/defect, heads/tails, success/failure—we need the function BINOMDIST or BINOM.DIST. All .DIST functions in Excel are statistical functions that return a probability or percentage—in this case for a binomial situation.

Simulations in Action

What you need to do

1. Place in cells C2:G8 the following formula: =BINOMDIST($B2,6,C$1,0). This specifies the number of successes (from 0-6 in B2:B8), out of 6 trials (6 coin tosses), with 50% probability of success, in a non-cumulative way.
2. Notice how certain references are "locked" (see Appendix for more details), so you can copy the formula to cell G8.
3. In column F, the highest percentage should be for 3 times "heads" (equal to 3 times "tails"), because this is a "fair" coin. In the other columns, the coins are not fair.
4. In cell C11, we simulate a random flip of the first coin: =IF(RAND ()<=C$10,"X","0"). Copy this formula to cell F16.
5. In C18:F18, we count the percentage of heads (X) or tails: =COUNTIF (C11:C16,"X")/6.
6. We expect cell F18, the fair coin, to be 50%, but because we flip the coin only 6x, chance kicks in—so "results may vary."
7. Place in cells C18:F18: =COUNTIF(C11:C16,"X")/6.
8. To repeat each session of 6 flips some 16 more times, we use a *Data Table*. Place in R2: =C18. In S2: = D18. In T2: =E18. In U2: =F18.
9. Select range Q2:U18 and start a *Data Table* with no row input and an empty cell (e.g. P2) for column input: =TABLE(,P2).
10. Place a conditional format in cells R3:U18: Cell Value | Equal to | =0.5.
11. Place in cells R20:U20: =COUNTIF(R2:R18,0.5).
12. In the simulation shown below, we were "lucky" enough to hit 12 rows of 50% (cell U20). Notice how hard it is to decide whether a coin is fair or not. We would need millions of tosses!

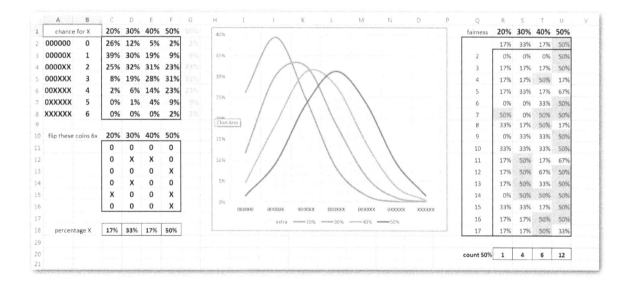

Chapter 27: Simulation of Sick Cases

What the simulation does

	A	B	C	D	E	F	G
1	Sample Size	100				Sick Cases	25
2	Confidence	95%					
3							
4	sick in popul.	Min sick of 100	Max sick of 100			sick in popul.	Prob. of finding up to 25 cases
5	5%	2	9			5%	0.00%
6	10%	5	15			10%	0.00%
7	15%	9	21			15%	0.30%
8	20%	14	27			20%	8.75%
9	25%	18	32			25%	44.65%
10	30%	23	38			30%	83.69%
11	35%	27	43			35%	97.89%
12	40%	32	48			40%	99.88%
13	45%	37	53			45%	100.00%
14	50%	42	58			50%	100.00%
15	55%	47	63			55%	100.00%

If a certain percentage of people is sick in the population (column A), we can find out with a 95% confidence (cell B2) how many in a sample of 100 persons (cell B1) will be sick, either as a minimum (column B) or as a maximum (column C) based on that confidence level.

We can also calculate what the probability is of finding up to a certain number of sick cases (cell G1), given a certain sample size (B1).

We can vary the sample size (B1) as well as the number of sick cases (G1) by using the scrollbar controls next to each cell. The confidence level can be manually adjusted on the sheet.

What you need to know

One of the functions we need in column G is BINOMDIST (or BINOM.DIST) again. As explained in the previous chapter, it returns a binomial distribution probability for problems with a fixed number of tests or trials, when the outcomes of any trial are either success or failure, when trials are independent, and when the probability of success is constant throughout the experiment.

The other crucial function is BINOM.INV (which replaces CRITBINOM in pre-2010 versions). It has 3 arguments: the number of trials, the probability of a success on each trial, and the criterion value (alpha).

The function IFERROR is also quite recent (ISERROR could be used in earlier versions, but is a bit more involved). If there is an error in a certain BINOMDIST calculation, the function IFERROR can make it display an empty string.

What you need to do

1. Place a scrollbar control next to cell B1: Min 10 | Max 100 | SmallChange 10 | LargeChange 10 | LinkedCell B1.
2. Place a scrollbar control next to cell G1: Min 0 | Max 25 | SmallChange 1 | LargeChange 1 | LinkedCell G1.
3. Place in cells B5:B15: =BINOM.INV($B$1,$A5,1-$B$2). You may need CRITBINOM instead if you have an older version.
4. Place in cells C5:C15: =BINOM.INV($B$1,$A5,$B$2). You may need CRITBINOM instead.
5. Place in cell G5:G15: =IFERROR(1-BINOMDIST(G$1,$B$1,$F5,TRUE),"").
6. Put conditional formatting in range A5:A15: =AND(A5>=($G$1/$B$1),A5<($G$1/$B$1)+0.05).
7. In cells B4, C4, and G4, you could place something like this: ="Min sick of " & $B$1. Notice the single space on both sides of the ampersand (&).

	A	B	C			F	G
1	Sample Size	75				Sick Cases	25
2	Confidence	95%					
3							
4	sick in popul.	Min sick of 75	Max sick of 75			sick in popul.	Prob. of finding up to 25 cases
5	5%	1	7			5%	0.00%
6	10%	3	12			10%	0.00%
7	15%	6	17			15%	0.00%
8	20%	9	21			20%	0.21%
9	25%	13	25			25%	3.93%
10	30%	16	29			30%	22.27%
11	35%	20	33			35%	56.73%
12	40%	23	37			40%	85.59%
13	45%	27	41			45%	97.33%
14	50%	30	45			50%	99.74%
15	55%	34	48			55%	99.99%

Chapter 28: Bean Machine Simulation

What the simulation does

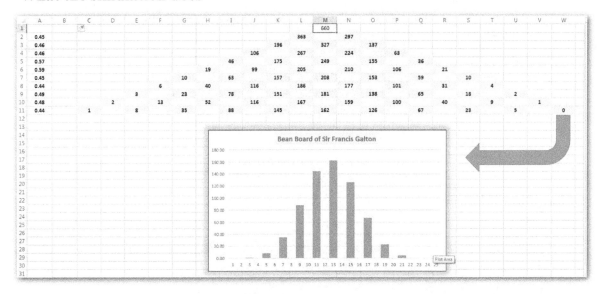

The Galton board, also known as a "quincunx" or "bean machine," is a device for statistical experiments named after English scientist Sir Francis Galton. It consists of an upright board with evenly spaced nails (or pegs) driven into its upper half, where the nails are arranged in staggered order, and a lower half divided into a number of evenly-spaced rectangular slots. The front of the device is usually covered with a glass cover to allow viewing of both nails and slots. In the middle of the upper edge, there is a funnel into which balls can be poured, where the diameter of the balls must be much smaller than the distance between the nails. The funnel is located precisely above the central nail of the second row so that each ball would fall vertically and directly onto the uppermost point of this nail's surface.

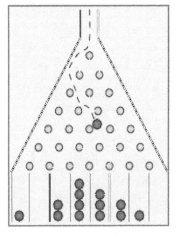

Each time a ball hits one of the nails, it can bounce either right or left. For symmetrically placed nails, balls will bounce left or right with equal probability. This process therefore gives rise to a binomial distribution of the heights of heaps of balls in the lower slots. If the number of balls is sufficiently large, then the distribution of the heights of the ball heaps will approximate a normal distribution.

What you need to know

This sheet simulates this process. All you have to do is using the *F9* key, and the 11 rows will fill as to be expected. The results of the last row are plotted in the chart and show a normal distribution.

At each branching point, the split is randomized by using a random number in row A. Another random number is located in cell L1. In the last row, we should have a total number of balls equal to cell M1.

What you need to do

1. Place in cells A2:A11: =RANDBETWEEN(40,60)/100.
2. You can hide column A or give its cells a white font, if you want to.
3. Select all the colored cells (with the *Ctrl* key after each selection), starting in cell W11 and ending at L2. Now cell L2 is the active cell in which you put this formula: =K1*$A2+M1*(1-$A2). Make sure you "lock" all references the proper way (see Appendix).
4. Accept this formula with *Ctrl Enter*, so it ends up in all selected cells at once.
5. Make sure that the totals of the last row equal the number in cell M1—otherwise you lost some balls in the process or created some from scratch!
6. The cells of the last row are plotted in the column chart.
7. When you hit *F9*, all cells update, but the last row remains close to a normal distribution.

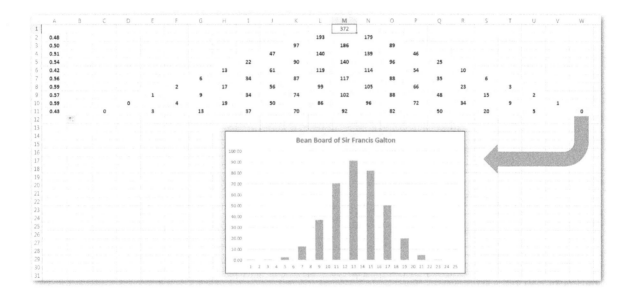

Chapter 29: Correlated Distributions

What the simulation does

	A	B	C	D	E	F	G
1	X	Z	Y		current correlation coefficient (r)		
2	9.15	8.85	11.26		-0.009744859		
3	8.97	11.83	11.92				
4	6.43	7.48	8.27				
5	11.29	8.3	13.16				
6	10.12	7.38	11.78		desired correlation coefficient (r)		
7	11.23	8.68	13.21		0.96	◀ ▶	
8	11.72	12.69	14.8				
9	9.73	9.34	11.96				
10	10.34	8.11	12.2				
11	7.43	11.8	10.44		new correlation coefficient (r)		
12	12.27	9.86	14.54		0.954810768		
13	10.38	9.47	12.62				
14	6.97	7.5	8.79				
15	9.72	8.54	11.72				

When you create multiple distributions, you may want to make this happen with a rather specific correlation coefficient between them. This simulation does so for you. In columns A:B, the sheet creates two independent sets of normally distributed values in columns A and B.

However, we want these two sets (X and Z) to be correlated as requested by cell E7. This simulation does so by using a transformation with the formula shown below. Then it compares the old correlation coefficient (in cell E2) with the new one (in cell E12). Notice how close the new correlation coefficient has come to the desired one in cell E7.

What you need to know

$$Y = r * X + \sqrt{1 - r^2} * Z$$

The formula to make this happen is shown to the left. It uses the desired correlation coefficient r in cell E7 as well as the X-value (in column A) plus the Z-value (in column B) in order to find the better correlated Y-value (in column C).

Correlation coefficients can be calculated with either CORREL or PEARSON. They both have two arguments: array1 and array2, provided they have the same number of data points. The equation for the correlation coefficient is:

$$Correl(X,Y) = \frac{\sum (x-\bar{x})(y-\bar{y})}{\sqrt{\sum (x-\bar{x})^2 \sum (y-\bar{y})^2}}$$

where $\bar{x}$ and $\bar{y}$ are the sample means AVERAGE(array1) and AVERAGE(array2).

What you need to do

1. Place a spinbutton control next to cell E7: Min 80 | Max 100 | SmallChange1 | LinkedCell F7.
2. Place in cell E7: =F7/100.
3. Place in cells A2:A31: =ROUND(NORM.INV(RAND(),10,2),2).
4. Place in cells B2:B31: =ROUND(NORM.INV(RAND(),10,2),2).
5. Place in cells C2:C31: =ROUND($E$7*A2+SQRT(1-$E$7^2)*B2,2).
6. Place in cell E2: =CORREL(A2:A31,B2:B31).
7. Place in cell E12: =CORREL(A2:A31,C2:C31).
8. Notice that most of the time the match between cells E7 and E12 is very close, even if the original correlation coefficient was pretty bad.
9. The key *F9* will change things, of course.
10. Notice also that for *r*=1, the values for Y are equal to the values for X.

	A	B	C	D	E	F	G
1	X	Z	Y		correlation coefficient (r) b/w X and Z		
2	10.31	5.85	11.84		-0.206601778		
3	6.51	8.39	9.62				
4	8.8	10.21	12.49				
5	12.1	12.51	16.47				
6	8.74	9.65	12.18		desired correlation coefficient (r)		
7	10.55	8.85	13.42		0.89		
8	9.61	11.01	13.57				
9	12.47	10.73	15.99				
10	8.74	8.71	11.75				
11	10.64	8.3	13.25		new correlation coefficient (r)		
12	9.23	11.34	13.39		0.913056635		
13	8.87	11.55	13.16				
14	13.81	7.52	15.72				
15	11.34	11.42	15.3				

Chapter 30: Transforming a LogNormal Distribution

What the simulation does

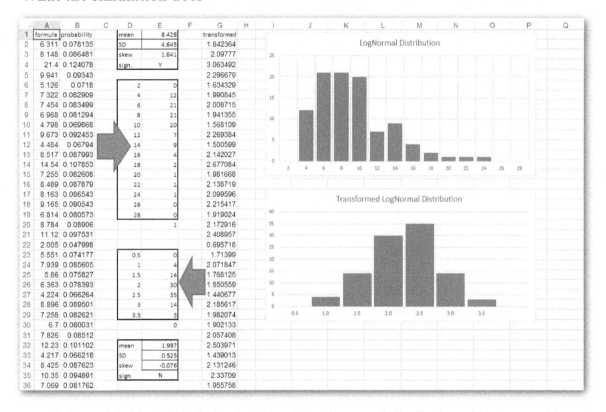

Column A holds 100 random values based on a lognormal distribution with a mean of 2 and a SD of 0.5. Column B shows the probability of each value. In column G, the lognormally distributed values are transformed by taking their natural logarithm with function LN.

In columns D:E, we calculate the mean and SD plus their frequencies—first of the values in A, then for the transformed values in G. We also calculate if and how skewed they are.

It turns out that the transformed lognormal distribution comes close to a normal distribution.

What you need to know

The function LOGNORM.INV allows us to create a series of values that have a lognormal distribution. It has this syntax: LOGNORM.INV(probability,mean,SD). You can transform lognormal data by using the LN function, which returns the natural logarithm of a number.

We also use in cell E3 (and also in E34) the SKEW function—which characterizes the degree of asymmetry of a distribution around its mean. Positive skewness indicates a distribution with an asymmetric tail extending toward higher values (to the right of the mean). Negative skewness indicates a distribution with an asymmetric tail extending toward lower values (to the left of the mean).

The rule of thumb is that if skewness is less than −1 or greater than +1, the distribution is highly skewed. However, this is an interpretation of your data. That's fine when you have data for the whole population. But when you have only a sample, the sample skewness does not necessarily apply to the whole population. A crude way to correct for this is: dividing by $\sqrt{(6/n)}$.

In cell E4 (and E35) we use this thumb rule. The formula is for E4 as follows: =IF(E3>(2*SQRT(6/COUNT(A:A))),"Y","N").

What you need to do

1. Place in cells A2:A101: =LOGNORM.INV(RAND(),2,0.5).
2. Place in cells B2:B101: =LOGNORM.DIST(A2,$E$1,$E$2,TRUE).
3. Place in cells G2:G101: =LN(A2).
4. Place in cell E3: =SKEW(A:A).
5. Place in cell E4: =IF(E3>(2*SQRT(6/COUNT(A:A))),"Y","N")
6. Place in cell E34: =SKEW(G:G).
7. Place in cell E35: =IF(ABS(E34)>(2*SQRT(6/COUNT(G:G))),"Y","N").
8. Select range E6:E20 and insert: =FREQUENCY(A2:A101,D6:D19). Use *Ctrl Shift Enter*.
9. The top chart is connected to this frequency table.
10. Select range E23:E30 and insert: =FREQUENCY(G:G,D23:D29). Use *Ctrl Shift Enter*.
11. The bottom chart is connected to this frequency table.
12. Notice how this last distribution resembles a normal distribution and is usually no longer skewed.

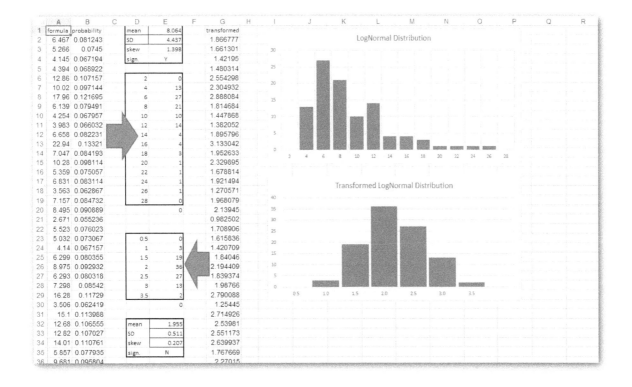

Chapter 31: Bootstrapping

What the simulation does

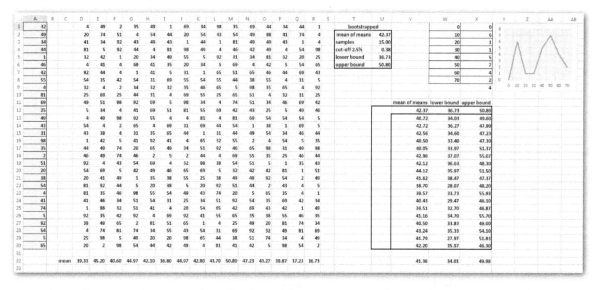

Sometimes you have a series of values that are not normally distributed. The 30 values, for example, shown in column A are not. The frequency table and chart to the far top right show this clearly. In such cases, it is not so simple to calculate a mean, a median, a SD, or a margin. You need some kind of technique such as bootstrapping. With this technique we pull ourselves, so to speak, "out of the swap of data by our own bootstraps."

This simulation uses the bootstrapping technique by randomly selecting values from the sample in A. We do that, for instance, 15 times: first in column D, then in column E, and so on up to column R. At the bottom of each column we calculate the average outcome. Based on these averages, we are able to come close to the statistical parameters we were looking for.

In cases of randomness it is essential to repeat such actions multiple times. We can do so by using a *Data Table* as shown to the far right. The averages of these outcomes are even more reliable, for larger numbers of drawings are obviously less susceptible to random fluctuations. The averages of these repeated runs are shown in cells V32:X32 below the *Data Table*.

What you need to know

To find a cell in a random row of column A, we need the INDEX function (see also Chapter 8). Whereas VLOOKUP works only with column numbers, INDEX also uses row numbers, which is essential when we want to look at a cell that is located in a random row.

Based on all the numbers pulled randomly from column A in the middle section, we can calculate in cell U2 a mean of the means from D32:R32. Then we calculate a cut-off value at a 2-tailed 95% confidence level: 0.025 * the number of means. (P.S. We can't use regular t-values or z-values, as the original values are not normally distributed.)

To calculate the lower-bound and upper-bound, we use two new functions. The function SMALL returns the k-th smallest value in a data set. It uses the syntax SMALL(array, k). The function LARGE returns the k-th largest value in a data set. It uses the syntax LARGE(array, k).

Simulations in Action — STATISTICS

What you need to do

1. Each cell in D1:R30 has this: =INDEX($A$1:$A$30,ROWS($A$1:$A$30)*RAND()+1).
2. In cell U2 is the mean of means: =AVERAGE(D32:R32).
3. In cell U3 is the number of samples: =COUNT(D32:R32).
4. In cell U4 is the 2.5% cut off on either side: =U3*0.025.
5. In cell U5 is the lower bound: =SMALL($D$32:$R$32,ROUNDUP($U$4,0)).
6. In cell U6 is the upper bound: =LARGE($D$32:$R$32,ROUNDUP($U$4,0)).
7. Create links in V12:X12 to U2, U5, and U6.
8. Select range U12:X30 and implement a *Data Table* with no row input and a column input of an empty cell, e.g. T12. So we end up with: =TABLE(,T12).
9. Press *F9* and notice how the 95% lower bound and upper bound do change, but certainly not dramatically.

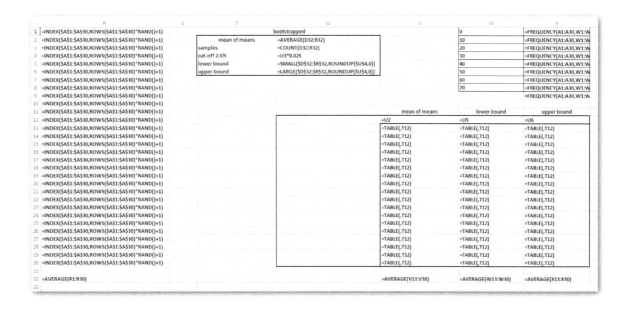

Chapter 32: Outlier Detection

What the simulation does

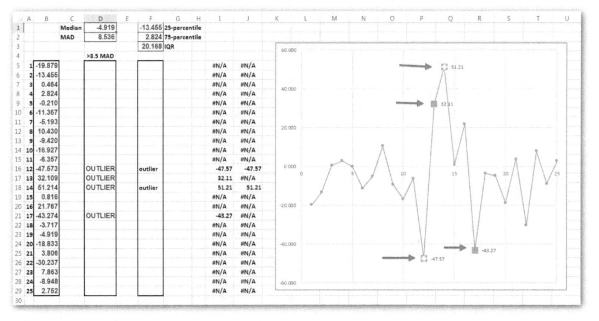

Outliers are defined as numeric values in any random data set that have an unusually high deviation from either the statistical mean or the median value. In other words, these numbers are relatively extreme. It requires sound statistics—not intuition—to locate them. A rather simple rule is that all values outside a range of three times the standard deviation around the mean could be considered outliers—provided they follow a normal distribution.

In this simulation, however, we will use a more robust statistical detection of outliers by calculating the deviation for each number, expressed as a "modified Z-score," and testing it against a predefined threshold. Z-scores stand for the amount of standard deviation relative to the statistical median (in D1). MAD (in D2) stands for *Median Absolute Deviation*. Any number in a data set with the absolute value of modified Z-scores exceeding 3.5 times MAD is considered an outlier. Column D shows the outcome.

What you need to know

In the 1970's the famous statistician John Tukey decided to give the term outlier a more formal definition. He called any observation value an outlier if it is smaller than the first quartile (F1) minus 1.5 times the *IQR* (F3), or larger than the third quartile (F2) plus 1.5 times the *IQR*. The Inter-Quartile Range, *IQR*, is the width of the interval that contains the middle half of the data set. Column F shows the outcome.

The graph to the right shows the observed values marked with a *square* shape if it is an outlier according to the first method, or with a *diamond* shape if it is an outlier according to the second method. Most of the time, the first method detects more outliers than the second one.

Simulations in Action — STATISTICS

The marked data points in the chart are based on column I for the MAD method and on column J for the Tukey method. The "trick" used in these columns works with the function NA. This function returns #N/A, which does not show up as a data point in a chart—so the chart only shows the data points with a real value. Apparently, there are *three* series of values behind the chart: the columns B, I, and J.

What you need to do

1. In cell B5:B29 we create normally distributed values between around 30 with SD 15 and manipulate them randomly: =NORMINV(RAND(),30,15)*(1-2*RAND()).
2. Cell D1 shows the median of these numbers: =MEDIAN(B5:B29).
3. MAD in cell D2: =MEDIAN(ABS(MEDIAN(B5:B29)-B5:B29)). This is a single-cell array formula requiring *Ctrl Shift Enter*.
4. Place in cells D5:D29: =IF(ABS(D$1-B5)>(3.5*D$2), "OUTLIER", ""). We consider any number with the absolute value of the modified Z-score exceeding 3.5 times MAD to be an outlier.
5. Cell F1 has the 25th percentile: =PERCENTILE($B$5:$B$29,0.25). QUARTILE for quart #1 equals PERCENTILE for 25%.
6. Cell F2 has the 75th percentile: =PERCENTILE($B$5:$B$29,0.75). QUARTILE for quart #3 equals PERCENTILE for 75%.
7. Calculate IQR in cell F3: =AVERAGE($B$5:$B$29)+(1.5*(F2-F1)). IQR is the width of the interval that contains the data's middle half.
8. Place in cells F5:F29: =IF(OR(B5>($F$2+1.5*$F$3),B5<($F$1-1.5*$F$3)),"outlier","").
9. The markers in the graph for the 1st method (in column D) are based on column I Perhaps hidden behind the chart). Place in cells I5:I29: =IF(D5="OUTLIER",B5,NA()).
10. The markers in the graph for the second method (in column F) are based on a (hidden) column J behind the graph. Place in cells J5:J29: =IF(F5="outlier",B5,NA()).
11. With *F9* you can simulate new situations. Sometimes both methods generate the same verdict (see below).

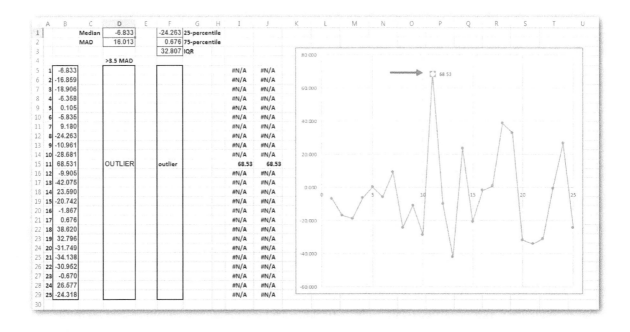

Chapter 33: Chi-Squared Test

What the simulation does

	A	B	C	D	E	F	G	H	I
1		Observed frequencies:							
2									
3		Diabetes	No diabetes	TOTAL					
4	Overweight	1200	800	2000					
5	Normal weight	919	1081	2000					
6	TOTAL	2119	1881	4000					
7									
8									
9		Expected frequencies (if indep.):							
10							Null Hypothesis: No dependence		
11		Diabetes	No diabetes	TOTAL					
12	Overweight	1059.5	940.5	2000			CHITEST ⇨ "p"	0.00000000%	
13	Diabetes	1059.5	940.5	2000			confidence	highly significant	
14	TOTAL	2119	1881	4000			overweight	increases risk	
15									

Researchers often have to deal with *frequencies* instead of means and binomial proportions because they have their cases categorized in bins. The *Chi-squared* distribution allows them to compare observed frequencies with expected frequencies. The *Chi-squared* distribution (*Chi-squared*, or χ^2) is the perfect distribution for frequencies.

$$\chi^2 = \sum \left[\frac{(f_{obs} - f_{exp})^2}{f_{exp}} \right]$$

In this simulation we test whether there is a significant relationship between diabetes and overweight. We use a cohort of 4000 persons and enter the *observed* frequencies in the top table (cells B4:C5). With the two scrollbar controls you can change the number of persons who have diabetes in your sample. The so-called *null-hypothesis* assumes there is no dependence between diabetes and overweight. Based on this assumption of a random relationship, we calculate a table of *expected* frequencies (in cells B12:C13).

The *Chi-squared* test (in cell H12) compares the observed frequencies with the expected frequencies on the assumption there is no dependency (*null-hypothesis*). It calculates the probability that the observed frequencies are random: high probabilities mean that dependence is very unlikely; very low probabilities mean there is some dependence between diabetes and overweight. So in the case shown above, the null-hypothesis is rejected, because the observed frequencies could hardly have happened by mere chance.

What you need to know

The test can easily be done by using the function CHISQ.TEST. It has this syntax: CHISQ.TEST(observed_range,expected_range). A low value of χ^2 is an indicator of independence. As can be seen from the formula, χ^2 is always positive or 0.

The table of observed frequencies (A3:D6) has total calculations in the end row and column. The table of expected frequencies (A11:D14) is an exact replica of the table above it, except for the observed frequencies (B12:C13). The observed frequencies have to be replaced by calculated, expected frequencies. Here's how to do this: =Subtotal$_{Row}$ * Subtotal$_{Column}$ / Total.

So the totals in each row and column should remain the same, but the cells inside would differ. By the way, in the table of expected frequencies, decimals do matter!

What you need to do

	A	B	C	D
1		Observed frequencies:		
2				
3		Diabetes	No diabetes	TOTAL
4	Overweight	1200	=D4-B4	2000
5	Normal weight	919	=D5-B5	2000
6	TOTAL	=SUM(B4:B5)	=SUM(C4:C5)	=SUM(D4:D5)
7				
8				
9		Expected frequencies (if indep.):		
10				
11		Diabetes	No diabetes	TOTAL
12	Overweight	=$D4*B$6/$D$6	=$D4*C$6/$D$6	=SUM(B12:C12)
13	Diabetes	=$D5*B$6/$D$6	=$D5*C$6/$D$6	=SUM(B13:C13)
14	TOTAL	=SUM(B12:B13)	=SUM(C12:C13)	=SUM(D12:D13)

1. Place a scrollbar control in row 4: Min 800 | Max 1200 | SmallChange 5 | LargeChange 10 | LinkedCell B4.
2. Place a scrollbar control in row 5: Min 800 | Max 1200 | SmallChange 5 | LargeChange 10 | LinkedCell B4.
3. Place in cells C4:C5: =D5-B5.
4. Place in cells B12:C13: =$D4*B$6/$D$6.
5. Place in cell H12: =CHISQ.TEST(B4:C5,B12:C13).
6. Place in cell H13: =IF(H12<1%,"highly significant",IF(H12<5%,"significant","random")).
7. Place in cell H14: =IF(H13="random","no impact",IF(B4>B5,"increases risk","decreases risk")).
8. In the case below, we cannot detect a significant dependence between diabetes and overweight.

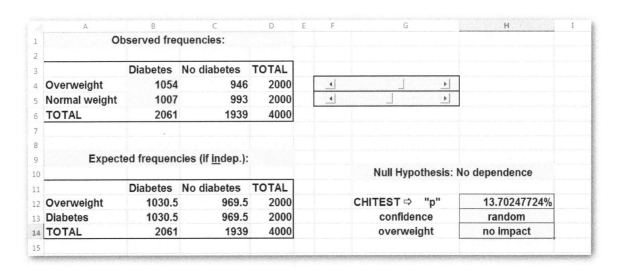

Chapter 34: Unbiased Sampling

What the simulation does

	A	B	C	D	E	F	G	H	I	J	K	L	M	N	O	P	Q
	mere random			25% of random			only 10 codes			10 weighted area codes							
1	random	area code		area code	25%		area code	10x		cumul.	area code	weight	bar		sample of 10	weighted	
3	0.069	701		670	FALSE		670	417		0	203	1	+		217	+	
4	0.151	405		611	TRUE		611	270		1	204	4	++++		224	++++	
5	0.612	649		757	FALSE		757	811		5	205	2	++		210	+++	
6	0.930	310		216	FALSE		216	504		7	206	1	+		224	++++	
7	0.939	630		411	FALSE		411	709		8	207	1	+		205	++	
8	0.716	484		307	FALSE		307	816		9	208	1	+		204	++++	
9	0.997	660		805	FALSE		805	450		10	209	4	++++		215	++++	
10	0.719	320		905	FALSE		905	513		14	210	3	+++		219	+	
11	0.400	425		803	FALSE		803	937		17	212	1	+		203	+	
12	0.160	868		606	FALSE		606	612		18	213	1	+		215	++++	
13	0.115	441		843	TRUE		843			19	214	1	+				
14	0.178	882		308	FALSE		308			20	215	4	++++				
15	0.715	860		360	FALSE		360			24	216	2	++				
16	0.992	311		917	FALSE		917			26	217	1	+				
17	0.796	309		314	FALSE		314			27	218	1	+				
18	0.855	831		784	FALSE		784			28	219	1	+				
19	0.350	915		920	FALSE		920			29	224	4	++++				
20	0.302	847		267	FALSE		267			33	225	2	++				
21	0.641	780		417	FALSE		417			35	228	1	+				
22	0.127	708		419	FALSE		419			36	240	1	+				
23	0.064	301		612	TRUE		612			37	Total						
24	0.618	540		201	FALSE		201										
25	0.706	214		765	FALSE		765										

When taking samples, the problem is that some are more likely to be chosen than others—so we call them potentially "biased" samples. Unbiased sampling requires some bias-proof techniques. Therefore, we need the unbiased verdict of mathematical tools.

In this simulation, we use four different techniques to select telephone area codes at random. Technique #1 assigns a random number, so after sorting by that number, you take the first or last N cases. Technique #2 selects $X\%$ of the area codes randomly. Technique #3 produces N cases randomly. Technique #4 "weighs" each area code (depending on population density, for instance) and then performs a *weighted* random sampling of N cases.

What you need to know

Case #4 may need some extra explanation. In column J, we calculate the cumulative total of all previous weights. So area code 204 (in K4) is four times included in that total. In column O, we multiply the grand total (J23) with a random number between 0 and 1, and then we look up that value in range J3:J23 and determine its corresponding area code. In other words, the second area code, 204, can be found through the random numbers between >=1 and <5; this amounts to 4 chances of being picked (4x more than the first area code, 203).

The function REPT repeats text a given number of times. For instance, =REPT("-",10) would display a dash (-) 10 times.

What you need to do

1. Place in cell A1: =RAND (). Copy down to the last area code.
2. In order to sort by column A, without RAND recalculating again, we copy column A and paste it back as a value: Paste Special | Values.
3. Now select columns A and B, then Data | Sort | Sort by "mere random".
4. Consider the top or bottom *N* cases as your random samples.
5. For case #2, we want a certain percentage of area codes (say, 25% in cell E2). To do so, place in cell E3: =RAND()<$E$2. Copy down. Take the TRUE cases for your 25% sampling, after you do something that is similar to steps 2 and 3, but this time sorting by column E.
6. For case #3, we use an Excel tool: Data | Data Analysis | Sampling | Input Range: $G$3:$G$269 | ⊙ Random: 10 | Output Range: H3.
7. Case #4 is more complicated. Each area code was manually given a certain "weight" in column L, depending on population density or so. This weight was translated into some kind of bar symbol (column M). Place in cell M3: =REPT("+",L3).
8. Column J is for a cumulative total. Place in J3 the value 0. Place in J4: =J3+L3. Copy this last formula downwards to cell J23.
9. Column O creates a series of 10 (or more) random area codes in accordance with their weight. To do so, place in cells O3:O12: =VLOOKUP($J$23*RAND(), $J$3:$K$23, 2).
10. If you want to see also their bar codes, place in P3:P12: =VLOOKUP(O3,$K$3:$M$22,3,0).
11. Hitting *F9* should give you each time a new set of weighted random area codes. Most of the time, you will see more four- and three-plusses than any other cases.
12. See below the results after pasting values and sorting.

	A	B	C	D	E	F	G	H	I	J	K	L	M	N	O	P	Q
1	mere random			25% of random			only 10 codes								10 weighted area codes		
2	random area code			611	TRUE		area code	10x		cumul.	area code	weight	bar		sample of 10 weighted		
3	0.995	323		314	TRUE		670	417		0	203	1	+		204	++++	
4	0.993	208		417	TRUE		611	270		1	204	4	++++		210	+++	
5	0.993	805		419	TRUE		757	811		5	205	2	++		209	++++	
6	0.992	602		612	TRUE		216	504		7	206	1	+		217	+	
7	0.989	503		416	TRUE		411	709		8	207	1	+		207	+	
8	0.985	925		661	TRUE		307	816		9	208	1	+		213	+	
9	0.982	651		614	TRUE		805	450		10	209	4	++++		209	++++	
10	0.976	864		506	TRUE		905	513		14	210	3	+++		208	+	
11	0.975	807		954	TRUE		803	937		17	212	1	+		203	+	
12	0.973	828		402	TRUE		606	612		18	213	1	+		216	++	
13	0.971	207		424	TRUE		843			19	214	1	+				
14	0.961	913		345	TRUE		308			20	215	4	++++				
15	0.957	419		705	TRUE		360			24	216	2	++				
16	0.953	806		218	TRUE		917			26	217	1	+				
17	0.950	757		903	TRUE		314			27	218	1	+				
18	0.950	405		712	TRUE		784			28	219	1	+				
19	0.945	809		869	TRUE		920			29	224	4	++++				
20	0.937	670		882	TRUE		267			33	225	2	++				
21	0.927	740		203	TRUE		417			35	228	1	+				
22	0.923	406		828	TRUE		419			36	240	1	+				
23	0.922	610		559	TRUE		612			37	Total						
24	0.916	717		910	TRUE		201										

Chapter 35: Sorted Random Sampling

What the simulation does

	A	B	C	D	E	F	G	H	I	J	K	L	M	N	O
1	0.6494	1			lot size		50								
2	0.1218				sample size		15								
3	0.3170			hide with white font											
4	0.8258	4					random, no duplicates, sorted								
5	0.8313	5		1	1	30									
6	0.9654	6		2	4	43									
7	0.3713			3	5	45									
8	0.7197	8		4	6	48									
9	0.3213			5	8	50									
10	0.0205			6	14										
11	0.5754			7	21										
12	0.4970			8	23										
13	0.1174			9	25										
14	0.6591	14		10	29										
15	0.4394				0	10	20	30	40	50	60	70	80	90	
16	0.1521														
17	0.3011				0.6494	0.8689									
18	0.5267				0.8258	0.7621									
19	0.5015				0.8313	0.8109									
20	0.0534				0.9654	0.9007									
21	0.6993	21			0.7197	0.8542									
22	0.0119				0.6591										
23	0.7047	23			0.6993										
24	0.2491				0.7047										
25	0.8930	25			0.8930										
26	0.3891				0.9047										

This simulation takes random samples from values in column A—but without any duplicates, and in a sorted order. The sampling is based on a specific lot size (G1) and sample size (G2), which can be regulated though two scrollbar controls. All of this is done by sampling the numbers in column A, then manipulating them in column B, and finally displaying them orderly in E5:N14.

What you need to know

Column A runs from A1 to A100, and displays random numbers between 0 and 1, but only for the number of cells determined by the lot size (G1).

The sampling of numbers is done by using the function RANK. It returns the rank of a number in a list of numbers. The rank of a number is its size relative to other values in a list. Its syntax is: RANK(number,array,[order]). If [order] is 0 (zero) or omitted, the function ranks numbers as if it were a list sorted in an descending order.

The center table on top uses an extra column to the left and an extra row at the bottom to accommodate a maximum of 100 entries in an orderly fashion. For instance, entry 15 is in the column with 10 at the bottom and in the row with 5 to the far left—so 10+5=15. Then it finds one of the sampled values in column B in a sorted way by using the RANK function again.

The center table at the bottom finds the corresponding number in column A by using INDEX. INDEX works also with row numbers: INDEX(array,row#,column#). We can find a row number (or column number for that matter) by using a nested MATCH function (see Appendix for more information on nesting). MATCH returns the relative position of some item in a range. For example, if the range A1:A3 contains the values 5, 25, and 38, then the formula =MATCH(25,A1:A3,0) returns the row number 2, because 25 is the second item in the range.

Simulations in Action — STATISTICS

What you need to do

1. Place a scrollbar control next to cell G1: Min 5 | Max 100 | LinkedCell G1.
2. Place a scrollbar control next to cell G2: Min 5 | Max 100 | LinkedCell G2.
3. Place in cells A1:A100: =IF(ROW(A1)>$G$1,"",RAND()).
4. Place in cells B1:B100: =IF(A1="","",IF(RANK(A1,$A$1:$A$101)>$G$2,"",ROW(A1))).
5. Place in cells E5:N14: =IF($D5+E$15>$G$2,"",SMALL($B$1:$B$100,$D5+E$15)).
6. If you want, hide the row and column numbers on the outside of the table with a white font.
7. Place in cells E17:N26: =IF(E5="","",INDEX($A$1:$B$100,MATCH(E5,$B$1:$B$100,0),1)).
8. Test the scroll bars and notice how everything adjusts nicely.
9. Hitting *F9* on its own will run a new random sample for the same lot and sample sizes.

	A	B	C	D	E	F	G	H	I	J	K	L	M	N	O
1	0.7999	1				lot size	73								
2	0.4440					sample size	35								
3	0.6343	3			hide with white font										
4	0.6399	4							random, no duplicates, sorted						
5	0.9388	5			1	28	45	61							
6	0.0182				3	30	47	62							
7	0.2176				4	31	49	67							
8	0.7304	8			5	32	52	69							
9	0.1738				8	34	53	70							
10	0.8696	10			10	36	54								
11	0.5158				12	39	55								
12	0.8978	12			13	40	57								
13	0.9771	13			22	43	59								
14	0.3549				24	44	60								
15	0.3641														
16	0.2360														
17	0.3301				0.7999	0.7846	0.7127	0.8855							
18	0.0955				0.6343	0.6757	0.7048	0.9413							
19	0.6088				0.6399	0.8885	0.9184	0.8576							
20	0.5935				0.9388	0.6692	0.6123	0.7900							
21	0.5642				0.7304	0.9265	0.7436	0.6169							
22	0.9818	22			0.8696	0.7324	0.9432								
23	0.2598				0.8978	0.8944	0.6408								
24	0.6202	24			0.9771	0.6108	0.7963								
25	0.1035				0.9818	0.7399	0.9551								
26	0.3018				0.6202	0.9090	0.6502								

Chapter 36: Sorted Random Dates

What the simulation does

	C	D	E	F	G	H	I	J	K	L	M	N	O	P
1	13-Feb-10			lot size	50									
2	9-Mar-10			sample size	25									
3	20-Mar-10													
4	25-Mar-10							random positions						
5	1-Apr-10		1	3	22	43								
6	3-Apr-10		2	6	23	46								
7	5-Apr-10		3	8	25	47								
8	13-Apr-10		4	9	27	48								
9	28-Apr-10		5	11	30	50								
10	29-Apr-10		6	13	38									
11	25-May-10		7	16	39									
12	19-Aug-10		8	17	40									
13	27-Aug-10		9	19	41									
14	29-Aug-10		10	20	42									
15	27-Sep-10			0	10	20	30	40	50	60	70	80	90	
16	22-Oct-10													
17	24-Nov-10							look up dates at random positions						
18	30-Nov-10		1	20-Mar-10	6-Mar-11	17-May-12								
19	19-Dec-10		2	3-Apr-10	22-Mar-11	16-Jul-12								
20	14-Jan-11		3	13-Apr-10	19-Apr-11	17-Jul-12								
21	23-Feb-11		4	28-Apr-10	29-Apr-11	16-Aug-12								
22	6-Mar-11		5	25-May-10	7-May-11	23-Sep-12								
23	22-Mar-11		6	27-Aug-10	9-Dec-11									
24	4-Apr-11		7	22-Oct-10	1-Jan-12									
25	19-Apr-11		8	24-Nov-10	10-Jan-12									
26	25-Apr-11		9	19-Dec-10	17-Mar-12									
27	29-Apr-11		10	14-Jan-11	17-May-12									
28	30-Apr-11			0	10	20	30	40	50	60	70	80	90	

This simulation does something similar to what was shown in the previous chapter, but this time specifically for dates. The sorted and unique randomly chosen dates are in the bottom table.

This time there is an extra secret: two hidden rows before column C. The hidden columns A and B do the same work as they did in the previous simulation. The range F18:O27 displays the dates corresponding to the sorted and unique random positions shown in cells F5:O14.

What you need to know

Make sure you have the two columns A and B, which you probably want to hide afterwards. Through these two columns, the simulation can populate the top center table with entries randomly selected from column B.

Based on these entries the second center table can display the corresponding dates.

	A	B	C	D	E	F	G	H	I	J	K	L	M	N	O	P
1	0.43951		13-Feb-10			lot size	50									
2	0.4518		9-Mar-10			sample size	25									
3	0.66728	3	20-Mar-10													
4	0.00834		25-Mar-10							random positions						
5	0.08305		1-Apr-10		1	3	22	43								
6	0.77755	6	3-Apr-10		2	6	23	46								
7	0.38611		5-Apr-10		3	8	25	47								
8	0.76747	8	13-Apr-10		4	9	27	48								
9	0.59675	9	28-Apr-10		5	11	30	50								
10	0.40784		29-Apr-10		6	13	38									
11	0.73208	11	25-May-10		7	16	39									
12	0.1412		19-Aug-10		8	17	40									
13	0.6844	13	27-Aug-10		9	19	41									
14	0.20443		29-Aug-10		10	20	42									
15	0.05088		27-Sep-10			0	10	20	30	40	50	60	70	80	90	
16	0.97813	16	22-Oct-10													

What you need to do

1. Place a scrollbar control next to cell G1: Min 5 | Max 100 | LinkedCell G1.
2. Place a scrollbar control next to cell G2: Min 5 | Max 100 | LinkedCell G2.
3. Place in cells A1:A100: =IF(ROW(A1)>$G$1,"",RAND()).
4. Place in cells B1:B100: =IF(A1="","",IF(RANK(A1,$A$1:$A$101)>$G$2,"",ROW(A1))).
5. Column C holds the series of dates you want to randomly sample.
6. Place in cells F5:O14: =IF($E5+F$15>$G$2,"",SMALL($B$1:$B$100,$E5+F$15)).
7. Place in cells F18:O27 a formula that uses VLOOKUP instead of INDEX: =IF($E18+F$28>$G$2,"",VLOOKUP(SMALL($B$1:$B$100,$E18+F$28),$B$1:$C$100,2)).

	A	B	C	D	E	F	G	H	I	J	K	L	M	N	O	P
1	0.60621	1	13-Feb-10			lot size	56	◄		►						
2	0.645	2	9-Mar-10			sample size	56	◄		►						
3	0.4306	3	20-Mar-10													
4	0.67696	4	25-Mar-10							random positions						
5	0.20198	5	1-Apr-10		1	1	11	21	31	41	51					
6	0.49831	6	3-Apr-10		2	2	12	22	32	42	52					
7	0.07946	7	5-Apr-10		3	3	13	23	33	43	53					
8	0.91343	8	13-Apr-10		4	4	14	24	34	44	54					
9	0.21179	9	28-Apr-10		5	5	15	25	35	45	55					
10	0.39883	10	29-Apr-10		6	6	16	26	36	46	56					
11	0.86216	11	25-May-10		7	7	17	27	37	47						
12	0.08826	12	19-Aug-10		8	8	18	28	38	48						
13	0.7341	13	27-Aug-10		9	9	19	29	39	49						
14	0.11657	14	29-Aug-10		10	10	20	30	40	50						
15	0.94934	15	27-Sep-10			0	10	20	30	40	50	60	70	80	90	
16	0.47914	16	22-Oct-10													
17	0.32708	17	24-Nov-10						look up dates at random positions							
18	0.01568	18	30-Nov-10		1	13-Feb-10	25-May-10	23-Feb-11	20-May-11	17-Mar-12	4-Oct-12					
19	0.58625	19	19-Dec-10		2	9-Mar-10	19-Aug-10	6-Mar-11	18-Jul-11	17-May-12	16-Oct-12					
20	0.28332	20	14-Jan-11		3	20-Mar-10	27-Aug-10	22-Mar-11	30-Jul-11	17-May-12	22-Nov-12					
21	0.35763	21	23-Feb-11		4	25-Mar-10	29-Aug-10	4-Apr-11	24-Aug-11	2-Jul-12	15-Jan-13					
22	0.1013	22	6-Mar-11		5	1-Apr-10	27-Sep-10	19-Apr-11	12-Sep-11	8-Jul-12	21-Feb-13					
23	0.17789	23	22-Mar-11		6	3-Apr-10	22-Oct-10	25-Apr-11	20-Oct-11	16-Jul-12	4-Mar-13					
24	0.90304	24	4-Apr-11		7	5-Apr-10	24-Nov-10	29-Apr-11	23-Nov-11	17-Jul-12						
25	0.39762	25	19-Apr-11		8	13-Apr-10	30-Nov-10	30-Apr-11	9-Dec-11	16-Aug-12						
26	0.56328	26	25-Apr-11		9	28-Apr-10	19-Dec-10	5-May-11	1-Jan-12	4-Sep-12						
27	0.13459	27	29-Apr-11		10	29-Apr-10	14-Jan-11	7-May-11	10-Jan-12	23-Sep-12						
28	0.23925	28	30-Apr-11			0	10	20	30	40	50	60	70	80	90	

III. Monte Carlo Simulations

Chapter 37: The Law of Large Numbers

What the simulation does

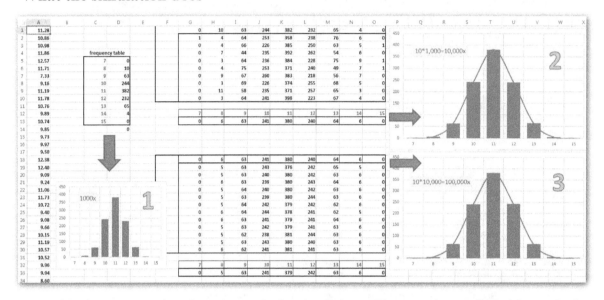

This is an example of a Monte Carlo simulation. Why are they called *Monte Carlo* simulations? The name came up in the 1940s when Los Alamos physicists John von Neumann, Stanislaw Ulam, and Nicholas Metropolis were working on nuclear weapon research during the Manhattan Project in the Los Alamos National Laboratory. They were unable to solve their problems using conventional, deterministic mathematical methods. Then one of them, Stanisław Ulam, had the idea of using random simulations based on random numbers (see Appendix). The Monte Carlo simulations required for the Manhattan Project were severely limited by the computational tools at the time. Nowadays we have Excel!

Currently, the technique is used by professionals in such widely disparate fields as finance, project management, energy, manufacturing, engineering, research and development, insurance, and transportation. Monte Carlo simulation furnishes you as a decision-maker with a range of possible outcomes and the probabilities they will occur for any choice of action. Always run at least 1,000 iterations of Monte Carlo models to reduce the risk of random impact.

What you need to know

This simulation shows the effect of large numbers. Column A contains "only" 1,000 numbers (plotted in chart #1). Then we run the results of those 1,000 numbers 10 more times in a *Data Table*, which makes for 10,000 cases (plotted in chart #2). Finally we repeat these results another 10 times with another *Data Table*, which makes for 100,000 random numbers (plotted in chart #3).

Needless to say that this is a time consuming process—mostly because of cell manipulation on the sheet in the *Data Table*s. But because there is much randomness involved, and therefore much uncertainty, Monte Carlo simulations can harness the uncertainty and give us a bit more certainty in the midst of much uncertainty.

The function TRANSPOSE converts a vertical range of cells to a horizontal, or vice versa. It is an array function that has to be entered at once for all cells and requires *Ctrl Shift Enter*.

What you need to do

1. Place in cells A1:A1000: =NORMINV(RAND(),10.5,1).
2. Create a frequency table in C5:D13: =FREQUENCY(A1:A1000,C5:C13). Use *Ctrl Shift Enter*.
3. Plot C5:D13 in a column chart (#1).
4. Select cells G1:O1: =TRANSPOSE(D5:D13). This is an array formula, so use *Ctrl Shift Enter*.
5. Select cells F1:O10 for a *Data Table* (see Appendix) with no row imput and a column input from an empty cell (e.g. E1).
6. Place in G12:O12: =TRANSPOSE(C5:C13). This is an array formula: use *Ctrl Shift Enter*.
7. Place in G13:O13: =AVERAGE(G1:G10).
8. Plot G12:O13 in a column chart (#2).
9. Place in cells G18:O18: =G13.
10. Select cells F18:O30 for a *Data Table* (see Appendix) with no row imput and a column input from an empty cell (e.g. E18).
11. Place in G32:O32: =TRANSPOSE(C5:C13). This is an array formula: use *Ctrl Shift Enter*.
12. Place in G33:O33: =AVERAGE(G18:G30).
13. Plot G32:O33 in a column chart (#3).
14. Notice how all three charts change during execution, but the third one stays rather stable.

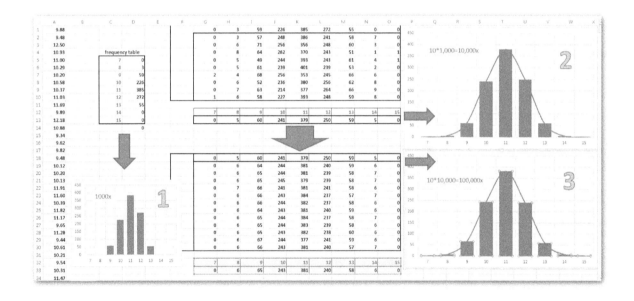

Chapter 38: Random Walk

What the simulation does

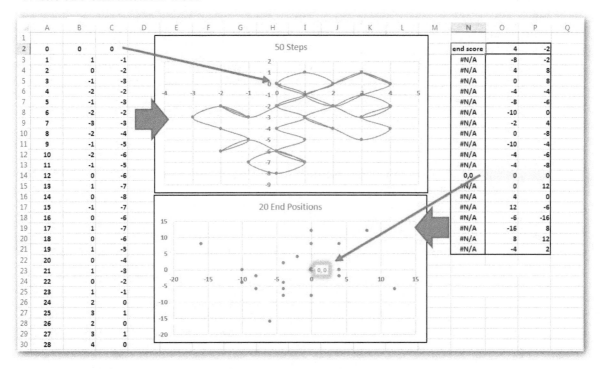

This simulation uses a *random-walk* approach. Imagine we are leaving home (position 0). When we flip a coin and get heads, we go one block north or east (position +1); when we flip tails, we go one block south or west (position -1). We keep doing this many times and then check how far we end up being from home. (We may also ask what the probability is that we return to where we started—believe it or not, that probability is 100% if the walk is long enough!).

First we will simulate 50 steps in columns B and C, plotted in the top graph. All walks start at position (0,0) in cells B2 and C2. In the *Data Table* to the right, we repeat all 50 steps some 20 times and show where each walk ended. If a certain walk ends where it started, we mark that outcome with conditional formatting. The columns O and P of the *Data Table* are plotted in the bottom graph. For a situation like this see the figure on the facing page.

As it turns out, we could potentially make big "gains" and drift far away from where we started. But not always! If this random-walk were interpreted as a case of gambling, we could encounter many negative, perhaps even huge negative outcomes—"losses" in gambling terms. Random walks are just fascinating and ideal candidates for Monte Carlo simulation.

What you need to know

In Range N3:N22, we use a formula with a nested NA function. This function returns #N/A. The advantage of doing so is that a curve in the chart does not display #N/A, but just "skips" it. Besides, the NA function is also very helpful to avoid the problem of unintentionally including empty cells in our calculations.

When this column represents a return home (0,0), we plot that in the chart as a new series, and attach a *Data Callout* label which reads "0,0" (see picture above).

What you need to do

1. Place in cell B3:B1007: =IF(RAND()<0.5,B2-1,B2+1). RAND determines whether we go one down or one up (north or south).
2. We do this also for the 2nd dimension in C3:C1007: =IF(RAND()<0.5,C2-1,C2+1). RAND determines whether we go one to the left or one to the right (east or west).
3. The top chart shows how the walk usually meanders all over the place.
4. Select range N2:P21 for a *Data Table* with no row input and an empty cell (e.g. cell M1) for the column input. This creates the following array formula in the *Data Table*: =TABLE(,M1)).
5. Place in N3:N21: =IF(AND(O3=0,P3=0),"0,0",NA()). This marks all returns back to the point of departure (0,0), if there are any.
6. Apply conditional formatting to range O2:P21: =AND($O2=0,$P2=0). Select a fill color.
7. Set the font color of range N3:N21 to *white*.
8. Apply conditional formatting to range N3:N21 with a *black* font: =AND($O3=0,$P3=0).
9. Some "walks" veer off quite a bit (see below, for instance).

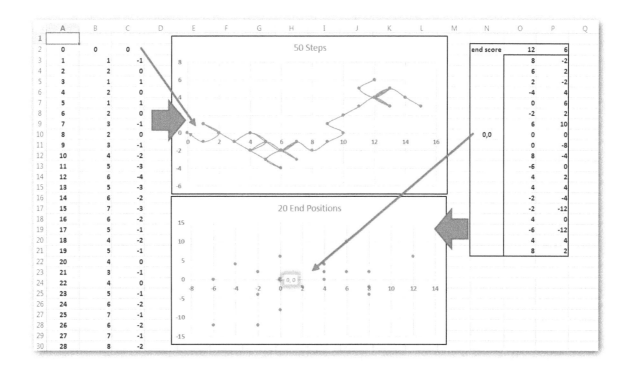

Chapter 39: Brownian Motion

What the simulation does

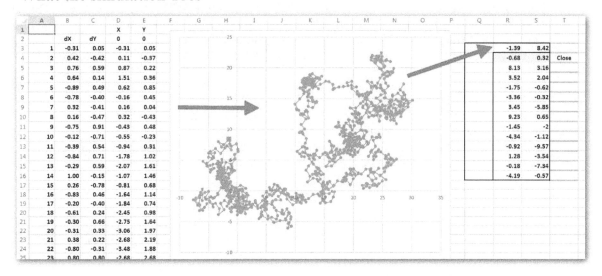

Brownian motion was discovered in the early 1800s by botanist Robert Brown, who noticed under his microscope how grains of pollen appeared to constantly and randomly move in a jittery way on the surface of the water. In his 1905 paper, Albert Einstein hypothesized that Brownian motion was caused by actual atoms and molecules hitting the grains of pollen, impelling them to take a "random walk" on the surface of the liquid. Einstein's work eventually led to the inherently probabilistic nature of quantum mechanics.

This simulation shows how a grain of pollen—or a molecule, for that matter—takes a "random walk" on the surface of the water. Brownian motion is basically a *random-walk* simulation (see the previous chapter).

Dealing with the uncertain and the unknown is the realm of probability, which helps us to put a meaningful numerical value on things we do not know. Although a single random event is not predictable, the aggregate behavior of numerous random events is.

What you need to know

Column B displays random X-changes and column C displays random Y-changes. In D and E, we start at coordinates 0,0 and keep adding the random changes from the previous columns. In P:Q we repeat each run 14 times and mark runs in column T that ended up close to 0,0 again.

A	B	C	D	E
			X	Y
	dX	dY	0	0
1	=ROUND(1-2*RAND(),2)	=ROUND(1-2*RAND(),2)	=D2+B3	=E2+C3
2	=ROUND(1-2*RAND(),2)	=ROUND(1-2*RAND(),2)	=D3+B4	=E3+C4
3	=ROUND(1-2*RAND(),2)	=ROUND(1-2*RAND(),2)	=D4+B5	=E4+C5
4	=ROUND(1-2*RAND(),2)	=ROUND(1-2*RAND(),2)	=D5+B6	=E5+C6
5	=ROUND(1-2*RAND(),2)	=ROUND(1-2*RAND(),2)	=D6+B7	=E6+C7

What you need to do

1. Place in B3:B1002: =ROUND(1-2*RAND(),2). For rounding functions, see Chapter 67.
2. Do the same for column C.
3. Place in D3:E1002: =D2+B3.
4. Link R3 to D52 and T3 to E52.
5. Select range Q3:S16 and start a *Data Table* with no row input and an empty cell (e.g. Q1) as column input: =TABLE(,Q1).
6. In cells T3:T16: =IF(AND(R3>-1,R3<1,S3>-1,S3<1),"Close","").
7. Apply Conditional Formatting to cells R3:R16 with: =AND($R4>-1,$R4<1,$S4>-1,$S4<1).
8. Notice how Brownian motions can be very jittery—sometimes they center around the coordinates 0,0 but more often they veer to the sides or to the corners. The chance that they end up close to the spot where they had started is very improbable.
9. In the case shown below, begin and end of the random walk are close together, but most of the walk is done in the left lower quadrant.

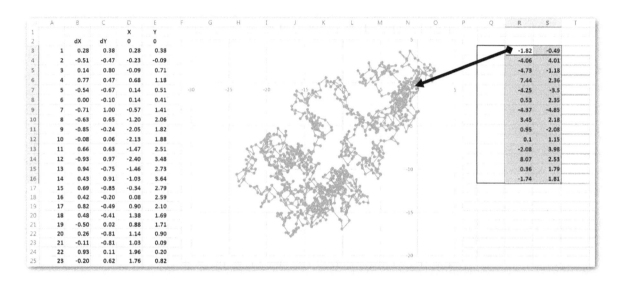

Chapter 40: Ehrenfest Urn

What the simulation does

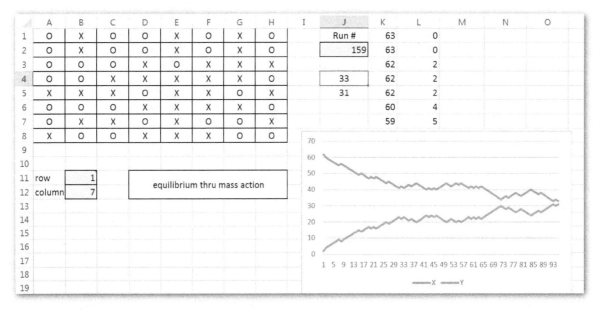

Consider two urns A and B. Urn A contains N marbles and urn B contains none. The marbles are labelled 1,2,...N. At each step of the algorithm, a number between 1 and N is chosen randomly, with all values having equal probability. The marble corresponding to that value is moved to the opposite urn. Hence the first step of the algorithm will always involve moving a marble from urn A to urn B.

What will the two urns look like after k steps? If k is sufficiently large, we may expect the urns to have equal numbers of morbles, as the probabilities of drawing a marble from A or from B become increasingly similar. States in which one urn has many more marbles than the other may be said to be unstable, as there is an overwhelming tendency to move marbles to the urn that contains fewer. This phenomenon is called the "Ehrenfest Urn," achieving equilibrium through mass action.

Ehrenfest sometimes used the image of two dogs; the one with fleas gradually infects the other one. In the long-time run, the mean number of fleas on both dogs converges to the equilibrium value.

What you need to know

Instead of using two urns, we use a "board" that has X's at all positions. Each time, at a random row and column position (cells B11 and B12), an X is replaced by an O, or vice-versa. Gradually, we reach an equilibrium where the number of X's and O's have become very similar, albeit with some oscillations of course.

During each run, the simulation finds a random row and column position to replace an X with an O or reversed. It keeps track of the number of runs in cell J2. It also counts the number of X's and Y's after each change and places those two numbers sequentially in row K (for X's) and in row L for O's. These two columns gradually feed the progressing curves in the chart.

All of this can be done with simple, but long formulas based on the functions IF, RAND or RANDBETWEEN, AND, ROW, COLUMN, and COUNTIF.

What you need to do

1. First you need to turn iteration ON, with only 1 iteration.
2. Place in cell B11 and B12: =RANDBETWEEN(1,8). If you don't have RANDBETWEEN, use =INT(RAND()*8+1).
3. Place in range A1:H8 a formula that populates each cell: =IF(AND(ROW(A1)=$B$11,COLUMN(A1)=$B$12),IF(A1="X","O","X"),IF(A1=0,"X",A1)).
4. Be aware in all formulas: O is not 0.
5. Place in cell J2: =J2+1. This counts the number of runs.
6. Place in cell J4: =COUNTIF($A$1:$H$8,"X"). This counts X's.
7. Place in cell J5: =COUNTIF($A$1:$H$8,"O"). This counts O's.
8. Place in cells K1:K536: =IF(ROW(A1)=$J$2,COUNTIF($A$1:$H$8,"X"),K1).
9. Place in cells L1:L536: =IF(ROW(B1)=$J$2,COUNTIF($A$1:$H$8,"O"),L1).
10. The chart is based on columns K and L. It runs from $K$6:$K$536 and from $L$6:$L$536. This way it skips the first adjustments when cleaning the slate.
11. Keep holding *F9* until the chart stops building (assuming the X-axis has a max of 536).
12. To reset the simulation, work in this order:
    a. Select cell J2, click in the formula bar, and hit *Ctrl Enter*.
    b. Select cells K1:K536, click in the formula bar, and hit *Ctrl Enter*.
    c. Select cells L1:L536, click in the formula bar, and hit *Ctrl Enter*.
    d. Select cells A1:H8, click in the formula bar, and hit *Ctrl Enter* (this places the formula in all selected cells at once).

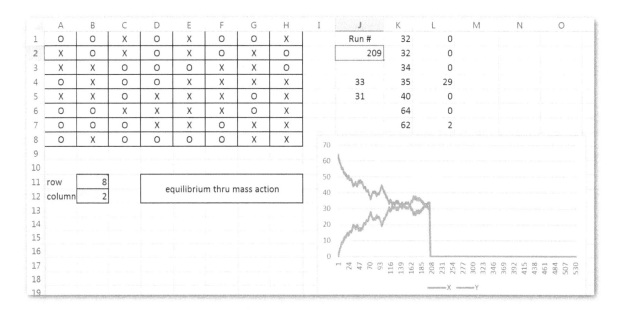

Chapter 41: A Data Table with Memory

What the simulation does

	A	B	C	D	E	F	G	H	I	J
1	0		1%			14		Min	Max	
2	0				2%	16		11	37	
3	0				3%	36		29	59	
4	0				4%	81		54	92	
5	0				5%	105		91	133	
6	0				6%	153		138	183	
7	0				7%	225		196	242	
8	0				8%	310		258	333	
9	0				9%	390		343	403	
10	0				10%	448		410	500	
11	0									
12	0							iterations on		
13	0									

In column A, we randomly choose 0's or 1's, with a chance for 1's based on cell C1. This is done 1,000 times. The number of 1's is calculated in cell F1. Based on this calculation, a *Data Table* in columns E and F runs all of this again for the next 9 percentages. So, when the percentage in C1 has been chosen to be 15%, column C shows the next 9 percentages from 16% to 24%.

Columns H and I serve as some kind of memory and keep track of the highest and lowest values reached so far. Each time you get a value in column F that is the same as the value for either the maximum or minimum, the max or min cell in column H or I gets marked (see picture on the next page). When the value in column F goes below the minimum or above the maximum, the corresponding values in column H and I are updated.

What you need to know

Each time you hit *F9*, the columns A and F will be recalculated. Whether the columns H and I change depends on the outcome in column F. The range from minimum to maximum can be pretty wide because we use only 1000 cases in column A

The formulas in columns H and I contain circular references. So you need to turn iteration ON with some 1000 iterations or so.

The formulas in column E use the ROW function to increase the percentage by 1%.

The formulas in columns H and I use an IF function nested inside another IF function (see Appendix for more information on nested functions).

Simulations in Action — MONTE CARLO

What you need to do

	A	B C D	E	F	G	H	I
1	=IF(RAND()<=$C$1,1,0)	0.01		=COUNTIF(A:A,1)	Min		Max
2	=IF(RAND()<=$C$1,1,0)		=$C$1+ROW(A1)/100	=TABLE(,C1)		=IF(H2=0,F2,IF(F2<H2,F2,H2))	=IF(I2=0,F2,IF(F2>I2,F2,I2))
3	=IF(RAND()<=$C$1,1,0)		=$C$1+ROW(A2)/100	=TABLE(,C1)		=IF(H3=0,F3,IF(F3<H3,F3,H3))	=IF(I3=0,F3,IF(F3>I3,F3,I3))
4	=IF(RAND()<=$C$1,1,0)		=$C$1+ROW(A3)/100	=TABLE(,C1)		=IF(H4=0,F4,IF(F4<H4,F4,H4))	=IF(I4=0,F4,IF(F4>I4,F4,I4))
5	=IF(RAND()<=$C$1,1,0)		=$C$1+ROW(A4)/100	=TABLE(,C1)		=IF(H5=0,F5,IF(F5<H5,F5,H5))	=IF(I5=0,F5,IF(F5>I5,F5,I5))
6	=IF(RAND()<=$C$1,1,0)		=$C$1+ROW(A5)/100	=TABLE(,C1)		=IF(H6=0,F6,IF(F6<H6,F6,H6))	=IF(I6=0,F6,IF(F6>I6,F6,I6))
7	=IF(RAND()<=$C$1,1,0)		=$C$1+ROW(A6)/100	=TABLE(,C1)		=IF(H7=0,F7,IF(F7<H7,F7,H7))	=IF(I7=0,F7,IF(F7>I7,F7,I7))
8	=IF(RAND()<=$C$1,1,0)		=$C$1+ROW(A7)/100	=TABLE(,C1)		=IF(H8=0,F8,IF(F8<H8,F8,H8))	=IF(I8=0,F8,IF(F8>I8,F8,I8))
9	=IF(RAND()<=$C$1,1,0)		=$C$1+ROW(A8)/100	=TABLE(,C1)		=IF(H9=0,F9,IF(F9<H9,F9,H9))	=IF(I9=0,F9,IF(F9>I9,F9,I9))

1. Turn iterations ON and set to 1000 iterations.
2. Place in cells A1:A1000: =IF(RAND()<=$C$1,1,0).
3. Place in cell F1: =COUNTIF(A:A,1).
4. Place in cells E2:E10: =$C$1+ROW(A1)/100.
5. Select E1:F10 and implement a *Data Table* with only a column input for C1: =TABLE(,C1).
6. Place in cells H2:H10: =IF(H2=0,F2,IF(F2<H2,F2,H2)).
7. Place in cells I2:I10: =IF(I2=0,F2,IF(F2>I2,F2,I2)).
8. Implement Conditional Formatting for H2:I10: =$F2
9. To reset the memory, select H2:H10, click in the formula bar, then hit *Ctrl Enter*.
10. Do the same for I2:I10.
11. In the beginning the difference between min and max is small (shown below), but then gradually grows (shown at the beginning of this chapter).

	A	B	C	D	E	F	G	H	I	J
1	0		1%			11		Min	Max	
2	0				2%	25		16	25	
3	0				3%	36		36	42	
4	0				4%	76		66	76	
5	0				5%	105		99	123	
6	0				6%	150		150	153	
7	0				7%	197		197	221	
8	0				8%	290		288	319	
9	0				9%	375		348	386	
10	0				10%	483		448	483	
11	0									
12	0							**iterations on**		
13	0									

Chapter 42: Juror Selection in Court

What the simulation does

	A	B	C	D	E	F	G	H	I
1	Candidates	100						Needed	24
2									
3		No opinion	No witness	Yes death		qualified			
4		0.4	0.3	0.6	Juror?	5		Pool	5
5	Juror 1			+	0			100	7
6	Juror 2			+	0			200	15
7	Juror 3				0			300	22
8	Juror 4			+	0			400	25
9	Juror 5	+	+		0			500	39
10	Juror 6			+	0			600	45
11	Juror 7		+	+	0			700	53
12	Juror 8		+	+	0			800	47
13	Juror 9	+	+	+	1			900	61
14	Juror 10				0			1000	63
15	Juror 11	+	+	+	1				
16	Juror 12				0				
17	Juror 13			+	0				
18	Juror 14			+	0				
19	Juror 15	+		+	0				

Countries with a juror system in court have to face the fact that they must choose 12+12=24 jurors from a larger pool of candidates after checking each candidate for certain criteria.

We assume we need 24 jurors (cell I1) from a pool of 100 (cell B1). We also use the following criteria: #1 they have no opinion yet whether the defendant is guilty (column B); #2 they were not witness to the crime (column C); #3 they accept the possibility of the death penalty (column D). These criteria have a probability of occurring in the population as shown in range B4:D4. Column E decides whether all three conditions have been met. Cell F4 counts how many in the pool of candidates actually qualified to be a juror in the case.

Finally we run this setup 10 more times (H:I), but for different pool sizes (from 100 to 1000). In column H, we mark pool sizes that meet the needed number of candidates (F2).

What you need to know

All gray cells have a formula in it. This is done by selecting all cells and implementing Conditional Formatting based on this formula: =ISFORMULA(A1).

In the run shown above, a pool of 300 candidates would not be enough to reach the 24 jurors needed, given the three conditions in B:D and their probabilities. But 400 would! If the probabilities in the population would be higher (B4:D4), the required pool of jurors would probably be smaller. And again, we are dealing with probabilities here, so results may vary!

The function TEXT converts a value to text in a specific number format. Its syntax is: TEXT(value,format_text).

What you need to do

1. All cells with a formula in it have a gray background: =ISFORMULA(A1).
2. Place in cells A5:A1005: =IF(ROW(A1)<=$B$1,TEXT(ROW(A1), "Juror 0"),"").
3. Place in cells B5:B1005: =IF(ROW(A1)<=$B$1,IF(RAND()<B$4,"+",""),"").
4. Place in cells C5:C1005: =IF(ROW(B1)<=$B$1,IF(RAND()<C$4,"+",""),"").
5. Place in cells D5:D1005: =IF(ROW(C1)<=$B$1,IF(RAND()<D$4,"+",""),"").
6. Place in cells E5:E1005: =IF(COUNTIF(B5:D5,"+")=3,1,0).
7. Place in cell F4: =SUM(E5:E1006).
8. Place in cell I4: =F4.
9. Select range H4:I14 for a *Data Table* with only column input from cell B1 (the pool size of candidates).
10. Use Conditional Formatting for range H5:I14: =$I5>=$I$1.
11. Sometimes, we may need a larger pool by mere chance. But if you raise the probabilities in cells B4:D4, smaller pools would be sufficient.

	A	B	C	D	E	F	G	H	I
1	Candidates	100						Needed	24
2									
3		No opinion	No witness	Yes death		qualified			
4		0.6	0.7	0.6	Juror?	27		Pool	27
5	Juror 1		+	+	0			100	23
6	Juror 2		+	+	0			200	50
7	Juror 3	+	+		0			300	86
8	Juror 4		+		0			400	94
9	Juror 5	+	+	+	1			500	147
10	Juror 6				0			600	158
11	Juror 7	+	+		0			700	186
12	Juror 8				0			800	223
13	Juror 9	+			0			900	202
14	Juror 10	+	+		0			1000	260
15	Juror 11	+	+	+	1				
16	Juror 12	+	+		0				
17	Juror 13	+	+	+	1				
18	Juror 14	+		+	0				
19	Juror 15		+	+	0				

Chapter 43: Running Project Costs

What the simulation does

	A	B	C	D	E	F	G	H	I	J	K	L
1	Estimates	SubProject1	SubProject2	SubProject3	SubProject4	SubProject5	Total		Mean	$ 222,500		
2	Max. Costs	$ 30,000	$ 10,000	$ 50,000	$ 80,000	$ 100,000	$ 270,000		SD	$ 38,784		
3	Min. Costs	$ 20,000	$ 5,000	$ 25,000	$ 50,000	$ 75,000	$ 175,000		Margin	$ 742	◄ ►	
4												
5	average	$ 25,021	$ 7,492	$ 37,517	$ 65,030	$ 87,478	$ 222,538		Z or t 95%	1.96		
6	upper bound	$ 30,684	$ 10,312	$ 51,728	$ 82,035	$ 101,504	$ 249,582					
7	lower bound	$ 19,359	$ 4,672	$ 23,306	$ 48,024	$ 73,452	$ 195,493					
8									Min. Runs	10,505		
9		$ 29,850	$ 9,228	$ 44,396	$ 63,490	$ 78,603	$ 225,568					
10		$ 22,832	$ 8,060	$ 49,349	$ 63,831	$ 99,209	$ 243,281					
11		$ 25,864	$ 6,493	$ 32,289	$ 75,040	$ 77,654	$ 217,340					
12		$ 27,157	$ 8,018	$ 30,988	$ 78,444	$ 80,199	$ 224,805					
13		$ 21,358	$ 9,321	$ 36,079	$ 65,431	$ 78,474	$ 210,663					
14		$ 23,643	$ 9,292	$ 44,428	$ 63,012	$ 81,899	$ 222,273					
15		$ 28,842	$ 9,521	$ 26,930	$ 62,541	$ 96,772	$ 224,605					
16		$ 22,490	$ 8,933	$ 32,575	$ 57,490	$ 81,470	$ 202,957					

This Monte Carlo simulation deals with risks we encounter when we have project costs that we anticipate to be between a maximum value and a minimum value for several sub-projects or various products.

Given the mean of total costs (J1), their SD (J2), and the margin (J3) we want based on a 95% confidence level, the simulation calculates in cell J8 how many runs are needed. A spinbotton control allows us to increase or decrease the margin.

Based on this number of runs, the sheet starts calculations beginning in row 9 down to the needed number of rows (in this case 10,505 rows in J8, which would end up in row 9 + 10,505).

The average of all these calculations is calculated in row 5, the upper bound in row 6, and the lower bound in row 7. The cells G5:G7 give us a cost estimate with a 95% confidence.

Manually changing maximum and minimum costs in rows 2 and 3 should affect the outcome.

What you need to know

To determine how far down the calculations should go, we need OFFSET (see Chaper 14).

The minimum number of runs (J8) can be calculated (see Chapter 24) as follows: $((1.96/(margin/mean))^2) * ((SD/mean)^2)$.

The mean (J1) is: =AVERAGE(G2:G3).

The Standard Deviation (J2) is: =STDEVP(G2:G3,J1). Notice we did not use STDEVS but STDEVP, which is for the entire population (in this case only two values).

The Margin (J3) is: =J1/K3. The cell K3 is regulated by a spinbutton control, which goes from 50 to 300 (with intervals of 50).

The Z or t value (J5) is based on a 95% confidence level and will be used to calculate the upper and lower bound of the costs in rows 6 and 7.

What you need to do

1. Place a spinbutton control next to cell J3: Min 50 | Max 300 | SmallChange 50 | LinkedCell K3 (not J3).
2. Place in cell J1: =AVERAGE(G2:G3).
3. Place in cell J2: =STDEVP(G2:G3,J1). It uses 3 values.
4. Place in cell J3: =J1/K3.
5. Place in cells B9:F14426 (or so): =IF(ROW(A1)<=$J$8,RAND()*(B$2-B$3)+B$3,"").
6. Place in cells G9:G14426: =IF(ROW(A1)<=$J$8,SUM(B9:F9),"").
7. Place in cells B5:G5: =AVERAGE(B9:OFFSET(B9,$J$6-1,0)).
8. Place in cells B6:G6: =B5+$J$4*STDEV.S(B9:OFFSET(B9,$J$6-1,0)).
9. Place in cells B7:G7: =B5-$J$4*STDEV.S(B9:OFFSET(B9,$J$6-1,0)).
10. Hitting *F9* reveals how the cells G5:G7 give us a rather reliable cost estimate.
11. Changing the scrollbar control shows us that smaller margins require a larger number of runs, and reversed, oscillating between 292 and 10,505 (see below).

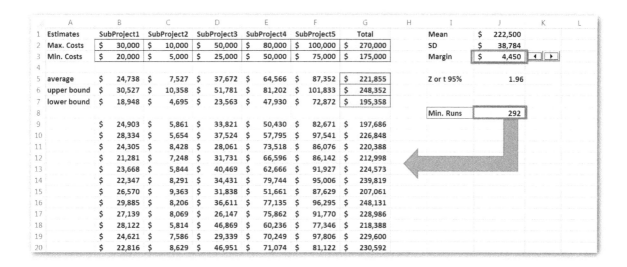

Chapter 44: Forecasting Profits

What the simulation does

	A	B	C	D	E	F	G	H	I	J	K
1	produced	60,000	=RAND()		demand probabilities						
2	rand#	0.86166547		0.00	20,000	10%					
3	demand	60,000		0.10	30,000	35%					
4	unit cost	$1.50		0.45	40,000	30%					
5	unit price	$4.00		0.75	60,000	25%					
6	unit disposal	$0.20									
7											
8	revenues	$240,000.00									
9	prod. costs	$90,000.00									
10	dispos. Costs	$0.00									
11	profit	$150,000.00									
12											
13	mean profit	$50,000.00	$71,094.00	$77,698.00	$70,694.00	$62,010.00	$49,714.00		production		
14	SD profits	$0.00	$12,204.27	$27,395.61	$38,994.76	$54,917.06	$56,356.92		40,000	best profit	
15	lower 95%	$50,000.00	$70,337.57	$76,000.00	$68,277.08	$58,606.21	$46,220.96		70,000	most risky	
16	upper 95%	$50,000.00	$71,850.43	$79,396.00	$73,110.92	$65,413.79	$53,207.04				
17											
18	$150,000.00	20,000	30,000	40,000	50,000	60,000	70,000	units produced			
19	1	$50,000.00	$75,000.00	$100,000.00	$83,000.00	-$18,000.00	$49,000.00				
20	2	$50,000.00	$75,000.00	$58,000.00	$41,000.00	$24,000.00	$7,000.00				
21	3	$50,000.00	$75,000.00	$100,000.00	$83,000.00	$24,000.00	$7,000.00				
22	4	$50,000.00	$75,000.00	$100,000.00	$41,000.00	$150,000.00	$7,000.00				
23	5	$50,000.00	$75,000.00	$58,000.00	$83,000.00	$150,000.00	$133,000.00				
24	6	$50,000.00	$75,000.00	$100,000.00	$125,000.00	-$18,000.00	$7,000.00				
25	7	$50,000.00	$75,000.00	$16,000.00	$83,000.00	$150,000.00	$133,000.00				
26	8	$50,000.00	$75,000.00	$16,000.00	$83,000.00	$150,000.00	$7,000.00				
27	9	$50,000.00	$75,000.00	$58,000.00	-$1,000.00	$150,000.00	$49,000.00				
28	10	$50,000.00	$75,000.00	$16,000.00	$41,000.00	$66,000.00	$49,000.00				

Let's say we are trying to the figure out the optimal amount of production needed in order to maximize our profits. If the demand for this product is regulated by a range of estimated probabilities, then we can determine optimal production by simulating demand within that range of probabilities and calculating profit for each level of demand.

The simulation uses three tables to set up this calculation. The table top right (E:F) sets up the estimated probabilities of various demand levels. The table top left (A:B) calculates the profit for one trial production quantity. Cell B1 contains the trial production quantity. Cell B2 generates a random number. In cell B3, we simulate demand for this product with the function VLOOKUP.

The third table, on the lower left, is a *Data Table* which simulates each possible production quantity (20,000, 30,000, to 70,000) some 1,000 times and calculates profits for each trial number (1 to 1,000) and each production quantity (10,000, etc.).

Finally, row 13 calculates the mean profit for the six different production quantities. In this example, the figures show that a production of 40,000 units results in maximum profits (D13).

What you need to know

The VLOOKUP function in B3 matches the value in B1 with the closest previous match in the first column of table D2:E5; column D has cumulative totals.

In cell A18 starts a *Data Table*. A18 has a link to the profit in B11. Then it uses cell B1 (20,000) for the row input, and an empty cell (say, H12) for the column input.

What you need to do

1. Place in cells D3(!):D5: =SUM($F$2:F2). Cell D2 has 0 in it.
2. Place in cell B3: =VLOOKUP(B2,D2:F5,2). It uses the random number in cell B2.
3. Place in cell B8: =MIN(B1,B3)*B5.
4. Place in cell B9: =B1*B4.
5. Place in cell B10: =B6*IF(B1>B3,B1-B3,0).
6. Place in cell B11: =B8-B9-B10.
7. Place in cell B18: =B11.
8. Select cells A18:G1018 and implement a *Data Table* with B1 as row input and an empty cell as column input.
9. Place in cells B13:G13: =AVERAGE(B19:B1018).
10. Place in cells B14:G14: =STDEV(B19:B1018).
11. Place in cells B15:G15: =B13-1.96*B14/SQRT(1000).
12. Place in cells B16:G16: =B13+1.96*B14/SQRT(1000).
13. Place in cell I14: =INDEX(B18:G18,1,MATCH(MAX(B13:G13),B13:G13,0)).
14. Place in cell I15: =INDEX(B18:G18,1,MATCH(MAX(B14:G14),B14:G14,0)).
15. Unless you change some values manually, *F9* keeps showing the best profit for a production of 40,000 units. The most risky outcome fluctuates between 60,000 and 70,000 units.

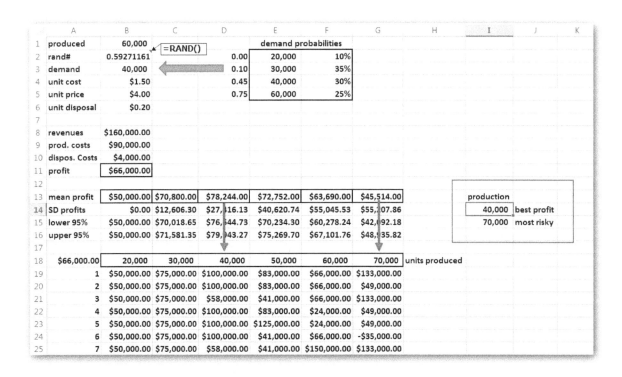

Chapter 45: Uncertainty in Sales

What the simulation does

As said before, Monte Carlo simulations are computerized mathematical techniques that allow people to account for risks in quantitative analysis and decision making. They create more certainty in the midst of many uncertainties.

In this case, the decision-maker supplies sales data and probabilities (the shaded cells in columns A and B).

Based on this information, the simulation creates some 10,000 distributions with a range of possible outcomes (center section) and with the probabilities they will occur for any choice of action (right section).

What you need to know

The situation is basically simple. The major functions we need to achieve such kinds of predictions in this case are RAND, VLOOKUP, COUNT, and COUNTIF. Again we use 1,000 runs in the center section (F:I) to reach more reliable predictions.

What you need to do

1. Use the formulas as shown in columns C and D on the previous picture.
2. In cells F3:F10002: =VLOOKUP(RAND(),$C$3:$D$5,2).
3. In cells G3:G10002: =VLOOKUP(RAND(),$C$10:$D$13,2).
4. In cells H3:H10002: =VLOOKUP(RAND(),$C$18:$D$20,2).
5. In cells I3:I10002: =F3*G3*H3.
6. In cells M8:M24: =$M$2+($M$2*K8).
7. In cells N8:N24: =$M$2+($M$2*L8).
8. Place in O8:O24: =(COUNTIF($I$3:$I$10002,"<="&M8)-(COUNTIF($I$3:$I$10002,"<"&N8)))/(COUNT($I$3:$I$10002)).
9. Place in cells Q2, Q3, and Q4: =AVERAGE(I3:I10002), followed by =MIN(…) and =MAX(…).
10. Place in cell Q7: =(COUNTIF($I$3:$I$10002,">"&M2) /(COUNT($I$3:$I$10002))).
11. Place in cell Q8: =(COUNTIF($I$3:$I$10002,"<"&M2) /(COUNT($I$3:$I$10002))).
12. In cell P15 and P21: =M2. This was last year's base.
13. In cells Q12:Q17: =(COUNTIF($I$3:$I$10002,">"&P12) /(COUNT($I$3:$I$10002))).
14. In cells Q19:Q24: =(COUNTIF($I$3:$I$10002,"<"&P19) /(COUNT($I$3:$I$10002))).

	K	L	M	N	O	P	Q
2	Last year's base	569993		Average Sales Day			=AVERAGE(I:I)
3	Change this year	=Q2-M2		Minimum Sales Day			=MIN(I:I)
4				Maximum Sales Day			=MAX(I:I)
5							
6					Probabilities		
7	% range		Sales range		Probability	Positive	=(COUNTIF(I:I,">"&M2)/(COUNT(I:I)))
8	-0.25	-0.3	=$M$2+($M$2*K8)	=$M$2+($M$2*L8)	=(COUNTIF(I:I,"<="&M8)-(COUNTIF(I:I,"<"&N8)))/(COUNT(I:I))	Negative	=(COUNTIF(I:I,"<"&M2)/(COUNT(I:I)))
9	-0.2	-0.25	=$M$2+($M$2*K9)	=$M$2+($M$2*L9)	=(COUNTIF(I:I,"<="&M9)-(COUNTIF(I:I,"<"&N9)))/(COUNT(I:I))		
10	-0.15	-0.2	=$M$2+($M$2*K10)	=$M$2+($M$2*L10)	=(COUNTIF(I:I,"<="&M10)-(COUNTIF(I:I,"<"&N10)))/(COUNT(I:I))		
11	-0.1	-0.15	=$M$2+($M$2*K11)	=$M$2+($M$2*L11)	=(COUNTIF(I:I,"<="&M11)-(COUNTIF(I:I,"<"&N11)))/(COUNT(I:I))	Sales will exceed:	
12	-0.07	-0.1	=$M$2+($M$2*K12)	=$M$2+($M$2*L12)	=(COUNTIF(I:I,"<="&M12)-(COUNTIF(I:I,"<"&N12)))/(COUNT(I:I))	400000	=(COUNTIF(I:I,">"&P12)/(COUNT(I:I)))
13	-0.05	-0.07	=$M$2+($M$2*K13)	=$M$2+($M$2*L13)	=(COUNTIF(I:I,"<="&M13)-(COUNTIF(I:I,"<"&N13)))/(COUNT(I:I))	450000	=(COUNTIF(I:I,">"&P13)/(COUNT(I:I)))
14	-0.02	-0.05	=$M$2+($M$2*K14)	=$M$2+($M$2*L14)	=(COUNTIF(I:I,"<="&M14)-(COUNTIF(I:I,"<"&N14)))/(COUNT(I:I))	500000	=(COUNTIF(I:I,">"&P14)/(COUNT(I:I)))
15	0	-0.02	=$M$2+($M$2*K15)	=$M$2+($M$2*L15)	=(COUNTIF(I:I,"<="&M15)-(COUNTIF(I:I,"<"&N15)))/(COUNT(I:I))	=M2	=(COUNTIF(I:I,">"&P15)/(COUNT(I:I)))
16	0	0	=$M$2+($M$2*K16)	=$M$2	=(COUNTIF(I:I,"<="&M16)-(COUNTIF(I:I,"<"&N16)))/(COUNT(I:I))	600000	=(COUNTIF(I:I,">"&P16)/(COUNT(I:I)))
17	0	0.02	=($M$2+($M$2*K17))	=$M$2+($M$2*L17)	=(COUNTIF(I:I,"<="&M17)-(COUNTIF(I:I,"<"&N17)))/(COUNT(I:I))	650000	=(COUNTIF(I:I,">"&P17)/(COUNT(I:I)))
18	0.02	0.05	=$M$2+($M$2*K18)	=$M$2+($M$2*L18)	=(COUNTIF(I:I,"<="&M18)-(COUNTIF(I:I,"<"&N18)))/(COUNT(I:I))	Sales will be under:	
19	0.05	0.07	=$M$2+($M$2*K19)	=$M$2+($M$2*L19)	=(COUNTIF(I:I,"<="&M19)-(COUNTIF(I:I,"<"&N19)))/(COUNT(I:I))	600000	=(COUNTIF(I:I,"<"&P19)/(COUNT(I:I)))
20	0.07	0.1	=$M$2+($M$2*K20)	=$M$2+($M$2*L20)	=(COUNTIF(I:I,"<="&M20)-(COUNTIF(I:I,"<"&N20)))/(COUNT(I:I))	575000	=(COUNTIF(I:I,"<"&P20)/(COUNT(I:I)))
21	0.1	0.15	=$M$2+($M$2*K21)	=$M$2+($M$2*L21)	=(COUNTIF(I:I,"<="&M21)-(COUNTIF(I:I,"<"&N21)))/(COUNT(I:I))	=M2	=(COUNTIF(I:I,"<"&P21)/(COUNT(I:I)))
22	0.15	0.2	=$M$2+($M$2*K22)	=$M$2+($M$2*L22)	=(COUNTIF(I:I,"<="&M22)-(COUNTIF(I:I,"<"&N22)))/(COUNT(I:I))	500000	=(COUNTIF(I:I,"<"&P22)/(COUNT(I:I)))
23	0.2	0.25	=$M$2+($M$2*K23)	=$M$2+($M$2*L23)	=(COUNTIF(I:I,"<="&M23)-(COUNTIF(I:I,"<"&N23)))/(COUNT(I:I))	450000	=(COUNTIF(I:I,"<"&P23)/(COUNT(I:I)))
24	0.25	0.3	=$M$2+($M$2*K24)	=$M$2+($M$2*L24)	=(COUNTIF(I:I,"<="&M24)-(COUNTIF(I:I,"<"&N24)))/(COUNT(I:I))	425000	=(COUNTIF(I:I,"<"&P24)/(COUNT(I:I)))

Chapter 46: Exchange Rate Fluctuations

What the simulation does

	A	B	C	D	E	F	G	H	I	J
1		Input			1000x	Profit				
2	Units Sold	100,000				$ 126,434,782.61		Average F2:F1008	$ 126,492,050.24	
3					0.908	$ 129,037,694.01		0.975 percentile	$ 131,869,593.07	
4	Unit price U$	$ 1,200.00			0.931	$ 126,151,843.82		0.025 percentile	$ 121,391,849.53	
5	Exchange Rate A$/U$	0.92			0.910	$ 125,449,838.19				
6	SD exchange rate	0.02			0.956	$ 126,718,954.25				
7					0.887	$ 123,253,446.45		exchange rate	frequency	
8	Unit Cost	$ 40.00			0.931	$ 126,718,954.25		0.86	3	
9					0.930	$ 123,118,644.07		0.88	12	
10	Total Cost U$	4,000,000			0.913	$ 123,931,769.72		0.90	142	
11					0.915	$ 121,918,153.20		0.92	354	
12	Revenue U$	130,434,783			0.898	$ 126,718,954.25		0.94	339	
13					0.910	$ 128,890,365.45		0.96	132	
14	Profit	$ 126,434,782.61			0.922	$ 129,333,333.33		0.98	22	
15					0.915	$ 125,310,344.83		1.00	2	
16					0.906	$ 125,729,729.73		not covered	0	
17					0.920	$ 129,630,289.53				
18					0.934	$ 127,147,540.98				
19					0.913	$ 127,291,028.45				
20					0.976	$ 125,449,838.19				

The profit of a certain company depends on a fluctuating exchange rate between the American and Australian dollar—or any other foreign currency. The average profit we predict in cell B14 is based on a fixed exchange rate (B5). But in reality this rate has normally distributed fluctuations with a Standard Deviation shown in cell B6. So we need to simulate such variations.

This simulation is done by using a *Data Table* that simulates exchange rates (in E3:E1008) that fluctuate around a rate of 0.92 (B5) with a SD of 0.02 (B6). The frequency table of these fluctuations is shown in range H8:I16. The average of profits is shown in cell I3, which is in-between the values of cell I3 and cell I4 at a confidence level of 95%. The outcome is obviously affected by uncertainty, but also by any manual changes in B2:B8.

What you need to know

An essential part of this simulation is the first column of the *Data Table* (column D). It holds this formula: =NORM.INV(RAND(),0.92,0.02)—or whatever the fixed numeric values should be. The column input cell of the *Data Table* is the exchange rate value in cell B5.

The problem is that calculations in column E make column F recalculate, which in turn recalculates column E. So the two columns do not completely match, but that won't affect the total outcome because of the law of large numbers. However, if this bothers you, then replace the formulas in column E with their values. The drawback is that *F9* will no longer cause recalculations, because the values in column F are now fixed (unless you change values in column B manually).

For the percentile scores, we use the function PERCENTILE in column L. This function works in all Excel versions. In version 2010 and later, it can be replaced with PERCENTILE.EXC or PERCENTILE.INC. The former function does not include k=1, whereas the latter one does. So the latter one is equivalent to the older function PERCENTILE.

What you need to do

	E	F	G	H	I
1	1000x		Profit		
2		=B14		Average F2:F1008	=AVERAGE($F$2:$F$1008)
3	=ROUND(NORMINV(RAND(),0.92,0.02),3)	=TABLE(,B5)		0.975 percentile	=PERCENTILE.EXC($F$2:$F$1008,0.975)
4	=ROUND(NORMINV(RAND(),0.92,0.02),3)	=TABLE(,B5)		0.025 percentile	=PERCENTILE.EXC($F$2:$F$1008,0.025)
5	=ROUND(NORMINV(RAND(),0.92,0.02),3)	=TABLE(,B5)			
6	=ROUND(NORMINV(RAND(),0.92,0.02),3)	=TABLE(,B5)			
7	=ROUND(NORMINV(RAND(),0.92,0.02),3)	=TABLE(,B5)		exchange rate	frequency
8	=ROUND(NORMINV(RAND(),0.92,0.02),3)	=TABLE(,B5)		0.86	=FREQUENCY(E3:E1008,H8:H15)
9	=ROUND(NORMINV(RAND(),0.92,0.02),3)	=TABLE(,B5)		0.88	=FREQUENCY(E3:E1008,H8:H15)
10	=ROUND(NORMINV(RAND(),0.92,0.02),3)	=TABLE(,B5)		0.9	=FREQUENCY(E3:E1008,H8:H15)

1. Cell F2 has a link to the profit in cell B14.
2. Place in cells E3:E1008: =NORM.INV(RAND(),0.92,0.02).
3. Select range E2:G1008 and implement a *Data Table* with no row input and cell B5 for column input: =TABLE(,B5).
4. Calculate in cell I2 the average profit of all 1,000 runs: =AVERAGE($F$3:$F$1008).
5. Calculate in cell I3 the 0.975 percentile: =PERCENTILE.INC($F$2:$F$1008,0.975).
6. Calculate in cell I4 the 0.025 percentile: =PERCENTILE.INC($F$2:$F$1008,0.025).
7. To prove that NORM.INV did create a normally distributed set of exchange rates, we calculate frequencies. Select I11:I18: =FREQUENCY(E3:E1008,H8:H15) with *Ctrl Shift Enter*.
8. Hitting *F9* will run 1,000 times again. In spite of uncertainty about exchange rate oscillations, we have a bit more certainty in I2:I4 of what to expect.
9. As shown below, we have 95% confidence that our profit will be between I2 and I3.

H	I
Average F2:F1008	$ 126,594,972.37
0.975 percentile	$ 132,674,259.68
0.025 percentile	$ 121,391,849.53
exchange rate	frequency
0.86	5
0.88	27
0.90	155
0.92	314
0.94	338
0.96	144
0.98	22
1.00	1
not covered	0

H	I
Average F2:F1008	$ 126,672,178.25
0.975 percentile	$ 132,054,421.77
0.025 percentile	$ 121,523,012.55
exchange rate	frequency
0.86	1
0.88	22
0.90	158
0.92	320
0.94	347
0.96	138
0.98	20
1.00	0
not covered	0

Chapter 47: Monte Carlo Stock Values

What the simulation does

	A	B	C	D	E	F	G	H	I	J	K
1	drift (annual)	10.00%		drift (daily)	0.04%		drift (expected)	0.01%			
2	volatility (annual)	40.00%		volatility (daily)	2.52%		Initial Stock	100			
3											
4	average of 1000	$ 100.15	$ 100.14	$ 100.36	$ 100.43	$ 100.62	$ 100.74	$ 100.75	$ 100.65	$ 100.75	$ 100.69
5	baseline	$ 100.00	$ 100.00	$ 100.00	$ 100.00	$ 100.00	$ 100.00	$ 100.00	$ 100.00	$ 100.00	$ 100.00
6											
7											
8		day 1	day 2	day 3	day 4	day 5	day 6	day 7	day 8	day 9	day 10
9	N(0,1)	-1.5008	0.0269	0.4519	0.6218	0.7066	-2.5999	0.6450	0.8958	-0.0416	-0.1283
10	Log Return	-3.769%	0.080%	1.151%	1.579%	1.793%	-6.538%	1.638%	2.270%	-0.092%	-0.311%
11	Price	$ 96.30	$ 96.38	$ 97.49	$ 99.05	$ 100.84	$ 94.46	$ 96.02	$ 98.22	$ 98.13	$ 97.83
12		$ 98.64	$ 99.49	$ 100.93	$ 101.51	$ 100.92	$ 96.83	$ 93.73	$ 93.06	$ 90.28	$ 91.51
13		$ 99.45	$ 97.56	$ 102.03	$ 105.68	$ 107.20	$ 107.10	$ 100.40	$ 99.37	$ 98.19	$ 93.35
14		$ 98.75	$ 100.04							$ 101.53	$ 103.91
15		$ 105.04	$ 104.21							$ 93.55	$ 91.98
16		$ 98.26	$ 96.07							$ 105.99	$ 108.41
17		$ 102.10	$ 101.91							$ 107.89	$ 112.54
18		$ 102.18	$ 99.65							$ 94.13	$ 97.69
19		$ 101.78	$ 101.35							$ 110.60	$ 113.45
20		$ 100.19	$ 104.38							$ 110.33	$ 108.26
21		$ 99.74	$ 102.63							$ 93.11	$ 90.04
22		$ 99.27	$ 100.55							$ 109.52	$ 111.36
23		$ 100.65	$ 98.74							$ 101.61	$ 102.41
24		$ 101.03	$ 103.20							$ 106.37	$ 108.03
25		$ 98.43	$ 97.74							$ 97.47	$ 96.01
26		$ 100.96	$ 101.01							$ 108.50	$ 109.65
27		$ 98.92	$ 99.34							$ 99.69	$ 101.12
28		$ 97.80	$ 96.30							$ 99.20	$ 101.25
29		$ 101.25	$ 98.66	$ 100.97	$ 101.23	$ 99.73	$ 100.18	$ 98.32	$ 97.63	$ 96.53	$ 94.35
30		$ 102.77	$ 103.40	$ 103.34	$ 104.42	$ 105.29	$ 106.80	$ 108.45	$ 112.15	$ 111.35	$ 112.00

The development of stock prices is subject to volatility (B2) and drift (B1). Drift means that stock prices continue to climb if earnings are good—or fall if earnings are bad—for months after company earnings announcements.

Based on the annual drift and volatility, we can calculate the daily drift (E1) and volatility (E2), plus the expected drift (H1). This allows us to project for 10 consecutive days (row 8) a random factor (row 9), a lognormal return (row 10), and a stock price (row 11).

It is a lognormal diffusion process equivalent to the lognormal of today's price divided by yesterday's price: $ln(S_t/S_{t-1}) = \alpha + z_t\sigma$. The deterministic factor is α, which is the expected drift (H1). The non-deterministic factor is the volatility (σ in E2) times a random number (z_t) generated in row 9. The new price of the stock on each next trading day is the initial value times the EXP function of the lognormal return in row 10.

Obviously, the prices in row 11 keep changing when you press *F9*. Therefore, we repeat these price calculations with 1,000 more runs. The chart shows us that individual runs (e.g. rows 11:13) can vary widely, but the results of 1,000 runs are rather stable slightly upwards (see next page).

What you need to know

The function EXP returns *e* raised to the power of number. The constant *e* equals 2.71828182845904, the base of the natural logarithm.

		day 1	day 2	day 3	day 4	day 5
8						
9	N(0,1)	=NORM.S.INV(RAND())	=NORM.S.INV(RAND())	=NORM.S.INV(RAND())	=NORM.S.INV(RAND())	=NORM.S.INV(RAND())
10	Log Return	=$H$1+$E$2*B9	=$H$1+$E$2*C9	=$H$1+$E$2*D9	=$H$1+$E$2*E9	=$H$1+$E$2*F9
11	Price	=$H$2*EXP(B10)	=B11*EXP(C10)	=C11*EXP(D10)	=D11*EXP(E10)	=E11*EXP(F10)
12		=TABLE(,A8)	=TABLE(,A8)	=TABLE(,A8)	=TABLE(,A8)	=TABLE(,A8)

What you need to do

1. Place in cell E1: =B1/252. (assuming a year has 252 trading days
2. Place in cell E2: =B2/SQRT(252).
3. Place in cell H1: =E1-0.5*E2^2.
4. Place in cells B9:K9: =NORM.S.INV(RAND()).
5. Place in cells B10:K10: =$H$1+$E$2*B9.
6. Place in cell B11: =$H$2*EXP(B10).
7. Place in cells C11:K11: =B11*EXP(C10).
8. Select range A11:K1011 and implement a *Data Table*: =TABLE(,A8).
9. Place in cells B4:K4: =AVERAGE(B11:B1011).
10. Place in cells B5:K5: =$H$2. This is the baseline, the original stock value.
11. The picture below shows the baseline, the mean of 1000 runs, and 3 individual runs.

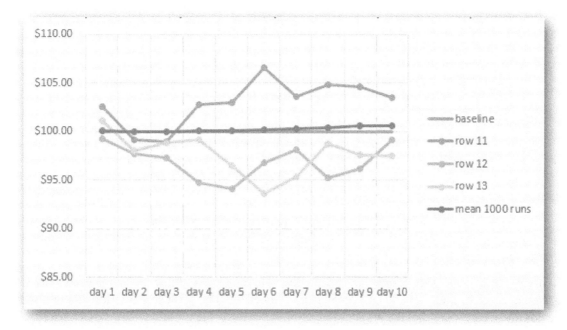

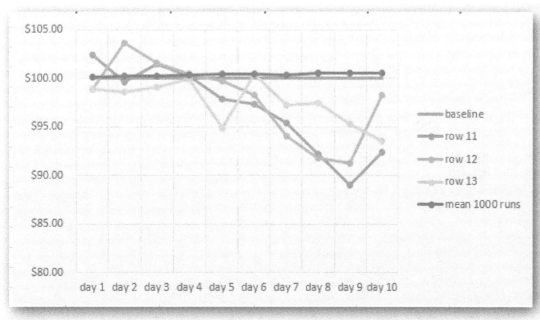

Chapter 48: Monte Carlo Retirement

What the simulation does

	A	B	C	D	E	F	G	H	I	J	K	L
1	Start investment	$ 100,000				1,000 repeats						
2	Avg. return	11.20%			end value:	$ 128,039.02		mean	$ 120,859.83			
3	SD of return	18%				$ 131,135.35		median	$ 120,136.34			
4	Years to retirement	30				$ 132,541.59		5%	$ 91,534.49			
5	Annual investment	$ 10,000				$ 147,066.14				95% confidence of >=91K		
6						$ 127,727.43						
7						$ 105,269.44						
8	Year	Return	End of year			$ 125,830.57						
9	1	0.73%	$ 110,732.33			$ 99,667.18						
10	2	10.34%	$ 120,342.79			$ 119,977.13						
11	3	30.56%	$ 140,564.20			$ 112,377.28						
12	4	16.12%	$ 126,119.80			$ 116,942.89						
13	5	13.03%	$ 123,028.08			$ 148,078.93						
14	6	16.48%	$ 126,482.15			$ 96,993.02						
15	7	3.76%	$ 113,760.51			$ 132,868.44						
16	8	28.04%	$ 138,039.27			$ 99,154.56						
17	9	27.13%	$ 137,132.07			$ 107,608.06						
18	10	3.87%	$ 113,866.08			$ 116,140.83						
19	11	5.21%	$ 115,209.44			$ 123,995.32						
20	12	7.69%	$ 117,691.40			$ 118,196.94						

This simulation[3] starts with a certain investment in a pension plan (B1) that comes with a certain average return (B2) and a certain SD of returns (B3). At the end of each year a fixed new investment is made (B5). What is the amount of money available at the time of retirement? The question is of course how many years are left up to retirement. Cell B4 contains that information.

Obviously, there is quite some uncertainty involved. Therefore, the end amount after 30 years in column C is not very reliable. To gain more certainty, a Monte Carlo simulation might be the best tool to gain a bit more confidence.

This is done in the *Data Table* of column E:F where we run column C some 1,000 times more. The average of these 1,000 runs is calculated in cell I2. The 5% percentile tells us that we have a confidence of 95 % that the amount in cell I4 is the lowest amount we may expect after the number of years in cell B4.

What you need to know

The *Data Table* must start in F2 with a link to the end amount in column C reached after n years. Since column C can have a variable height depending on the number of years chosen in cell B4, we need the function OFFSET again (see Chapter 14): =OFFSET(C9,B4-1,0).

For the 5% percentile scores, we used the function PERCENTILE in column L. In version 2010 and later, it can be replaced with PERCENTILE.EXC or PERCENTILE.INC. The former function does not include k=1, whereas the latter one does. In this case, we can use PERCENTILE or PERCENTILE.INC.

---

[3] My special thanks for part of this simulation go to Matt Macarty.

What you need to do

1. Place a scrollbar control next to cell B1: Min 500 | Max 30000 | SmallChange 100 | LargeChange 10000 | LinkedCell C1.
2. Place in cell B1: =C1*10.
3. Place a spinbutton control next to cell B4: Min 5 | Max 40 | SmallChange 1 | LinkedCell B4.
4. Place in cells A9:A38: =IF(ROW(A1)<=$B$4,ROW(A1),"").
5. Place in cells B9:B38: =IF(ROW(A1)<=$B$4,NORM.INV(RAND(),$B$2,$B$3),"").
6. Place in cell C9: =IF(ROW(A1)<=$B$4,$B$1*(1+B9)+$B$5, "").
7. Place in cells C10:C38: =IF(ROW(A2)<=$B$4,$B$1*(1+B10)+$B$5, "").
8. Place in cell F1: =OFFSET(C9,B4-1,0)
9. Select the cells E2:E1002 and implement a *Data Table*: =TABLE(,D2).
10. Place in cell I2: =AVERAGE(F2:F1002).
11. Place in cell I3: =MEDIAN(F2:F1002). Mean and average are close, so little skewness.
12. Place in cell I4: =PERCENTILE.INC(F2:F1002,5%).
13. Place in cell J5: ="95% confidence of >=" & INT(I4/1000) & "K".
14. Below is shown the outcome for retirement in 15 years.

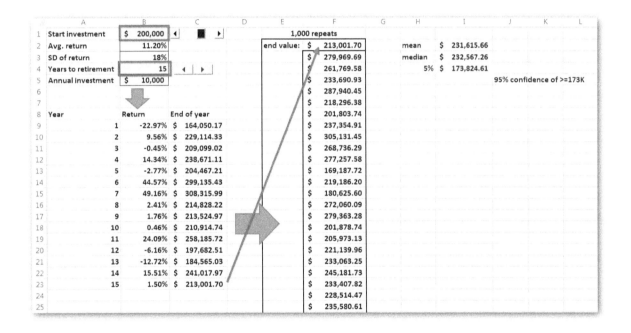

Chapter 49: Monte Carlo and Pi

What the simulation does

	A	B	C	D	E	F
1	Pi	3.14159		10,000,000x	3.1416	
2						
3	1			10,000x	3.16800	
4	1				3.23200	
5	1				3.13600	
6	1				3.02400	
7	1				3.14400	
8	1				3.14000	
9	0				3.14800	
10	1				3.18000	
11	1				3.05200	
12	0				3.15200	
13	0				3.13600	
14	1				3.10400	
15	0				3.09200	

Excel has a function to calculate *pi* (π)—not surprisingly, it's the function PI. Instead of using that function, we could also use a Monte Carlo simulation to approach the *pi* value.

Because Excel does have a PI function, we can compare its value (cell A1) with the value we received through our simulation (E1). There are only very minor deviations, because of the large number of runs we used in this Monte Carlo simulation (10,000,000 runs).

What you need to know

The Monte Carlo approach uses the formula *RAND()^2 + RAND()^2*. If this formula returns a value that is less than or equal to 1, we place the number 1 in column A—otherwise the number 0: *=IF(RAND()^2 + RAND()^2<=1,1,0)*. We do this 1,000 times in column A.

Then, in cell E3, we sum all 0s and 1s in column A, multiply them by 4, and divide this by the numbers of 0s and 1s: *=4*SUM(A3:A1002)/1000*. Next we repeat this calculation 10,000 times in a *Data Table*. So the end result is reached after 10 million times

The mean of all these results is calculated in cell E1, and can be compared with the result of the Excel function PI.

What you need to do

1. Place in cell B1: =PI().
2. Place in cells A3:A10002: =IF(RAND()^2 + RAND()^2<=1,1,0).
3. Place in cell E3: =4*SUM(A3:A10002)/10000.
4. Select range D3:E10002 and implement a *Data Table* with no row input and a column input of an empty cell (e.g. F3): =TABLE(,F3).
5. Place in cell E1: =AVERAGE(E3:E10002).
6. Because of the numerous repeats, it will take longer to complete the calculations. Be patient!
7. Notice that individual runs of 1,000 in column E vary, but the mean of means of 10,000,000 repeats comes rather close to the outcome of the function PI.

	A	B	C	D	E	F
1	Pi	3.14159		10,000,000x	3.14192	
2						
3	1			10,000x	3.14800	
4	1				3.10800	
5	1				3.09200	
6	1				3.08000	
7	1				3.18400	
8	1				3.17600	
9	1				3.16000	
10	1				3.14800	

Chapter 50: Integration Simulated

What the simulation does

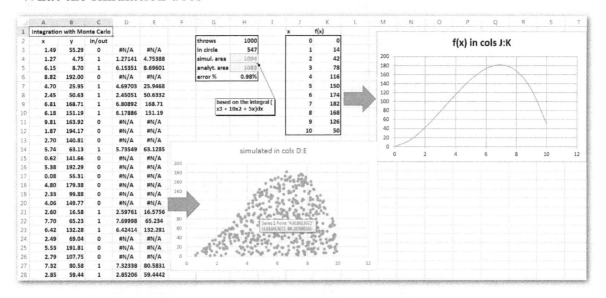

Consider a circle inscribed within a square with sides of *s* units. The radius of the circle equates to *s*/2. This is basically an integration problem with an analytical solution (H5). The analytical curve is plotted in the XY chart to the right.

However, we can simulate this outcome with a Monte Carlo technique that gives us an approximation of the analytical integral. One-thousand "darts" (H2) are randomly thrown at the diagram and then we count the number that fall inside the circle (H3). So the simulated area (H4) is *20*10*F3/F2*. The result is shown in the Scatter chart to the left.

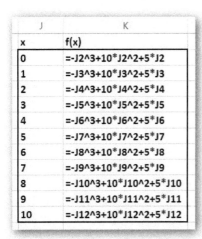

What you need to know

I won't explain this part, but the integral would be: $-x^3 + 10x^2 + 5x)dx$. This formula is used in the cells of columns C and K. The XY chart to the right plots the analytic solution based on columns J and K (see left). The curve is within a 10 by 200 rectangle (columns A and B).

We will use the RAND function in columns A and B to determine the position of all 1,000 "darts."

Cell H6 shows us how far the simulated solution deviates from the analytical solution.

What you need to do

1. Place in cells A3:A1002: =RAND()*10. This is for the X-position of the dart.
2. Place in cells B3: B1002: =RAND()*200. This is for the Y-position of the dart.
3. Place in cells C3:C1002: =IF(B3>-A3^3+10*A3^2+5*A3,0,1). This calculation determines if the dart is inside or outside the circle by using the integral formula: 1 is "in," 0 is "out."
4. Place in cells D3:D1002: =IF(C3=1,A3,NA()). This column is used for the Scatter chart.
5. Place in cells E3:E1003: =IF(C3=1,B3,NA()).This column is also used for the Scatter chart.
6. Insert a Scatter chart based on the columns D and E.
7. Cell H2 counts the number of darts thrown: =COUNT(A:A).
8. Cell H3 sums all the 1s for "in": =SUM(C:C).
9. Cell H4 calculates the area under the curve: =2000*H3/H2.
10. Cell H5 tells us what the analytical result would be. We do this only for comparison reasons: =-(1/4)*10^4+(10/3)*10^3+(5/2)*10^2.
11. Cell H6 calculates the error percentage: =(H4-H5)/H5.
12. Each time you hit *F9*, the columns A:H recalculate. Notice how the error keeps changing too, since we "only" used 1,000 simulations. Sometimes you may hit the "perfect" solution.
13. An error value of ±4% (see to the left below, for instance) is very unusual but never impossible when dealing with probabilities.

throws	1000
in circle	520
simul. area	1040
analyt. area	1083
error %	-4.00%

throws	1000
in circle	534
simul. area	1068
analyt. area	1083
error %	-1.42%

Chapter 51: Two Monte Carlo Integrations

What the simulation does

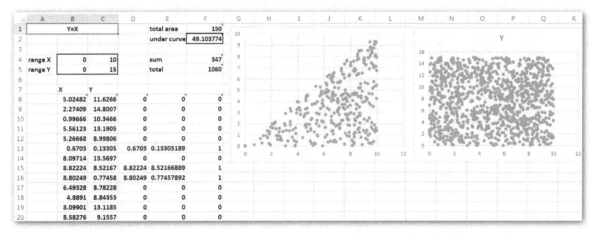

If you don't feel comfortable with integration equations, you may want to consider Monte Carlo simulations to calculate the area under a curve. We did a case in the previous chapter, but we did so by using an integration formula.

This time, we discuss only two equations as an example: Y=X (on the 1st sheet) and Y=X^2 (on the 2nd sheet), and without using any integration formula. That will probably help you to tackle similar situations. The range we want to cover for X and Y is set in the cells B4:C5.

What you need to know

On the 1st sheet, we generate random X-values between B4 and C4 in column B, plus random Y-values between B5 and C5 in column C. They are plotted in the right graph.

In column D, we place the X-value when Y is smaller than X. In column E, we place the corresponding Y-value when there is an X-value in the previous column. Both columns are plotted in the left graph. In column F, we assign 1's when the two previous columns have X- and Y-values in it, so we can calculate the area under the curve with the cells F2, F6, and F7.

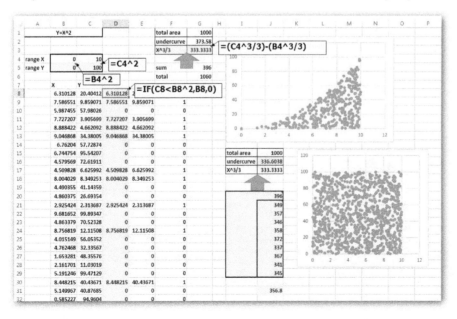

On the 2nd sheet we do something similar, but now for equation Y=X^2. Everything is the same as on the 1st sheet except for the marked cells with comments (see to the left).

Simulations in Action — MONTE CARLO

What you need to do

1. Place in cells B8:B1067: =$B$4+($C$4-$B$4)*RAND().
2. Place in cells C8:C1067: =$B$4+($C$4-$B$4)*RAND().
3. Place in cells D8:D1067: =IF(C8<B8,B8,0).
4. Place in cells E8:E1067: =IF(D8=0,0,C8).
5. Place in cells F8:F1067: =IF(E8=0,0,1).
6. Sum in cell F4 all 1's in column F below: =SUM(F8:F1067).
7. Count in cell F5 the number of values: =COUNT(F8:F1067).
8. Calculate in cell F1 the total area: =(C4-B4)*(C5-B5).
9. Determine in cell F2 what is under the curve: =(C4-B4)*(C5-B5).
10. The 2nd sheet is the same as the 1st sheet except for the marked cells (see below).
11. Cell B5: =B4^2. Cell C5: =C4^2.
12. Place in cell D8:D1067: =IF(C8<B8^2,B8,0).
13. Cell G3 has the integration formula for comparison with cell G2: =(C4^3/3)-(B4^3/3).
14. To improve the Monte Carlo results, we use a *Data Table*.
15. The start cell of the *Data Table* in J19 has in it: =G5
16. Select range I19:J28, implement a *Data Table* with only column input of any empty cell outside the range: =TABLE(,H18).
17. Cell J30 has the mean of all 10 runs.
18. Cell J16 uses the result of 10 runs: =G1*J30/G6.
19. Very often the *Data Table* gives better results (see below).

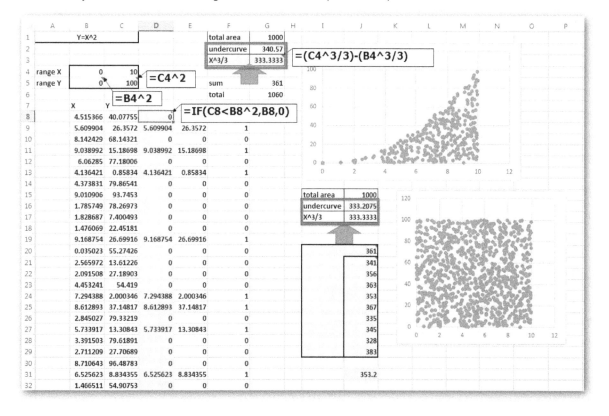

IV. GENETICS

Chapter 52: Shuffling Chromosomes

What the simulation does

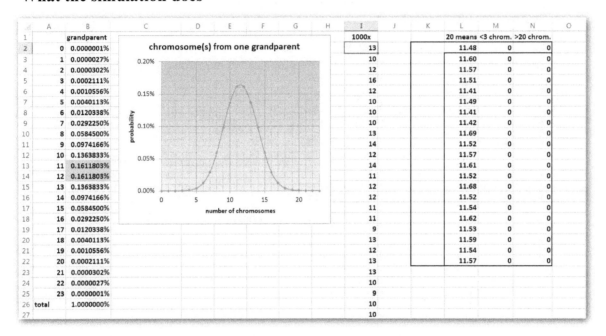

This simulation shows what the probability is that an individual still has the original chromosomes from one particular grandparent. Since we humans have 23 pairs of chromosomes, on average we have 11 or 12 chromosomes that were handed down to us from one particular grandparent, two generations ago—actually a 16% chance (row 13 and 14). But the outcome can vary between 0 chromosomes or the entire set of 23 chromosomes—but extremes like these are extremely unlikely (see columns M and N).

The basic idea is that parents randomly contribute part of their genetic material—chromosomes, genes, and DNA—to their children (and grandchildren, etc.). As a consequence, genetics, the science of inheritance of traits and characteristics, is modeled probabilistically.

As an aside, the situation is much more complicated. One problem is that chromosomes do not remain identical during the formation of reproductive cells, but they can exchange parts between the two of each pair—which is called crossing-over or recombination. In this simulation, we stay clear of that issue.

What you need to know

We will also use the new function BINOM.INV in this simulation. There is no pre-2010 version of this function, so if you use a file with this function in 2007, you will get an error message. In Excel 2007, an alternative would be the function CRITBINOM.

Cells B2:B25 hold the following formula: =BINOM.DIST(A2,23,0.5,0)/100. The function BINOMDIST needs to know the number of "successes" (running from 0 to 23 in column A), out of 23 trials (23 chromosomes), with a 50% probability of "success" in each trial, and with a non-cumulative setting in our case. Make sure to divide this by 100.

What you need to do

1. Place in cell B2:B25: =BINOMDIST(A2,23,0.5,0)/100. BINOMDIST needs to know the number of "successes" (running from 0 to 23 in column A), out of 23 trials (23 chromosomes), with a 50% probability of "success" in each trial, and with a non-cumulative setting in our case. Don't forget to divide by 100.
2. In column I, we simulate 1,000 times how many chromosomes someone received from a grandparent, ranging from none (0) to all (23).
3. To do so, place in cells I2:I1001: =BINOM.INV(23,0.5,RAND()). The last argument is a criterion value (alpha) between 0 and 1.
4. Place in cell L2: =AVERAGE(I:I).
5. Place in cell M2: =COUNTIF(I:I,"<3").
6. Place in cell N2: =COUNTIF(I:I,">20").
7. Select K2:N22 and start a *Data Table* with no row input and an empty cell (say, K1) as column input: {=TABLE(,K1)}.
8. Give range M2:N22 conditional formatting: Cell Value > 0.
9. When the sheet recalculates (*F9*), notice how rare it is that descendants have received less-than-3 or more-than-20 chromosomes from a grandparent (in columns M and N).
10. In the picture to the left, two such rare cases were marked with conditional formatting.

K	L	M	N
	20 means	<3 chrom.	>20 chrom.
	11.37	0	0
	11.58	0	0
	11.62	0	0
	11.54	0	0
	11.51	0	0
	11.42	0	0
	11.58	0	0
	11.53	0	0
	11.46	0	0
	11.46	0	0
	11.50	0	0
	11.50	0	0
	11.46	0	0
	11.50	0	0
	11.47	0	0
	11.53	0	0
	11.50	0	0
	11.53	0	0
	11.50	1	0
	11.57	0	1
	11.46	0	0

Chapter 53: Sex Determination

What the simulation does

	A	B	C	D	E	F	G	H	I	J	K	L
1			XY*	x	XX							
2				⊥								
3				XX	x	XY						
4					⊥							
5					XX	x	XY					
6						⊥						
7						XX	x	XY				
8							⊥					
9							XY	x	XX			
10								⊥				
11								XY	x	XX		
12									⊥			
13									XY	x	XX	
14												

This sheet simulates what happens when a father (XY) and a mother (XX) have one descendant, who has in turn another descendant, and so forth. It is something like a family tree.

If the descendant is a female (XX), that cell gets marked with a color. If the descendant still has the original Y-chromosome (Y*) from the (great-great-grand-) father, that chromosome is marked with an asterisk (*). In the figure above, there happen to be three female descendants, and the ancestral Y-chromosome got already "lost" by mere chance after the 1st generation.

It is possible, by mere unlikely change, that the paternal X-chromosome persists for six generations (see picture at the end)—or even longer.

What you need to know

One of the 23 pairs of chromosomes is called the sex-chromosome pair. It either holds two similar chromosomes (XX) or two unlike chromosomes (XY; Y is actually a very short chromosome). Simply put, the presence of the Y-chromosome determines maleness.

The father (XY) produces sperm cells with either an X-chromosome (50% chance) or a Y-chromosome (50% chance). If the egg cell—which has always one X-chromosome—is fertilized by a sperm cell with a Y-chromosome, the descendant will be a male. So there is a 50% chance for either a male or a female descendant (in reality, there is a slight difference in chance, though).

	C	D	E	F
1	XY*	x	XX	
2		⊥		
3		=IF(RAND()>0.5,"XX",IF(C1="XY*","XY*","XY"))	x	=IF(D3="","",IF(OR(D3="XY",D3="XY*"),"XX","XY"))
4			⊥	
5			=IF(RAND()>0.5,"XX",IF(D3="XY*","XY*","XY"))	
6				⊥
7				=IF(RAND()>0.5,"XX",IF(E5="XY*","XY*","XY"))
8				

What you need to do

1. Place in cell D3 the following formula: =IF(RAND()>0.5,"XX",IF(C1="XY*","XY*","XY")). Do not forget an asterisk (*) inside the double quotes.
2. This formula creates a 50% chance for either a male or a female. If it is a male, we check whether the father had an ancestral Y-chromosome; if so, this male inherits it.
3. Copy this formula into the cells E5, F7, G9, H11, and I13.
4. Place in cell F3 the following formula: =IF(D3="","",IF(OR(D3="XY",D3="XY*"),"XX","XY")).
5. This formula checks whether there is a descendant (D3), and if so, it determines whether the partner (F3) of this descendant must be a female (XX) or a male (XY).
6. Copy this formula into the cells G5, H7, I9, J11, and K13.
7. Apply conditional formatting to the cells $D$3, $E$5, $F$7, $G$9, $H$11, and $I$13. Choose "Format only cells that contain": Specific Text | Containing | XX (no quotes).
8. After hitting *F9*, the ancestral Y-chromosome may disappear immediately, or after one or more generations. It is very unlikely, but not impossible, that the ancestral Y-chromosome remains present all the way down (see below).

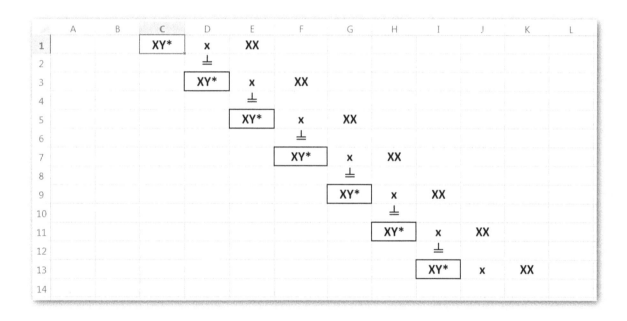

Chapter 54: Mendelian Laws

What the simulation does

	A	B	C	D	E	F	G	H	I	J	K	L	M	N	O	P	Q	R	S	T
1	dominant A							recessive a							X-linked, recessive h					
2	Aa	x	aa					Aa	x	Aa						Hh	x	H-		
3		⊥							⊥							⊥			
4	'Aa	'Aa	'Aa	aa	50%			AA	AA	'aa	Aa	25%			H'h	H'h	'h-	H-	25%
5																				
6								Aa	aa	h-					Aa	aa	h-			
7							100x%	75%	25%	25%					47%	25%	25%			
8								75%	0%	0%										
9								25%	50%	0%										
10								75%	0%	0%										
11								75%	25%	0%										
12								50%	0%	25%										
13								25%	100%	0%										
14								25%	0%	25%										
15								50%	0%	25%										

Certain diseases, such as a particular form of dwarfism, are based on a *dominant* allele (say, *A*). Anyone who carries such an allele (*Aa*) is called a heterozygote and has the disease.

Other diseases, such as cystic fibrosis, are based on a *recessive* allele (say, *a*). Only a person with two of those alleles (*aa*) shows the disease and is called a homozygote. So someone can be a carrier (*Aa*) of the disease without showing its symptoms.

Then there are also diseases, such as a known form of hemophilia, that are called sex-linked because they are based on a recessive allele (say, *h*) located on the X-chromosome; such alleles come always to expression in males (XY)—because there is no matching chromosome to counteract it—but in females (XX) only when both X-chromosomes have that recessive allele.

What you need to know

This sheet simulates the chances for passing on such alleles to the next generation. When the allele does come to expression, it is marked with conditional formatting. Because conditional formatting cannot distinguish between lowercase and uppercase characters—it's not case sensitive—we need to mark the capital with an apostrophe ('), or something like it.

The 1st case: Parents with *Aa* and *aa* have 50% *Aa* children and 50% *aa* children. The chance that a dominant allele (*A*) from such parents comes to expression in the next generation is 50%.

The 2nd case: The offspring of parents who are both *Aa* is *AA* (25%), *Aa* (50%), and *aa* (25%). The chance that a recessive allele (*a*) comes to expression in the next generation is 25%.

The 3rd case: The offspring of a mother with *Hh* and a father with *H-* would be *HH* (25%), *Hh* (25%), *H-* (25%), and *h-* (25%). The chance that a recessive, X-linked allele (*h*) comes to expression in the next generation is therefore 25% (*h-*).

The simulation applies Mendelian laws in row 4, and then uses a *Data Table* with 100 runs to calculate the percentage of *Aa* in the first diagram, of *aa* in the second one, and of *h-* in the third one. The average of these 100 runs is calculated in cells O7:Q7. These percentages should be rather close to the ones predicted according to Mendelian laws to the right of each diagram.

What you need to do

1. Because conditional formatting cannot distinguish between lowercase and uppercase characters, we will mark the diseased genotypes with an apostrophe (').
2. Place in cells A4: D4: =IF(RAND()<0.5,"'Aa","aa"). Notice the single apostrophe in front of *Aa*.
3. Place in cells H4:K4 the following nicely nested formula: =IF(RAND()<0.5,"Aa",IF(RAND()<0.25,"AA","'aa")). Notice the single apostrophe at the end.
4. Place in cells O4:R4 a formula that is even more heavily nested: =IF(RAND()<0.25,"HH",IF(RAND()<=0.33,"H'h",IF(RAND()<0.5,"H-","'h-"))).
5. Format the cells A4:D4, H4:K4, and O4:R4 as follows: Specific Text | Beginning With | an apostrophe (').
6. Hitting *F9* shows you when the abnormal allele kicks in (shaded cells in row 4).
7. Because there is much randomness involved (see below), we add a Data Table.
8. H7: =COUNTIF(A4:D4,"'Aa")/4. I7: =COUNTIF(H4:K4,"'aa")/4. J7: =COUNTIF(O4:R4,"'h-")/4.
9. Select G7:J106 for a Data Table with an empty cell for column input: =TABLE(,K6).
10. Place in cells O7:Q7: =AVERAGE(H7:H106).

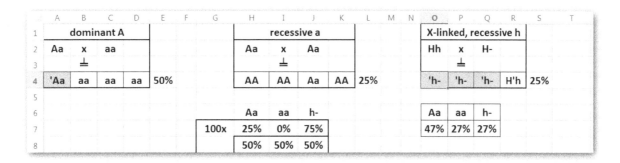

Chapter 55: The Hardy-Weinberg Law

What the simulation does

	A	B	C	D	E	F	G	H	I	J	K	L	M	N	O	P	Q	R
1		cumul.	type	%				parents		offspring					parent1	parent2	offspring	
2		0%	aa	10%	=2*SQRT(D2)*			A'A'A'A'	A'A'	A'A'	A'A'	A'A'		1000x	aa	A'a	aa	
3		10%	A'a	43%	SQRT(D4)			A'A'A'a	A'A'	A'A'	A'a	A'a			A'A'	aa	A'a	
4		53%	A'A'	47%				A'A'aa	A'a	A'a	A'a	A'a			A'A'	A'a	A'a	
5					=(1-SQRT(D2))^2			A'aA'A'	A'A'	A'A'	A'a	A'a			A'A'	A'A'	A'A'	
6								A'aA'a	A'A'	A'a	A'a	aa			A'a	aa	A'a	
7								A'aaa	A'a	A'a	aa	aa			aa	aa	aa	
8								aaA'A'	A'a	A'a	A'a	A'a			A'A'	A'a	A'A'	
9								aaA'a	A'a	A'a	aa	aa			aa	A'A'	A'a	
10								aaaa	aa	aa	aa	aa			A'a	aa	aa	
11															aa	A'a	A'a	
12											1000 generations				A'A'	aa	A'a	
13										aa	10%				A'A'	aa	A'a	
14										A'a	43%				aa	aa	aa	
15										A'A'	47%				A'A'	A'a	A'A'	
16															A'A'	A'A'	A'a	
17															A'a	A'A'	A'a	
18															A'A'	A'A'	A'A'	
19															A'A'	A'a	A'A'	
20															A'A'	A'A'	A'A'	

A gene can carry various alleles. Let us assume there are only two alleles, *A* and *a*. People who have two of the same alleles are homozygotes (*AA* or *aa*). Those who carry both alleles are heterozygotes (*Aa*). Let us take the example of an allele for albinism (*a*), which is recessive, so albinos must be *aa*, whereas individuals with the genotypes *AA* and *Aa* are not albinos. If we know the percentage (q^2) of albinos (*aa*), we can calculate the frequency q of allele *a*, as well as the frequency p of allele *A*—provided there are no other alleles—since $p=1-q$.

As a consequence, the frequency would be p^2 for the homozygotes *AA* (cell D4), q^2 for the homozygotes *aa* (cell D2), and $2pq$ for the heterozygotes (in cell D3: pq for *Aa* and qp for *aA*). So if we know that *aa* has a frequency of 10%, we can deduce what the frequencies are for *Aa* and *AA* (see the comments in those cells shown in the figure above).

What you need to know

The Hardy-Weinberg law states that if these genotypes would *randomly* mate, the frequencies would stay the same in the next generations. We are going to simulate this. We know, based on Mendelian laws, what the offspring would be for certain pairs of parents (see H1:L10). The simulation is going to randomly create these combinations and randomly determine what their offspring would be. The result, based on 1,000 runs (in columns O:Q), is displayed in cells K13:L15. Notice how the frequencies remain extremely close to the frequencies of the parent generation—which is exactly what the Hardy-Weinberg law states.

The VLOOKUP function plays an important role in this simulation. Its 2nd argument can specify a column number in which to search. It finds randomly the genotype of each parent and then finds randomly (with a random number between 2 and 5) the child's genotype in one of the 2nd to 5th columns of range H:L.

If you were to change the frequency of *aa* to 40% (in D2), the next generation will more or less keep that frequency because of random mating. Obviously, the total of the frequencies should be 100%.

Simulations in Action — GENETICS

What you need to do

1. Place in cell B2: 0%.
2. Place in cells B3:B4: =SUM($D$2:D2).
3. {;ace in cell D2: 10%.
4. Place in cell D3: =2*SQRT(D2)*SQRT(D4).
5. Place in cell D4: =(1-SQRT(D2))^2.
6. The cells H1:L10 are all manually done (according to Mendelian laws).
7. Place in cell O2: =VLOOKUP(RAND(),$B$2:$C$4,2,TRUE).
8. Place in cell P2: =VLOOKUP(RAND(),$B$2:$C$4,2,TRUE).
9. Place in cell Q2: =VLOOKUP(O2 & P2,H2:L10,RANDBETWEEN(2,5),FALSE).
10. Select range N2: Q1001 and implement a *Data Table* with no row input and a column input of an empty cell (e.g. R1): =TABLE(,R1).
11. Place in cells L13:L15: =COUNTIF($Q$2:$Q$1002,K13)/1000.
12. Notice how stable the percentages are after each generation by comparing D2:D4 with L13:L15.
13. Change the frequency in D2 and notice the outcome.

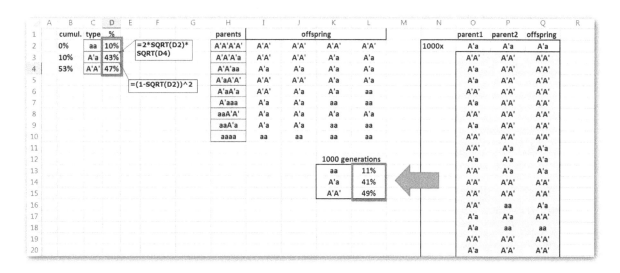

Chapter 56: Genetic Drift

What the simulation does

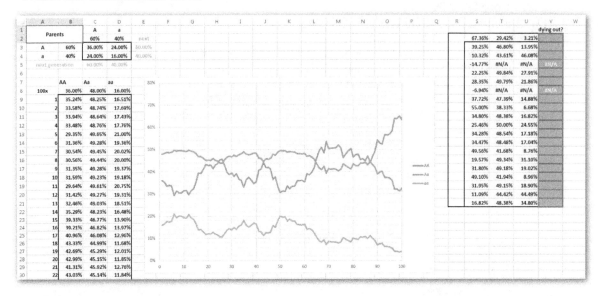

The Hardy-Weinberg law (see the previous chapter) states that allele frequencies remain the same over the next generations. Even in case of a recessive allele, this allele will not entirely disappear. However, by random chance, the percentage of alleles may, and usually does, change in the next generations. This is called "genetic drift." The effect increases when the population size decreases—the so-called "founder effect."

The table to the left simulates what happens for 100 generations when frequencies randomly fluctuate with a SD of 2% for each generation. During this ongoing process, recessive homozygotes (*aa*) may eventually, by mere chance, disappear from stage, to the advantage of the dominant homozygotes (*AA*). This happened in the picture at the end of this chapter.

When we repeat the left table (which has 100 runs) some 20 more times in the *Data Table* to the right, we see how much the outcome of genetic drift can vary. In column U, we flag situations in which a certain genotype disappears completely ("out") or had disappeared already ("#N/A").

What you need to know

If the frequency of allele *A* is 0.6 (=*p*), then the frequency of allele *a* must be 1-0.6=0.4 (=*q*)—assuming there are only two alleles for this gene. So the frequency of genotype *AA* would be p^2 and the frequency of genotype *aa* would be q^2. The frequency of *Aa* and *aA* would be $2pq$.

The only functions we need for this simulation are NORMINV, RAND, SQRT, and IFERROR. All of these were already used and explained before.

Simulations in Action — GENETICS

What you need to do

	A	B	C	D	E
1		Parents	A	a	
2			0.6	=1-C2	next
3	A	0.6	=B3*C2	=B3*D2	=SUM(C3:D3)
4	a	=1-B3	=B4*C2	=B4*D2	=SUM(C4:D4)
5		next generation	=SUM(C3:C4)	=SUM(D3:D4)	
6					
7			AA	Aa	aa
8		100x	=C3	=C4+D3	=D4
9	1	=NORMINV(RAND(),B8,0.02)	=IFERROR(2*SQRT(B9)*(1-SQRT(B9)),NA())	=IFERROR((1-SQRT(B9))^2,NA())	
10	2	=NORMINV(RAND(),B9,0.02)	=IFERROR(2*SQRT(B10)*(1-SQRT(B10)),NA())	=IFERROR((1-SQRT(B10))^2,NA())	
11	3	=NORMINV(RAND(),B10,0.02)	=IFERROR(2*SQRT(B11)*(1-SQRT(B11)),NA())	=IFERROR((1-SQRT(B11))^2,NA())	

1. Place in cells B9:B108: =NORM.INV(RAND(),B8,0.02). It uses the frequency of the previous generation and makes it fluctuate with a SD of 2%. That is going to be the new frequency of genotype AA (p^2) in the next generation.
2. The frequency of genotype Aa ($2pq$) would be $2 * \sqrt{p^2} * (1 - \sqrt{p^2})$. So place in cells C9:C108: =IFERROR(2*SQRT(B9)*(1-SQRT(B9)),NA()). If there is an error (e.g., because the allele had already disappeared), IFERROR places "#N/A" in that cell.
3. Place in cell D9:D108: =IFERROR((1-SQRT(B9))^2,NA()). This calculates the new frequency of genotype aa (q^2).
4. In cells R2:T2, place a link to the cells B109:D109.
5. Select range S2:U21 (not V21), and start a *Data Table* with no row input and an empty cell (e. g., cell P2) as column input: =TABLE(,P2).
6. Place in cell U2: =IF(T2<1%,"out","").
7. Notice how significant—and unpredictable—genetic drift can be. In the situation below, the recessive homozygote disappeared completely in the first run (V2) and had disappeared already in the next to last run (V20). This is basically another example of random walk.

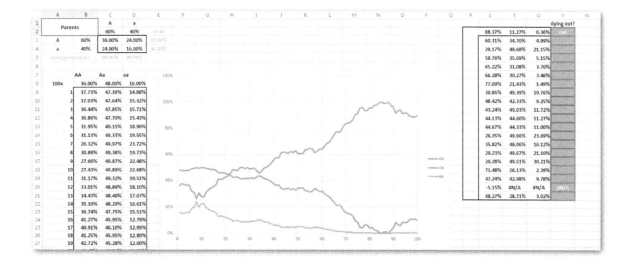

Chapter 57: Two Selective Forces

What the simulation does

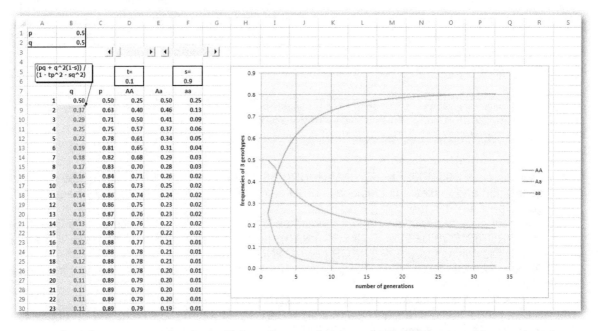

It is rather common that both alleles of a gene have a selection factor working against them; let's designate those two selection factors with the symbols s and t. The most well-known case is sickle-cell anemia. Because there is strong selection pressure (s) against the homozygote (aa), who suffers from anemia, we would expect allele a to disappear from the population. However, in malaria areas it has a rather stable frequency (q). The explanation is that there is also a selection pressure (t) against the other homozygote (AA), who is more vulnerable to malaria than other individuals, especially the heterozygotes (Aa). With two scrollbar controls you can change the selection factors t and s, so you can watch their effects in the chart.

What you need to know

In areas where malaria occurs, the heterozygote (Aa) has a higher level of fitness to resist both malaria and anemia. This leads to new frequencies according to the following formula: $(pq + q^2(1-s)) / (1 - tp^2 - sq^2)$.

With the help of some mathematical manipulations, we are able to deduce that the frequency of alleles will become stable as soon as $tp = sq$. This is a form of balanced polymorphism—an equilibrium mixture of homozygotes and heterozygotes maintained by negative selection pressure against both homozygotes.

What you need to do

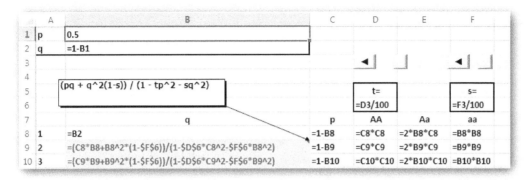

1. Place in B8 a link to cell B2.
2. Place in cells B9:B40: =(C8*B8+B8^2*(1-$F$6))/(1-$D$6*C8^2-$F$6*B8^2).
3. Place in cells C8:C40: =1-B8.
4. Place in cells D8:D40: =C8*C8.
5. Place in cells E8:E40: =2*B8*C8.
6. Place in cells F8:F40: =B8*B8.
7. Add two scroll-bar controls (see Appendix). Both have Min set to 0 and Max to 100. The left one is linked to D3, the right one to F3.
8. The formulas in D6 (*t*) and F6 (*s*) divide the settings of D3 and F3 respectively by 100.
9. Test the outcome for different settings. Below is the situation where t=0.72 and s=0.32. After some 15 generations, equilibrium seems to have set in.

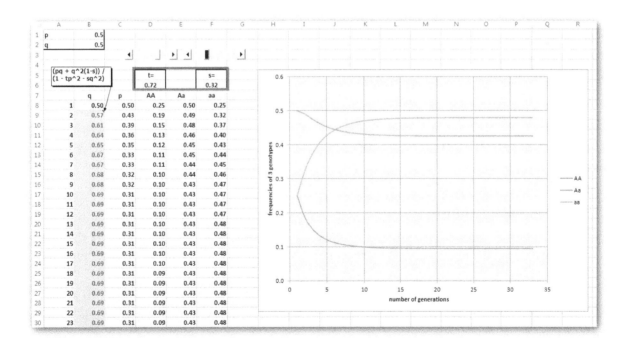

Chapter 58: Balanced Polymorphism

What the simulation does

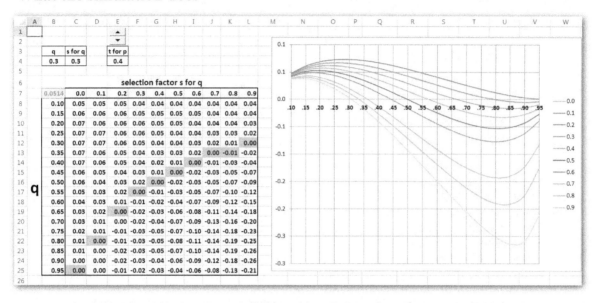

In the previous simulation we discussed how, with the help of some mathematical manipulations, we are able to deduce that the frequencies of two alleles, *p* and *q*, with each one having a different selection factor, *s* and *t*, will become stable in a population as soon as *tp* = *sq*.

This phenomenon is called balanced polymorphism—an equilibrium mixture of homozygotes and heterozygotes maintained by negative selection pressure against both homozygotes.

The formula for Δq is: *(tp²q - spq²) / (1 - tp² - sq²)*.

This formula is used in cell B7 at the origin of a *Data Table*: =($E$4*(1-$B$4)^2*$B$4-$C$4*(1-$B$4)*$B$4^2)/(1-$E$4*(1-$B$4)^2-$C$4*$B$4^2)

With the help of this *Data Table*, we can find out when we reach equilibrium, given a certain value for *q* (in column B; *p = 1 - q*), a certain value for *s* (in row 7), and a certain value for *t* (cell E4). Those situations are marked with conditional formatting in the *Data Table*.

What you need to know

Since *Data Table*s can only hold two dimensions at the most, we could simulate the third variable with a spinbutton control (see Appendix for more details). This control regulates the value of variable *t* in cell E4.

Notice how the curves in the graph intersect with the X-axis at some point. Until it reaches that point, the frequency *q* will either increase (to the right) or decrease (to the left) for each next generation.

What you need to do

1. Place in cell B7 the formula for Δq: =($E$4*(1-$B$4)^2*$B$4-$C$4*(1-$B$4)*$B$4^2)/(1-$E$4*(1-$B$4)^2-$C$4*$B$4^2).
2. Select the range B7:L25 and start a *Data Table* with cell C4 as row input and B4 for column input: =TABLE(C4,B4).
3. Apply conditional formatting to range C8:L25 with a formula that looks for the lowest value in the positive range (which is very close to 0): =ABS(C8)=MIN(ABS(C$8:C$25))).
4. Place a spinbutton control over cells E1:E2 (see Appendix for more details). Set Min to 0, Max to 10, and LinkedCell to E1.
5. Place in cell E4: =E1/10. Now this cell listens to the spinbutton control.
6. Whenever a cell in the *Data Table* shows 0 or whenever the curve reaches the X-axis, a balanced state of equilibrium has been reached.
7. If calculation is set to automatic, you can click the spin button and watch the changes in the table and the graph. Otherwise, you must hit each time *F9* after each button change—but only after you have activated the sheet again.
8. In the case below, *t* has been set to 0.9. Equilibrium can only be reached when *q* is greater than 0.50 for any value of *s*.

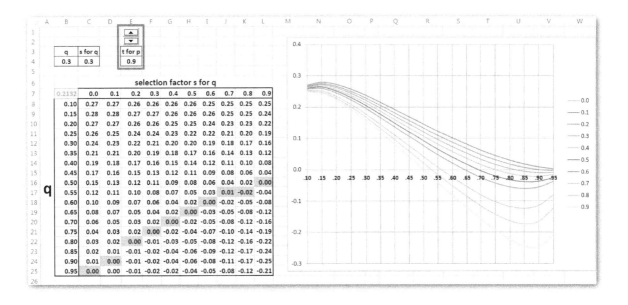

Chapter 59: Differential Fitness

What the simulation does

	A	B	C	D	E	F	G	H	I	J	K	L	M	N	O	P	Q	R	S	T	U	V	W	X	Y
1		cumul.	type	%		parents						fitness			parents							parent1	parent2	child	
2		0%	SS	10%		AAAA	AA	AA	AA	AA		SS	0.4		AAAA	AA	AA				1000x	AA	AA		
3		10%	AA	47%		AAAS	AA	AA	AS	AS		AA	0.7		AAAS	AA	AA	AS	AS			AA	SS	AS	
4		57%	AS	43%		AASS	AS	AS	AS	AS		AS	1.0		AASS	AS	AS	AS	AS			AA	AS	AS	
5				100%		ASAA	AA	AA	AA	AS					ASAA			AS	AS			AS	AS	SS	
6						ASAS	AA	AS	AS	SS					ASAS	AA	AS					AS	AA	AA	
7						ASSS	AS	AS	SS	SS					ASSS	AS	AS	SS	SS			AS	AS	AA	
8						SSAA	AS	AS	AS	AS					SSAA	AS	AS	AS	AS			AS	AS	AS	
9						SSAS	AS	AS	SS	SS					SSAS	AS	AS					AS	AS	AA	
10						SSSS	SS	SS	SS	SS					SSSS			SS				AS	AA	AS	
11																						AA	SS	AS	
12																	frequencies					AA	AA		
13																	new	old				AA	AA	AA	
14																SS	5%	10%				AA	AA	AA	
15																AA	31%	47%				SS	AA	AS	
16																AS	45%	43%				AA	AS	AS	
17																						AS	AS	SS	
18																						AA	AS		
19																						AS	AA	AS	
20																						AS	AA	AS	

This simulation is similar to the one used in Chapter 55. Again, we assign relative fitness factors—for instance, genotype AS (fitness factor 1 in cell M4) is more "fit" than genotype *SS* (fitness factor 0.4 in cell M2). So gradually, up to a certain point, the frequency of *AS* will increase, while the frequency of genotype *SS* (sickle cell anemia, for instance) will decrease in future generations.

All the gray cells on the sheet have formulas in it. We assume that each combination of parents has up to 4 children per generation (columns G:J). Most formulas are identical to the ones used in Chapter 55. The main difference is that the range P2:S10 is based on the different fitness factors for each genotype. Columns G:J show offspring without fitness impact, whereas columns P:S do show fitness impact. The offspring is not only determined by Mendel's laws but also by the fitness of that specific genotype. That's why certain cells remain empty in P2:S10.

This will obviously affect frequencies in the next generation. The simulation calculates the average frequencies of the three genotypes based on 1,000 couples with each couple having up to 4 children (O2:S10). The simulation calculates through a *Data Table* the results for the next generation and compares them with the original frequencies in the 1st generation of the parents (in cells Q13:S16). It is to be expected that there is a change of frequencies—but again, not always, for there is still randomness involved. Sometimes, the effect is quite dramatic (see the picture at the end of this chapter).

What you need to know

Only the gray cells on the sheet have formulas in it; the rest is manual input. To mark the cells with formulas in them, conditional formatting can be a helpful tool. Select all the cells and then use conditional formatting with the following formula: =ISFORMULA(A1). The function ISFORMULA became available in more recent versions of Excel.

The pivotal functions are VLOOKUP, RAND, RANDBETWEEN, and COUNTIF.

Simulations in Action — GENETICS

What you need to do

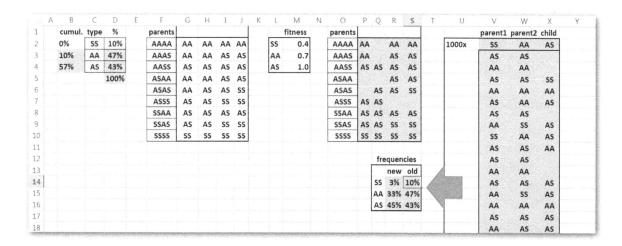

1. The first 4 columns are similar to Chapter 55 (see picture to the right).
2. Place in cells P2:S10 this formula: =IF(RAND()<VLOOKUP(H6,$L$2:$M$4,2,0),H6,"")
3. Place in cell V2 this formula: =VLOOKUP(RAND(),$B$2:$C$4,2,TRUE).
4. Place in cell W2: =VLOOKUP(RAND(),$B$2:$C$4,2,TRUE).
5. Place in cell X2: =VLOOKUP(V2 & W2,O2:S10,RANDBETWEEN(2,5),TRUE).
6. Select range U2:X1001 and implement a *Data Table* with no row input and an empty cell (e.g. Y1) as column input.
7. Place in cells R14:R16: =COUNTIF($X$2:$X$1001,Q14)/1000.
8. Place in cells S14:S16: =D2 (which changes into D3 and D4 in the next 2 rows).
9. *F9* simulates new parents and their offspring with frequencies that are typically different from the previous generation.

Chapter 60: Random Mating

What the simulation does

In this file we simulate what happens when different genotypes (cells C2:C5) randomly mate with each other (columns B and C), and then produce an offspring of 1 to 4 individuals (columns F:I) with an average of 2 individuals (columns K and L).

Then we repeat this process some 20 more times with a *Data Table* (far to the right), to find out that random mating has hardly any impact on the frequencies of each genotype (see the means below the *Data Table*). This is known as the Hardy-Weinberg law (see Chapter 55).

What you need to know

We assume both alleles have the same fitness and that mating is completely random. If that is not the case, we would have to deal with a simulation like in Chapter 56 or 57.

What you need to do

1. The first 4 columns are similar to Chapter 55 (see picture to the right).
2. Range N1:R10 contains manual input.
3. Select the range B6:C30 and implement: =VLOOKUP(RAND(),$B$2:$C$4,2,1).
4. Place in the cell range F6:I30 the following heavily nested formula: =IF(RANDBETWEEN(0,6)>COLUMN(A1),VLOOKUP($B6&$C6,$N$2:$R$10,RANDBETWEEN(2,5),FALSE),"").
5. Place in the cells K6:K30: =4-COUNTBLANK(F6:I6).
6. Place in the merged cell L6: =AVERAGE(K6:K30).
7. Place in the cells B32:C34: =COUNTIF(B$6:B$30,$A32)/COUNTA($B$6:$B$30).
8. Place in the cells F32:I34: =COUNTIF(F$6:F$30,$A32)/(COUNTA(F$6:F$30)-COUNTBLANK(F$6:F$30)).
9. Place in the cells K32:K34: =AVERAGE(F32:I32).
10. Place in cell L32: =SUM(K32:K34).
11. Place in the cells Q13:S13: =TRANSPOSE(K32:K34). Don't forget *Ctrl Shift Enter*.
12. Select the range P13:S33 and implement a *Data Table* with no row input and an empty cell (e.g. O13) for column input: =TABLE(,O13).
13. Place in the cells Q34:S34: =AVERAGE(Q13:Q33).
14. Use *F9* and notice how the frequencies after 1 generation may vary slightly for 1 run (K32:K34) but remain pretty stable for 10 repeats (Q34:S34).

Chapter 61: Molecular Clock

What the simulation does

	A	B	C	D	E	F	G	H	I	J	K
1	Comparing two individuals with a common ancestor										
2	individuals		2								
3	mutation rate/yr		0.0000001								
4	unchanged		0.9999999			target ± .5%					
5	number of years		50000			10%					
6	mutation percentage		1%								
7											
8		1%	0.9999999	0.9999998	0.9999997	0.9999996	0.9999995	0.9999994	0.9999993	0.9999992	0.9999991	1-mutation rate
9	50000	1.0%	2.0%	3.0%	4.0%	4.9%	5.9%	6.9%	7.8%	8.8%	
10	100000	2.0%	4.0%	5.9%	7.8%	9.8%	11.6%	13.5%	15.4%	17.2%	
11	150000	3.0%	5.9%	8.8%	11.6%	14.5%	17.2%	19.9%	22.6%	25.3%	
12	200000	4.0%	7.8%	11.6%	15.4%	19.0%	22.6%	26.1%	29.6%	32.9%	
13	250000	4.9%	9.8%	14.5%	19.0%	23.5%	27.9%	32.1%	36.3%	40.3%	
14	300000	5.9%	11.6%	17.2%	22.6%	27.9%	32.9%	37.9%	42.7%	47.3%	
15	350000	6.9%	13.5%	19.9%	26.1%	32.1%	37.9%	43.5%	48.8%	54.0%	
16	400000	7.8%	15.4%	22.6%	29.6%	36.3%	42.7%	48.8%	54.8%	60.5%	
17	450000	8.8%	17.2%	25.3%	32.9%	40.3%	47.3%	54.0%	60.5%	66.6%	
18	500000	9.8%	19.0%	27.9%	36.3%	44.2%	51.8%	59.1%	65.9%	72.5%	
19	550000	10.7%	20.8%	30.4%	39.5%	48.1%	56.2%	63.9%	71.2%	78.1%	
20	years ago										

Genes may undergo changes, called mutations. Mutations to non-essential portions of the DNA are useful for measuring time—the so-called molecular clock. It is assumed that such mutations occur with a uniform probability per unit of time in a particular portion of DNA, because they are not exposed to selection. If P is the percentage of *no*-mutations in a year, then P^N is the probability of *no*-mutations over N years.

On average, given two individuals who had a common ancestor many generations ago, you would expect—assuming that mutations are so rare that it is very unlikely that a mutation in the same segment has occurred in two individuals—that the percentage of segments that are mutated in one or the other is, on average, $2(1 - P^N)$. This is an estimate of the percentage of segments to be found different when comparing two individuals with a common ancestor N years ago.

This simulation provides a simplified version of the technique that has been used to locate the first common ancestors of all human beings in evolution—the most recent common female and the most recent common male, so to speak. Non-essential DNA sections can be tested for single-nucleotide-polymorphisms (SNPs, pronounced "snips"), which are single base pair changes in DNA that occur throughout the genome, including its "silent" DNA sections.

What you need to know

Place in cell C6: *=2*(1-C4^C5)*. This is the mutation percentage after a certain number of years—in this case after 50,000 years as shown in cell C5.

Notice in the *Data Table* the following: If two individuals have a 10% difference (F5), their most recent common ancestor lived 100,000 years ago if the mutation rate for those DNA segments is 0.9999995 (F10), but 250,000 years ago based on a rate of 0.9999998 (C13), or even 500,000 years ago based on a rate of 0.9999999 (B18). So small differences in mutation rate can have an enormous impact. Apparently, the accuracy of the molecular clock depends heavily on the accuracy of the mutation rate.

What you need to do

1. Place in cell C4: =1-C3.
2. Place in cell C6: =2*(1-C4^C5). This is the mutation percentage after a certain numbers of years (in this case 50,000 years as shown in cell C4).
3. Cell A8 is linked to cell C6.
4. Select range A8:I19 and start a *Data Table* with cell C4 as row input and cell C5 for column input: =TABLE(C4,C5).
5. In cell F5 users can enter their target (± 0.5%). This target determines which cells in the *Data Table* match the target.
6. Highlight the cells B9:J19 and implement conditional formatting with the color of your choice: =AND(B9>=($F$5-0.005),B9<=($F$5+0.005))
7. Notice the following: If two individuals have a 10% difference, their most recent common ancestor lived 100,000 years ago if the mutation rate for those DNA segments is 0,9999995, but 250,000 years ago based on a rate of 0,9999998. So small differences in mutation rate can have an enormous impact.
8. For 25% (see below), this would be 150,000 years ago at a mutation rate per year of .9999991, or 450,000 years ago at a rate of 0.9999997. Apparently, the accuracy of the molecular clock depends heavily on the accuracy of the mutation rate.

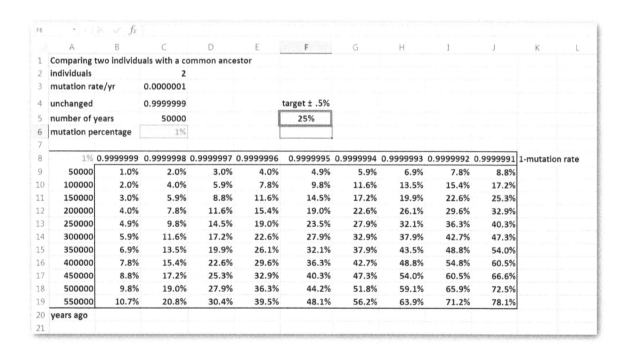

Chapter 62: DNA Sequencing

What the simulation does

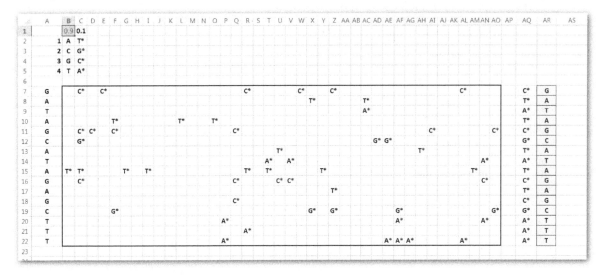

This is a rather simplified simulation of what was done in the Human Genome Project. Today, "dideoxy sequencing" is the method of choice to sequence very long strands of DNA. DNA is composed of 4 different nucleotides—A, C, G, and T. The composition of a DNA string is randomly generated in column A. It is clear that this composition is not known yet until we use a technique in the middle section that we are going to describe soon. The end result is shown in the columns AQ and AR by using formulas on the sheet.

What you need to know

To determine the unknown sequence of nucleotides in a DNA section of interest, the double-stranded DNA is separated into single strands (denaturation). In the next step, a new DNA strand is made, complementary to the template strand, by using the bacterial enzyme DNA polymerase. During this step, A-nucleotides will be "paired" with T-nucleotides, and C-nucleotides with G-nucleotides—they are called complementary.

Then follows a key step. In addition to the four regular single nucleotides, the reaction mixture also contains small amounts of four dideoxy-nucleotides which lack a group necessary for chain extension. Once in a while—by low chance, because of its much lower concentration—a dideoxy-nucleotide will be incorporated into the growing DNA strand instead of the regular nucleotide. This will prevent the DNA chain from growing further. Since each of these four special nucleotides is labeled with a different fluorescent dye, a certain type of laser can later detect them. We marked them with an asterisk (*) in our simulation.

So, by chance, DNA chains end up being very short, very long, and of every possible length in-between. The newly synthesized DNA strands are then passed through a laser beam that excites the fluorescent dye attached to the dideoxy-nucleotide at the end of each strand. This color is then detected by a photocell, which feeds the information to a computer. Finally, the computer does the rest of the work by piecing the short sequences together like a puzzle.

What you need to do

	A	B	C	D	E
1		0.9	=1-B1		
2	1	A	T*		
3	2	C	G*		
4	3	G	C*		
5	4	T	A*		
6					
7	=VLOOKUP(RANDBETWEEN(1,4),$A$2:$B$5,2,0)	=IF(RAND()>$B$1,VLOOKUP($A7,$B$2:$C$5,2,0),"")	=IF(RAND(	=IF(RAI	=IF(RAI
8	=VLOOKUP(RANDBETWEEN(1,4),$A$2:$B$5,2,0)	=IF(RAND()>$B$1,VLOOKUP($A8,$B$2:$C$5,2,0),"")	=IF(RAND(	=IF(RAI	=IF(RAI
9	=VLOOKUP(RANDBETWEEN(1,4),$A$2:$B$5,2,0)	=IF(RAND()>$B$1,VLOOKUP($A9,$B$2:$C$5,2,0),"")	=IF(RAND(	=IF(RAI	=IF(RAI
10	=VLOOKUP(RANDBETWEEN(1,4),$A$2:$B$5,2,0)	=IF(RAND()>$B$1,VLOOKUP($A10,$B$2:$C$5,2,0),"")	=IF(RAND(	=IF(RAI	=IF(RAI
11	=VLOOKUP(RANDBETWEEN(1,4),$A$2:$B$5,2,0)	=IF(RAND()>$B$1,VLOOKUP($A11,$B$2:$C$5,2,0),"")	=IF(RAND(	=IF(RAI	=IF(RAI

1. The following formula in the cells A7:A22 generates nucleotides A, C, G, or T: =VLOOKUP(RANDBETWEEN(1,4),$A$2:$B$5,2,0).
2. Assuming that 90% (B1) is not dyed, we simulate in cells B7:AO22 the chance that a dyed nucleotide is inserted and then stops the chain from growing further: =IF(RAND()>$B$1,VLOOKUP($A7,$B$2:$C$5,2,0),"").
3. Each column simulates a new chance for creating strands of different lengths, terminated by a dyed nucleotide (*).
4. In AQ7 we locate the first dyed nucleotide in that row by using an array formula: =INDEX(B7:AO7,0,MATCH(TRUE,(B7:AO7)<>"",0)). This is a single-cell array formula (so you must use *Ctrl Shift Enter*).
5. Copy this formula downwards (the normal way) to AQ22.
6. In cell AR7:AR22, we display what the complementary code for the nucleotide is at a specific position in the chain: =INDEX($B$2:$C$5,MATCH(AQ7,$C$2:$C$5,0),1).
7. The values found in column AR should match the values in column A, which were initially unknown and had to be determined!
8. Setting cell B1 to a slightly lower value creates shorter strands.
9. If there are cells with #N/A in the columns AQ and AR (see below), then the strand was too long to be displayed. Setting B1 lower, will reduce the chances of this happening.

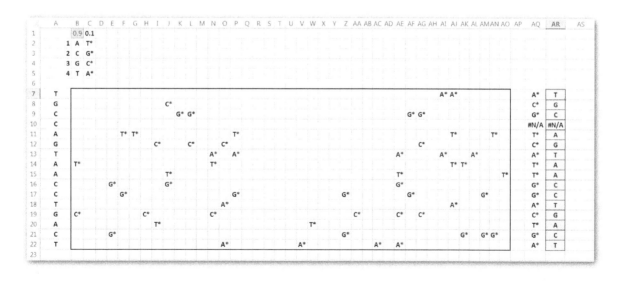

V. SCIENCE

Chapter 63: Matrix Elimination

What the simulation does

	A	B	C	D	E	F	G	H
1		4 equations with 4 unknown X's:			Y = $a_1X_1 + a_2X_2 + a_3X_3 + a_4X_4$			
2								
3			a_1	a_2	a_3	a_4		Y's
4								
5	2 equations		9.375	3.042			=	9.231
6	with 2		3.042	6.183			=	8.202
7	unknowns		0.659	1.002				
8								
9	3 equations		9.375	3.042	-2.437		=	9.231
10	with 3		3.042	6.183	1.216		=	8.202
11	unknowns		-2.437	1.216	8.443		=	3.931
12	3 X's		0.896	0.765	0.614			
13								
14	4 equations		9.375	3.042	-2.437	-1.234	=	9.231
15	with 4		3.042	6.183	1.216	4.654	=	8.202
16	unknowns		-2.437	1.216	8.443	5.731	=	3.931
17			1.234	4.453	8.443	-3.453	=	4.576
18	4 X's		1.01858	0.39285	0.38032	0.47534		

If you need to solve equations, it can be helpful to use *matrixes*. This file has a few examples of such equations. E.g., 4 equations with 4 unknown X's: Y = $a_1X_1 + a_2X_2 + a_3X_3 + a_4X_4$.

Let's focus on rows 14-18, which use four different coefficients for *a*, as shown in matrix *[A]* (C14:F17). These four equations should equate to the Y-values shown in matrix *[Y]* (H14:H17).

What you need to know

You need to determine what the four X-values must be to solve the equations. Here's what you do. #1: Invert matrix *[A]* by using the multi-cell array function MINVERSE. #2: Multiply the matrix *Inv[A]* with the matrix *[Y]* by using the array function MMULT. #3: You could have combined both steps by using a nested function instead: =MMULT(MINVERSE([A]),[Y]). #4: This creates vertical array results, so to plot them horizontally you need TRANSPOSE as well.

So we end up with: =TRANSPOSE(MMULT(MINVERSE([A]),[Y]))). Thanks to this technique of matrix elimination, you can solve the equations and find the four X-values for a_1 through a_4 in the cells C18:F18. These X-values make the four equations, based on the *a* values specified in matrix *[A]*, equate to the Y-values specified in matrix *[Y]*. Test them in J14:J17.

								test
4 equations		9.375	3.042	-2.437	-1.234	=	9.231	→ 9.231
with 4		3.042	6.183	1.216	4.654	=	8.202	8.202
unknowns		-2.437	1.216	8.443	5.731	=	3.931	3.931
		1.234	4.453	8.443	-3.453	=	4.576	4.576
4 X's		1.019	0.393	0.380	0.475			

What you need to do

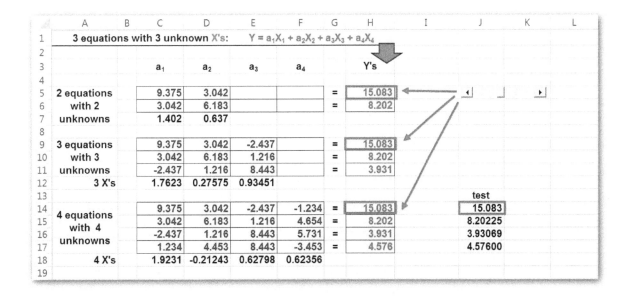

1. The rows 5:6, 9:11, and 14:17 have manual input.
2. Place in cells C7:D7: =TRANSPOSE(MMULT(MINVERSE(C5:D6),H5:H6)). Do this all at once with *Ctrl Shift Enter*.
3. Place in cells C12:E12: =TRANSPOSE(MMULT(MINVERSE(C9:E11),H9:H11)). Do this all at once with *Ctrl Shift Enter*.
4. Place in cells C18:F18: =TRANSPOSE(MMULT(MINVERSE(C14:F17),H14:H17)). Do this all at once with *Ctrl Shift Enter*.
5. If you want to test the results for the 3rd example, place in cells J14:J17: =C14*$C$18+D14*$D$18+E14*$E$18+F14*$F$18.
6. To make the sheet more dynamic, place a scrollbar control over J5, linked to J5 (keep the other properties default).
7. Place in cells H5, H9, and H14: -$J$5/1000.

Chapter 64: Interpolation

What the simulation does

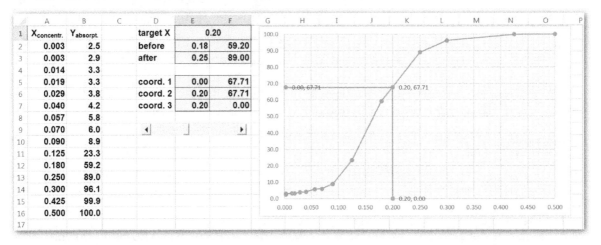

Columns A and B display 15 sets of observation points for the relationship between the concentration of some solution and the absorption for a certain wave length. Plotting this out results in a sigmoidal or S-shaped curve.

In order to find out what the absorption (Y) would be for a specific concentration (X) that was *not* observed or measured, we need to perform interpolation between the two closest observation points on both sides of our target value of X. In this simulation we set our target value in cell E1—either manually or by using a scrollbar control. Then formulas in cells E2:F3 determine the observed X- and Y-values just before and just after the target value in columns A and B. Based on this information, the interpolated Y-value can be found in cells F5:F6.

In order to plot this point in the sigmoidal curve as an insert, we need to calculate 3 sets of coordinates in cells E5:F7. Cells E5 and F7 should be 0 if both axes start at 0. Then we add these new data points to the chart and fix the chart type for this insert.

What you need to know

To find certain row and column positions in an array, we need the function INDEX with a nested function MATCH for row position numbers.

To find a non-observed data point between two close data points, the ideal function is TREND. It assumes a *linear* relationship—that's why we need the closest neighboring values on both sides of the target value. TREND is a multi-cell array function, which can return multiple values at the same time (if that's the case, you must select multiple cells first and finish the formula with *Ctrl Shift Enter* at once). In our case it returns only one value. The function only needs to know the observed X-values (in this case E2:E3) and the observed Y-values (in F2:F3).

The syntax is: TREND(known_y's,[known_x's],[new_x's],[const]). In this case, we know the 2 *known-x's* (E2:E3) and the 2 *known-y's* (F2:F3). Essential here is one *new-x*: the target value in cell E1. The 4th and last argument of TREND are optional and can usually be ignored. The outcome of TREND is pretty accurate if the two neighboring values on both sides are not too far apart from each other.

What you need to do

	D	E	F
1	target X	=D9/100	
2	before	=INDEX($A$2:$B$16,MATCH($E$1,$A$2:$A$16,1),1)	=INDEX($A$2:$B$16,MATCH($E$1,$A$2:$A$16,1),2)
3	after	=INDEX($A$2:$B$16,MATCH($E$1,$A$2:$A$16,1)+1,1)	=INDEX($A$2:$B$16,MATCH($E$1,$A$2:$A$16,1)+1,2)
4			
5	coord. 1	=MIN(A2:A16)	=TREND($F$2:$F$3,$E$2:$E$3,$E$7)
6	coord. 2	=E1	=TREND($F$2:$F$3,$E$2:$E$3,$E$7)
7	coord. 3	=E1	=E5
8			
9	27 ◄		►
10			

1. Place a scrollbar control over cell D9: Min 0 | Max 50 | SmallChange1 | LinkedCell D9.
2. Place in cell E1: =D9/100.
3. Place in cell E2: =INDEX($A$2:$B$16,MATCH($E$1,$A$2:$A$16,1),1). It looks for a value in column 1 of the array (see the last argument).
4. Place in cell F2: =INDEX($A$2:$B$16,MATCH($E$1,$A$2:$A$16,1),2). It looks for a value in column 2 of the array (see the last argument).
5. Place in cell E3: =INDEX($A$2:$B$16,MATCH($E$1,$A$2:$A$16,1)+1,1). This formula looks 1 row farther down (+1) in column 1.
6. Place in cell F3: =INDEX($A$2:$B$16,MATCH($E$1,$A$2:$A$16,1)+1,2). This formula looks 1 row farther down in column 2.
7. So we end up with two sets of coordinates closest to our target X-value. Now we need to find the corresponding Y-value.
8. We do so in the cells F5 and F6: =TREND($F$2:$F$3,$E$2:$E$3,$E$7). Use *Ctrl Shift Enter*!
9. The other elements of the 3 sets of coordinates are rather straightforward.
10. Use the scrollbar control and see how the insert nicely, and rather accurately, follows the sigmoidal curve.

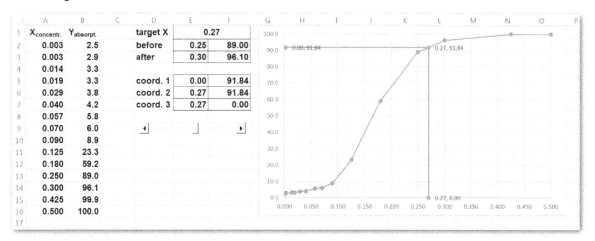

Chapter 65: Extrapolation

What the simulation does

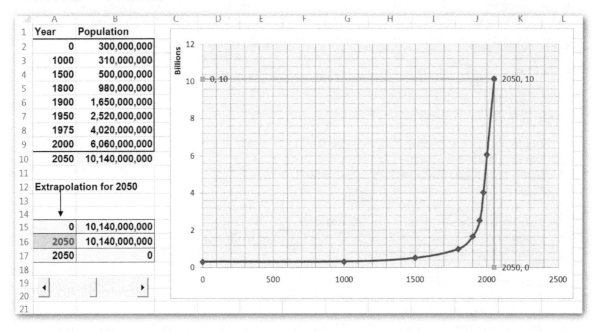

Extrapolation is a process of estimating a value beyond or outside the range of existing, observed values. For example, in a graph, you might want to mark a specific point on the curve that is located in the future.

In this simulation we have data about the size of the world population in the past 2000 years. The simulation allows you to extrapolate what the size of the world population would be in the years to come. A scrollbar control lets us extrapolate what the world population would be up to 100 years ahead, if the current trend would continue.

What you need to know

Extrapolation can be done in two ways. If you can figure out the equation behind the observed, or known, values—but often you don't—you can apply that equation to find the value you are trying to extrapolate (for example, the year 2050).

If you do *not* know the equation, you can use the two most recent observations (in this case, 1975 and 2000), assuming a linear relationship between the two, and then calculate the new, approximate value in cell B10.

The function to do the latter is TREND. We used it before, in the previous chapter, for a case of interpolation, but it also works for extrapolation, although extrapolation is always more risky than interpolation. Based on observed X-values and observed Y-values, it can be used for a new, unobserved X-value to predict what the extrapolated Y-value would be.

Then we figure out what the three sets of coordinates would be (A15:B17), so you can create an insert for the extrapoleted value.

What you need to do

1. Place in cell B10: =TREND(B8:B9,A8:A9,A10).
2. Place in cells A15 and B17: 0.
3. Place in cells A16 and A17: =A10.
4. Place in cells B15 and B16: =B10
5. Add a scrollbar control. (For more details see Appendix). Set Min to 2000, Max to 2100, Small and Large change to 5, and LinkedCell to cell A10.
6. The farther away the extrapolation goes, the more unreliable the outcome is, of course (see below).

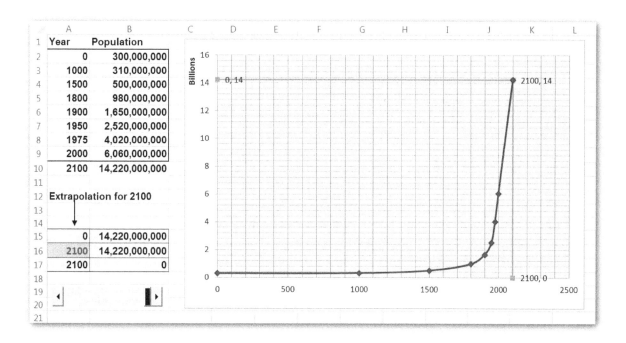

Chapter 66: Boltzmann Equation for Sigmoidal Curves

What the simulation does

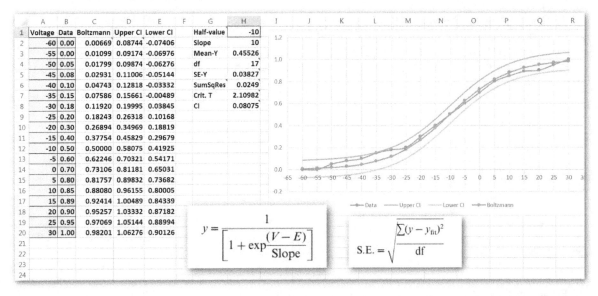

This simulation deals with curves that are of the logistic, s-shaped, or sigmoidal type, so we could use the Boltzmann equation as explained in the figure above (where E is the independent variable in column A, and V the half-way activity). The values in columns C:E and H are calculated (see next page), except for the values in H1 and H2, which are two educated guesses.

Something similar can be done for EC50 or IC50 determination. The term "half maximal effective concentration" (EC50) refers to the concentration of a drug, antibody, or toxicant which induces a response *halfway* between the baseline and maximum after a specified exposure time. It is commonly used as a measure of a drug's *effective* potency. (IC50, on the other hand, is the "halfway maximal *inhibitory* response.")

Based on the confidence interval (*CI* in H8), the columns D and E calculate the confidence margin on both sides of the curve of the observed values: (mean + *CI*) or (mean − *CI*).

What you need to know

In order to get a more accurate value for the half-way value and the slope, we need to set the *Sum of Squared Residuals* (H6) to a minimum, which means that the difference between what we observed and what we expected according to the equation is minimal.

We can do so by using Excel's *Solver* tool. Make sure *Solver* is active in VBA: Tools | References | Solver ON. Now you should be able to call *Solver*. On the screen shot to the left, cell H6 is set to a minimum by changing the variable cells H1:H2 (the educated guesses). Since there can be several solutions to this problem, it is wise to add some constraints—for instance, that H1 should be between -5 and -15.

What you need to do

	G	H
1	Half-value	-10
2	Slope	10
3	Mean-Y	=AVERAGE(B:B)
4	df	=COUNT(B:B)-COUNT(H1:H2)
5	SE-Y	=SQRT(SUM((B2:B20-C2:C20)^2)/H4)
6	SumSqRes	=SUM((B2:B20-C2:C20)^2)
7	Crit. T	=TINV(0.05,H4)
8	CI	=H7*H5

1. Place in C the Boltzmann equation: =(1/(1+EXP(($H$1-A2)/$H$2)))
2. Place in D the upper confidence margin (mean + CI): =C2+$H$8.
3. Place in E the lower confidence margin (mean - CI): =C2-$H$8.
4. Plot columns A:E in a line chart.
5. Fill the cells G1:H8 as shown left.
6. Use Excel's *Solver* with the settings show above to get a better estimate of the halfway value and the slope.
7. See below what *Solver* came up with.

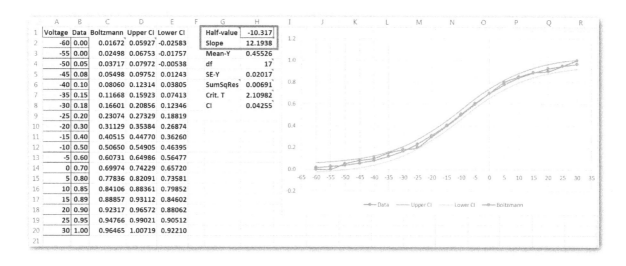

Chapter 67: Rounding in Excel

What the simulation does

	A	B	C	D	E	F	G	H
1		8.6478306	4.8125463	0.8523772	0.469982	9.2356314	-8.3026789	-1.1735252
2								
3	ABS	8.6478306	4.8125463	0.8523772	0.469982	9.2356314	8.30267894	1.17352522
4	INT	8	4	0	0	9	-9	-2
5	TRUNC	8	4	0	0	9	-8	-1
6	QUOTIENT	4	2	0	0	4	-4	0
7	MOD	0.6478306	0.8125463	0.8523772	0.469982	1.2356314	1.69732106	0.82647478
8								
9								
10	FLOOR(..., 0.5)	8.5	4.5	0.5	0	9	-8.5	-1.5
11	FLOOR(..., -0.5)	#NUM!	#NUM!	#NUM!	#NUM!	#NUM!	-8	-1
12	CEIL(..., 0.5)	9	5	1	0.5	9.5	-8	-1
13	CEIL(..., -0.5)	#NUM!	#NUM!	#NUM!	#NUM!	#NUM!	-8.5	-1.5
14								
15	EVEN	10	6	2	2	10	-10	-2
16	ODD	9	5	1	1	11	-9	-3
17								
18	ROUND(..., 2)	8.65	4.81	0.85	0.47	9.24	-8.3	-1.17
19	ROUNDDOWN	8.64	4.81	0.85	0.46	9.23	-8.3	-1.17
20	ROUNDUP	8.65	4.82	0.86	0.47	9.24	-8.31	-1.18
21	ROUNDEVEN	-	-	-	-	-	-	-
22								
23	n signif. digits	1	2	3	4	5	6	7
24	ROUNDn	9.00000000	4.80000000	0.85200000	0.47000000	9.23560000	-8.30268000	-1.17352500
25								

This simulation shows how many rounding functions Excel offers and how they round numbers.

Row 1 has a series of random numbers between 0 and 1. The other rows show how a specific function rounds the values in row 1. Some round up or down, others round toward 0.

What you need to know

INT rounds a number *down* to the nearest integer.

TRUNC truncates a number to an integer by removing the fractional part of the number. It has a 2nd argument specifying the precision of the truncation—default value is 0 (zero).

QUOTIENT returns the integer portion of a division. Use this function when you want to discard the remainder of a division.

MOD returns the remainder after number is divided by divisor. The result has the same sign as divisor. So MOD(3,2) = 1.

FLOOR and CEILING round numbers either down or up, toward zero, to the nearest multiple of significance. Their two arguments must be both positive, or both negative (otherwise #NUM!).

ODD rounds a positive number up and a negative number down to the nearest odd integer. EVEN does the same to the nearest even integer.

Then there are three ROUND-ing functions. See how they round numbers differently.

If you want to round to a specific number of *significant* digits, you need to do a bit more work. Here is the formula: *=ROUND(x,n-1-INT(LOG10(ABS(x))))*.

What you need to do

1. Place in cells B1:H1: =RAND()*10.
2. Place in cells B3:H3: =ABS(B1).
3. Place in cells B4:H4: =INT(B1).
4. Place in cells B5:H5: =TRUNC(B1,2).
5. Place in cells B6:H6: =QUOTIENT(B1,2).
6. Place in cells B7:H7: =MOD(B1,2).
7. Place in cells B10:H10: =FLOOR(B1,0.5).
8. Place in cells B11:H11: =FLOOR(B1,-0.5).
9. Place in cells B12:H12: =CEILING(B1,0.5).
10. Place in cells B13:H13: =CEILING(B1,-0.5).
11. Place in cells B15:H15: =EVEN(B1).
12. Place in cells B16:H16: =ODD(B1).
13. Place in cells B18:H18: =ROUND(B1,2).
14. Place in cells B19:H19: =ROUNDDOWN(B1,2).
15. Place in cells B20:H20: =ROUNDUP(B1,2).
16. Place in cells B21:H21: =ROUNDUP(B1,2).
17. Place in cells B24:H24: =ROUND(B1,B23-1-INT(LOG10(ABS(B1)))).
18. Using the key *F9*, you will see how rounding works each time.

	A	B	C	D	E	F	G
1		=RAND()*10	=RAND()*10	=RAND()*10	=RAND()*10	=RAND()*10	=-RAND()*10
2							
3	ABS	=ABS(B1)	=ABS(C1)	=ABS(D1)	=ABS(E1)	=ABS(F1)	=ABS(G1)
4	INT	=INT(B1)	=INT(C1)	=INT(D1)	=INT(E1)	=INT(F1)	=INT(G1)
5	TRUNC	=TRUNC(B1,2)	=TRUNC(C1)	=TRUNC(D1)	=TRUNC(E1)	=TRUNC(F1)	=TRUNC(G1)
6	QUOTIENT	=QUOTIENT(B1,2)	=QUOTIENT(C1,2)	=QUOTIENT(D1,2)	=QUOTIENT(E1,2)	=QUOTIENT(F1,2)	=QUOTIENT(G1,2)
7	MOD	=MOD(B1,2)	=MOD(C1,2)	=MOD(D1,2)	=MOD(E1,2)	=MOD(F1,2)	=MOD(G1,2)
8							
9							
10	FLOOR(..., 0.5)	=FLOOR(B1,0.5)	=FLOOR(C1,0.5)	=FLOOR(D1,0.5)	=FLOOR(E1,0.5)	=FLOOR(F1,0.5)	=FLOOR(G1,0.5)
11	FLOOR(..., -0.5)	=FLOOR(B1,-0.5)	=FLOOR(C1,-0.5)	=FLOOR(D1,-0.5)	=FLOOR(E1,-0.5)	=FLOOR(F1,-0.5)	=FLOOR(G1,-0.5)
12	CEIL(..., 0.5)	=CEILING(B1,0.5)	=CEILING(C1,0.5)	=CEILING(D1,0.5)	=CEILING(E1,0.5)	=CEILING(F1,0.5)	=CEILING(G1,0.5)
13	CEIL(..., -0.5)	=CEILING(B1,-0.5)	=CEILING(C1,-0.5)	=CEILING(D1,-0.5)	=CEILING(E1,-0.5)	=CEILING(F1,-0.5)	=CEILING(G1,-0.5)
14							
15	EVEN	=EVEN(B1)	=EVEN(C1)	=EVEN(D1)	=EVEN(E1)	=EVEN(F1)	=EVEN(G1)
16	ODD	=ODD(B1)	=ODD(C1)	=ODD(D1)	=ODD(E1)	=ODD(F1)	=ODD(G1)
17							
18	ROUND(..., 2)	=ROUND(B1,2)	=ROUND(C1,2)	=ROUND(D1,2)	=ROUND(E1,2)	=ROUND(F1,2)	=ROUND(G1,2)
19	ROUNDDOWN	=ROUNDDOWN(B1,2)	=ROUNDDOWN(C1,2)	=ROUNDDOWN(D1,2)	=ROUNDDOWN(E1,2)	=ROUNDDOWN(F1,2)	=ROUNDDOWN(G1,2)
20	ROUNDUP	=ROUNDUP(B1,2)	=ROUNDUP(C1,2)	=ROUNDUP(D1,2)	=ROUNDUP(E1,2)	=ROUNDUP(F1,2)	=ROUNDUP(G1,2)
21	ROUNDEVEN	-	-	-	-	-	-

Chapter 68: Simple Decay Simulation

What the simulation does

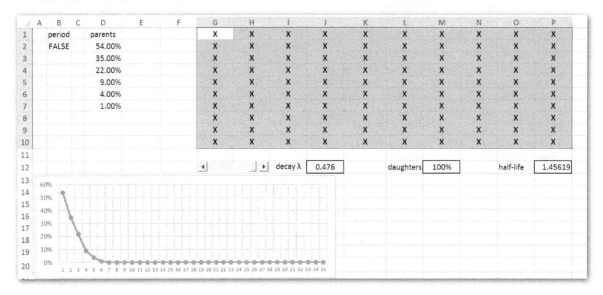

Everything in the microscopic world happens according to probabilities. A very clear example of this is radioactive decay. This is a process in which an atomic nucleus that is not stable converts itself into a different isotope. For example, a carbon 14 nucleus (^{14}C: 6 protons and 8 neutrons) converts itself into a nitrogen 14 nucleus (^{14}N: 7 protons and 7 neutrons) because ^{14}N is more stable. In this particular process, a neutron turns into a proton.

The radioactive elements can be referred to as *parent* nuclei; the nuclei they disintegrate to are called *daughter* products. The board G1:P10 shown above replaces at each period (B2) the original parent nuclei with daughter nuclei ("X") according to a decay constant λ (J12) until there are no parent nuclei left and the daughter nuclei have reached 100% (M12).

At each period, column D keeps track of the percentage of parent atoms that are still left. This process is then plotted in an exponential decay chart.

What you need to know

The half-lives of some radioactive isotopes	
Radioactive isotope	**Half-life**
Uranium-238, $^{238}_{92}$U	4.5×10^9 years
Carbon-14, $^{14}_{6}$C	5.7×10^3 years
Radium-226, $^{226}_{88}$Ra	1.6×10^3 years
Strontium-90 $^{90}_{38}$Sr	28 years
Iodine-131, $^{131}_{53}$I	8.1 days
Bismuth-214, $^{214}_{83}$Bi	19.7 minutes
Polonium-214, $^{214}_{84}$Po	1.5×10^{-4} seconds

The half-life, $T_{1/2}$, is the time required for the number of radioactive nuclei to decrease to one-half of the initial number of radioactive nuclei. So the half-life, $T_{1/2}$, is defined as the time for one-half of the radioactive nuclei to decay.

$$t_{1/2} = \tau \ln(2) = \frac{0.693}{\lambda}$$

The half-life is considerably different for various isotopes, as the table to the left shows.

What you need to do

1. Set iteration to 1x.
2. Place a scrollbar control (see Appendix) next to cell I12: Min 100 (!) | Max 500 | SmallChange 1 | LargeChange 10 | Linked to cell H12.
3. Place in cell J12: =H12/1000.
4. Place in cell B2: =IF($M$12=100%,B2=1,B2+1).
5. Place in cells D2:D36: =IF(ROW(A1)>$B$2,"",IF(ROW(A1)=$B$2,1-$M$12,D2)).
6. Place in cells G1:P10: =IF(G1<>"X",IF(RAND()<$J$12,"X",""),"X").
7. Place in cell M12: =COUNTIF(G1:P10,"X")/100.
8. Place in cell P12: =LN(2)/J12.
9. Plot D2:D36 in the chart.
10. Regulate the decay constant with the scrollbar control, with a minimum of 0.1 in J12.
11. To start from scratch again, select G1:P10, click in the formula bar, and finish with *Ctrl Enter*.
12. The first *F9* hit shows the first decay result on the board; but the rest lags 1 run behind.
13. Next, after hitting (or holding) *F9*, cell B2 keeps track of each period, and column D adds the new percentage of parents. The chart, linked to column D updates automatically.
14. When cell M12 reaches 100%, cell B2 is set back to FALSE. You don't have to touch columns B or D. Just refresh range G1:P10 through the formula bar with *Ctrl Enter*.

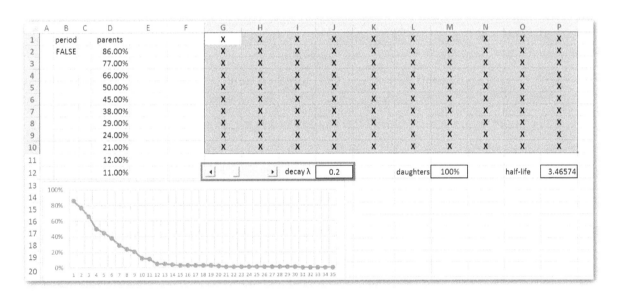

Chapter 69: Radioactive Decay

What the simulation does

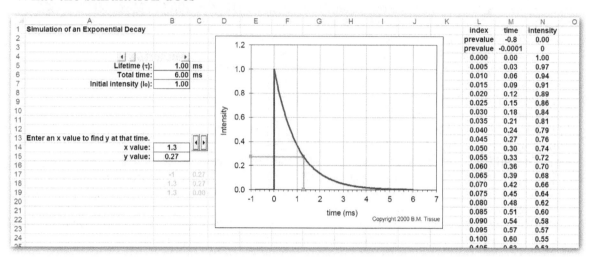

This simulation[4] is again about exponential radioactive decay. With a scrollbar control, you can regulate the life-time of an isotope in cell B5. For high values, you may want to increase the maximum time scale in the chart (according to cell B6).

With a spinbutton control, you can find for a specific x-value (in cell B14) what the corresponding y-value would be (in cell B15). An insert in the chart shows that position.

Calculations are done in columns L:N. The chart plots the values from columns M and N.

What you need to know

The minimum x-axis value is set to -1. The maximum x- and y-axis values will autoscale. The *ms* time scale on the chart is arbitrary.

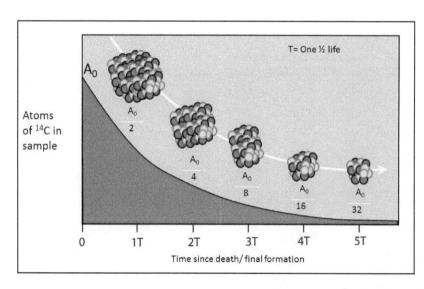

A rather well-known example of a radioactive isotope is carbon-14 (^{14}C). It has a half-life of 5730 years. Once a plant or animal dies, its carbon-14 content gradually decreases. Using the half-life for carbon-14 and comparing the amount of carbon-14 in any ancient artifact with the amount of carbon-14 that we would expect in a fresh sample today, we can date an object.

---

[4] My special thanks for this simulation goes to Brian M. Tissue from Virginia Tech.

What you need to do

1. Place a scrollbar control above cells A5:B5: Min 10 | Max 5000 | SmallChange 1 | LargeChange 5 | LinkedCell B4.
2. Place in cell B5: =B4/100.
3. Place a spinbutton control next to cells B13:B14: Min 0 | Max 100 | SmallChange 1 | LinkedCell C14.
4. Place in cell B14: =C14/10.
5. Create 3 sets of coordinates for the insert in cells B17:C19 with the following settings: B17 -1 | B18 =B14 | B19 =B14 | C17 =B15 | C18 =B15 | C19 0.
6. Place in the cells L4:L5 two manual entries: 0.000 and 0.005. Select both cells at the same time and copy them downwards to cell L204.
7. Place in the cells M4:M204: =L4*$B$6.
8. Place in the cells N4:N204: =B$7*EXP(-$M4/B$5).

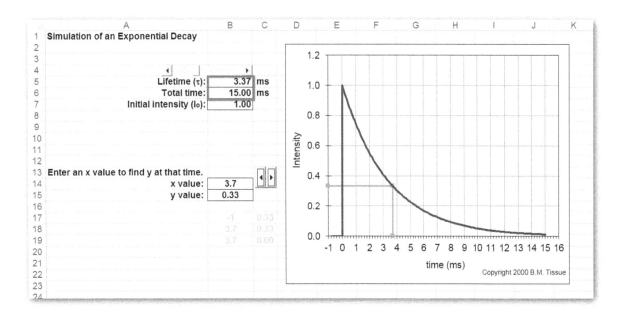

Chapter 70: Michaelis-Menten Equation

What the simulation does

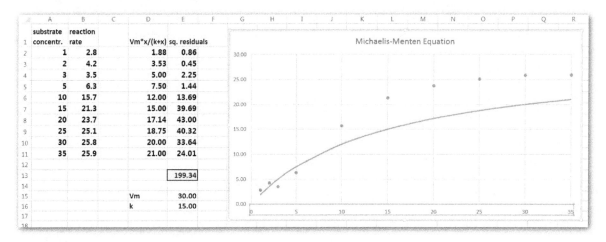

This is one of the best-known models of enzyme kinetics. It describes the rate of enzymatic reactions, by relating reaction rate (r) to the concentration of a substrate (C).

$$r = \frac{V_m C}{K + C}$$

In the formula shown to the left, C is the substrate concentration, and V_m and K are the Michaelis-Menten parameters to be fit. V_m is the maximum rate in the system, and K is the concentration at which the reaction rate is $V_m/2$.

What you need to know

The curve does not fit very well yet. So we need to go for a better fit.

The problem is that the Michaelis-Menten parameters V_m (in cell E15) and K (in cell E16) are unknown but have to be based on an educated guess. Apparently this guess is still off.

To find out how much "off" they are, we use the sum of the squared residuals in cell E13: the difference between what was observed and what is expected according to the Michaelis-Menten equation. We need the *Solver* tool (see Chapter 66) to set E13 to a minimum by changing the two parameters (see picture to the left).

The function RSQ calculates the square of the correlation coefficient through data points in two arrays of values. The *r-squared* value can be interpreted as the proportion of the variance in y attributable to the variance in x.

What you need to do

1. Place in cells D2:D11: =($E$15*A2)/($E$16+A2).
2. Place in cells E2:E11: =(B2-D2)^2.
3. Place in cell E13: =SUM(E2:E12).
4. Call *Solver*: Data | Solver (see Chapter 66).
5. If you accept the solution, the sum of the squared residuals has been reduced from 199.34 to 26.53 by setting V_m to 42.43 and K to 18.39 (see below).
6. If you want to see how close the predictions are in column D, use the Excel function RSQ: =RSQ(D2:D11,B2:B11). The result would be 0.97418 in this case, which is very close to the "ideal" value of 1.

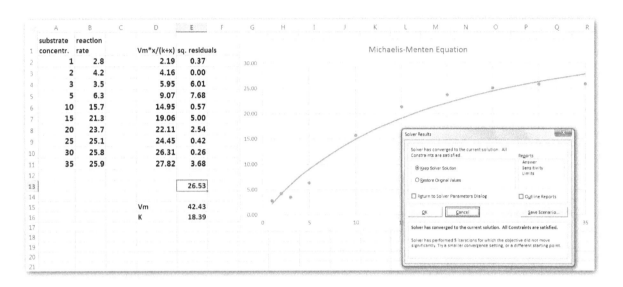

Chapter 71: Chemical Equilibria

What the simulation does

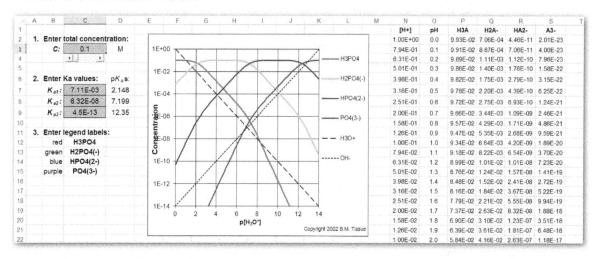

This simulation[5] plots the logarithmic concentration of a polyprotic acid such as phosphoric acid (*H3PO4*), which forms tripotic acids: H2PO4(-), HPO4(2-), and PO4(3-). Other forms of triprotic acids are, after their dissociation into H⁺ ions: *H2S* (Hydrogen sulfide) | *H2SO4* (Sulfuric acid) | *H2SO3* (Sulfurous acid) | *H2C2O4* (Oxalic acid) | *H2CO3* (Carbonic acid) | *H2C3H2O4* (Malonic acid).

Polyprotic acids contain more than one mole ionizable hydronium ions per mole of acids. They ionize to give more than one H⁺ ions per molecule. These acids ionize in several stages, giving out one proton at each stage.

1. Determine the total concentration in cell C3 by using a scrollbar control.

2. Enter the K_a values in the gray boxes for different polyprotic acids. (Leave K_{a3} blank for a diprotic acid.)

3. Change the acid labels to change the legend on the plot.

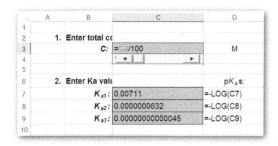

What you need to know

The columns B:D are basically simple, and partially done manually (see left).

The hard work is done in columns N:S (see next page).

The function LOG returns the logarithm of a number to a base you specify (typically 100).

---

[5] My special thanks for this simulation goes to Brian M. Tissue from Virginia Tech.

What you need to do

	N	O	P	Q
1	[H+]	pH	H3A	H2A-
2	1	0	=$C$3*$N2^3 / ($N2^3+($C$7*$N2^2)+($C$7*$C$8*$N2)+($C$7*$C$8*$C$9))	=$C$3*$C$7*$N2^2 / ($N2^3+($C$7*$N2^2)+($C$7*$C$8*$N2)+($C$7*$C$8*$C$9))
3	=10^(-03)	0.1	=$C$3*$N3^3 / ($N3^3+($C$7*$N3^2)+($C$7*$C$8*$N3)+($C$7*$C$8*$C$9))	=$C$3*$C$7*$N3^2 / ($N3^3+($C$7*$N3^2)+($C$7*$C$8*$N3)+($C$7*$C$8*$C$9))
4	=10^(-04)	0.2	=$C$3*$N4^3 / ($N4^3+($C$7*$N4^2)+($C$7*$C$8*$N4)+($C$7*$C$8*$C$9))	=$C$3*$C$7*$N4^2 / ($N4^3+($C$7*$N4^2)+($C$7*$C$8*$N4)+($C$7*$C$8*$C$9))
5	=10^(-05)	0.3	=$C$3*$N5^3 / ($N5^3+($C$7*$N5^2)+($C$7*$C$8*$N5)+($C$7*$C$8*$C$9))	=$C$3*$C$7*$N5^2 / ($N5^3+($C$7*$N5^2)+($C$7*$C$8*$N5)+($C$7*$C$8*$C$9))
6	=10^(-06)	0.4	=$C$3*$N6^3 / ($N6^3+($C$7*$N6^2)+($C$7*$C$8*$N6)+($C$7*$C$8*$C$9))	=$C$3*$C$7*$N6^2 / ($N6^3+($C$7*$N6^2)+($C$7*$C$8*$N6)+($C$7*$C$8*$C$9))
7	=10^(-07)	0.5	=$C$3*$N7^3 / ($N7^3+($C$7*$N7^2)+($C$7*$C$8*$N7)+($C$7*$C$8*$C$9))	=$C$3*$C$7*$N7^2 / ($N7^3+($C$7*$N7^2)+($C$7*$C$8*$N7)+($C$7*$C$8*$C$9))
8	=10^(-08)	0.6	=$C$3*$N8^3 / ($N8^3+($C$7*$N8^2)+($C$7*$C$8*$N8)+($C$7*$C$8*$C$9))	=$C$3*$C$7*$N8^2 / ($N8^3+($C$7*$N8^2)+($C$7*$C$8*$N8)+($C$7*$C$8*$C$9))
9	=10^(-09)	0.7	=$C$3*$N9^3 / ($N9^3+($C$7*$N9^2)+($C$7*$C$8*$N9)+($C$7*$C$8*$C$9))	=$C$3*$C$7*$N9^2 / ($N9^3+($C$7*$N9^2)+($C$7*$C$8*$N9)+($C$7*$C$8*$C$9))

1. Place a scrollbar control under cell C3: Min 10 | Max 10o | SmallChange 1 | LinkedCell C4.
2. Place in cell C3: =C4/100.
3. Place in cells D7:D9: =-LOG(C7).
4. Place in cells N2:N142: =10^(-O2).
5. Place in cells O2:O142: 0.0 to 14.0 in steps of 0.1.
6. Place in cells P2: P142 the following somewhat sophisticated formula:
   =$C$3*$N2^3 / ($N2^3+($C$7*$N2^2)+($C$7*$C$8*$N2)+($C$7*$C$8*$C$9)).
7. Place in cells Q2:Q142 the following somewhat sophisticated formula:
   =$C$3*$C$7*$N2^2 / ($N2^3+($C$7*$N2^2)+($C$7*$C$8*$N2)+($C$7*$C$8*$C$9)).
8. Place in cells R2:R142 the following somewhat sophisticated formula:
   =$C$3*$C$7*$C$8*$N2 / ($N2^3+($C$7*$N2^2)+($C$7*$C$8*$N2)+($C$7*$C$8*$C$9)).
9. Place in cells S2:S142 the following somewhat sophisticated formula:
   =$C$3*$C$7*$C$8*$C$9 / ($N2^3+($C$7*$N2^2)+($C$7*$C$8*$N2)+($C$7*$C$8*$C$9)).
10. Make the vertical axis in the chart logarithmic.
11. Below we changed the cells to another acid: oxalic acid.

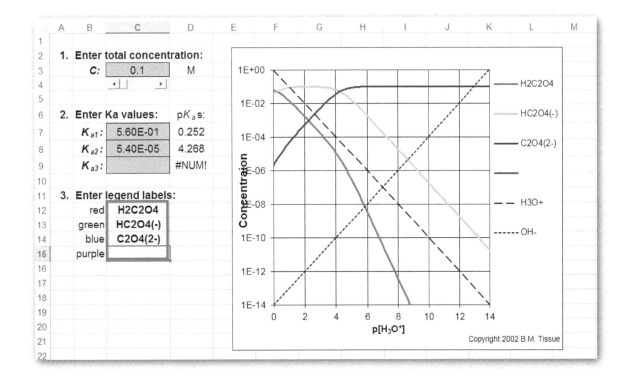

Chapter 72: Spectrum Simulation

What the simulation does

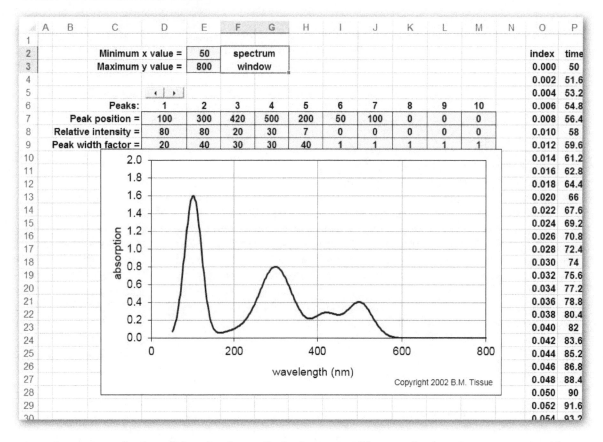

A spectrum is a condition that is not limited to a specific set of values but can vary, without steps, across a continuum. The word was first used scientifically in optics to describe the rainbow of colors in visible light after passing through a prism. As scientific understanding of light advanced, it came to apply to the entire electromagnetic spectrum.

In this simulation,[6] the spectrum shown in the chart is the sum of 10 Gaussian peaks (cells D6:M8). The shaded cells can be entered manually and then the chart will update. The cells E2:E3 determine the spectrum window on the horizontal axis of the chart.

What you need to know

The main calculations are done in columns O:AA, as shown on the next page.

---

[6] My special thanks for this simulation goes to Brian M. Tissue from Virginia Tech.

What you need to do

	O	P	Q	R	S	
1			width factor =	=Simulation!D$9	=Simulation!E$9	=Simulation!
2	index	time	sum	************ Raw Data ************		
3	0	=$E$2+O3*$E$3	=SUM(R3:AA3)	=D$8*(1/(2*PI()*R$1^2)^0.5)*EXP(-(($P3-D$7)^2)/(2*R$1^2))	=E$8*(1/(2*PI()*S$1^2)^0.5)*EXP(-(($P3-E$7)^2)/(2*S$1^2))	=F$8*(1/(2*PI
4	0.002	=$E$2+O4*$E$3	=SUM(R4:AA4)	=D$8*(1/(2*PI()*R$1^2)^0.5)*EXP(-(($P4-D$7)^2)/(2*R$1^2))	=E$8*(1/(2*PI()*S$1^2)^0.5)*EXP(-(($P4-E$7)^2)/(2*S$1^2))	=F$8*(1/(2*PI
5	0.004	=$E$2+O5*$E$3	=SUM(R5:AA5)	=D$8*(1/(2*PI()*R$1^2)^0.5)*EXP(-(($P5-D$7)^2)/(2*R$1^2))	=E$8*(1/(2*PI()*S$1^2)^0.5)*EXP(-(($P5-E$7)^2)/(2*S$1^2))	=F$8*(1/(2*PI
6	0.006	=$E$2+O6*$E$3	=SUM(R6:AA6)	=D$8*(1/(2*PI()*R$1^2)^0.5)*EXP(-(($P6-D$7)^2)/(2*R$1^2))	=E$8*(1/(2*PI()*S$1^2)^0.5)*EXP(-(($P6-E$7)^2)/(2*S$1^2))	=F$8*(1/(2*PI
7	0.008	=$E$2+O7*$E$3	=SUM(R7:AA7)	=D$8*(1/(2*PI()*R$1^2)^0.5)*EXP(-(($P7-D$7)^2)/(2*R$1^2))	=E$8*(1/(2*PI()*S$1^2)^0.5)*EXP(-(($P7-E$7)^2)/(2*S$1^2))	=F$8*(1/(2*PI
8	0.01	=$E$2+O8*$E$3	=SUM(R8:AA8)	=D$8*(1/(2*PI()*R$1^2)^0.5)*EXP(-(($P8-D$7)^2)/(2*R$1^2))	=E$8*(1/(2*PI()*S$1^2)^0.5)*EXP(-(($P8-E$7)^2)/(2*S$1^2))	=F$8*(1/(2*PI
9	0.012	=$E$2+O9*$E$3	=SUM(R9:AA9)	=D$8*(1/(2*PI()*R$1^2)^0.5)*EXP(-(($P9-D$7)^2)/(2*R$1^2))	=E$8*(1/(2*PI()*S$1^2)^0.5)*EXP(-(($P9-E$7)^2)/(2*S$1^2))	=F$8*(1/(2*PI
10	0.014	=$E$2+O10*$E$3	=SUM(R10:AA10)	=D$8*(1/(2*PI()*R$1^2)^0.5)*EXP(-(($P10-D$7)^2)/(2*R$1^2))	=E$8*(1/(2*PI()*S$1^2)^0.5)*EXP(-(($P10-E$7)^2)/(2*S$1^2))	=F$8*(1/(2*PI
11	0.016	=$E$2+O11*$E$3	=SUM(R11:AA11)	=D$8*(1/(2*PI()*R$1^2)^0.5)*EXP(-(($P11-D$7)^2)/(2*R$1^2))	=E$8*(1/(2*PI()*S$1^2)^0.5)*EXP(-(($P11-E$7)^2)/(2*S$1^2))	=F$8*(1/(2*PI
12	0.018	=$E$2+O12*$E$3	=SUM(R12:AA12)	=D$8*(1/(2*PI()*R$1^2)^0.5)*EXP(-(($P12-D$7)^2)/(2*R$1^2))	=E$8*(1/(2*PI()*S$1^2)^0.5)*EXP(-(($P12-E$7)^2)/(2*S$1^2))	=F$8*(1/(2*PI
13	0.02	=$E$2+O13*$E$3	=SUM(R13:AA13)	=D$8*(1/(2*PI()*R$1^2)^0.5)*EXP(-(($P13-D$7)^2)/(2*R$1^2))	=E$8*(1/(2*PI()*S$1^2)^0.5)*EXP(-(($P13-E$7)^2)/(2*S$1^2))	=F$8*(1/(2*PI
14	0.022	=$E$2+O14*$E$3	=SUM(R14:AA14)	=D$8*(1/(2*PI()*R$1^2)^0.5)*EXP(-(($P14-D$7)^2)/(2*R$1^2))	=E$8*(1/(2*PI()*S$1^2)^0.5)*EXP(-(($P14-E$7)^2)/(2*S$1^2))	=F$8*(1/(2*PI
15	0.024	=$E$2+O15*$E$3	=SUM(R15:AA15)	=D$8*(1/(2*PI()*R$1^2)^0.5)*EXP(-(($P15-D$7)^2)/(2*R$1^2))	=E$8*(1/(2*PI()*S$1^2)^0.5)*EXP(-(($P15-E$7)^2)/(2*S$1^2))	=F$8*(1/(2*PI
16	0.026	=$E$2+O16*$E$3	=SUM(R16:AA16)	=D$8*(1/(2*PI()*R$1^2)^0.5)*EXP(-(($P16-D$7)^2)/(2*R$1^2))	=E$8*(1/(2*PI()*S$1^2)^0.5)*EXP(-(($P16-E$7)^2)/(2*S$1^2))	=F$8*(1/(2*PI
17	0.028	=$E$2+O17*$E$3	=SUM(R17:AA17)	=D$8*(1/(2*PI()*R$1^2)^0.5)*EXP(-(($P17-D$7)^2)/(2*R$1^2))	=E$8*(1/(2*PI()*S$1^2)^0.5)*EXP(-(($P17-E$7)^2)/(2*S$1^2))	=F$8*(1/(2*PI
18	0.03	=$E$2+O18*$E$3	=SUM(R18:AA18)	=D$8*(1/(2*PI()*R$1^2)^0.5)*EXP(-(($P18-D$7)^2)/(2*R$1^2))	=E$8*(1/(2*PI()*S$1^2)^0.5)*EXP(-(($P18-E$7)^2)/(2*S$1^2))	=F$8*(1/(2*PI
19	0.032	=$E$2+O19*$E$3	=SUM(R19:AA19)	=D$8*(1/(2*PI()*R$1^2)^0.5)*EXP(-(($P19-D$7)^2)/(2*R$1^2))	=E$8*(1/(2*PI()*S$1^2)^0.5)*EXP(-(($P19-E$7)^2)/(2*S$1^2))	=F$8*(1/(2*PI
20	0.034	=$E$2+O20*$E$3	=SUM(R20:AA20)	=D$8*(1/(2*PI()*R$1^2)^0.5)*EXP(-(($P20-D$7)^2)/(2*R$1^2))	=E$8*(1/(2*PI()*S$1^2)^0.5)*EXP(-(($P20-E$7)^2)/(2*S$1^2))	=F$8*(1/(2*PI

1. Place a spinbutton control above cell D6: Min 50 | Max 800 | SmallChange 50 | LinkedCell D7.
2. This control only regulates cell D7, but you can also add controls to the other cells in the shaded range, if you want to.

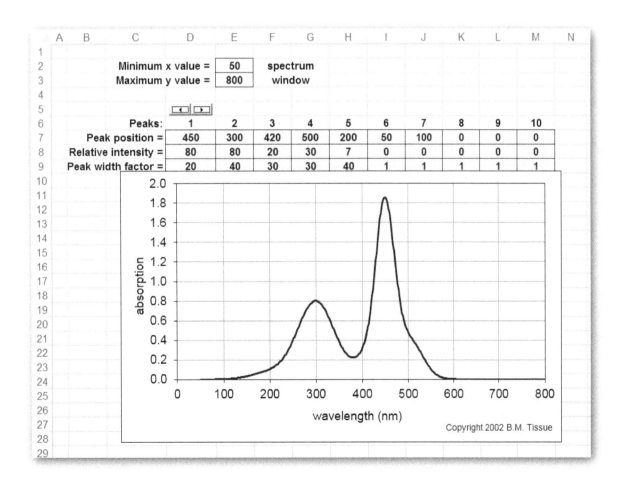

Chapter 73: Oscillations

What the simulation does

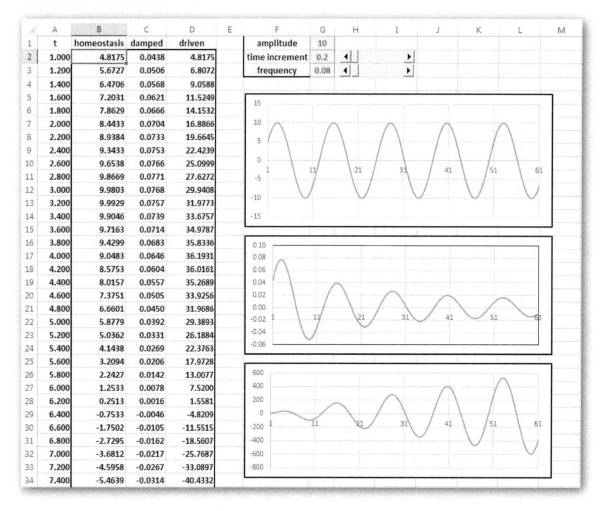

Oscillation is the repetitive variation, typically in time, of some measure about a central value (often a point of equilibrium) or between two or more different states.

A simple harmonic oscillator (shown in column B and in the top curve) will continue to oscillate with no decrease in amplitude—on the unrealistic condition there is no form of "friction."

Therefore, in all real-world oscillator systems, energy is taken from the system and so the amplitude decays. In real oscillators, friction, or damping, slows the motion of the system. This is called *damped* oscillation (column C and middle chart). Thus, oscillations tend to decay with time unless there is some net source of energy into the system. Examples of damped oscillation are pendulums and spring absorbers in cars.

In addition to damped oscillation, an oscillating system may be subject to some external force, as when an AC circuit is connected to an outside power source. In this case the oscillation is called *driven* (column D and bottom chart). Examples of driven oscillations are driving a child's swing or soldiers marching in cadence across a bridge, which has been known to set up resonant vibrations in the structure and thereby causes it to collapse. Whenever any real physical system is driven near its resonance frequency, you can expect oscillations towards very large amplitudes.

A simple harmonic oscillator is an oscillator system that is neither driven nor damped, which never happens in real life. A harmonic oscillator needs both a driving force and a damping force. Examples of this can be found in cases of *homeostasis* in living organisms. An example would be keeping the glucose level in the body within a specific amplitude range: insulin lowers and glucagon elevates the glucose level in the blood. So the ideal end result of a good oscillating system is what is shown in column B and the top chart.

What you need to know

Oscillations are determined by amplitude, frequency, and time increments. We can dynamically regulate these with scrollbar controls in this simulation.

Because these oscillations are sinusoidal, we need the function SIN as well as the function PI. With the help of these two functions, we can simulate very simple oscillations, without going into much more sophisticated physical and mathematical issues.

What you need to do

1. Place a scrollbar control next to cell G2: Min 2 | Max 9 | SmallChange 1 | LinkedCell H2.
2. Place in cell G2: =H2/10.
3. Place a scrollbar control next to cell G3: Min 2 | Max 150 | SmallChange 10 | LargeChange 10 | LinkedCell H3.
4. Place in cell G3: =H3/100.
5. Place in cells B2:B305: =$G$1*SIN(2*PI()*A2*$G$3).
6. Place in cells C2:C305: =(1/(A2+$G$1))*SIN(2*PI()*A2*$G$3).
7. Place in cells D2:D305: =($G$1*A2)*SIN(2*PI()*A2*$G$3).
8. Test various settings for amplitude, time increment, and frequency.

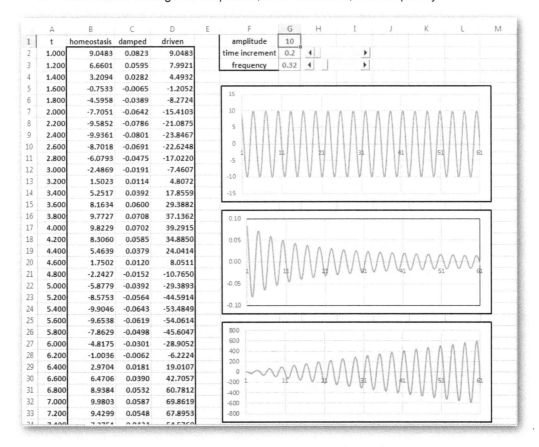

Chapter 74: Ballistic Trajectories

What the simulation does

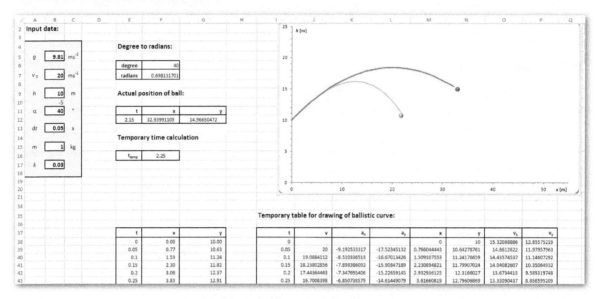

This simulation[7] is a dynamic visualization of mechanical motion—the trajectory of ballistic shots. The result is a ballistic curve plotted in an XY graph.

The ballistic trajectory is given by equations of motion. The equations of motion in the x, resp. y directions are: $ma_x = -kv_x$ and $ma_y = -mg-kv_y$, where m is mass of the projectile, k is coefficient of the air resistance, ax and ay are accelerations, vx and vy are velocities, and g is gravity acceleration. It is a time dependent system with a time dependent motion. The system changes its variables during the time.

What you need to know

The main parameter responsible for iterative recalculation is time t. The trajectory will be drawn step by step from time $t = 0$ with the time increment dt. The value of the time t is saved in cell F16 by using a circular reference formula: =IF(G12<0,B13,F16+B13).

The iterative recalculation of time t is changed within the range from a minimum value (t_0) to a maximum value (t_{max}) with a certain iteration step (the value of dt given in cell B13) by repeatedly pressing or holding the key *F9*.

The chart is based on *Range Names* which use OFFSET functions (see to the left).

You can find much more detailed explanations in the article of the two authors: http://www.wseas.us/e-library/conferences/2013/Valencia/CSA/CSA-16.pdf.

---

[7] A special thanks for this simulation goes to Marie Hubálovská and Štěpán Hubálovský.

Simulations in Action

What you need to do

1. Turn iterations on, set to a maximum of 1.
2. Place in cell F6: =B11.
3. Place in cell F7: =(F6*PI())/180.
4. Place in cell E12: =F16-B13.
5. Place in cell F12: =B7*(E12)*COS(F7).
6. Place in cell G12: =B9+(B7*(E12)*SIN(F7))-(0.5*B5*(E12)*(E12)).
7. Place in cell F16: =IF(G12<0,B13,F16+B13).
8. The rows 22:33 are empty and were hidden on the sheet.
9. Place in cells E39:E657: =IF(E38<>"",IF($E$12>=(E38+$B$13),(E38+$B$13),""),"").
10. Place in cells F39:F657: =IF(E39<>"",$B$7*(E39)*COS($F$7),"").
11. Place in cell G38: =B9+(B7*(E38)*SIN(F7))-(0.5*B5*(E38)*(E38)).
12. In G39:G657: =IF(E39<>"",$B$9+($B$7*(E39)*SIN($F$7))-(0.5*$B$5*(E39)*(E39)),"").
13. Place in cells I38:I657: =E38.
14. Place in cells J39:J657: =IF(I39<>"",SQRT(($O$38*$O$38)+($P$38*$P$38)),"").
15. Place in cells K39:K657: =IF(I39<>"",-$B$17*$O$38*$J$39,"").
16. Place in cells L39:L657: =IF(I39<>"",-$B$5-($B$17*$P$38*$J$39),"").
17. Place in cell M38: =$I$26.
18. Place in cells M39:M657: =IF(I39<>"",I26+($O$38*$B$13),"").
19. Place in cell N38: =$B$9.
20. Place in cells N39:N657: =IF(I39<>"",$B$9+($P$38*$B$13),"").
21. Place in cell O38: =$B$7*COS($F$7).
22. Place in cells O39:O657: =IF(I39<>"",$O$38+(K39*$B$13),"").
23. Place in cell P38: =$B$7*SIN($F$7).
24. Place in cells P39:P657: =IF(I39<>"",$P$38+(L39*$B$13),"").
25. The top curve is linked to x and y in columns F and G. The lower curve is linked to x and y in columns M and N.
26. Holding or pressing *F9* sets the process in motion. Ignore any error message.

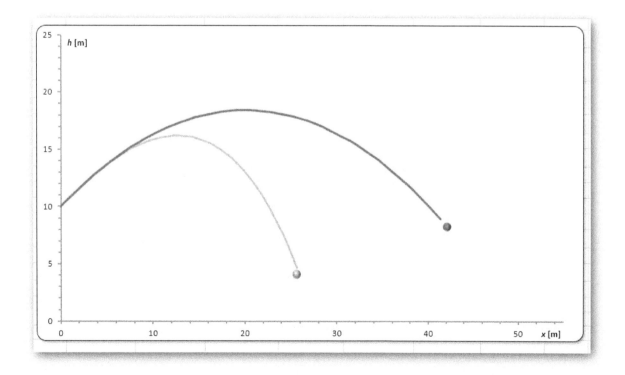

Chapter 75: Logistic Bacterial Growth

What the simulation does

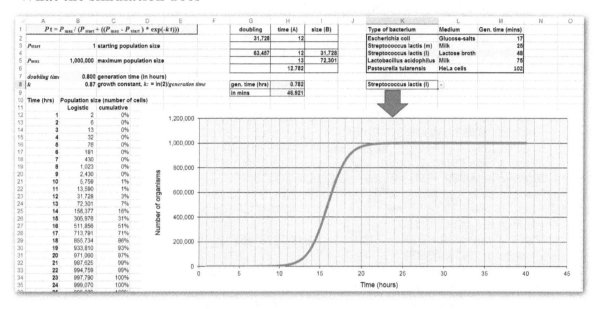

During active bacterial growth, the number of bacterial cells continuously doubles at specific time intervals. This "specific time interval" is known as *generation time* (or doubling time). This makes for exponential growth. But as the bacterial population continues to grow, all the nutrients in the growth medium are used up and there is accumulation of waste materials, toxic metabolites and inhibitory compounds such as antibiotics in the medium. So growth slows down and leads to a logistic, sigmoidal, or s-shaped curve, which can be simulated with a logistic equation (column B).

Typically the microbial growth in liquid cultures is monitored by turbidity. Data is obtained with a spectrophotometer to measure optical density at 600nm. The degree of turbidity in the broth culture is directly related to the number of microorganisms present, either viable or dead cells.

This simulation has two parts. On the one hand, it simulates the growth of 5 types of bacteria which have a known generation time (K1:M6). In cell K8, we determine which type of bacteria to use so as to calculate its logistic population growth (columns A:B), and to plot its logistic curve.

On the other hand, the simulation also demonstrates how to use data received through a spectrophotometer in order to derive generation time. This is done in columns G:I.

What you need to know

There are several logistic equations. The following one is a good one for bacterial growth in a medium: $Pt = Pmax / (Pstart + ((Pmax - Pstart) * exp(-kt)))$. P stands for the population size.

The pivotal factors are the generation time (in B7 given and in H9 derived) plus the growth constant k, which is $ln(2)/genertion\_time$.

The time values used in column A (t) are in units of days, but can be changed to units of hours, which is often more appropriate for bacterial growth.

To derive the generation time—the time to double population size—we need one population size at an early exponential stage in the curve (in G2) and for its doubled size (in G5). Then we determine the times of these two sizes on the horizontal axis in order to find the generation time.

What you need to do

1. Validate cells K8: List | Source =$K$2:$K$6.
2. Select cells K2:M6 for conditional formatting: =$K2=$K$8.
3. Place in cell B7: =VLOOKUP(K8,K2:M6,3,FALSE)/60. This converts from mins to hours.
4. Place in cell B8: =LN(2)/B7.
5. Place in cells B12:B51: =$B$5/($B$3+(($B$5-$B$3)*EXP(-$B$8*A12))).
6. Place in cells C12:C51: =B12/$B$51.
7. Place in cell G2: =INDEX(B12:C51,MATCH(3%,C12:C51,1)+1,1). The value 3% is basically a rule of thumb that you may want to change. It is the population size early in the process.
8. Place in cell H2: =INDEX($A$12:$B$47,MATCH($G$2,$B$12:$B$47,1),1). This is the hour when the size of G2 was reached.
9. Place in cell G4: =G2*2. This is double the size of G2, one generation later.
10. Place in cell H4: =INDEX($A$12:$B$47,MATCH($G$4,$B$12:$B$47,1),1). This finds the time of reaching the population size just *before* the size in G4 (see Chapter 64).
11. Place in cell I4: =INDEX($A$12:$B$47,MATCH($G$4,$B$12:$B$47,1),2). This finds the population size reached at that time.
12. Place in cell H5: =INDEX($A$12:$B$47,MATCH($G$4,$B$12:$B$47,1)+1,1). This finds the time of reaching the population size just *after* the size in G4.
13. Place in cell I5: =INDEX($A$12:$B$47,MATCH($G$4,$B$12:$B$47,1)+1,2). This finds the population size reached at that time.
14. Place in cell H6: =TREND(H4:H5,I4:I5,G4). Here TREND finds the exact time, with decimals, between the hour in H4 and the hour in H5 (in the case shown below, not 20 or 21 but 20.270). For the TREND function see Chapter 64.
15. Place in cell H8: =H6-H2. This is the generation time needed to double the population size.
16. Place in cell H9: =H8*60. This changes the hours from the time scale of the chart into the minutes used in column M.
17. Notice that the results in H8:H9—derived from density measurements—come very close to what we found with the logistic equations based on the known generation times in column M.

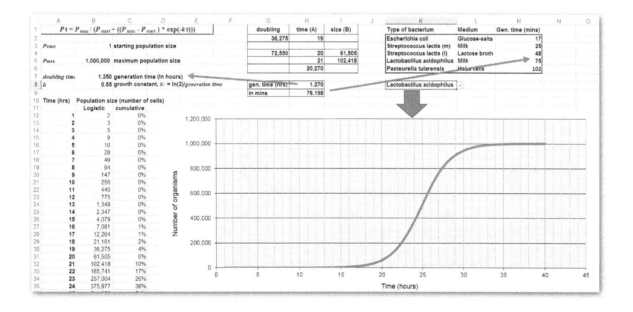

Chapter 76: Predator-Prey Cycle

What the simulation does

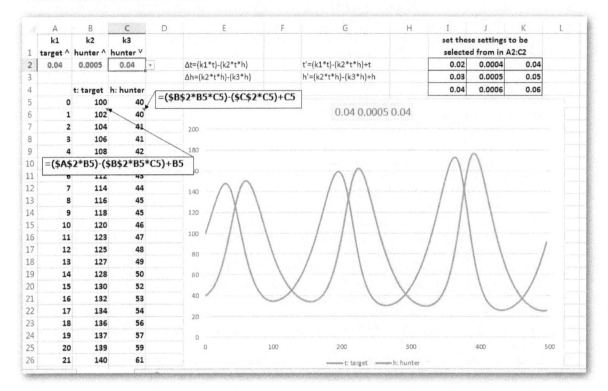

The so-called Lotka-Volterra model, dealing specifically with the relationship between predator and prey (or hunter and target) makes the following simplified assumptions: The change in the prey's numbers is given by its own growth minus the rate at which it is preyed upon (E2). On the other hand, the change in growth of the predator population is fueled by the food supply, minus natural death (E3). The equations that were used are explained on the sheet.

The cells A2:C2 can be set to values manually entered in cells I2:I4 (or by using controls).

What you need to know

In "real" life, populations do not grow in an exponential and unlimited way as they would under artificial circumstances (such as raising mice and rabbits in laboratories), for there are always limiting factors such as food supply and the presence of predators.

This idea has led to the so-called Lotka-Volterra model, dealing specifically about the relationship between predator and prey. It makes a number of assumptions: 1. The prey population finds ample food at all times. 2. The food supply of the predator population depends entirely on the prey populations. 3. The rate of change is proportional to the population size.

After some manipulation, we could deduce two simplified equations for the size of the prey population (done in column B) and the size of the predator population (in column C) for a certain generation (column A). Notice how this may lead to a stable relationship: Each species goes to a minimum before rising to a maximum, but the two curves are shifted relative to each other.

Simulations in Action

What you need to do

1. Apply Data Validation to cell A2: Data | Data Validation | List | =$I$2:$I$4.
2. Apply Data Validation to cell B2: Data | Data Validation | List | =$J$2:$J$4.
3. Apply Data Validation to cell C2: Data | Data Validation | List | =$K$2:$K$4.
4. Place in cells A6(!):A500: =ROW(A1). Cell A5 has: 0.
5. Place in cells B6(!):B500: =($A$2*B5)-($B$2*B5*C5)+B5. Cell B5 has: 5.
6. Place in cells C6(!):C500: =($B$2*B5*C5)-($C$2*C5)+C5. Cell C5 has: 40.
7. The chart title has in the formula bar: =$A$2:$C$2.
8. Changing A2:C2 through their dropdown boxes simulates new situations.

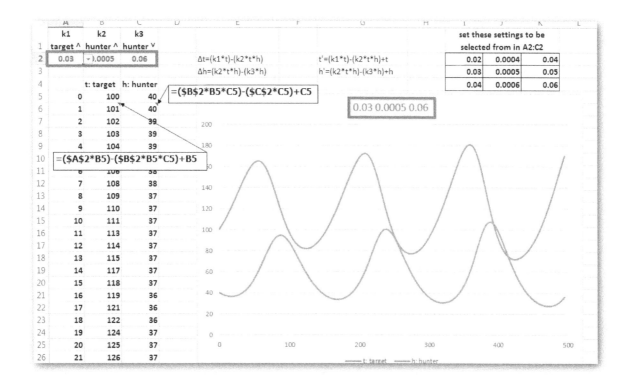

Chapter 77: The Course of an Epidemic

What the simulation does

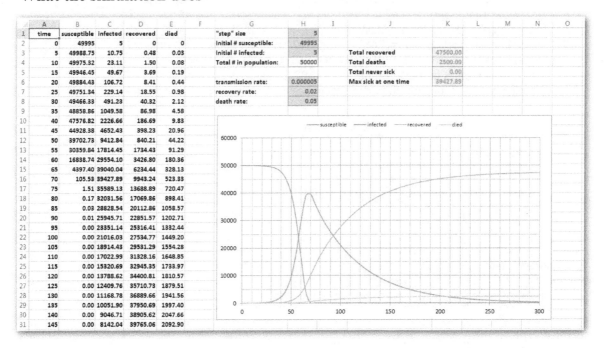

In this simple simulation, we follow the course of an epidemic (e.g. the flu) based on certain variables in column H. In general, epidemics follow a more or less fixed pattern. Initially only a few people get sick, but soon the number of sick cases rises exponentially until stabilization sets in, and more and more people have recovered.

We need some essential parameters, although they may not always be exactly known. We will only focus on transmission rate, recovery rate, and death rate—without going into issues such as mutation rate for the agent causing the infection.

What you need to know

The model that we apply is the standard *SIR* model, commonly used for many infectious diseases. The name of the model reflects the three groups of individuals that it models: *S*usceptible people, *I*nfected people, and *R*ecovered people. There are a number of important thresholds in this model. Reaching, or failing to reach, these thresholds is a crucial feature of managing the spread of infectious diseases. The system is sensitive to some changes, but not to others, so this may give us some insight as to when and where the problem should be attacked.

In order to make the appropriate calculations, we use the Euler's method, without explaining it much further. Euler's Method provides us with an approximation for the solution of a differential equation by using multiple small line segments so that they make up an approximation of the actual curve. It is a first-order method, which means that the error per step is proportional to the square of the step size, and the error at a given time is proportional to the step size. You can find the method explained elsewhere in more detail.

What you need to do

1. Place in cells A3:A302: =A2+$H$1.
2. Place in cell B2: =H2.
3. Place in cell C2: =H3.
4. Place in cells B3:B302: =B2-($H$6*B2*C2)*$H$1.
5. Place in cells C3:C302: =C2+($H$6*B2*C2-$H$7*C2)*$H$1.
6. Place in cells D3:D302: =D2+((1-$H$8)*$H$7*C2)*$H$1.
7. Place in cells E3:E302: =E2+($H$8*$H$7*C2)*$H$1.
8. Place in cell K3: =D302.
9. Place in cell K4: =E302.
10. Place in cell K5: =B302.
11. Place in cell K6: =MAX(C2:C302).
12. The cells in column H are all manually entered, except for H4: =H2+H3.
13. Some manual changes may cause weird results, because of many simplifying assumptions.

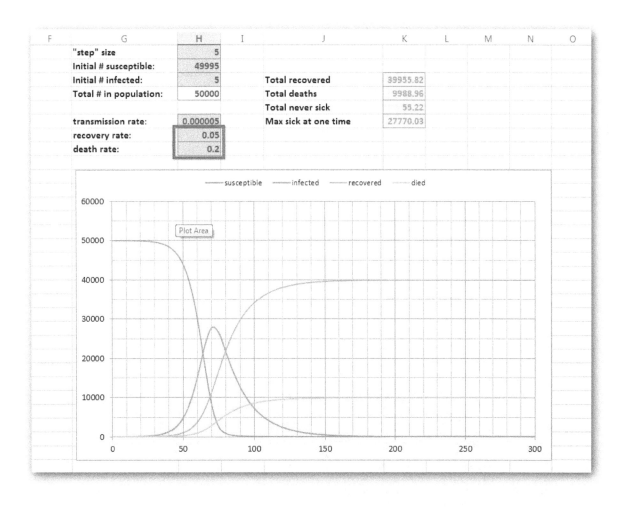

Chapter 78: Taking Medication

What the simulation does

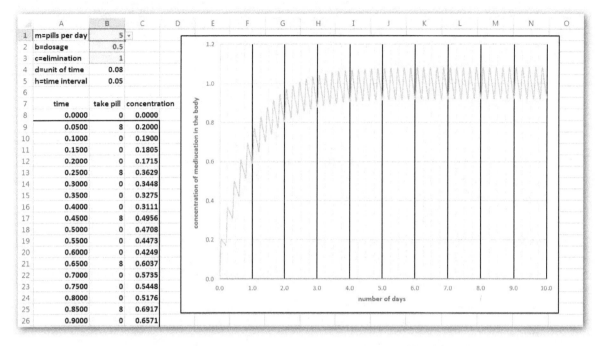

When taking medication, we want to reach a rather steady concentration of the medicine inside the body. The concentration rises each time we take a pill, but then also declines because the body metabolizes and/or excretes it (a so-called "trough").

We simulate this process based on at least 5 parameters. The three important ones are the number of pills a day (B1), the strength of each pill (B3), and the elimination factor (B4). You may want to change these variables manually to find out what the best regimen is.

What you need to know

The simplest model would be as follows: If $u(t)$ is the concentration of the medication in the body, then $du = b\, f(t)\, dt - cu\, dt$. In words: the change in concentration equals (the amount of medication entering the body at time t during the period dt) minus (the amount of medication leaving the body during a small time interval dt). Instead of differentiating the equation, we use an Excel simulation.

What you need to do

1. Apply Data Validation to cell B1: Data | Data Validation | List | Source: 1,2,3,4,5.
2. Place zeros in cells A8:C8.
3. Place in cells A9(!):A208: =A8+$B$5.
4. Place in cells B9:B208 a rather complicated formula with IF, AND, and INT: =IF(AND(A9>INT($B$1*A9)/$B$1,A9<INT($B$1*A9)/$B$1+$B$4),8,0).
5. Place in cells C9:C208: =C8+$B$5*($B$2*B9-$B$3*C8).

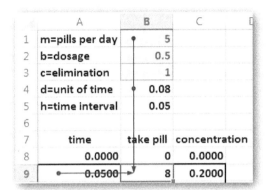
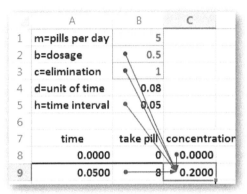

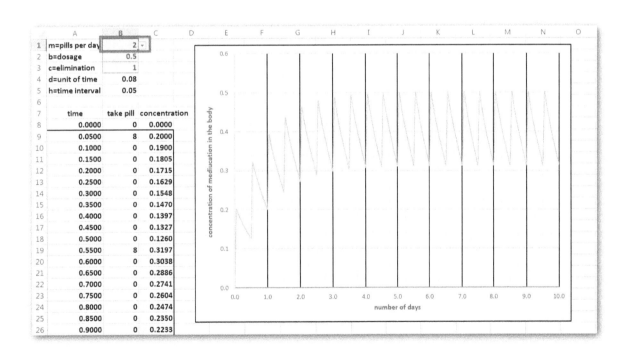

Chapter 79: A Hawk-Dove Game

What the simulation does

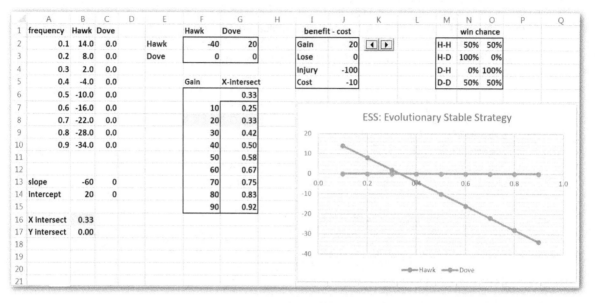

Game theory is the study of mathematical models of conflict and cooperation. The name "Hawk-Dove" refers to a situation in which there is a competition for a shared resource and the contestants can choose either conciliation or conflict; this terminology is most commonly used in biology and economics.

The traditional payoff matrix for the Hawk-Dove game includes the value of the contested resource, and the cost of an escalated fight. It is assumed that the value of the resource is less than the cost of a fight. Sometimes the players are supposed to split the payoff equally, at other times the payoff is assumed to be zero. These values can be found in columns J, M, and N.

A "mixed" evolutionary strategy (ESS) is where two strategies permanently coexist. For a given set of payoffs, there will be one set of frequencies where this mix is stable. A mixed ESS can be achieved if individuals either play one strategy all the time in a population where the two strategies are at the equilibrium frequencies (for example, 60% of the individuals always call and 40% always act as satellites), or all individuals play a mixed strategy where each behavior in the mix is performed at the equilibrium frequency.

Every ESS is a so-called Nash equilibrium, called after the game theorist, mathematician, and Nobel Laureate John Nash whose life story was turned into the biopic *A Beautiful Mind* starring Russell Crowe.

What you need to know

We need at least two sets of assumptions. One set is regarding benefits and costs in a fight (I2:J5). Another set (N2:O5) determines the chances of winning for hawks (H) and for doves (D).

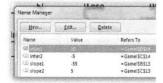

We also need the functions SLOPE and INTERCEPT. In a linear regression equation, $Y = slope * X + intercept$. We used *Range Names* for the four cells with slope and intercept (see to the left). For hawks (in column B): $Y = slope1*X + interc1$. For doves (in column C): $Y = slope2*X + interc2$.

Besides, we need to know where X and Y intersect. The intersect on the X-axis would be as follows: = *(interc2 - interc1)/(slope1-slope2)*; on the Y-axis: = *slope1 * intersectX + interc1*.

What you need to do

	A	B	C	D	E	F	G
1	frequency	Hawk		Dove		Hawk	Dove
2	0.1	=A2*$F$2+(1-A2)*$G$2	=A2*$F$3+(1-A2)*$G$3		Hawk	=($N$2*$J$2)+(($O$2*$J$4))	=$N$3*$J$2-0
3	0.2	=A3*$F$2+(1-A3)*$G$2	=A3*$F$3+(1-A3)*$G$3		Dove	=$N$4*$J$2+$O$4*$J$3	=$N$5*($J$2+$J$5)-$O$5*-$J$5
4	0.3	=A4*$F$2+(1-A4)*$G$2	=A4*$F$3+(1-A4)*$G$3				
5	0.4	=A5*$F$2+(1-A5)*$G$2	=A5*$F$3+(1-A5)*$G$3			Gain	X-Intersect
6	0.5	=A6*$F$2+(1-A6)*$G$2	=A6*$F$3+(1-A6)*$G$3				=B16
7	0.6	=A7*$F$2+(1-A7)*$G$2	=A7*$F$3+(1-A7)*$G$3			10	=TABLE(,J2)
8	0.7	=A8*$F$2+(1-A8)*$G$2	=A8*$F$3+(1-A8)*$G$3			20	=TABLE(,J2)
9	0.8	=A9*$F$2+(1-A9)*$G$2	=A9*$F$3+(1-A9)*$G$3			30	=TABLE(,J2)
10	0.9	=A10*$F$2+(1-A10)*$G$2	=A10*$F$3+(1-A10)*$G$3			40	=TABLE(,J2)
11						50	=TABLE(,J2)
12						60	=TABLE(,J2)
13	slope	=SLOPE(B2:B10,$A$2:$A$10)	=SLOPE(C2:C10,$A$2:$A$10)			70	=TABLE(,J2)
14	intercept	=INTERCEPT(B2:B10,$A$2:$A$10)	=INTERCEPT(C2:C10,$A$2:$A$10)			80	=TABLE(,J2)
15						90	=TABLE(,J2)
16	X Intersect	=(Inter2-Inter1)/(slope1-slope2)					
17	Y intersect	=slope1*B16+inter1					

1. Place a spinbutton control next to cell J2: Min 10 | Max 90 | SmallChange 10 | LinkedCell J2.
2. Place in cell F2: =($N$2*$J$2)+(($O$2*$J$4)).
3. Place in cell F3: =$N$4*$J$2+$O$4*$J$3.
4. Place in cell G2: =$N$3*$J$2-0.
5. Place in cell G3: =$N$5*($J$2+$J$5)-$O$5*-$J$5.
6. Place in cell B2: =A2*$F$2+(1-A2)*$G$2, and copy down.
7. Place in cell C2: =A2*$F$3+(1-A2)*$G$3, and copy down.
8. Place in cell B13: =SLOPE(B2:B10,$A$2:$A$10), and copy one cell to the right. I named cell B13 *slope1* and cell C13 *slope2*.
9. Place in cell B14: =INTERCEPT(B2:B10,$A$2:$A$10), and copy to next cell. Cell B14 is named *inter1* and cell C14 *inter2*.
10. Place in cell B16: =(inter2-inter1)/(slope1-slope2).
11. Place in cell B17: =slope1*B16+inter1.
12. For the *Data Table*, place in G6: =B16.
13. Select range F6:G15 for a *Data Table* with only a column input from cell J2 (the gain factor).
14. Select cells F7:G15 and implement conditional formatting with a formula: =$G7=$G$6.

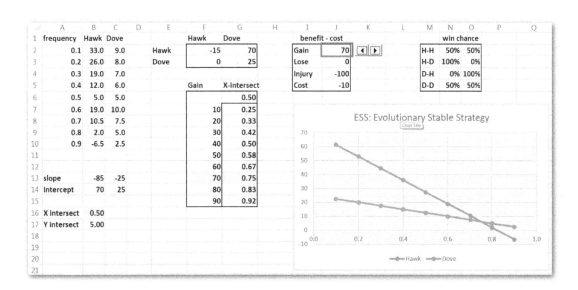

Chapter 80: A Population Pyramid

What the simulation does

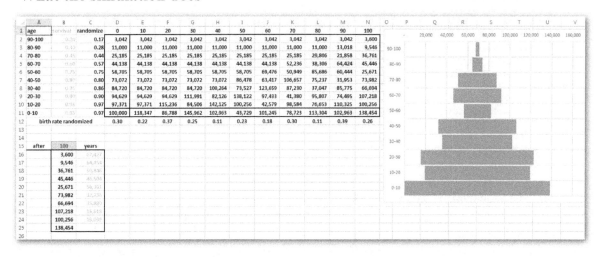

This simulation shows how a population pyramid may change over the course of 100 years. The simulation is based on several grossly oversimplified assumptions.

Assumption #1: The population starts at 100,000 (cell D11).

Assumption #2: The birth rate is partially randomized (row 12) and is based on participation by everyone over 20 years old.

Assumption #3: Every age group has a certain survival value (column B) which is subject to small fluctuations, determined by a randomize factor (in column C).

The randomize factor in column C is by default 0.02, the minimum birth rate is by default 0.1, and the maximum birth rate is by default 0.4. Then the simulation loops through 100 years in steps of 10 (row 1) and shows the situation after that particular number of years.

What you need to know

In cell B15, you determine after how many years (from 0 to 100) you would like to plot a population pyramid in the chart shown to the right.

The cells B16:B25 show the results in column N if you choose 100 years, or column M for 90 years, etc. They determine the width/length of each bar in the chart. The cells C16:C25 calculate how far each bar in the chart should be offset to the right, which is done with the formula: =(MAX($B$16:$B$25)-B16)/2.

The cells B16:B25 use the function HLOOKUP, which searches for a value in the top row of a table or an array of values, and then returns a value in the same column from a row you specify in the table or array. It has the following syntax: HLOOKUP(value,table or array,row index number,exact match or not). So the formula in B16 would be as follows: =HLOOKUP($B$15,$D$1:$N$11,ROW(A2),0), where ROW(A2), copied down, becomes ROW(A3), etc. So it finds the number of years horizontally in the first row of D1:N11, and then returns the 2nd cell down, 3rd cell, etc. For 100 years, B16:B25 should be the same as N2:N11.

The chart is a *stacked bar* chart, and plots A2:A11 against B6:B25 and C6:C25.

Simulations in Action

What you need to do

	A	B	C	D	E	F	G	H	I
1	age	survives	randomize	0	10	20	30	40	50
2	90-100		0.171980966799729	=D3*$C3	=D3*$C3	=E3*$C3	=F3*$C3	=G3*$C3	=H3*$C3
3	80-90		0.280546786281342	=D4*$C4	=D4*$C4	=D3*$C3	=F4*$C4	=G4*$C4	=H4*$C4
4	70-80		0.42903522784283	=D5*$C5	=D5*$C5	=E5*$C5	=F5*$C5	=G5*$C5	=H5*$C5
5	60-70		0.606789828050401	=D6*$C6	=D6*$C6	=E6*$C6	=F6*$C6	=G6*$C6	=H6*$C6
6	50-60		0.739340989717628	=D7*$C7	=D7*$C7	=E7*$C7	=F7*$C7	=G7*$C7	=H7*$C7
7	40-50		0.783153132476069	=D8*$C8	=D8*$C8	=E8*$C8	=F8*$C8	=G8*$C8	=H8*$C8
8	30-40		0.8560191527801	=D9*$C9	=D9*$C9	=E9*$C9	=F9*$C9	=G9*$C9	=H9*$C9
9	20-30		0.904631646496482	=D10*$C10	=D10*$C10	=SUM(D$2:D$9)*D$12			10*$C10
10	10-20		0.95193645948201	=D11*$C11	=D11*$C11	=E11*$C11	=F11*$C11	=G11*$C11	=H11*$C11
11	0-10		0.957059937681503	100000	=SUM(D$2:D$9)*D$12	=SUM(E$2:E$9)*E$12	=SUM(F$2:F$9)*F$12	=SUM(G$2:G$9)*G$1	=SUM(H$2:H$9
12		birth rate randomized:		0.4	0.25	0.28	0.29	0.25	0.39

1. Place in cells C2:C11: =NORMINV(RAND(),B2,0.02). This randomizes the survival rate of each cohort with a default SD of 0.02.
2. Place in cell D12:N12: =RANDBETWEEN(10,40)/100. This assumes birth rates vary between 0.1 and 0.4 per adult per 10 years.
3. Place in cell D10: =D11*$C11. Copy *upwards* to D2. This calculates the volume of each ten-year cohort, based on a gross oversimplification (but good enough for now).
4. Place in cell E11:N11: =SUM(D$2:D$9)*D$12. This assumes that all adults are included in the birth rate multiplier.
5. Place in cell E2: =D3*$C3. Copy this formula all the way to N10.
6. Place in cells B16:B25: =HLOOKUP($B$15,$D$1:$N$11,ROW(A2),0). This looks up all age group sizes after the number of years chosen in cell B15.
7. Place in cells C16:C25 =(MAX($B$16:$B$25)-B16)/2. This calculates the offset for each bar in the bar chart.
8. Using *F9* can create an enormous variety of population pyramids. Some pyramids have a solid basis, others a rather weak one. Famine and other disasters can leave their marks on certain age groups.

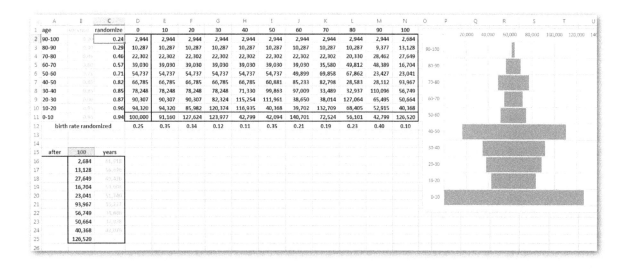

Chapter 81: False Positives

What the simulation does

	A	B	C	D	E	F	G	H	I	J	K	L	M	N	O	P	Q
1		from data to diagnostics								from diagnostics to universal testing							
2																	
3		T+	T-	Total													
4	D+	283	51	334		new	population	300,000,000			T+	T-	Total				
5	D-	27	612	639		disease	w/ AIDS	100,000	◄ ►	D+	95,000	5,000	100,000				
6	Total	310	663	973			prevalence	0.00033333		D-	5,998,000	293,902,000	299,900,000				
7						new	sensitivity	0.95		Total	6,093,000	293,907,000	300,000,000				
8	sensitivity T+	SE =B2/D2	0.84731			test	specificity	0.98									
9	specificity T+	SP =C3/D3	0.95775				P(D+|T+)	1.56%			1.56%	P(D+|T+)					
10	prevalence D+	PR =D2/D4	0.34327														
11							P(D+|T+)										
12		T+	T-	Total			1.56%	80.0%	82.0%	84.0%	86.0%	88.0%	90.0%	92.0%	94.0%	96.0%	98.0%	SE
13	D+	SE*PR	(1-SE)*PR	PR			80.0%	0.13%	0.14%	0.14%	0.14%	0.15%	0.15%	0.15%	0.16%	0.16%	0.16%	
14	D-	(1-SP)*(1-PR)	SP*(1-PR)	(1-PR)			82.0%	0.15%	0.15%	0.16%	0.16%	0.16%	0.17%	0.17%	0.17%	0.18%	0.18%	
15	Total	P(T+)	P(T-)	1			84.0%	0.17%	0.17%	0.17%	0.18%	0.18%	0.19%	0.19%	0.20%	0.20%	0.20%	
16							86.0%	0.19%	0.19%	0.20%	0.20%	0.21%	0.21%	0.22%	0.22%	0.23%	0.23%	
17	P(D+|T+)	P(D+|T-)	P(D-|T+)	P(D-|T-)			88.0%	0.22%	0.23%	0.23%	0.24%	0.24%	0.25%	0.25%	0.26%	0.27%	0.27%	
18	=P(D+ and T+)/P(T+)	=P(D+ and T-)/P(T-)	=P(D- and T+)/P(T+)	=P(D- and T-)/P(T-)			90.0%	0.27%	0.27%	0.28%	0.29%	0.29%	0.30%	0.31%	0.31%	0.32%	0.33%	
19							92.0%	0.33%	0.34%	0.35%	0.36%	0.37%	0.37%	0.38%	0.39%	0.40%	0.41%	
20	P(D+|T+)	SE*PR / SE*PR + (1-SP)*(1-PR)					94.0%	0.44%	0.45%	0.46%	0.48%	0.49%	0.50%	0.51%	0.52%	0.53%	0.54%	
21	P(D+|T-)	(1-SE)*PR / (1-SE)*PR + SP*(1-PR)					96.0%	0.66%	0.68%	0.70%	0.71%	0.73%	0.74%	0.76%	0.78%	0.79%	0.81%	
22	P(D-|T+)	(1-SP)*(1-PR) / SE*PR + (1-SP)*(1-PR)					98.0%	1.32%	1.35%	1.38%	1.41%	1.45%	1.48%	1.51%	1.54%	1.58%	1.61%	
23	P(D-|T-)	SP*(1-PR) / (1-SE)*PR + SP*(1-PR)					SP											

Most tests for certain diseases produce sometimes positive results (T+), even though the person tested does *not* have the disease (D-). Those "positive" results are called "*false* positives."

In the left panel above, we calculate the *sensitivity* (C8) and the *specificity* (C9) of a certain test based on known test results—for instance based on a trial (B4:C5).

In the cells H4:H8 from the right panel, we use existing information about a certain test for a certain disease (in this case AIDS, but the same would hold for a drug test) and then we calculate what number of affected people we would find if we went for *universal* testing (in cells H9 and K9). You will be surprised to discover how low this percentage is! Then we use a *Data Table* to check the effect of changes in the test's sensitivity (row 12) and specificity (column F).

What you need to know

This is basically an issue of "conditional probability." We want to find, for instance, the probability of having a disease (D^+) "on condition of" having a positive test (T^+). This is expressed as: $P(D^+|T^+)$, which you read as follows: the probability of event D^+ given event T^+. Or we want to find the probability of *not* having a disease given a (*false*) positive test: $P(D^-|T^+)$. An analysis like this is done with the so-called Bayes Theorem.

This kind of analysis is explained in the left panel. Based on trial data (B4:C5), we can calculate how good the test is in *excluding* a disease (which is the *sensitivity* of the test, in cell C8) and how good the test is in *finding* a disease (which is the *specificity* of the test, in cell C9). The *prevalence* of D^+ is the relative number of disease cases in a sample or population (in cell C10). The Hayes Theorem allows us to calculate the four different conditional probabilities based on sensitivity, specificity, and prevalence—as shown in the lower part of the left section. The basic "rule" is shown in A17:D18: $P(D^+|T^+) = P(D^+ \text{ and } T^+) / P(T^+)$.

What you need to do

1. The left panel explains the basics of the Bayes Theorem.
2. The right calculations in the left panel are already done. They are based on the simple panel estimates that, in a population of 300 million people (H4), 500,000 individuals have AIDS (H5). A certain test for AIDS has a sensitivity of 0.95 (H7) and a specificity of 0.98 (H8). The rest is based on calculations explained next.
3. Place a spinbutton control next to cell H5: Min 100 | Max 1000 | Small 100 | LinkedCell I5.
4. Place in cell H5: =I5*1000.
5. Place in H6: =H5/H4. This calculates the prevalence of the disease (the percentage of AIDS people in the population).
6. Place in cell H9: =(H7*H6)/(H7*H6+(1-H8)*(1-H6)). This is the calculation for P(D+|T+), based on the formula in B18. In other words, if we would do general testing for AIDS in the entire population, we would find that the probability of having the disease, if one gets a positive test result, is only 7.35%. Consequently, doing *universal* testing for a relatively rare disease is not good policy because of the probability of false-positives.
7. We could have calculated this also with the grid of K5:M7. Place in M5: =H5. In M7: =H4. In M6: =M7-M5. In K5: =$H$7*M5. In L5: =M5-K5. In K6: =M6-L6. In L6: =H8*M6. In K7: =SUM(K5:K6). In L7: =SUM(L5:L6).
8. Based on this, we can calculate P(D+|T+) in K9: =K5/K7.
9. In cell F12, we start an overview table for various test sensitivities (row 12) and specificities (column F): =H9 (or: =K9). To do so, select range F12:P22 and start a *Data Table* with H7 for row input and H8 for column input: =TABLE(H7,H8).

P(D+|T+)											
13.71%	80.0%	82.0%	84.0%	86.0%	88.0%	90.0%	92.0%	94.0%	96.0%	98.0%	SE
80.0%	1.32%	1.35%	1.39%	1.42%	1.45%	1.48%	1.52%	1.55%	1.58%	1.61%	
82.0%	1.46%	1.50%	1.54%	1.57%	1.61%	1.64%	1.68%	1.72%	1.75%	1.79%	
84.0%	1.64%	1.69%	1.73%	1.77%	1.81%	1.85%	1.89%	1.93%	1.97%	2.01%	
86.0%	1.88%	1.92%	1.97%	2.01%	2.06%	2.10%	2.15%	2.20%	2.24%	2.29%	
88.0%	2.18%	2.23%	2.29%	2.34%	2.39%	2.45%	2.50%	2.55%	2.61%	2.66%	
90.0%	2.61%	2.67%	2.73%	2.80%	2.86%	2.92%	2.99%	3.05%	3.11%	3.17%	
92.0%	3.24%	3.31%	3.39%	3.47%	3.55%	3.63%	3.70%	3.78%	3.86%	3.94%	
94.0%	4.27%	4.37%	4.47%	4.57%	4.68%	4.78%	4.88%	4.98%	5.08%	5.18%	
96.0%	6.27%	6.42%	6.56%	6.71%	6.85%	7.00%	7.14%	7.29%	7.43%	7.57%	
98.0%	11.80%	12.06%	#####	#####	12.83%	13.08%	13.33%	13.58%	13.83%	14.08%	
SP											

VI. BUSINESS

Chapter 82: Cycle Percentiles

What the simulation does

	A	B	C	D	E	F	G	H
1		Sunday	Monday	Tuesday	Wednesday	Thursday	Friday	Saturday
2	Jan	$ 21,156.00		$ 13,602.00	$ 14,363.00	$ 13,573.00	$ 17,779.00	$ 16,921.00
3	Feb	$ 12,750.00	$ 14,798.00	$ 18,562.00	$ 10,273.00	$ 24,043.00	$ 24,310.00	$ 20,154.00
4	Mar	$ 13,695.00		$ 16,676.00	$ 14,154.00		$ 21,121.00	
5	Apr	$ 18,451.00				$ 10,611.00	$ 12,655.00	$ 15,348.00
6	May	$ 17,756.00	$ 18,157.00		$ 20,094.00	$ 13,731.00	$ 24,807.00	$ 23,797.00
7	Jun	$ 24,290.00	$ 24,505.00	$ 22,918.00	$ 13,960.00		$ 12,111.00	$ 23,007.00
8	Jul	$ 10,515.00		$ 22,584.00		$ 24,846.00	$ 15,429.00	
9	Aug	$ 18,010.00	$ 12,663.00	$ 15,648.00		$ 12,420.00	$ 12,619.00	$ 21,737.00
10	Sep		$ 18,495.00	$ 18,978.00	$ 14,235.00	$ 15,345.00	$ 16,216.00	$ 11,548.00
11	Oct				$ 16,808.00	$ 17,393.00	$ 14,806.00	
12	Nov	$ 12,394.00	$ 15,879.00	$ 11,605.00	$ 17,420.00		$ 11,010.00	$ 23,347.00
13	Dec	$ 20,898.00	$ 24,152.00	$ 19,505.00	$ 23,232.00			$ 16,429.00
14								
15	above	percentile:	25%	$ 10,238.00			Total:	$ 1,090,294.00
16								
17								

This is a simple simulation to let the user "glide" with a scrollbar control through the 25th, 50th, and 75th percentile to show all the sales above or below that percentile, depending on the setting in cell A15, which has a dropdown box.

The simulation does so by cycling stepwise through 5 different percentile views of the sales report. It also calculates the total amount of sales for each percentile view (in cell H15).

What you need to know

For the percentile scores, we used the Excel function PERCENTILE (see Chapters 46 and 48). This function works in all Excel versions. In version 2010 and later, it can be replaced with PERCENTILE.EXC or PERCENTILE.INC. The former function does not include $k=1$, whereas the latter one does. So the latter one is equivalent to the older function PERCENTILE.

Depending on the percentile step, certain numbers are "hidden" by giving them a white font. This is done with conditional formatting.

Cell H15 uses the function SUMIF. It has this syntax: SUMIF(range,criteria,[sum_range]). The last argument is optional and only required when the sum range is different from the criteria range. The 2nd argument for criteria requires a string with double quotes—for instance, ">25%". If you want to replace the value 25% with a reference to the cell that has such value in it (e.g. C15), then you need to use an ampersand (&) with space before and after it—this way: ">" & C15.

What you need to do

1. Apply Data Validation to cell A15: Data | Data Validation | List | Source: above,below.
2. Place a scrollbar control under cell C15: Min 0 | Max 100 | SmallChange 25 | LargeChange 25 | LinkedCell B16.
3. Place in cell C15: =B16/100.
4. Place in cell D15: =PERCENTILE.INC(B2:H13,C15).
5. Place in cell H15: =SUMIF(B2:H13,IF(A15="above",">=" & D15,"<=" & D15)).
6. Select range B2:H13 and apply conditional formatting with the following formula: =IF($A$15="above",B2<$D$15,B2>$D$15).

	A	B	C	D	E	F	G	H
1		Sunday	Monday	Tuesday	Wednesday	Thursday	Friday	Saturday
2	Jan	$ 21,156.00						
3	Feb					$ 24,043.00	$ 24,310.00	$ 20,154.00
4	Mar						$ 21,121.00	
5	Apr							
6	May				$ 20,094.00		$ 24,807.00	$ 23,797.00
7	Jun	$ 24,290.00	$ 24,505.00	$ 22,918.00				$ 23,007.00
8	Jul			$ 22,584.00		$ 24,846.00		
9	Aug							$ 21,737.00
10	Sep			$ 18,978.00				
11	Oct							
12	Nov							$ 23,347.00
13	Dec	$ 20,898.00	$ 24,152.00	$ 19,505.00	$ 23,232.00			
14								
15	above	percentile:	75%	$ 18,666.00			Total:	$ 473,481.00
16								
17								

	A	B	C	D	E	F	G	H
1		Sunday	Monday	Tuesday	Wednesday	Thursday	Friday	Saturday
2	Jan		$ 8,310.00	$ 13,602.00	$ 14,363.00	$ 13,573.00	$ 17,779.00	$ 16,921.00
3	Feb	$ 12,750.00	$ 14,798.00	$ 18,562.00	$ 10,273.00			
4	Mar	$ 13,695.00	$ 8,005.00	$ 16,676.00	$ 14,154.00	$ 6,036.00		$ 5,724.00
5	Apr	$ 18,451.00	$ 6,964.00	$ 6,513.00	$ 6,445.00	$ 10,611.00	$ 12,655.00	$ 15,348.00
6	May	$ 17,756.00	$ 18,157.00	$ 9,004.00		$ 13,731.00		
7	Jun				$ 13,960.00	$ 5,575.00	$ 12,111.00	
8	Jul	$ 10,515.00	$ 5,017.00		$ 10,133.00		$ 15,429.00	$ 9,445.00
9	Aug	$ 18,010.00	$ 12,663.00	$ 15,648.00	$ 7,464.00	$ 12,420.00	$ 12,619.00	
10	Sep	$ 9,615.00	$ 18,495.00		$ 14,235.00	$ 15,345.00	$ 16,216.00	$ 11,548.00
11	Oct	$ 6,217.00	$ 5,125.00	$ 5,168.00	$ 16,808.00	$ 17,393.00	$ 14,806.00	$ 9,839.00
12	Nov	$ 12,394.00	$ 15,879.00	$ 11,605.00	$ 17,420.00	$ 7,623.00	$ 11,010.00	
13	Dec					$ 8,414.00	$ 9,733.00	$ 16,429.00
14								
15	below	percentile:	75%	$ 18,666.00			Total:	$ 773,182.00
16								
17								

Chapter 83: Profit Estimates

What the simulation does

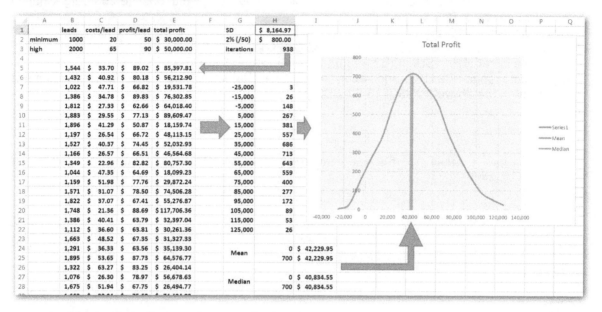

In this simulation[8], we estimate profits based on projected minimum and maximum values in the rows 2:3. We need a certain number of leads (column B), we expect certain costs per lead (column C), we forecast a certain profit per lead (column D), and we calculate what the total profit would be (column E).

Obviously, there is a wide range of uncertainty between E2 and E3. So we want to find out how many random repeats or iterations we need to get a more reliable estimate of the total profit with a 95% confidence: at least 938 (cell H3). All of this is done in the lower part of columns B:E.

The table in cells G7:H20 summarizes the frequencies of all 938 (or more) total profits in column E. These frequencies are plotted in the XY-chart to the right. When we compare the mean with the median of all the profit calculations, we notice they are very close together, which indicates that the results follow more or less a normal distribution. So the total profit is expected to hover around these two values.

What you need to know

In cell H1, we use the function STDEV.P (not STDEV.S), because the two values in E2 and E3 cover the entire "population."

The total error (ε) is given by *3 x SD / $\sqrt{n}$*. An absolute error of 2% in cell H1 is the mean of minimum profit (E2) and the maximum profit (E3) divided by 50 (to get to an error of less than 2%). So the minimum number of repeats or iterations (n) should be: *(3 x SD/ε)^2*.

Another new function is MEDIAN. It returns the number in the middle of a set of numbers. In a perfectly symmetrical distribution of a group of numbers, the measures of mean and median are the same. So comparing the mean with the median is a simple way of showing how symmetrical the distribution of the data is.

---

[8] A special thanks for part of this simulation goes to Rob Jeges.

For the number of repeats, assuming a uniform distribution, we use the RAND function to generate numbers in the interval (0,1) and multiply these by the range of each variable. This range is the difference between maximum and minimum: RAND*(max-min)+min.

What you need to do

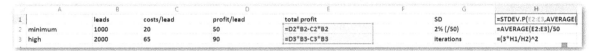

1. Place in cells E2:E3: =D2*B2-C2*B2.
2. Place in cell H1: =STDEV.P(E2:E3,AVERAGE(E2:E3)).
3. Place in cell H2: =AVERAGE(E2:E3)/50.
4. Place in cell H3: =(3*H1/H2)^2. In what follows, we actually used a potential of 5000 repeats.
5. Place in cells B5:B5004: =IF(ROW(A1)<=$H$3,RAND()*($B$3-$B$2)+$B$2, "").
6. Place in cells C5:C5004: =IF(ROW(A1)<=$H$3,RAND()*($C$3-$C$2)+$C$2,"").
7. Place in cells D5:D5004: =IF(ROW(A1)<=$H$3,RAND()*($D$3-$D$2)+$D$2,"").
8. Place in cells E5:E5004: =IF(ROW(A1)<=$H$3,D5*B5-C5*B5, "").
9. Place in cells H7:H22 at once: =FREQUENCY(E5:E5004,G7:G21). Use *Ctrl Shift Enter*.
10. Now we create the inserts in the graph for the mean and median with 2 sets of coordinates.
11. Place in cells H25 and H28: =MAX($H$7:$H$22).
12. Place in cells I24:I25: =AVERAGE($E$5:$E$5004).
13. Place in cells I27:I28: =MEDIAN($E$5:$E$5004).
14. Using *F9* creates some variation, but not much.

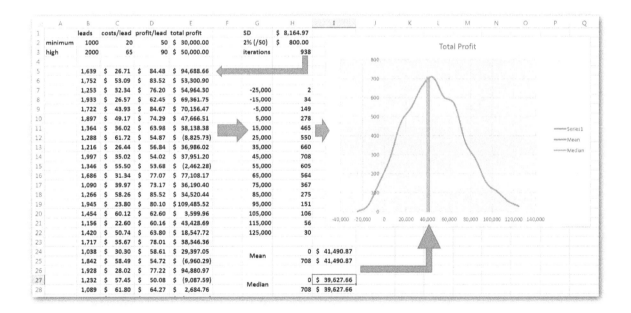

Chapter 84: Production Costs

What the simulation does

This is basically a simple simulation. It gives a prognosis for a specific product based on several parameters: unit price, units sold, costs per unit, and overhand costs.

The simulation shows in two *Data Table*s various values for each parameter and then highlights where the total profit would be higher than what was projected in cell B9.

We also added scrollbar controls to change individual parameter values.

What you need to know

There are no spectacular new features in this simulation. However, the *Data Table*s and the controls are powerful in themselves.

What you need to do

1. Add 4 scrollbar controls with your own settings. Make sure the controls cover the ranges used in the margins of the *Data Tables*.
2. Place in cell B3: =B1*B2.
3. Place in cell B7: =B6+B5*B2.
4. Place in cell B9: =B3-B7.
5. Place in cell D1 and in cell D11 a link to cell B9: =B9.
6. Apply a *Data Table* to range D1:I8, with B2 for row input and B1 for column input: =TABLE(B2,B1).
7. Apply a *Data Table* to range D11:I16, with B6 for row input and B5 for column input: =TABLE(B6,B5).
8. Select range E2:I8 and apply conditional formatting with the formula: =E2>$D$1.
9. Select range E12:I16 and apply conditional formatting with the formula: =E12>$D$11.
10. Manipulate the scrollbar controls for updates.

	A	B	C	D	E	F	G	H	I	J	K
1	Price per unit	$75.00		$ 640,626.00	10,000	15,000	20,000	25,000	30,000	sold	
2	Units Sold	10,666		$20.00	$50,000	$80,000	$110,000	$140,000	$170,000		
3	Total Revenue	$ 799,950.00		$30.00	$150,000	$230,000	$310,000	$390,000	$470,000		
4				$40.00	$250,000	$380,000	$510,000	$640,000	$770,000		
5	Costs per unit	$14.00		$50.00	$350,000	$530,000	$710,000	$890,000	$1,070,000		
6	Overhead Costs	$10,000.00		$60.00	$450,000	$680,000	$910,000	$1,140,000	$1,370,000		
7	Total Costs	$ 159,324.00		$70.00	$550,000	$830,000	$1,110,000	$1,390,000	$1,670,000		
8				$80.00	$650,000	$980,000	$1,310,000	$1,640,000	$1,970,000		
9	Profit	$ 640,626.00		unit price							
10											
11	Price per unit	◂ ▸		$640,626.00	$1,000.00	$5,000.00	$10,000.00	$13,000.00	$17,000.00	overhead	
12	Units Sold	◂ ▸		$6	$734,954.00	$730,954.00	$725,954.00	$722,954.00	$718,954.00		
13	Costs per unit	◂ ▸		$8	$713,622.00	$709,622.00	$704,622.00	$701,622.00	$697,622.00		
14	Overhead Costs	◂ ▸		$10	$692,290.00	$688,290.00	$683,290.00	$680,290.00	$676,290.00		
15				$12	$670,958.00	$666,958.00	$661,958.00	$658,958.00	$654,958.00		
16				$14	$649,626.00	$645,626.00	$640,626.00	$637,626.00	$633,626.00		
17				unit cost							
18											

Chapter 85: Profit Changes

What the simulation does

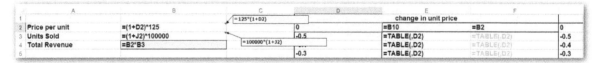

This simulation creates and populates five different *Data Table* ranges. The top three have a column input of D2, J2, and G2 respectively, but these three cells have only 0 in it.

However, we use a powerful "trick" here: there are no hard values in cells B2, B2, and B6. Instead they hold a formula that multiplies a certain value with *(1+D2)*, *(1+J2)*, or *(1+G2)*. As a consequence, the *Data Table* can use changes in percentages in its 1st table column, for its corresponding value in each table's 3rd column.

What you need to know

Since the formula in cells B2, B3, and B6 uses hard-coded values, we probably want to make those values updatable. We could do so by linking them to 3 scrollbar controls (see picutre on the next page).

Simulations in Action — BUSINESS

What you need to do

1. Place in cell B2: =(1+D2)*125.
2. Place in cell B3: =(1+J2)*100000.
3. Place in cell B6: =(1+G2)*25.
4. Place in cell B4: =B2*B3.
5. Place in cell B8: =B3*B6+B7.
6. Place in cell B10: =B4-B8.
7. Place in E2, H2, K2 a link to cell B10.
8. Place in cells F2, I2, L2 a link to the corresponding cell in column B.
9. Select range D2:F13 and start a *Data Table*: =TABLE(,D2).
10. Select range G2:I13 and start a *Data Table*: =TABLE(,G2).
11. Select range J2:L13 and start a *Data Table*: =TABLE(,J2).
12. Select range D16:I20 and start a *Data Table*: =TABLE(G2,D2).
13. Select range D23:I28 and start a *Data Table*: =TABLE(J2,D2).
14. Place 3 scrollbar controls over the cells B13, B14, B15 so you can regulate cell B2, B3, and B6. Each one is linked to the cell behind the control.
15. Adjust the formulas as follows: =(1+D2)*B13 | =(1+J2)*B14 | =(1+G2)*B15.
16. Each time you change scrollbar positions, the sheet performs *two* rather quick updates.

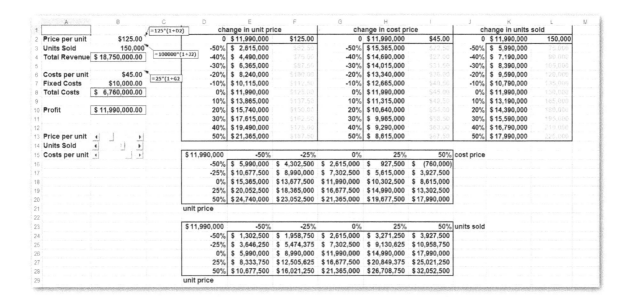

Chapter 86: A Filtering Table

What the simulation does

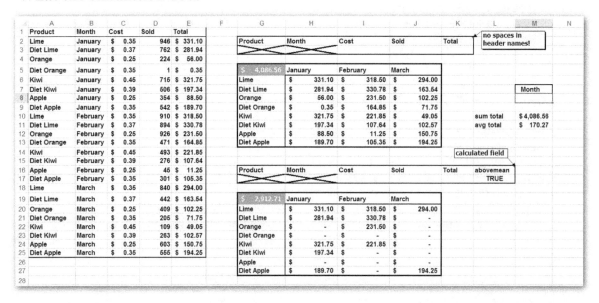

Range G5:J13 contains a 2-dimensional *Data Table* with information extracted from the database A1:E25. There is also a filter in G2:K3, which regulates what the table G5:J13 displays by using the same headers as the database in its 1st row (in the above case, the 2nd row of the filter is still empty). We could fill it like it is done below. Settings in the same 2nd row of the filter are treated as an "and" condition: both *Sold* as >200 and *Total* as >100 (as shown below)

Product	Month	Cost	Sold	Total
			>200	>100

The 2nd *Data Table* (G19:J27) uses another filter (J16:L17), but this time with an added label (with any name, but no spaces). The added label ("abovemean") creates a *calculated* field—for instance, totals above the mean of all totals, so the *Data Table* shows only totals above the mean. Cells M10:M11 use a very simple filter (M7:M8) which is based on the name of the month.

What you need to know

The filter works through the labels, or headers, of the database. The function used in this simulation is DSUM. Like all other database functions (such as DAVERAGE, DCOUNT, etc.)—but unlike SUM—it accepts also certain criteria as to what to sum. It has 3 arguments: DSUM(database,field,criteria). The 2nd argument indicates which field in the databse to sum (e.g. "Total", or E1, or just 5 for its column position).

A computed field in a filter (e.g. L17) contains a formula that may look like this: =E2>AVERAGE($E$2:$E$25). It starts at the 1st record in the database (e.g. E2 or D2, etc.), but then works automatically through all the other records. So its displayed result (TRUE of FALSE) applies only to the first record, but has no other implications.

The two *Data Table*s use DSUM at their origin (G5 or G19) and then use their rows and columns to let DSUM work for each category.

Simulations in Action BUSINESS 173

What you need to do

1. Make sure the labels in the 1st row of the database have no spaces in it, for then the filters will not work.
2. Make sure all filters use the same labels as the database does (or new labels for computed fields that carry formulas).
3. Place in cell G5: =DSUM(A1:E25,E1,G2:K3).
4. Select cells G5:J13 and start a *Data Table* with H3 for row input and G3 for column input: =TABLE(H3,G3).
5. Place in cell L17: =E2>AVERAGE($E$2:$E$25). The result is either TRUE or FALSE, depending on the 1st record in the database.
6. Place in cell G19: =DSUM(A1:E25,E1,G16:L17).
7. Select cells G19:J27 and start a *Data Table* with H17 for row input and G17 for column input: =TABLE(H17,G17).
8. Place in cell M10: =DSUM($A$1:$E$25,E$1,L$7:M$8).
9. Place in cell M11: =DAVERAGE($A$1:$E$25,E$1,L$7:M$8).
10. Check whether all calculations return correct results.
11. If you want to test the filters, enter some criteria in cells J3, K3, M8, or wherever (see below).

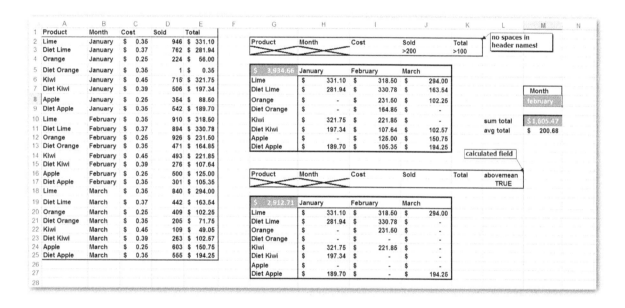

Chapter 87: Risk Analysis

What the simulation does

	A	B	C	D	E	F	G
1		produced	20000			probability	demand
2		rand#	0.753344708			0%	10,000
3		demand	60,000			10%	20,000
4		unit prod cost	$ 2.50			25%	40,000
5		unit price	$ 6.00			60%	60,000
6							
7		revenue	$ 120,000.00				
8		total var cost	$ 50,000.00				
9		profit	$ 70,000.00				
10							
11	mean	$	35,000.00	$ 63,340.00	$107,180.00	$ 97,380.00	
12	st dev	$	-	$ 18,857.36	$ 61,856.88	$ 107,315.67	
13							
14	$70,000.00		10,000	20,000	40,000	60,000	
15	1		$35,000.00	$70,000.00	$20,000.00	$90,000.00	
16	2		$35,000.00	$70,000.00	$20,000.00	$30,000.00	
17	3		$35,000.00	$10,000.00	$20,000.00	$210,000.00	
18	4		$35,000.00	$70,000.00	$140,000.00	$90,000.00	

If the demand for some product is regulated by a range of probabilities (G2:H4), then you can determine your optimal production by simulating demand within that range of probabilities and calculating profits for each level of demand.

In this simulation, the top left section (B:C) calculates the profit for one trial production quantity. Cell C1 has a trial production quantity. Cell C2 has a random number. In cell C3, we simulate demand for this product with the function VLOOKUP.

A *Data Table* (A14:E1014) simulates each possible production quantity (10,000, 20,000, 40,000 or 60,000 in row 14) some 1,000 times and calculates profits for each trial number (1 to 1,000) and each production quantity (10,000, etc.). At the origin of the *Data Table* (A14) is a reference to the profit calculation in C9. The *Data Table* uses cell C1 (a specific production quantity) for the row input, and an empty cell for the column input (e.g. G14).

Finally, row 11 calculates the mean profit for the four different production quantities. In the example shown at the end, the results indicate that the production of 40,000 units results in maximum profits (D11). Row 12 does something similar, but this time for the standard deviation. Notice that the SD increases when the quantities increase.

What you need to know

The VLOOKUP function in C3 matches the value in C1 with the closest previous match in the first column of table F2:G5. The corresponding value from the second column in table F2:G5 is then entered into C3.

How does the *Data Table* work? Take cell D15 below as an example: the column input cell value of 1 (A15) is placed in a blank cell (G14) and the random number in cell C2 recalculates. The corresponding profit is then recorded in cell D14. Next the column cell input value of 2 is placed in the blank cell G14, and the random number in C2 again recalculates. The corresponding profit is entered in cell D15. And so the table grows quickly. A *Data Table* has an amazing power!

Simulations in Action — BUSINESS

What you need to do

	A	B	C	D	E	F	G
1		produced	20000			probability	demand
2		rand#	=RAND()			0	10000
3		demand	=VLOOKUP(C2,F2:G5,2,1)			0.1	20000
4		unit prod cost	2.5			0.25	40000
5		unit price	6			0.6	60000
6							
7		revenue	=MIN(C1,C3)*C5				
8		total var cost	=C1*C4				
9		profit	=C7-C8				
10							
11	mean	=AVERAGE(B15:B1014)	=AVERAGE(C15:C1014)	=AVERAGE(D15:D1014)	=AVERAGE(E15:E1014)		
12	st dev	=STDEV(B15:B1014)	=STDEV(C15:C1014)	=STDEV(D15:D1014)	=STDEV(E15:E1014)		
13							
14	=C9	10000	20000	40000	60000		
15	1	=TABLE(C1,G14)	=TABLE(C1,G14)	=TABLE(C1,G14)	=TABLE(C1,G14)		
16	2	=TABLE(C1,G14)	=TABLE(C1,G14)	=TABLE(C1,G14)	=TABLE(C1,G14)		
17	3	=TABLE(C1,G14)	=TABLE(C1,G14)	=TABLE(C1,G14)	=TABLE(C1,G14)		
18	4	=TABLE(C1,G14)	=TABLE(C1,G14)	=TABLE(C1,G14)	=TABLE(C1,G14)		

1. Place in cell C2: =RAND().
2. Place in cell C3: =VLOOKUP(C2,F2:G5,2,1).
3. Place in cell C7: =MIN(C1,C3)*C5.
4. Place in cell C8: =C1*C4.
5. Place in cell A14 a link to cell C9: =C9.
6. Place in cell C9: =C7-C8.
7. Select A14:E1014. Use a *Data Table* with C1 as row input and G14 (or any other empty cell) as column input. (See Appendix for more details). The formula is =TABLE(C1,G14).
8. Place in cells B11:E11: =AVERAGE(B15:B1014).
9. Place in cells B12:E12: =STDEV(B15:B1014).
10. Hit *F9* several times and notice, as shown in the picture below, that a production of 40,000 usually gives the best profit (in D11). Even if cell E11 is higher or very close (by mere chance), its risk factor is much higher (as expressed in the SD shown in cell E12).
11. Try changing input cells in the top section and check the outcome.

	A	B	C	D	E	F	G	H
1		produced	20000			probability	demand	
2		rand#	0.118855398			0%	10,000	
3		demand	20,000			10%	20,000	
4		unit prod cost	$ 2.50			25%	40,000	
5		unit price	$ 6.00			60%	60,000	
6								
7		revenue	$ 120,000.00					
8		total var cost	$ 50,000.00					
9		profit	$ 70,000.00					
10								
11	mean	$ 35,000.00	$ 64,360.00	$103,820.00	$ 106,080.00			
12	st dev	$ -	$ 17,518.48	$ 63,228.20	$ 105,389.47			
13								
14	$70,000.00	10,000	20,000	40,000	60,000			
15	1	$35,000.00	$70,000.00	$140,000.00	$90,000.00			
16	2	$35,000.00	$70,000.00	$140,000.00	$90,000.00			
17	3	$35,000.00	$70,000.00	$140,000.00	$90,000.00			
18	4	$35,000.00	$70,000.00	$140,000.00	$90,000.00			

Chapter 88: Scenarios

What the simulation does

	A	B	C	D	E	F	G	H	I	J	K	L	M
1	select likely scenario			select worst case		select best case		uncertainty			scenario combinations		
2		1			4		6				1-4-6	146	
3	Volume	1,500			1,400		2,200	1,491.77					
4	Cost/unit	$ 2.50		$	2.75	$	3.25	$2.76			Min	$ 73,151.79	
5	Profit/unit	$ 50.00		$	55.00	$	65.00	$58.76			25%	$ 90,049.75	
6	Overhead	$ 800.00									Median	$104,243.25	
7											75%	$112,623.31	
8	Revenues	$75,000.00		$77,000.00		$143,000.00		$87,649.64			Max	$125,792.56	
9	Expenses	$4,550.00		$4,650.00		$7,950.00		$4,922.73					
10									Volume	Revenues	Expenses	Profit	
11	Profit	$70,450.00		$72,350.00		$135,050.00		$82,726.92	1,492	$ 87,649.64	$4,922.73	$ 82,726.92	
12									1,847	$115,348.55	$6,296.57	$109,051.98	
13		most likely			worst case		best case		2,011	$120,996.95	$6,436.26	$114,560.69	
14	1	2	3		4	5	6		1,705	$100,328.60	$5,996.39	$ 94,332.21	
15	1,500	2,000	1,200		1,400	2,100	2,200		1,475	$ 95,559.95	$5,230.60	$ 90,329.35	
16	$ 2.50	$ 3.00	$ 2.30	$	2.75	$ 2.70	$ 3.25		1,834	$101,178.51	$6,082.88	$ 95,095.63	
17	$ 50.00	$ 60.00	$ 47.00	$	55.00	$ 53.00	$ 65.00		1,440	$ 92,782.08	$5,295.40	$ 87,486.67	
18									2,052	$129,783.11	$6,586.31	$123,196.81	
19		scenarios	worst		best				1,691	$ 95,835.20	$6,070.96	$ 89,764.24	
20		135	$ -	$	-				1,747	$ 97,176.88	$5,610.02	$ 91,566.86	
21		136	$56,843.66	$	132,417.02		turn		1,742	$ 97,257.80	$5,932.12	$ 91,325.69	
22		145	$ -	$	-		Iterations		1,991	$109,692.45	$7,223.36	$102,469.09	
23		146	$73,151.79	$	125,792.56		ON, set to		1,540	$ 90,138.50	$5,674.57	$ 84,463.93	
24		235	$ -	$	-		a max of		1,660	$102,376.66	$5,568.70	$ 96,807.96	
25		236	$55,059.33	$	130,774.96		1		1,451	$ 92,150.02	$5,495.39	$ 86,654.63	
26		245	$ -	$	-				2,071	$127,406.64	$6,672.72	$120,733.91	
27		246	$ -	$	-				1,806	$114,191.70	$6,221.33	$107,970.37	
28									1,858	$117,416.80	$6,316.16	$111,100.64	
29			$55,059.33	$	132,417.02				1,938	$116,691.00	$6,216.41	$110,474.59	
30									1,469	$ 90,640.70	$5,060.62	$ 85,580.07	

Predictions of expenses and revenues are subject to lots of uncertainty. Nevertheless, let's say we want to predict these under a few defined scenarios, such as the most likely, the best case, and the worst case scenario, in order to project a range of possible profit levels.

We use several tables to set up this calculation. The top left table (A1:F6) shows the 3 scenarios that were actually chosen. There are actually six scenarios—two for each case—with settings as displayed in the 2nd table (A13:F17). Cell B2 has a dropdown button to select scenario 1 or 2, cell D2 has one for selecting scenario 3 or 4, and cell F2 for scenario 5 or 6.

The main calculations occur in the *Data Table* in the lower-right corner (H11:L111). It is two-dimensional, but has a "hidden" third dimension: the 3 scenarios that were actually chosen in the top left table. All values in column H depend on these 3 scenarios.

Since the user has a choice of six different scenarios—1 and 2 for the most likely scenario, 3 and 4 for the worst-case scenario, and 5 and 6 for the best-case scenario—there are actually 8 possible combinations as is shown in B20:B27 (135, 136, etc.). The simulation uses these combinations and shows the results for each combination in the table B19:D27.

What you need to know

The cells B3:F5 use the function HLOOKUP, which stands for a *horizontal* lookup. It is similar to VLOOKUP, only it searches horizontal data rather than columnar data. HLOOKUP is used in the top left table to locate the correct input in the scenario table A14:F17. Because the scenario numbers are in a row (row 14), we need a *horizontal* lookup—so HLOOKUP, not VLOOKUP.

In cells H3:H5, we simulate random values between the worst and best case scenario: =D3+RAND()*(F3-D3).

What you need to do

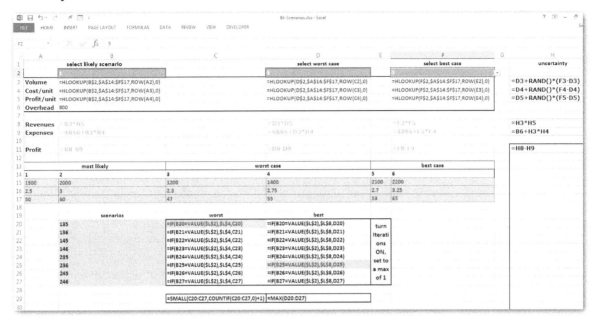

1. There is Data Validation in B2 (1,2), D2 (3,4), and F2 (5,6).
2. Place in cell B3 a lookup formula that we can copy down to cell B5: =HLOOKUP(B$2,$A$14:$F$17,ROW(A2),0).
3. Place in cells D3:D5: =HLOOKUP (D$2,$A$14:$F$17,ROW(C2),0).
4. Place in cells F3:F5: =HLOOKUP (F$2,$A$14:$F$17,ROW(E2),0).
5. In H3 we simulate random values between the worst and best case scenario: =D3+RAND()*(F3-D3). Copy down to H5.
6. Place in cell H8: =H3*H5.
7. Place in cell H9: =B6+H3*H4.
8. In cell H11: =H8-H9. This calculates the prediction for the given scenarios based on a single random run.
9. Create links in I11 (=H3), J11 (=H8), K11 (=H9), and L11 (=H11). These will regulate the outcome of 100 runs in the *Data Table*.
10. Select range H11:L111 at once and implement a *Data Table* with no row input and an empty cell (e.g. F11) for column input: =TABLE(,F11).
11. In the cells L4 through L8 we create an overview of the 100 profits generated in the *Data Table*: =MIN($L$11:$L$111) and =PERCENTILE ($L$11:$L$111, 0.25), and so on.
12. K2 shows the chosen scenarios: =B2 & "-" & D2 & "-" & F2.
13. Cell L2 changes this into a 3-digit number: =B2&D2&F2.
14. Turn iteration ON, set to a maximum of 1.
15. Place in cells C20:C27: =IF(B20=VALUE($L$2),$L$4,C20).
16. Place in cells D20:D27: =IF(B20=VALUE($L$2),$L$8,D20).
17. Place in cell C29: =SMALL(C20:C27,COUNTIF(C20:C27,0)+1). This is the worst of the worst.
18. Place in cell D29: =MAX(D20:D27). This is the best of the best.
19. *F9* will show you how each scenario combination has still some uncertainty in its outcome.
20. Try also to change scenario combinations.

Chapter 89: Market Growth

What the simulation does

	A	B	C	D	E	F	G	H	I	J	K	L	M	N
1			Market	4,000,000	Share	40%								
2	GDP Growth	Multiple	Market Growth	New Market Size	Market Share Growth	New Market Share	Sales Volume		100 x 100 = 10,000 runs only					
3	0.4946	1.8488	0.9144	7,657,536	0.038	0.438	3,357,267		8,789,299.35	8,787,981		MIN	2,404,339	
4	1.7073	4.3678	7.4569	33,827,676	0.024	0.424	14,350,522		2	5,078,937		MED	6,466,411	
5	0.9371	4.0694	3.8134	19,253,608	0.020	0.420	8,087,509		3	6,450,730		MAX	11,650,745	
6	1.8477	7.0473	13.0217	56,086,607	0.044	0.444	24,913,518		4	5,887,968				
7	1.9590	4.9538	9.7046	42,818,418	0.011	0.411	17,582,302		5	9,305,556				
8	0.6086	-2.6387	-1.6060	-2,423,957	0.019	0.419	-1,015,605		6	5,139,173				
9	2.0667	-4.0660	-8.4030	-29,611,830	0.027	0.427	-12,641,145		7	6,058,352				
10	1.9353	-3.8376	-7.4271	-25,708,368	-0.016	0.384	-9,868,767		8	8,726,582				

When talking about GDP growth (*Gross Domestic Product*) and the relationship between GDP growth and market growth, or the increase in market share, we are dealing with three uncertain inputs. The obvious approach is to use the best estimate for each of these inputs.

A better approach might be using a probability distribution, rather than using the single best estimate. Monte-Carlo modelling would use the probability distributions of the inputs. Rather than using the distributions themselves as inputs, we use the distributions to generate random inputs.

Based on a certain market volume (cell D1) and a certain market share (cell F1), the simulation calculates possible sales volumes (column G). It uses random distributions in 100 runs to estimate GDP growth (column A), the relationship between GDP and market size (column B), and the market share growth (column E).

Then it repeats this set of runs another 100 times, in columns I:J. After at least 10,000 runs, we get a reasonable estimate of the minimum and maximum sales volumes in column M. Needless to say that these figures can still vary quite a bit, because Monte Carlo simulations become more reliable when based on at least 1,000,000 runs.

What you need to know

The model we use is basically very simple:

- C3: market growth = GDP growth × multiple
- D3: market size = current size × (market growth + 1)
- F3: market share = current market share + gain
- G3: sales volumes = market size × market share

	A	B	C	D	E	F	G	H	I	J	K	L	M
1			Market	4000000		Share	0.4						
2	GDP Growth	Multiple	Market Growth	New Market Size	Market Share Growth	New Market Share	Sales Volume		100 x 100 = 10,000 runs only				
3	=NORMINV(RAND(),2,1)	=NORMINV(RAND(),1.5,5)	=A3*B3	=$D$1*(C3+1)	=NORMINV(RAND(),2%,2%)	=$F$1+E3	=D3*F3		=AVERAGE(G3:G102)	=G104		MIN	=MIN($J$3:$J$102)
4	=NORMINV(RAND(),2,1)	=NORMINV(RAND(),1.5,5)	=A4*B4	=$D$1*(C4+1)	=NORMINV(RAND(),2%,2%)	=$F$1+E4	=D4*F4		2	=TABLE(,H2)		MED	=MEDIAN($J$3:$J$102)
5	=NORMINV(RAND(),2,1)	=NORMINV(RAND(),1.5,5)	=A5*B5	=$D$1*(C5+1)	=NORMINV(RAND(),2%,2%)	=$F$1+E5	=D5*F5		3	=TABLE(,H2)		MAX	=MAX($J$3:$J$102)
6	=NORMINV(RAND(),2,1)	=NORMINV(RAND(),1.5,5)	=A6*B6	=$D$1*(C6+1)	=NORMINV(RAND(),2%,2%)	=$F$1+E6	=D6*F6		4	=TABLE(,H2)			
7	=NORMINV(RAND(),2,1)	=NORMINV(RAND(),1.5,5)	=A7*B7	=$D$1*(C7+1)	=NORMINV(RAND(),2%,2%)	=$F$1+E7	=D7*F7		5	=TABLE(,H2)			
8	=NORMINV(RAND(),2,1)	=NORMINV(RAND(),1.5,5)	=A8*B8	=$D$1*(C8+1)	=NORMINV(RAND(),2%,2%)	=$F$1+E8	=D8*F8		6	=TABLE(,H2)			
9	=NORMINV(RAND(),2,1)	=NORMINV(RAND(),1.5,5)	=A9*B9	=$D$1*(C9+1)	=NORMINV(RAND(),2%,2%)	=$F$1+E9	=D9*F9		7	=TABLE(,H2)			
10	=NORMINV(RAND(),2,1)	=NORMINV(RAND(),1.5,5)	=A10*B10	=$D$1*(C10+1)	=NORMINV(RAND(),2%,2%)	=$F$1+E10	=D10*F10		8	=TABLE(,H2)			

What you need to do

1. Place in cell A3: =NORMINV(RAND(),2,1).
2. Place in cell B3: =NORMINV(RAND(),1.5,5).
3. Place in cell C3: =A3*B3.
4. Place in cell D3: =$D$1*(C3+1).
5. Place in cell E3: =NORMINV(RAND(),2%,2%).
6. Place in cell F3: =$F$1+E3.
7. Place in cell G3: =D3*F3.
8. Place in the cells I3: =AVERAGE(G3:G102).
9. Place in cell J3: =G104.
10. Start in cell I3 a *Data Table* with no row input and an empty cell for column input: =TABLE(,H2).
11. Place in cell M3: =MIN($J$3:$J$102). (Or use the 5th percentile.)
12. Place in cell M4: =MEDIAN($J$3:$J$102).
13. Place in cell M5: =MAX($J$3:$J$102). (Or use the 95th percentile.)
14. Each time you hit *F9*, you will see new estimates. But again, "results may vary." Sometimes you may even get into a minimum that is negative.
15. Try many more runs if you want to reduce the uncertainty.

	A	B	C	D	E	F	G	H	I	J	K	L	M	N
1			Market	4,000,000	Share	40%								
2	GDP Growth	Multiple	Market Growth	New Market Size	Market Share Growth	New Market Share	Sales Volume		100 x 100 = 10,000 runs only					
3	1.8251	1.4404	2.6290	14,515,860	0.056	0.456	6,619,470		5,815,672.48	5,890,115		MIN	2,334,173	
4	1.6415	-1.4688	-2.4110	-5,644,183	0.005	0.405	-2,283,457		2	6,879,872		MED	6,521,046	
5	1.5838	-1.8330	-2.9031	-7,612,285	-0.001	0.399	-3,040,554		3	5,879,764		MAX	11,466,164	
6	1.8262	-9.5409	-17.4238	-65,695,043	0.011	0.411	-26,985,180		4	4,458,523				
7	1.5607	5.6632	8.8384	39,353,540	-0.006	0.394	15,510,348		5	5,963,870				
8	0.4294	-1.1352	-0.4875	2,050,147	0.001	0.401	821,162		6	7,397,457				
9	2.0012	-2.4679	-4.9388	-15,755,191	0.007	0.407	-6,411,044		7	6,789,779				
10	2.9496	3.2739	9.6564	42,625,762	0.032	0.432	18,423,471		8	7,237,505				
11	2.3603	4.3493	10.2658	45,063,373	-0.013	0.387	17,441,107		9	5,051,211				
12	1.5789	-4.9342	-7.7908	-27,163,194	-0.009	0.391	-10,619,939		10	4,299,496				
13	0.1429	-0.3470	-0.0496	3,801,625	0.065	0.465	1,765,942		11	10,221,823				
14	2.6343	-2.2400	-5.9007	-19,602,702	0.029	0.429	-8,418,161		12	4,928,353				
15	2.3502	-0.0998	-0.2346	3,061,586	-0.001	0.399	1,221,261		13	6,761,894				
16	-0.1238	2.5518	-0.3159	2,736,298	-0.002	0.398	1,089,799		14	7,763,959				
17	1.2743	1.1433	1.4568	9,827,389	0.011	0.411	4,043,563		15	8,447,301				
18	1.8864	5.0938	9.6087	42,434,984	0.047	0.447	18,983,034		16	5,635,992				
19	1.7834	4.4499	7.9359	35,743,730	0.021	0.421	15,044,140		17	7,160,668				
20	3.5473	-4.2427	-15.0502	-56,200,701	0.016	0.416	-23,361,548		18	6,093,768				
21	1.6014	5.1006	8.1679	36,671,619	0.016	0.416	15,248,379		19	6,647,488				
22	2.3919	5.5107	13.1811	56,724,230	0.046	0.446	25,280,946		20	5,009,377				
23	3.2945	3.2338	10.6537	46,614,748	0.020	0.420	19,557,658		21	6,074,604				
24	2.3762	4.9766	11.8251	51,300,355	0.041	0.441	22,646,710		22	7,014,495				
25	1.6185	5.3719	8.6943	38,777,370	0.021	0.421	16,328,756		23	5,516,548				
26	4.0709	7.8442	31.9331	131,732,535	0.036	0.436	57,407,062		24	9,917,210				

Chapter 90: Target Analysis

What the simulation does

	A	B	C	D	E	F	G	H	I	J	K	L
1		Amount	Growth rate									
2	Revenues	1,000,000	26%									
3	Expenses	1,400,000	3%									
4	Year	5	◀ ▶									
5												
6	$1,428,774.11	5.0%	10.0%	15.0%	20.0%	25.0%	30.0%	35.0%	40.0%	45.0%	50.0%	revenues
7	1.0%	-$195,132.51	$139,095.93	$539,943.12	$1,016,905.93	$1,580,343.74	$2,241,515.93	$3,012,619.37	$3,906,825.93	$4,938,319.99	$6,122,335.93	
8	1.5%	-$231,916.04	$102,312.39	$503,159.58	$980,122.39	$1,543,560.21	$2,204,732.39	$2,975,835.83	$3,870,042.39	$4,901,536.46	$6,085,552.39	
9	2.0%	-$269,431.56	$64,796.88	$465,644.06	$942,606.88	$1,506,044.69	$2,167,216.88	$2,938,320.31	$3,832,526.88	$4,864,020.94	$6,048,036.88	
10	2.5%	-$307,689.94	$26,538.50	$427,385.69	$904,348.50	$1,467,786.31	$2,128,958.50	$2,900,061.94	$3,794,268.50	$4,825,762.56	$6,009,778.50	
11	3.0%	-$346,702.14	-$12,473.70	$388,373.48	$865,336.30	$1,428,774.11	$2,089,946.30	$2,861,049.73	$3,755,256.30	$4,786,750.36	$5,970,766.30	
12	3.5%	-$386,479.27	-$52,250.83	$348,596.36	$825,559.17	$1,388,996.98	$2,050,169.17	$2,821,272.61	$3,715,479.17	$4,746,973.23	$5,930,989.17	
13	4.0%	-$427,032.60	-$92,804.06	$308,043.12	$785,005.94	$1,348,443.75	$2,009,615.94	$2,780,719.37	$3,674,925.94	$4,706,420.00	$5,890,436.94	
14	4.5%	-$468,373.15	-$134,144.71	$266,702.47	$743,665.29	$1,307,103.10	$1,968,275.29	$2,739,378.72	$3,633,585.29	$4,665,079.35	$5,849,095.29	
15	5.0%	-$510,512.63	-$176,284.19	$224,563.00	$701,525.81	$1,264,963.63	$1,926,135.81	$2,697,239.25	$3,591,445.81	$4,622,939.88	$5,806,955.81	
16	5.5%	-$553,462.45	-$219,234.01	$181,613.18	$658,575.99	$1,222,013.80	$1,883,185.99	$2,654,289.43	$3,548,495.99	$4,579,990.05	$5,764,005.99	
17	6.0%	-$597,234.25	-$263,005.81	$137,841.38	$614,804.19	$1,178,242.00	$1,839,414.19	$2,610,517.63	$3,504,724.19	$4,536,218.25	$5,720,234.19	
18	6.5%	-$641,839.77	-$307,611.33	$93,235.86	$570,198.67	$1,133,636.48	$1,794,808.67	$2,565,912.11	$3,460,118.67	$4,491,612.73	$5,675,628.67	
19	7.0%	-$687,290.86	-$353,062.42	$47,784.76	$524,747.58	$1,088,185.39	$1,749,357.58	$2,520,461.01	$3,414,667.58	$4,446,161.64	$5,630,177.58	
20	7.5%	-$733,599.49	-$399,371.06	$1,476.13	$478,438.94	$1,041,876.76	$1,703,048.94	$2,474,152.38	$3,368,358.94	$4,399,853.01	$5,583,868.94	
21	expenses											
22												

Let's say we are trying to predict the number of periods until a currently unprofitable company becomes profitable. With a spinbutton control we can extend the number of years in cell B4. Profitabilty most likely increases over a longer period of time.

We have a goal here for managing expense growth rates and a goal for increasing sales growth rates—but, of course, we do not know whether or not we will meet our objectives.

A what-if table can help us here: A6:K20. It has various growth rates for revenues in the top row and various growth rates for expenses in the left column.

This *Data Table* shows us at a glance the effects of missing and/or exceeding our target growth rates. In the above snapshot, the grayed numbers are losses after 5 years (cell B4), especially for growth rates in revenues below 10%.

A spinbutton control lets us easily manipulate the number of years for our projection.

What you need to know

A what-if table will show us profits or losses for two different growth rates—one for revenues (C2) and one for expenses (C3)—after a certain amount of years (B4).

Since what-if tables can only be two dimensional, the year variable has to be manually changed—for instance, with the help of a spinbutton control. (Previous simulations show you how to deal with 3 variables in a different way.)

The formula for profit in cell A6 is basically simple: *(Revenues * (1 + Growth Rate Revenues) ^ Years) – (Expenses * (1 + Growth Rate Expenses) ^ Years)*.

Simulations in Action — BUSINESS

What you need to do

	A	B	C	D	E	F
1		Amount	Growth rate			
2	Revenues	1000000	0.25			
3	Expenses	1400000	0.03			
4	Year	3				
5						
6	=(B2*(1+C2)^B4)-(B3*(1+C3)^B 0.05	0.1	0.15	0.2	0.25
7	0.01	=TABLE(C2,C3)	=TABLE(C2,C3)	=TABLE(C2,C3)	=TABLE(C2,C3)	=TABLE(C2,C3)
8	0.015	=TABLE(C2,C3)	=TABLE(C2,C3)	=TABLE(C2,C3)	=TABLE(C2,C3)	=TABLE(C2,C3)
9	0.02	=TABLE(C2,C3)	=TABLE(C2,C3)	=TABLE(C2,C3)	=TABLE(C2,C3)	=TABLE(C2,C3)
10	0.025	=TABLE(C2,C3)	=TABLE(C2,C3)	=TABLE(C2,C3)	=TABLE(C2,C3)	=TABLE(C2,C3)
11	0.03	=TABLE(C2,C3)	=TABLE(C2,C3)	=TABLE(C2,C3)	=TABLE(C2,C3)	=TABLE(C2,C3)
12	0.035	=TABLE(C2,C3)	=TABLE(C2,C3)	=TABLE(C2,C3)	=TABLE(C2,C3)	=TABLE(C2,C3)
13	0.04	=TABLE(C2,C3)	=TABLE(C2,C3)	=TABLE(C2,C3)	=TABLE(C2,C3)	=TABLE(C2,C3)

1. Place a spinbutton control next to cell B4: Min 1 | Max 10 | SmallChange 1 | LinkedCell B4.
2. Place in cell A6: =(B2*(1+C2)^B4)-(B3*(1+C3)^B4).
3. Select A6:K20 and create a *Data Table* with C2 for row input and C3 for column input: =TABLE(C2,C3). (See Appendix for more details.)
4. Select cells B7:K20 and apply Conditional Formatting: Highlight Cell Rules | Less Than | 0.
5. Select cells B7:K20 and apply Conditional Formatting: =B7=$A$6.
6. Check the target for various numbers of years.
7. In the short term (2 years below in B4) the prospects are not too good, by they turn out to improve for most growth rates when the years progress.

	A	B	C	D	E	F	G	H	I	J	K	L
1		Amount	Growth rate									
2	Revenues	1,000,000	25%									
3	Expenses	1,400,000	3%									
4	Year		2									
5												
6	$77,240.00	5.0%	10.0%	15.0%	20.0%	25.0%	30.0%	35.0%	40.0%	45.0%	50.0%	revenues
7	1.0%	-$325,640.00	-$218,140.00	-$105,640.00	$11,860.00	$134,360.00	$261,860.00	$394,360.00	$531,860.00	$674,360.00	$821,860.00	
8	1.5%	-$339,815.00	-$232,315.00	-$119,815.00	-$2,315.00	$120,185.00	$247,685.00	$380,185.00	$517,685.00	$660,185.00	$807,685.00	
9	2.0%	-$354,060.00	-$246,560.00	-$134,060.00	-$16,560.00	$105,940.00	$233,440.00	$365,940.00	$503,440.00	$645,940.00	$793,440.00	
10	2.5%	-$368,375.00	-$260,875.00	-$148,375.00	-$30,875.00	$91,625.00	$219,125.00	$351,625.00	$489,125.00	$631,625.00	$779,125.00	
11	3.0%	-$382,760.00	-$275,260.00	-$162,760.00	-$45,260.00	$77,240.00	$204,740.00	$337,240.00	$474,740.00	$617,240.00	$764,740.00	
12	3.5%	-$397,215.00	-$289,715.00	-$177,215.00	-$59,715.00	$62,785.00	$190,285.00	$322,785.00	$460,285.00	$602,785.00	$750,285.00	
13	4.0%	-$411,740.00	-$304,240.00	-$191,740.00	-$74,240.00	$48,260.00	$175,760.00	$308,260.00	$445,760.00	$588,260.00	$735,760.00	
14	4.5%	-$426,335.00	-$318,835.00	-$206,335.00	-$88,835.00	$33,665.00	$161,165.00	$293,665.00	$431,165.00	$573,665.00	$721,165.00	
15	5.0%	-$441,000.00	-$333,500.00	-$221,000.00	-$103,500.00	$19,000.00	$146,500.00	$279,000.00	$416,500.00	$559,000.00	$706,500.00	
16	5.5%	-$455,735.00	-$348,235.00	-$235,735.00	-$118,235.00	$4,265.00	$131,765.00	$264,265.00	$401,765.00	$544,265.00	$691,765.00	
17	6.0%	-$470,540.00	-$363,040.00	-$250,540.00	-$133,040.00	-$10,540.00	$116,960.00	$249,460.00	$386,960.00	$529,460.00	$676,960.00	
18	6.5%	-$485,415.00	-$377,915.00	-$265,415.00	-$147,915.00	-$25,415.00	$102,085.00	$234,585.00	$372,085.00	$514,585.00	$662,085.00	
19	7.0%	-$500,360.00	-$392,860.00	-$280,360.00	-$162,860.00	-$40,360.00	$87,140.00	$219,640.00	$357,140.00	$499,640.00	$647,140.00	
20	7.5%	-$515,375.00	-$407,875.00	-$295,375.00	-$177,875.00	-$55,375.00	$72,125.00	$204,625.00	$342,125.00	$484,625.00	$632,125.00	
21	expenses											

Chapter 91: Fiscal Year

What the simulation does

	A	B	C	D	E	F	G	H	I	J	K	L	M
1	Account	Sale	Date	Year	Fiscal Quarter		fiscal year starts in		1	January	3	2017	
2	Young	$146.91	February 3, 2001	2001	2001--Q4				2	February	4	2017	
3	Jones	$155.05	April 15, 2001	2001	2001--Q4		5		3	March	4	2017	
4	Burke	$ 41.55	June 25, 2001	2001	2002--Q1		◄ ►		4	April	4	2017	
5	O'Brian	$172.39	September 4, 2001	2001	2002--Q2				5	May	1	2018	
6	Brown	$189.73	November 14, 2001	2001	2002--Q3				6	June	1	2018	
7	Brown	$219.95	December 1, 2001	2001	2002--Q3				7	July	1	2018	
8	Roberts	$115.55	January 24, 2002	2002	2002--Q3				8	August	2	2018	
9	Brown	$ 15.27	April 5, 2002	2002	2002--Q4				9	September	2	2018	
10	Young	$ 56.45	June 15, 2002	2002	2003--Q1				10	October	2	2018	
11	Jones	$103.95	August 25, 2002	2002	2003--Q2				11	November	3	2018	
12	Minsky	$163.96	November 4, 2002	2002	2003--Q3				12	December	3	2018	
13	Minsky	$ 63.96	November 4, 2002	2002	2003--Q3				1	January	3	2018	
14	Jenkins	$ 48.29	January 14, 2003	2003	2003--Q3				2	February	4	2018	
15	Jenkins	$ 88.19	March 14, 2003	2003	2003--Q4				3	March	4	2018	
16	Russell	$ 19.43	March 26, 2003	2003	2003--Q4				4	April	4	2018	
17	Caruso	$109.40	June 5, 2003	2003	2004--Q1				5	May	1	2019	
18	Russell	$171.92	August 15, 2003	2003	2004--Q2				6	June	1	2019	
19	Roberts	$ 45.77	October 25, 2003	2003	2004--Q2				7	July	1	2019	
20	O'Brian	$146.32	January 4, 2004	2004	2004--Q3				8	August	2	2019	
21	Jones	$ 65.92	March 15, 2004	2004	2004--Q4				9	September	2	2019	
22	Young	$ 37.88	May 25, 2004	2004	2005--Q1				10	October	2	2019	
23	Jones	$ 93.87	August 4, 2004	2004	2005--Q2				11	November	3	2019	
24	Burke	$ 77.51	October 14, 2004	2004	2005--Q2				12	December	3	2019	
25	O'Brian	$224.22	December 24, 2004	2004	2005--Q3								
26	Brown	$144.15	March 5, 2005	2005	2005--Q4								
27	Roberts	$ 24.67	May 15, 2005	2005	2006--Q1								
28	Brown	$257.14	July 25, 2005	2005	2006--Q1								
29	Jones	$ 18.13	October 4, 2005	2005	2006--Q2								
30													

Excel has great functions to extract the year, month, and day part of a date—but amazingly enough, it has no function to find out to which *quarter* of the year such a date belongs.

Obviously, for summary overviews, that is quite a limitation. This problem can be solved, though, with a simple nested function such as *ROUNDUP(MONTH(any date)/3,0)*.

However, finding the correct quarter becomes much harder when your company does not have a regular fiscal year.

On this sheet, we determine in cell G2 when your fiscal year starts—let us assume it is in May (month 5). Column E has to do "the math."

What you need to know

This is going to be a heavily nested formula (see Appendix for more details). It uses the functions YEAR, MONTH, IF, MOD, and INT. The function MOD was explained in Chapters 4 and 75. The last one, INT, rounds a number down to the nearest integer (see Chapter 67).

In addition, you may want to use the function TODAY, which returns the current day, and therefore changes its outcome every day.

For more information on how Excel handles dates, see Chapter 126.

What you need to do

1. Place in cell G3 Data Validation based on a list: =$I$1:$I$12.
2. Place also a spinbutton control under cell G3, so the user has a choice: Min 1 | Max 12 | LinkedCell G3.
3. Place in cells D2:D29: =YEAR(C2).
4. The hard work is done in cell E2:E29 with the following heavily nested formula: =YEAR(C2) + IF (MONTH(C2)>=$G$2,1,0) & "--Q" & INT(1 + MOD(MONTH(C2) - $G$2,12)/3). This results in something like "2001--Q2". The ampersand (&) "hooks" all the pieces together. Adjust the formula to your needs.
5. Place in cells K1:K24 the following formula: =INT(1+MOD(I1-$G$2,12)/3).
6. Place in cells L1:L24: =YEAR(TODAY())+COUNTIF($I$1:I1,$G$2).
7. Range I1:L24 has a conditional formatting formula: =AND(ROW()>=$G$2,ROW()<$G$2+12). Assign a fill color.
8. Range I1:L24 has another conditional formatting formula: =$L2<>$L1. Assign a bottom border line.
9. A different fiscal year (say 10, for October) would result in different quarters, of course, and a different color range, as you can see below.

	A	B	C	D	E	F	G	H	I	J	K	L	M
1	Account	Sale	Date	Year	Fiscal Quarter		fiscal year starts in		1	January	2	2017	
2	Young	$146.91	February 3, 2001	2001	2001--Q2				2	February	2	2017	
3	Jones	$155.05	April 15, 2001	2001	2001--Q3		10		3	March	2	2017	
4	Burke	$ 41.55	June 25, 2001	2001	2001--Q3				4	April	3	2017	
5	O'Brian	$172.39	September 4, 2001	2001	2001--Q4				5	May	3	2017	
6	Brown	$189.73	November 14, 2001	2001	2002--Q1				6	June	3	2017	
7	Brown	$219.95	December 1, 2001	2001	2002--Q1				7	July	4	2017	
8	Roberts	$115.55	January 24, 2002	2002	2002--Q2				8	August	4	2017	
9	Brown	$ 15.27	April 5, 2002	2002	2002--Q3				9	September	4	2017	
10	Young	$ 56.45	June 15, 2002	2002	2002--Q3				10	October	1	2018	
11	Jones	$103.95	August 25, 2002	2002	2002--Q4				11	November	1	2018	
12	Minsky	$163.96	November 4, 2002	2002	2003--Q1				12	December	1	2018	
13	Minsky	$ 63.96	November 4, 2002	2002	2003--Q1				1	January	2	2018	
14	Jenkins	$ 48.29	January 14, 2003	2003	2003--Q2				2	February	2	2018	
15	Jenkins	$ 88.19	March 14, 2003	2003	2003--Q2				3	March	2	2018	
16	Russell	$ 19.43	March 26, 2003	2003	2003--Q2				4	April	3	2018	
17	Caruso	$109.40	June 5, 2003	2003	2003--Q3				5	May	3	2018	
18	Russell	$171.92	August 15, 2003	2003	2003--Q4				6	June	3	2018	
19	Roberts	$ 45.77	October 25, 2003	2003	2004--Q1				7	July	4	2018	
20	O'Brian	$146.32	January 4, 2004	2004	2004--Q2				8	August	4	2018	
21	Jones	$ 65.92	March 15, 2004	2004	2004--Q2				9	September	4	2018	
22	Young	$ 37.88	May 25, 2004	2004	2004--Q3				10	October	1	2019	
23	Jones	$ 93.87	August 4, 2004	2004	2004--Q4				11	November	1	2019	
24	Burke	$ 77.51	October 14, 2004	2004	2005--Q1				12	December	1	2019	
25	O'Brian	$224.22	December 24, 2004	2004	2005--Q1								
26	Brown	$144.15	March 5, 2005	2005	2005--Q2								
27	Roberts	$ 24.67	May 15, 2005	2005	2005--Q3								
28	Brown	$257.14	July 25, 2005	2005	2005--Q4								
29	Jones	$ 18.13	October 4, 2005	2005	2006--Q1								

Chapter 92: Resource Allocation

What the simulation does

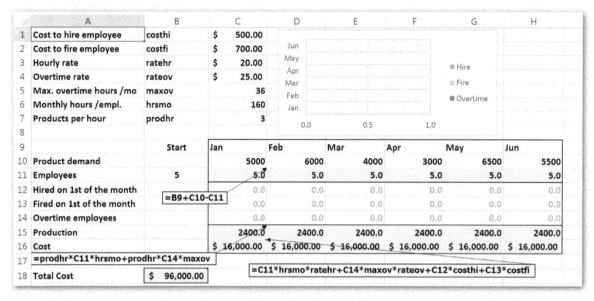

Let's pretend that for a series of months (row 9) you need a certain number of workers to fill the demand of products for each month (row 10). Since workers or employees come with costs, you want to find out how you can keep the total costs (cell B18) as low as possible by assigning overtime or by hiring and firing workers only as needed.

The costs for workers are entered in cells C1:C7. The cells with these values have been assigned a *Range Name* which is shown in B1:B7. Such Names are not necessary but they make the formulas easier to understand. We used the formulas as shown in the picture above. All the gray cells have formulas in them.

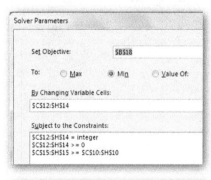

What you need to know

The tool we need to get to the lowest possible costs in cell B18 is *Solver* (see Chapter 70). Here are the settings:

1. Set B18 to a minimum.
2. The changing cells must have variables in them, not formulas: C12:H14, which are all zeros.
3. The production in row 15 must be higher than the product demand in row 19.
4. The number of workers in C12:H14 must be greater than or equal to 0.
5. We can't have "half" workers, so the numbers in C12:H14 must be integers.
6. However, this last constraint makes for a very long solving time.
7. So change some options. I decided on a *Constraint Precision* of 0.01 and an *Integer Optimality* of 5 (percent). Try other settings if you want. If solving time becomes very long, use *Ctrl Break* to stop the iteration process.

What you need to do

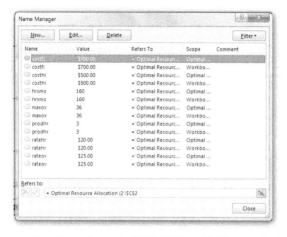

1. To mark all cells with formulas in them, select all cells in the left top corner where the row and column bars meet.
2. Apply Conditional Formatting to all cells with a function: =ISFORMULA(A1).
3. The easiest and fastest way of assigning *Range Names* is the following. Select B1:C7 | Formulas | in section Defined Names | Create from Selection | ☑ Left Column | OK.
4. Now these Names can be found in: Formulas | Name Manager (see left).
5. Place in cells C11:H11: =B11+C12-C13.
6. Place in cells C15:H15 the formula: =prodhr*C11*hrsmo+prodhr*C14*maxov.
7. Place in cells C16:H16: =C11*hrsmo*ratehr+C14*maxov*rateov+C12*costhi+C13*costfi.
8. Place in cell B18: =SUM(C16:H16).
9. Start *Solver* with the settings discussed on the previous page.
10. Accept or reject the solution.
11. The chart in the top right corner is a stacked bar chart for the range C12:H14.
12. The range C12:H14 has conditional formatting: Cell Value | Greater than | 0.
13. Make sure this condition kicks in *after* the ISFORMULA condition, otherwise you must use the arrow button in the Condition Formatting screen to change their order.
14. Sometimes it's wise to insert an extra row before row 15 for a "dummy" row—to take up any slack. This row makes sure all zero's there remain zero (see Chapter 95).

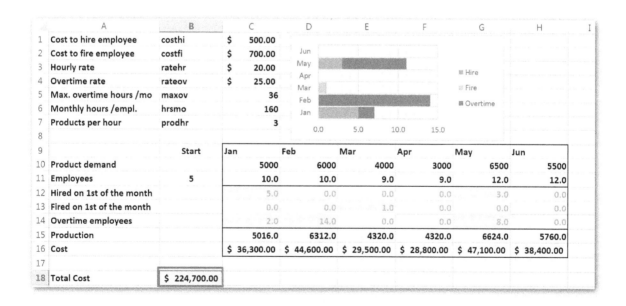

Chapter 93: A Traffic Situation

What the simulation does

	A	B	C	D	E	F	G	H	I	J	K	L
1	1st stretch	Traffic light	2nd stretch	seconds	minutes		cumul.	secs				
2	360	0.00	240	600.00	10.00		0	240		median	6.49	
3	111	0.00	240	351.00	5.85		70	360		average	6.92	
4	111	0.00	240	351.00	5.85		80	180		75%	7.07	
5	111	64.41	240	415.41	6.92		90	1800		100%	11.35	
6	111	35.97	240	386.97	6.45							
7	111	46.57	240	397.57	6.63							
8	111	80.96	240	431.96	7.20							
9	111	64.47	240	415.47	6.92							
10	111	28.03	240	379.03	6.32							

This simulation really illustrates how we can tame the uncertainty of commute traffic for your co-workers with ranges and probabilities, but not surprisingly, it also shows how impossible it is to be extremely precise.

Column A: We simulate driving 2 miles on a highway, with 90% probability we will drive with an average speed of 65 MPH, but with a 10% probability that a traffic jam will result in an average speed of 20 MPH (column A).

Column B: Then there is a traffic light that goes through a 120 second cycle with 90 seconds for "red" and 30 seconds for "green." If we hit it on green then there is no delay, but if we hit it on red we must wait for green.

Column C: Finally, we have 2 more miles to go: 70% of the time at 30 MPH, 10% at 20 MPH, 10% at 40 MPH, and 10% of the time it takes us 30 minutes. This can be calculated with a VLOOKUP function based on G2:H5.

Instead of using a fixed value for input variables, we can model an input variable with a probability distribution and then run the model a large number of times and see what impact the random variation has on the output.

Again, it is wise to run at least 1,000 iterations in the columns A:E. This is to ensure that we have a statistical chance of getting sufficient outliers (extreme values) to make the variance analysis meaningful. This is important because as the number of iterations increases, the variance of the average output decreases.

What you need to know

Since median (K2) and average (K3) are usually close together, we know we are dealing with a rather normal distribution of results. But under "unfavorable" circumstances, the toal driving time can go much higher (K5).

As you can see below, all the work is done with very basic functions and formulas.

	A	B	C	D	E
1	1st stretch	Traffic light	2nd stretch	seconds	minutes
2	=IF(RAND() < 0.9, 111, 360)	=MAX(0, (RAND() * 120) - 30)	=VLOOKUP(RAND(),$G$2:$H$5, 2)	=SUM(A2:C2)	=D2/60

What you need to do

1. Place in cells A2:A1001: =IF(RAND() < 0.9, 111, 360).
2. Place in cells B2:B1001: =MAX(0, (RAND() * 120) - 30).
3. Place in cells C2:C1001: =VLOOKUP(RAND(),$G$2:$H$5, 2).
4. Place in cells D2:D1001: =SUM(A2:C2).
5. Place in cells E2:E1001: =D2/60.
6. Place in cell K2: =MEDIAN(E:E).
7. Place in cell K3: =AVERAGE(E:E).
8. Place in cell K4: =PERCENTILE(E:E,J4). Or use a later version.
9. Place in cell K5: =PERCENTILE(E:E,J5).
10. If you wish, add a *Data Table* to G8:K22: =TABLE(,F7).
11. Place in range H7:K7: =TRANSPOSE(J2:J5). Don't forget to use *Ctrl Shift Enter*.
12. Place in range H8:K8: =TRANSPOSE(K2:K5). Don't forget to use *Ctrl Shift Enter*.
13. Place in the cells H24:K24: =AVERAGE(H8:H22). Use F9.

	A	B	C	D	E	F	G	H	I	J	K
1	1st stretch	Traffic light	2nd stretch	seconds	minutes		cumul.	secs			
2	111	40.31	240	391.31	6.52		0	240		median	6.47
3	111	24.08	240	375.08	6.25		70	360		average	6.88
4	111	6.75	240	357.75	5.96		80	180		75%	7.07
5	111	64.24	240	415.24	6.92		90	1800		100%	11.49
6	111	3.47	240	354.47	5.91						
7	111	21.64	240	372.64	6.21			median	average	0.75	1.00
8	111	0.00	240	351.00	5.85			6.47	6.88	7.07	11.49
9	111	4.38	240	355.38	5.92			6.46	6.77	6.97	11.48
10	111	82.09	240	433.09	7.22			6.41	6.79	7.00	11.46
11	111	1.88	240	352.88	5.88			6.49	6.81	7.02	11.46
12	111	82.24	240	433.24	7.22			6.54	6.90	7.06	11.50
13	360	27.64	240	627.64	10.46			6.47	6.82	7.01	11.47
14	111	81.29	240	432.29	7.20			6.51	6.84	7.03	11.50
15	111	39.19	240	390.19	6.50			6.49	6.83	7.04	11.48
16	111	72.44	240	423.44	7.06			6.41	6.83	7.00	11.50
17	111	20.79	240	371.79	6.20			6.45	6.82	7.00	11.41
18	111	0.00	240	351.00	5.85			6.45	6.80	7.03	11.45
19	111	24.46	240	375.46	6.26			6.43	6.84	7.02	11.47
20	111	39.35	240	390.35	6.51			6.42	6.77	6.97	11.46
21	360	0.00	240	600.00	10.00			6.48	6.79	6.99	11.50
22	111	8.63	240	359.63	5.99			6.45	6.85	7.01	11.48
23	111	23.72	240	374.72	6.25						
24	111	3.08	240	354.08	5.90		Mean	6.46	6.82	7.02	11.47
25	111	16.06	240	367.06	6.12						

Chapter 94: Quality Control

What the simulation does

	A	B	C	D	E	F	G	H	I	J	K	L	M	N	O	P	Q
1	Production	100		Sample	10%						mean products	mean sample	count samples	count rejects	max rejects	verdict	
2	Mean	15		Accept defect	2%												
3	SD	2		Confidence	95%					14.9727	14.9727	16.1672	9	0	1	+	
4											15.1108	15.2346	10	0	1	+	
5					samples	rejects	max rejects	verdict			15.0089	14.6424	5	0	1	+	
6	14.9727			16.1672	9	0	1	+			14.9158	15.2616	10	1	1	+	
7											14.5058	13.7190	10	1	1	+	
8	16.3608										14.9876	16.0739	9	0	1	+	
9	13.2087										15.2823	14.9717	10	0	1	+	
10	12.0580										15.0003	15.2678	8	0	1	+	
11	17.7391										15.1320	14.7109	10	2	1	reject	
12	13.4976										15.1808	15.5936	10	1	1	+	
13	16.8480										15.0330	14.1820	8	0	1	+	
14	12.4010										15.3118	16.6001	7	2	1	reject	
15	13.1061			13.1061	OK						15.5940	14.8418	6	1	1	+	
16	17.0386			17.0386	OK						14.7938	13.9935	5	1	1	+	
17	14.7797										14.9375	14.6459	9	3	1	reject	
18	14.4083										14.9644	16.1549	7	0	1	+	
19	16.2014										14.7065	13.7174	8	1	1	+	
20	16.1845										15.0177	14.8106	10	0	1	+	
21	14.6108										14.9956	15.5905	10	0	1	+	
22	14.4775										14.8781	15.0588	10	1	1	+	
23	16.9440										15.3415	15.2365	10	1	1	+	
24	15.1298										15.1628	15.4897	6	0	1	+	
25	14.5288																
26	18.4496										mean	15.0379	15.0893	8.5000			
27	17.2627			17.2627	OK												
28	17.2623																

Here we are dealing with an assembly line that creates between 100 and 1,000 products (B1) per period of time. One particular variable of this product is supposed to be close to a value of 15 (B2) but is allowed to vary with a SD of 2 (B3), as shown some 1,000 times in column A.

To ensure quality, we take a certain percentage of samples (E1) in which we accept 2% defects (E2, or whatever is in there). Based on such a sample we decide, with 95% confidence (E3), to accept or reject the entire production lot.

Since this process is far from certain but depends heavily on probabilities, we repeat this process at least some 20 times in the *Data Table* to the far right—so that's 20 times 1,000 runs.

What you need to know

Column A creates values normally distributed around the mean value that is shown in B2, with a SD as shown in cell B3. This column holds 1,000 records, but in order to allow for smaller production numbers, if so decided, we need the function OFFSET (see Simulation 14 for more information on this function).

Another function is CRITBINOM in cell G6. It can be used to determine the greatest number of defective parts that are allowed to come off an assembly line sample without rejecting the entire lot. It has 3 arguments: The number of trials, the probability of a success on each trial, and the criterion value (alpha). Recently, this function has been replaced with BINOM.INV.

	A	B	C	D	E
1	Production	100		Sample	0.1
2	Mean	15		Accept defect	0.02
3	SD	2		Confidence	0.95
4					
5					samples
6	=AVERAGE($A$8:OFFSET($A$8,$B$1-1,0))			=AVERAGE($D$8:OFFSET($D$8,$B$1-1,0))	=COUNT($D$8:OFFSET($D$8,$B$1-1,0))
7					
8	=NORMINV(RAND(),$B$2,$B$3)			=IF(AND(ROW(D7)+1<=($B$1+7),COUNT($D$7:D7)<($B$1*$E$1)),IF(RAND()<=$E$1,A8,""),"")	=IF(D8<>"",IF((ABS($B$2-D8)/$B$3)>1.96,"reject","OK"),"")
9	=NORMINV(RAND(),$B$2,$B$3)			=IF(AND(ROW(D8)+1<=($B$1+7),COUNT($D$7:D8)<($B$1*$E$1)),IF(RAND()<=$E$1,A9,""),"")	=IF(D9<>"",IF((ABS($B$2-D9)/$B$3)>1.96,"reject","OK"),"")
10	=NORMINV(RAND(),$B$2,$B$3)			=IF(AND(ROW(D9)+1<=($B$1+7),COUNT($D$7:D9)<($B$1*$E$1)),IF(RAND()<=$E$1,A10,""),"")	=IF(D10<>"",IF((ABS($B$2-D10)/$B$3)>1.96,"reject","OK"),"")

What you need to do

1. Place in cells A8:A1007: =NORMINV (RAND(),$B$2,$B$3). This creates normally distributed random values based on cells B2 and B3.
2. Place in A6: =AVERAGE($A$8:OFFSET ($A$8,$B$1-1,0)). This averages the normally distributed values for the number of products chosen in cell B1—that is, the range from A8 to A8-offset-by-B1-rows. The mean should be around 15 (B2).
3. In column D, we create samples—X% of the total number of products (e.g., 10%). This is a random process, so the number of samples can be lower than 10%, but should not be higher, and cannot go past the maximum number of products.
4. To achieve this, place in cell D8 a heavily nested function: =IF(AND(ROW (D7)+1<=($B$1+7),COUNT($D$7:D7)<($B$1*$E$1)),IF(RAND ()<=$E$1,A8,""),""). We use D7 instead of D8 to avoid circular reference. I assume you accept smaller random sample sizes but not larger ones.
5. Place in D6: =AVERAGE($D$8:OFFSET ($D$8,$B$1-1,0)).
6. In cell E8, we decide that, if the sample value (D8) is more than 1.96 SD-units away from the population mean (B2), the sample should be rejected. We do this with the following formula: =IF(D8<>"",IF((ABS($B$2-D8)/$B$3)>1.96,"reject","OK"),"").
7. Place in E6: =COUNT($D$8:OFFSET ($D$8,$B$1-1,0)). This counts the number of samples, which should be <=(B1*E1).
8. In cell F6, we count how many rejects were found: =COUNTIF ($E$8:OFFSET ($E$8,$B$1-1,0),"reject").
9. Place in cell G6: =IFERROR (CRITBINOM (E6,E2,E3),"?").
10. Place in cell H6 a verdict: =IF(F6>G6,"reject","+").
11. In J3: = A6. In K3: =A6. In L3: =D6. In M3: =E6. In N3: = F6. In O3: =G6. In P3: =H6.
12. Select range J3:P24 and start a *Data Table* with no row input and an empty cell (e.g. I3) for column input: =TABLE(,I3).
13. In K26:M26, calculate the mean of the columns above.
14. Test with different entries in B1:B3 and E1:E3.
15. As always, results may vary because of randomness.

Chapter 95: Logistics

What the simulation does

	A	B	C	D	E	F	G	H
1		Pharmacy Stores				total flow out		available
2	Warehouses	1	2	3	4			
3	A	0	0	0	0	0	=	80
4	B	0	0	0	0	0	=	75
5	C	0	0	0	0	0	=	90
6	D (dummy)	0	0	0	0	0	=	20
7	Total flow in	0	0	0	0			245
8	sign	=	=	=	=			265
9	Demand	60	80	70	55			265
10								
11		shipping costs per package						
12		Pharmacy Stores						
13	Warehouses	1	2	3	4			
14	A	$40	$50	$70	$60			
15	B	$50	$60	$40	$30			
16	C	$30	$70	$60	$50			
17	D (dummy)	$0	$0	$0	$0			
18								
19	total costs	$0						
20								

We have a logistical problem here. Pharmacies have a specific demand of a product (row 9). In the warehouses of some pharmaceutical company, there is a certain amount of packages available in stock (H3:H5).

Given the fact that shipment costs vary depending on the location of the warehouse and the location of the pharmacy (B14:E14), we need to minimize total shipping costs (in cell B19).

What you need to know

Only the shaded cells contain formulas. To make this task solvable we need a "dummy" warehouse in row 6 and row 17. A dummy destination (row 6) and a dummy source (row 17) take up the slack between the actual amounts and maximum amounts being distributed. In cell H6 we calculate the amount of fiction packs needed to make the task solvable.

This requires *Solver*, of course (see Chapter 66). The *Solver* settings are more or less obvious (see to the left). The objective cell must have a formula, but the changing cells cannot. Make sure that *Unconstrained Variables Non-Negative* is checked ON.

Solver tells us that one "dummy" warehouse (#3) has 20 packages below demand. To make all 4 stores share the insufficient amount—5 packages each—you can add an extra constraint: B6:E6=20/4.

What you need to do

1. To mark cells with a formula in it, select all cells and apply conditional formatting with this function: =ISFORMULA(A1).
2. Place in cells B7:E7: =SUM(B3:B6).
3. Place in cells F3:F6: =SUM(B3:E3).
4. Place in cell H7: =SUM(H3:H5).
5. Place in cell H8: =SUM(H3:H6).
6. Place in cell H9: =SUM(B9:E9).
7. Place in cell H6: =H9-H7.
8. Place in cell B19: =SUMPRODUCT(B14:E17,B3:E6). The function SUMPRODUCT returns the sum of the products of corresponding ranges.
9. All other cells have manual input.
10. Start *Solver* with the settings shown to the right.
11. The outcome is shown below with the lowest possible costs for transportation: $10,050.
12. But we are also 20 packages short (cell D6), unless you add an extra constraint: B6:E6=20/4.

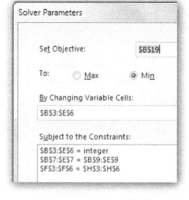

	A	B	C	D	E	F	G	H
1			Pharmacy Stores			total flow out		available
2	Warehouses	1	2	3	4			
3	A	0	80	0	0	80	=	80
4	B	0	0	36	39	75	=	75
5	C	60	0	14	16	90	=	90
6	D (dummy)	0	0	20	0	20	=	20
7	Total flow in	60	80	70	55			245
8	sign	=	=	=	=			265
9	Demand	60	80	70	55			265
10								
11		shipping costs per package						
12			Pharmacy Stores					
13	Warehouses	1	2	3	4			
14	A	$40	$50	$70	$60			
15	B	$50	$60	$40	$30			
16	C	$30	$70	$60	$50			
17	D (dummy)	$0	$0	$0	$0			
18								
19	total costs	$10,050						
20								

Chapter 96: Customer Flow

What the simulation does

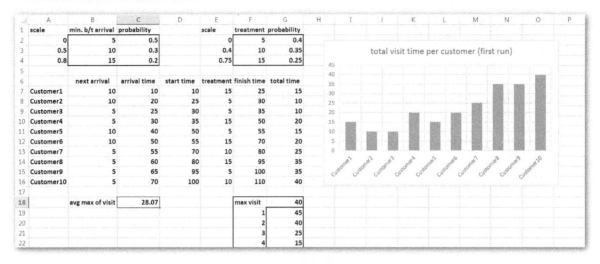

This simulation calculates the flow of patients in something like a walk-in clinic. Based on experience, we know the probabilities of patients coming in with 5, 10, or 15 minutes in-between arrivals (B2:C4). We also know the probabilities that the treatment takes 5, 10, or 15 minutes (F2:G4). Let's assume there are usually 10 patients in the morning (which we won't simulate, though). And there is only one nurse or doctor in the clinic.

Now we can simulate the flow of patients through the system (A7:G16). The chart shows how visit times can vary randomly. Because there is much volatility involved, we repeat this process some 1,000 times (F19:G1018), so we can calculate what the average maximum visit time is, based on waiting time and treatment time (cell C18) after 1,000 runs.

What you need to know

To randomly assign arrival times and treatment times, we need an extra column in front of the two probability tables shown on top of the sheet. These two columns must start at 0 and then cumulatively increase, so we can use VLOOKUP to assign these times in a random manner.

Other formulas on the sheet are shown in the screen shot below.

What you need to do

1. Place in cell A3(!): =SUM($C$2:C2), and copy 1 cell down.
2. Place in cell E3(!): =SUM($G$2:G2), and copy 1 cell down.
3. Place in cells B7:B16: =VLOOKUP(RAND(),$A$2:$B$4,2,TRUE).
4. Place in range C7:C16: =SUM($B$7:B7).
5. In D7: =C7. In D8:D16: =IF(C8<F7,F7,F7+(C8-F7)).
6. Place in cells E7:E16: =VLOOKUP(RAND(),$E$2:$F$4,2,TRUE).
7. Place in cells F7:F16: =D7+E7.
8. Place in cells G7:G16: =F7-C7.
9. Place in cell G18: =MAX(G7:G16).
10. Select range F18:G1018 for a *Data Table* with only column input from any empty cell outside the range.
11. Place in cell C18: =AVERAGE(G18:G1018).
12. The average MAX time in the clinic appears to oscillate around 27-28 minutes, but the time per patient may vary quite a bit (compare the two column charts shown below for 1 run).

Chapter 97: Project Delays

What the simulation does

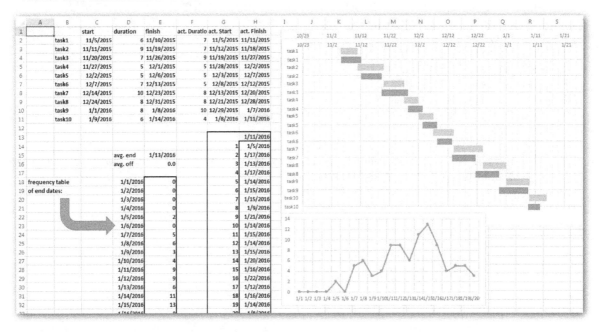

Here we have a sequence of tasks that start at a certain day, have an estimated duration, and then end, to be followed by the next task. So the entire project is supposed to be finished on the date shown in cell E11. For simplicity reasons, we treat all dates the same—as workdays, that is.

Usually, however, there are random changes in the duration (column F)—say, up to 2 days shorter or longer than anticipated. Such random changes would obviously affect the end date of the total project. In cell H11, we calculate what the actual end date of the project probably would be.

We run this project some 100 times in a *Data Table* (G14:H151), so we can calculate what on average the "real" end date of the project would be after random variations in duration per task. We then calculate how the final end dates for each run are distributed in a frequency chart (in the right lower corner of the sheet).

What you need to know

The only new function in this simulation is DAYS. It has two arguments: DAYS(end_date, start_date). It returns the number of days between end_date and start_date. If the number of days is negative, then the end-date is earlier than the start-date.

The chart in the upper right of the sheet is a so-called Gantt chart. In Excel, it is a *stacked* bar chart with two series of values, of which the first series, or stack, has no fill color or line color, so it is actually invisible.

We have actually 2 stacked charts here. They both use B2:B11 as categories. One is based on series G2:G11 (invisible) and series F2:F11. The other one is plotted from series C2:C11 (invisible) and series D2:D11. The second chart has a plot area with no fill, so it is transparent. You can lay it over the first one with a slight offset down.

What you need to do

1. Place in cell C3 (not C2): =E2+1, and copy down to cell C11.
2. Place in cell E2: =C2+D2-1, and copy down to cell E11.
3. Place in cell F1: =D2+RANDBETWEEN(-2,2). If you don't have RANDBETWEEN, use: =D2+(-2+INT(RAND()*5)).
4. Place in cell G2: =C2.
5. Place in cell H2: =G2+F2-1 and copy down.
6. Place in cell G3: =H2+1, and copy down.
7. Link cell H13 to cell H11.
8. Select the range G13:H114 for a *Data Table* with only column input from any empty cell outside the range.
9. Place in cell E15: =AVERAGE($H$13:$H$114).
10. Place in cell E16: =DAYS(E15,E11).
11. Select range E18:E37 at once and insert the following array formula: =FREQUENCY($H$13:$H$114,$D$18:$D$37). Don't forget *Ctrl Shift Enter*.
12. As always, results may vary!

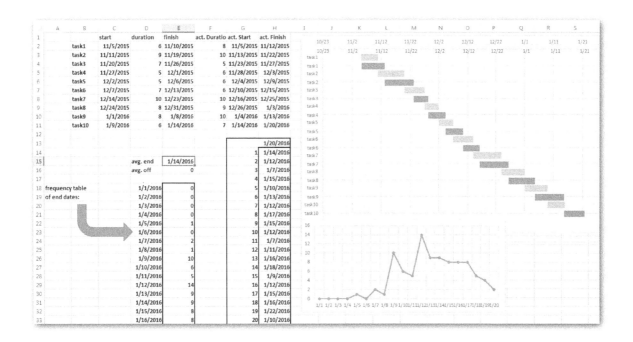

VII. Finance

Chapter 98: Smoothing Data

What the simulation does

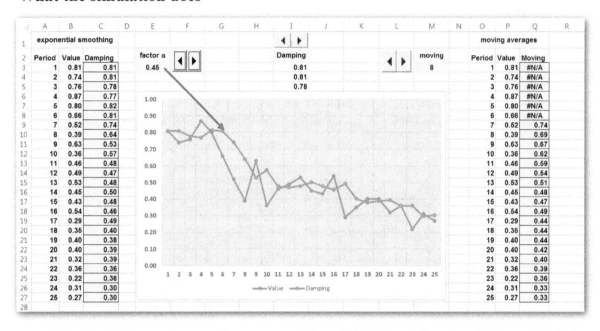

This simulation creates "moving averages" in column Q and "exponential smoothing" in column C for any financial values (columns B or P). In column I, the user can decide with a spinbutton control on top of cell I1 which one of the two options to display in the chart. With two other spinbutton controls the smoothing factor (E3) and the moving term factor (M3) can be changed. In either case, the sheet simulates what happens when we reduce the amount of "noise" in our data with a certain factor.

What you need to know

A moving average is often called a "smoothed" version of the original series of values because short-term averaging has the effect of smoothing out the bumps in the original series. By adjusting the degree of smoothing (the width of the moving average), we can hope to strike some kind of optimal balance between the performance of the mean and random walk models.

However, the simple moving average model has the undesirable property that it treats the last k observations the same as earlier ones, and thus completely ignores all preceding observations. Intuitively, past data should be discounted in a more gradual fashion—for example, the most recent observation should get a little more weight than 2nd most recent, and the 2nd most recent should get a little more weight than the 3rd most recent, and so on. The simple exponential smoothing (SES) model accomplishes this. Let α (alpha) denote a "smoothing constant" (a number between 0 and 1). So the formula used would look like the one shown above.

$$S_t = \alpha X_{t-1} + (1-\alpha) S_{t-1}$$

Both models assume that there is no trend of any kind in the data—which is usually OK or at least not-too-bad for 1-step-ahead forecasts when the data is relatively noisy. There are other exponential smoothing models that we will not discuss here. Keep in mind that trends evident today may slacken in the future due to various causes. For this reason, simple exponential smoothing often performs well enough, despite its "naïve" horizontal trend extrapolation.

What you need to do

1. Place a spinbutton control next to cell E3: Min 1 | Max 100 | LinkedCell F3.
2. Place in cell E3: =F3/100.
3. Place in cell C3: =B3.
4. Place in cells C4:C27: =$E$3*B3+(1-$E$3)*C3.
5. Place a spinbutton control next to cell M3: Min 1 | Max 100 | LinkedCell M3.
6. Place in cells Q3:Q27 the following formula with a nested OFFSET function: =IF(ROW()>=($M$3+1),AVERAGE(OFFSET(P3,-$M$3+1,0,$M$3)),NA()).
7. Place a spinbutton control over cell I1: Min 1 | Max 2 | LinkedCell I1.
8. Place in cells I2:I27: =IF($I$1=1,C2,Q2). These cells are partly behind the chart.
9. Now the spinbutton control on top of column I regulates whether column I displays the moving average values or the exponential smoothing values. And the chart in the center is linked to that column.

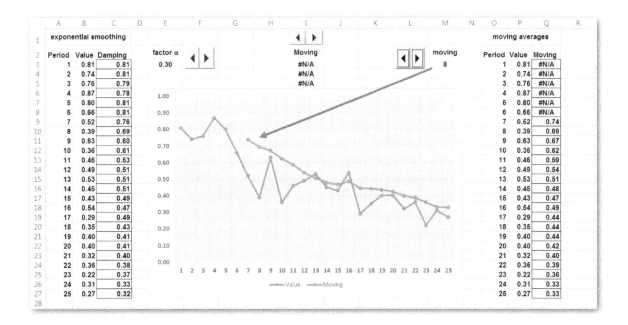

Chapter 99: Investing Optimized

What the simulation does

	A	B	C	D	E	F	G
1	Portfolio	2,000,000					CONSTRAINTS
2							
3	Investment	% Yield	Amount	Yield	% Portfolio		
4	Car Loans	7.50%	500,000	$ 37,500.00	25%		at least 2x CDs
5	Real Estate Loans	6.70%	500,000	$ 33,500.00	25%		
6	Unsecured Loans	9.10%	500,000	$ 45,500.00	25%		no more than 25% of portfolio
7	Bank CDs	4.30%	500,000	$ 21,500.00	25%		at least 10% of portfolio
8	Total		2,000,000	$ 138,000.00	100%		the portfolio fully spent
9							
10	Total Yield	6.90%					

Some person or company has a portfolio of $2,000,000 that has to be invested in certain loans or bank CDs in such a way that the total annual yield is as high as possible.

However, there are some conditions:

1. The investment in car loans should be at least 2x higher than the investment in bank CDs.
2. The investment in unsecured loans has to be less than 25% of the total portfolio.
3. The investment in bank CDs has to be at least 10% of the total portfolio.
4. The portfolio has to be fully invested.

What you need to know

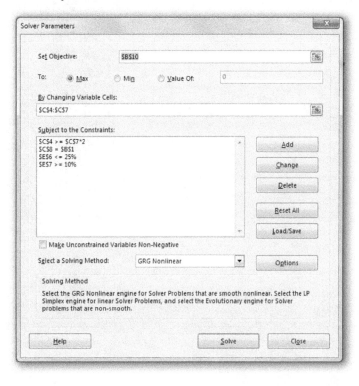

This is a perfect job for Excel's *Solver* (see Chapter 66).

This time the total yield (in cell B10 containing a formula) has to be maximized, by changing cells C4:C7 which contain no formulas.

The constraints are also rather obvious (see to the left), according to conditions the investor has.

Solver will come up with an optimal yield of 7.4% in cell B10.

Obviously changing conditions or manually changing yield percentages must have an impact on this outcome.

What you need to do

1. Give all cells containing a formula a conditional format: =ISNUMERIC(A1).
2. Place in cell C8: =SUM(C4:C7).
3. Place in cells D4:D7: =B4*C4.
4. Place in cells E4:E7: =C4/$C$8.
5. Place in cells C8:E8: =SUM(C4:C7).
6. Place in cell B10: =D8/C8.
7. Run with the settings we discussed already on the previous page.
8. The outcome is shown below: a highest yield of 7.4%.

	A	B	C	D	E	F	G	H
1	Portfolio	2,000,000					CONSTRAINTS	
2								
3	Investment	% Yield	Amount	Yield	% Portfolio			
4	Car Loans	7.50%	908,333	$ 68,125.00	45%		C4>=(C7*2)	
5	Real Estate Loans	6.70%	408,333	$ 27,358.33	20%			
6	Unsecured Loans	9.10%	483,333	$ 43,983.33	24%		E6<=25%	
7	Bank CDs	4.30%	200,000	$ 8,600.00	10%		E7>=10%	
8	Total		2,000,000	$ 148,066.67	100%		C8 = C1	
9								
10	Highest Yield	7.40%						

Chapter 100: Return on Investment (ROI)

What the simulation does

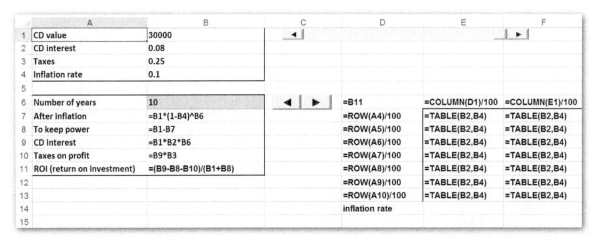

In this simulation, we want to calculate our return on an investment, but also take into consideration the cost of inflation and taxes for this investment.

The sheet simulates the return on investment (ROI) when buying bank CDs for a certain amount of money (B1, regulated by a scrollbar control), with the assumption that these have a fixed interest rate (B2), a certain fixed inflation rate (B4), and that we are taxed at 25% for CD profits (B3). We also assume that we want to keep our CD value at its original power by, at least theoretically, putting in more money each year (B8). We do all of this for a certain number of years (B6, regulated by a spinbutton control).

The core part of this simulation is calculating the return on investment (ROI) in cell B11, based on all the cells above it. The sheet also creates a *Data Table* to be placed in D6:K13. This table shows at what return rates and inflation rates our investment becomes profitable. It uses a link to that calculation in B11. Based on this calculation, the two-dimensional *Data Table* shows what the ROI is for a range of changes in CD interest (top row) and in inflation rate for a certain period (column D).

What you need to know

There is not much new on this sheet. Here are the formulas:

What you need to do

1. Place a scrollbar control next to cell B1: Min 1000 | Max 30000 | SmallChange 1000 | LargeChange 1000 | LinkedCell B1.
2. Place a spinbutton control next to cell B6: Min 1 | Max 1 | SmallChange 1 | LinkedCell B6.
3. Place in cell B7: =B1*(1-B4)^B6.
4. Place in cell B8: =B1-B7.
5. Place in cell B9: =B1*B2*B6.
6. Place in cell B10: =B9*B3.
7. Place in cell B11: =(B9-B8-B10)/(B1+B8).
8. Place in cell D6: =B11.
9. Place in cells D7:D143: =ROW(A4)/100.
10. Place in cells E6:K6: =COLUMN(D1)/100.
11. Select range D6:K13 and implement a *Data Table* with B2 for row input and B4 for column input: =TABLE(B2,B4).
12. Notice that ROI is affected by the number of years but not by the CD value, which shouldn't surprise you.
13. To mark interest rates and inflation rates that yield a positive ROI, use conditional formatting as shown in step 14 and 15.
14. For D7:D13: = $K7>0.
15. For E6:K6: =E$7>0.

	A	B	C	D	E	F	G	H	I	J	K	L
1	CD value	$ 30,000.00										
2	CD interest	8%										
3	Taxes	25%										
4	Inflation rate	10%										
5												
6	Number of years	2		-5.88%	4.00%	5.00%	6.00%	7.00%	8.00%	9.00%	10.00%	CD interest
7	After inflation	$ 24,300.00		4.00%	-1.71%	-0.32%	1.08%	2.47%	3.86%	5.25%	6.64%	
8	To keep power	$ 5,700.00		5.00%	-3.42%	-2.05%	-0.68%	0.68%	2.05%	3.42%	4.78%	
9	CD interest	$ 4,800.00		6.00%	-5.05%	-3.71%	-2.36%	-1.02%	0.32%	1.67%	3.01%	
10	Taxes on profit	$ 1,200.00		7.00%	-6.62%	-5.29%	-3.97%	-2.65%	-1.33%	-0.01%	1.31%	
11	ROI (return on investment)	-5.88%		8.00%	-8.11%	-6.81%	-5.51%	-4.21%	-2.91%	-1.61%	-0.31%	
12				9.00%	-9.55%	-8.27%	-6.99%	-5.71%	-4.43%	-3.15%	-1.87%	
13				10.00%	-10.92%	-9.66%	-8.40%	-7.14%	-5.88%	-4.62%	-3.36%	
14				inflation rate								

Chapter 101: Fluctuating APR

What the simulation does

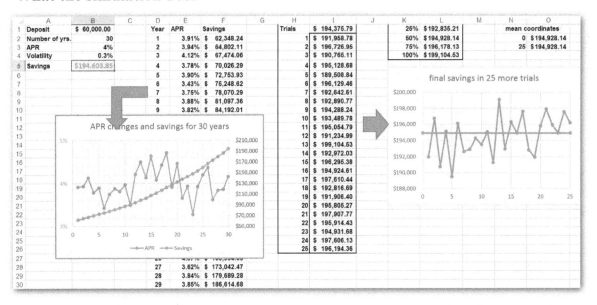

This sheet tries to simulate what the total savings would be over a period of years (B2) if the initial deposit (B1) is fixed and the annual percentage rate (APR in B3) is fluctuating with a known volatility (B4). So this sheet calculates how a fixed deposit compounds over a specific number of years with a fluctuating APR.

In column B, we set up our parameters and use a simple calculation of the final savings without considering any volatility. In the center table, we simulate how APR could fluctuate during the time period—in this case 30 years—if the volatility is 0.3% (cell B4). The left line chart shows the fluctuations of APR (column E) and uses a secondary Y-axis to plot the increase of savings (column J).

Since this center table represents only one of the many possible outcomes, we want to run additional repeats to model fluctuations. In the *Data Table* to the right, we run the calculations in columns D:F some 25 times. Column I shows the total savings of each run and plots these results in the XY chart to the right. It also plots the mean of all 25 runs, based on N2:O3.

What you need to know

Compounding a certain amount of money is based on a very simple formula: the starting amount multiplied by (1+APR) raised to the power of the number of years—or: $X*(1+APR)^{yrs}$.

The center table uses the function NORMINV or NORM.INV to simulate randomly distributed fluctuations in the annual percentage rate each year.

What you need to do

1. Place in cell B5: =B1*(1+B3)^B2. The savings are in this case: $194,603.85.
2. Place in cells D2:D31: =ROW(A1).
3. Place cells E2:E31: =NORMINV (RAND(),$B$3,$B$4).
4. Place in cell F2: =B1*(1+E2)^D2.
5. Place in cells F3:F31: =F2*(1+E3).
6. Place in cells H2:H26: =ROW(A1).
7. Place in cell I1: =F31 (this refers to the final savings amount after 30 years in the center table, based on a volatile APR).
8. Select range H1:I26 and implement a *Data Table* with no row input but any empty cell as column input (e.g. cell G1). This creates the array formula =TABLE(,G1) in range I2:I26.
9. Place in cells L1:L4: =PERCENTILE ($I$1:$I$26,K1).
10. Using *F9* recalculates the sheet and shows us some minor fluctuations around the mean (O2:O3) based on 25 runs.
11. The end result might cure you from ever doing this with your money, especially when inflation and low APRs become part of the picture.

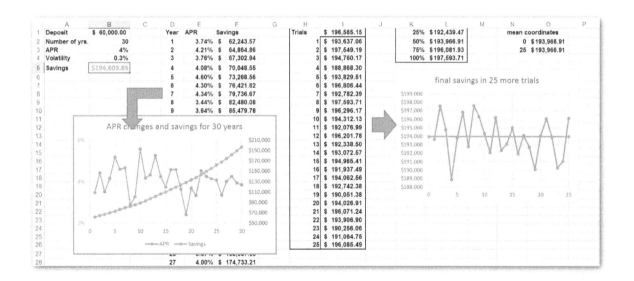

Chapter 102: Loan Payments

What the simulation does

	A	B	C	D	E	F	G	H	I	J
1			Loan	APR fixed	Years	Monthly		Total payments	$ 86,163.09	
2	◄	►	75,000.00	5.60%	5	($1,436.05)		Total interest	$ 11,163.09	
3					◄ ►					
4	start date		search for							
5	1/1/2018		Apr-18	$ 71,726.62	$(1,436.05)	$ (334.72)	$ (1,101.33)	$ (1,369.50)	$ (4,374.71)	
6										
7	Year	Month	Date	Balance	Payment	Interest	Principal	Cum.Interest	Cum.Principal	
8	1	1	Jan-18	75,000.00	($1,436.05)	($350.00)	($1,086.05)	($350.00)	($1,086.05)	
9	1	2	Feb-18	73,913.95	($1,436.05)	($344.93)	($1,091.12)	($694.93)	($2,177.17)	
10	1	3	Mar-18	72,822.83	($1,436.05)	($339.84)	($1,096.21)	($1,034.77)	($3,273.38)	
11	1	4	Apr-18	71,726.62	($1,436.05)	($334.72)	($1,101.33)	($1,369.50)	($4,374.71)	
12	1	5	May-18	70,625.29	($1,436.05)	($329.58)	($1,106.47)	($1,699.08)	($5,481.18)	
13	1	6	Jun-18	69,518.82	($1,436.05)	($324.42)	($1,111.63)	($2,023.50)	($6,592.81)	
14	1	7	Jul-18	68,407.19	($1,436.05)	($319.23)	($1,116.82)	($2,342.74)	($7,709.63)	
15	1	8	Aug-18	67,290.37	($1,436.05)	($314.02)	($1,122.03)	($2,656.76)	($8,831.65)	
16	1	9	Sep-18	66,168.35	($1,436.05)	($308.79)	($1,127.27)	($2,965.54)	($9,958.92)	
17	1	10	Oct-18	65,041.08	($1,436.05)	($303.53)	($1,132.53)	($3,269.07)	($11,091.45)	
18	1	11	Nov-18	63,908.55	($1,436.05)	($298.24)	($1,137.81)	($3,567.31)	($12,229.26)	
19	1	12	Dec-18	62,770.74	($1,436.05)	($292.93)	($1,143.12)	($3,860.24)	($13,372.38)	
20	2	1	Jan-19	61,627.62	($1,436.05)	($350.00)	($1,086.05)	($4,210.24)	($14,458.43)	
21	2	2	Feb-19	60,541.57	($1,436.05)	($344.93)	($1,091.12)	($4,555.17)	($15,549.55)	

This is basically a simple simulation. We enter estimates for loan amount (C2), for a fixed annual percentage rate (D2), and for the term of the loan (E2). The sheet calculates the monthly payments (F2). Two controls regulate the loan amount (C2) and the duration of the loan (E2).

In cell A5 we enter manually the start date of the loan. Then the simulation specifies the details for each month from row 7 down: date, balance, payment, interest, principal, cumulative interest, and cumulative principle. The length of this listing depends on the number of years (E2, with a maximum of 30 years).

In row 5 is a search option that displays the entire record (row) for a specific date.

What you need to know

This requires the Excel function PMT. Its syntax is: PMT(rate,nper,pv,[fv],[type]). It calculates the payment for a loan (*pv* or present value) based on constant monthly payments and a constant interest rate (*rate* per month) for a certain period of time (*nper* in months). The last two other arguments we can ignore here. Since we are dealing here with months, make sure to divide rate (APR) by 12, and multiply the number of years by 12. Be aware PMT returns a negative value (a value that is owed), unless you enter the present value as a negative amount (or use ABS).

In addition, we need the Excel functions IPMT to calculate the interest, and PPMT to calculate the principal. They have basically the same syntax.

We also use the function DATE with 3 arguments: DATE(year,month,day). All three arguments require integers. With the functions YEAR and MONTH we can find the year and the month integer of a certain date. Adding 1 to the month of December takes us automatically into the next year. We also use QUOTIENT again (see Chapter 67).

What you need to do

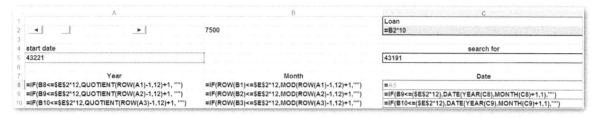

1. Place a scrollbar control next to cell C2: Min 500 | Max 30000 | SmallChange 100 | LargeChange 1000 | LinkedCell C2.
2. Place a spinbutton control below cell E2: Min 5 | Max 30 | SmallChange 5 | LinkedCell E2.
3. Place in cell F2: =PMT(D2/12,E2*12,C2).
4. Place in cell I2: =ABS(E2*12*F2).
5. Place in cell I3: =I1-C2
6. Place in A8:A364: =IF(B8<=$E$2*12,QUOTIENT(ROW(A1)-1,12)+1,""). See Chapter 115.
7. Place in B8:B364: =IF(ROW(B1)<=$E$2*12,MOD(ROW(A1)-1,12)+1,""). See Chapter 115.
8. Place in cell C8: =A5.
9. Place in cells C9:C364: =IF(B9<=($E$2*12),DATE(YEAR(C8),MONTH(C8)+1,1),"")
10. Place in cells D8: =C2. And then in cells C9:D364: =IF(B9<=($E$2*12),D8+G8,"").
11. Place in cells E8:E364: =IF(B8<=$E$2*12,$F$2,"").
12. Place in cells F8:F364: =IF(B8<=$E$2*12,IPMT($D$2/12,B8,$E$2*12,$C$2),"").
13. Place in cells G8:G364: =IF(B8<=$E$2*12,PPMT($D$2/12,B8,$E$2*12,$C$2),"").
14. Place in cells H8:H364: =IF(B8<=$E$2*12,SUM($F$8:F8),"").
15. Place in cells I8:I364: =IF(B8<=$E$2*12,SUM($G$8:G8),"").
16. In cells D5:I5: =IFERROR(INDEX($C$8:$I$364,MATCH($C$5,$C$8:$C$364,0),0),NA()).
17. Enter in C5 (manually) a full date such as 11/1/18 (formatting will change it).
18. To create a separator after each year in columns A:B, select range A8:B364 and implement conditional formatting with a formula: =$A8<>$A9. Choose a bottom border format.

	A	B	C	D	E	F	G	H	I	J
1			Loan	APR fixed	Years	Monthly		Total payments	$ 86,163.09	
2	◄	►	75,000.00	5.60%	5	($1,436.05)		Total interest	$ 11,163.09	
3					◄ ►					
4	start date		search for							
5	5/1/2018		Aug-18	$ 71,726.62	$(1,436.05)	$ (334.72)	$ (1,101.33)	$ (1,369.50)	$ (4,374.71)	
6										
7	Year	Month	Date	Balance	Payment	Interest	Principal	Cum.Interest	Cum.Principal	
8	1	1	May-18	75,000.00	($1,436.05)	($350.00)	($1,086.05)	($350.00)	($1,086.05)	
9	1	2	Jun-18	73,913.95	($1,436.05)	($344.93)	($1,091.12)	($694.93)	($2,177.17)	
10	1	3	Jul-18	72,822.83	($1,436.05)	($339.84)	($1,096.21)	($1,034.77)	($3,273.38)	
11	1	4	Aug-18	71,726.62	($1,436.05)	($334.72)	($1,101.33)	($1,369.50)	($4,374.71)	
12	1	5	Sep-18	70,625.29	($1,436.05)	($329.58)	($1,106.47)	($1,699.08)	($5,481.18)	
13	1	6	Oct-18	69,518.82	($1,436.05)	($324.42)	($1,111.63)	($2,023.50)	($6,592.81)	
14	1	7	Nov-18	68,407.19	($1,436.05)	($319.23)	($1,116.82)	($2,342.74)	($7,709.63)	
15	1	8	Dec-18	67,290.37	($1,436.05)	($314.02)	($1,122.03)	($2,656.76)	($8,831.65)	
16	1	9	Jan-19	66,168.35	($1,436.05)	($308.79)	($1,127.27)	($2,965.54)	($9,958.92)	
17	1	10	Feb-19	65,041.08	($1,436.05)	($303.53)	($1,132.53)	($3,269.07)	($11,091.45)	
18	1	11	Mar-19	63,908.55	($1,436.05)	($298.24)	($1,137.81)	($3,567.31)	($12,229.26)	
19	1	12	Apr-19	62,770.74	($1,436.05)	($292.93)	($1,143.12)	($3,860.24)	($13,372.38)	
20	2	1	May-19	61,627.62	($1,436.05)	($350.00)	($1,086.05)	($4,210.24)	($14,458.43)	
21	2	2	Jun-19	60,541.57	($1,436.05)	($344.93)	($1,091.12)	($4,555.17)	($15,549.55)	
22	2	3	Jul-19	59,450.45	($1,436.05)	($339.84)	($1,096.21)	($4,895.01)	($16,645.76)	
23	2	4	Aug-19	58,354.24	($1,436.05)	($334.72)	($1,101.33)	($5,229.73)	($17,747.09)	
24	2	5	Sep-19	57,252.91	($1,436.05)	($329.58)	($1,106.47)	($5,559.32)	($18,853.56)	
25	2	6	Oct-19	56,146.44	($1,436.05)	($324.42)	($1,111.63)	($5,883.74)	($19,965.19)	
26	2	7	Nov-19	55,034.81	($1,436.05)	($319.23)	($1,116.82)	($6,202.97)	($21,082.01)	
27	2	8	Dec-19	53,917.99	($1,436.05)	($314.02)	($1,122.03)	($6,516.99)	($22,204.04)	

Chapter 103: Buy or Sell Stock?

What the simulation does

	A	B	C	D	E	F	G	H	I	J	K	L	M	N	O	P	Q	R
1	Date	Value		last	30		0	30	last	25		5	30	last	20		10	30
2	1/6/2016	10.0000																
3	1/7/2016	10.1191		100x next value		30x100		9.8272	100x next value		30x100		9.7956	100x next value		30x100		9.8278
4	1/8/2016	9.8428		9.7035				9.8691	10.1405				9.8173	9.9893				9.8367
5	1/9/2016	9.7680		9.9508	mean			9.8791	9.8384	mean			9.8262	10.1778	mean			9.8766
6	1/12/2016	9.7327		10.0431	9.8277			9.8257	9.7914	9.8147			9.8387	10.0744	9.8451			9.8171
7	1/13/2016	9.5452		9.7705	SD			9.8330	9.7769	SD			9.7919	9.6057	SD			9.8414
8	1/14/2016	9.8715		9.7805	0.2085			9.8485	9.9120	0.2169			9.7950	9.8682	0.2254			9.8382
9	1/15/2016	9.7237		9.8531				9.7935	9.8444				9.8028	10.1322				9.8728
10	1/16/2016	9.6760		10.0916				9.8501	9.9682				9.8472	10.1272				9.8773
11	1/19/2016	9.7488		9.8722				9.8082	9.8283				9.8669	10.0038				9.8805
12	1/20/2016	10.0208		9.6979				9.8355	9.8476				9.7609	10.1260				9.8693
13	1/21/2016	9.9352		10.1445				9.7998	9.8072				9.8042	9.9503				9.8079
14	1/22/2016	9.7534		9.7576				9.8257	9.7313				9.8219	9.6194				9.8565
15	1/23/2016	9.5016		9.6143				9.8342	10.3164				9.8380	9.8219				9.8651
16	1/26/2016	9.3413		9.8684				9.8193	10.0420				9.8071	9.7908				9.8453
17	1/27/2016	9.5549		9.5406				9.8296	9.8291				9.8123	9.6531				9.8390
18	1/28/2016	9.6117		9.9862				9.8109	9.4475				9.8023	10.4529				9.8511
19	1/29/2016	9.7390		9.9978				9.8194	10.0000				9.8215	9.7450				9.8378
20	1/30/2016	9.7280		10.1594				9.8564	9.7957				9.8309	9.7455				9.8665
21	2/2/2016	9.8868		9.9351				9.8002	9.8039				9.8388	10.0903				9.8580
22	2/3/2016	9.7447		9.5852				9.8128	9.4926				9.8078	10.2956				9.8476
23	2/4/2016	9.8565		9.5422				9.8419	9.4119				9.8073	9.8840				9.8378
24	2/5/2016	10.1111		9.7042				9.8292	9.3135				9.8218	9.5825				9.8255
25	2/6/2016	10.1196		9.9816				9.8168	9.9281				9.8620	10.1308				9.8867
26	2/10/2016	10.0697		9.5152				9.8298	9.6681				9.8236	9.7396				9.8215
27	2/11/2016	10.0107		9.8886				9.7866	9.7216				9.8219	9.5016				9.8279
28	2/12/2016	9.8565		9.7961				9.8387	9.8082				9.8072	10.1860				9.8742
29	2/13/2016	10.1111		9.9352				9.8206	9.9716				9.8291	9.7391				9.8343
30	2/16/2016	10.1196		9.7336				9.7925	9.6726				9.8079	10.2564				9.7990
31	2/17/2016	9.8300		9.7699				9.8429	9.6541				9.8078	9.7003				9.8717
32				9.5065				9.8179	9.5843				9.8329	10.1447				9.8650
33				9.7850				9.8658	9.8517				9.8393	10.0889				9.8591
34				10.1509					9.9480					9.6947				
35				9.5854			mean of means	9.8278	9.9396			mean of means	9.8190	10.1464			mean of means	9.8488
36				9.3749			last value	9.8300	9.5011			last value	9.8300	9.1947			last value	9.8300
37				9.9801			buy or sell	sell	9.6401			buy or sell	sell	9.9345			buy or sell	buy
38				9.8731					9.9350					10.0943				

Based on the performance of a certain stock in the recent past, this simulation tries to anticipate its value the next day, so we can decide whether it is best to buy or to sell.

Since there is much uncertainty involved, we need to consider the mean and standard deviation of its past performance, and based on this information, the simulation projects some 100 (or more) normally distributed values in order to somewhat harness volatility.

Part of the decision is determined by how far we want to go back in history. So the simulation offers us three time frames of past history: 30 days back in columns D:G, 25 days back in columns I:L, and 20 days back in columns N:Q. These time frames can be manually adjusted.

Based on this information of previous performance, the simulation uses the following rule: if the projected value (after 30x100 runs) is greater than the most recent value plus 0.01 times the SD, go for "buy"; if it is less than the most recent value minus 0.01 times the SD, then go for "sell," otherwise don't do anything. (Adjust this rule to what you deem more appropriate.)

The simulation displays the verdict for each period in row 37, so the user can determine which decision to make based on this information.

What you need to know

Since we need to step back in time, the function OFFSET is essential here (or INDEX for that matter; see Chapter 14). I decided on OFFSET over INDEX.

For example, *OFFSET(A1,0,0):OFFSET(A1,9,0)* would refer to A1:A10.

What you need to do

	D	E	F	G
1	last 30		=COUNT($B:$B)-E1	=COUNT($B:$B)
2				
3	100x next value		30x100	=AVERAGE(D:D)
4	=NORM.INV(RAND(),$E$6,$E$8)			=TABLE(,E3)
5	=NORM.INV(RAND(),$E$6,$E$8)	mean		=TABLE(,E3)
6	=NORM.INV(RAND(),$E$6,$E$8)	=AVERAGE(OFFSET($B$2,$F$1,0):OFFSET($B$2,$G$1,0))		=TABLE(,E3)
7	=NORM.INV(RAND(),$E$6,$E$8)	SD		=TABLE(,E3)
8	=NORM.INV(RAND(),$E$6,$E$8)	=STDEV.S(OFFSET($B$2,$F$1,0):OFFSET($B$2,$G$1,0))		=TABLE(,E3)
9	=NORM.INV(RAND(),$E$6,$E$8)			=TABLE(,E3)
10	=NORM.INV(RAND(),$E$6,$E$8)			=TABLE(,E3)
11	=NORM.INV(RAND(),$E$6,$E$8)			=TABLE(,E3)
12	=NORM.INV(RAND(),$E$6,$E$8)			=TABLE(,E3)
13	=NORM.INV(RAND(),$E$6,$E$8)			=TABLE(,E3)

1. Place in cells F1, K1, and P1: =COUNT($B:$B)-E1.
2. Place in cells G1, L1, and Q1: =COUNT($B:$B).
3. Place in cells D4:D103: =NORM.INV(RAND(),$E$6,$E$8).
4. Place in cells I4:I103: =NORM.INV(RAND(),$J$6,$J$8).
5. Place in cells N4:N103: =NORM.INV(RAND(),$O$6,$O$8).
6. Place in cell E6: =AVERAGE(OFFSET($B$2,$F$1,0):OFFSET($B$2,$G$1,0)).
7. Place in cell E8: =STDEV.S(OFFSET($B$2,$F$1,0):OFFSET($B$2,$G$1,0)).
8. Place in cell J6: =AVERAGE(OFFSET($B$2,$K$1,0):OFFSET($B$2,$L$1,0)).
9. Place in cell J8: =STDEV.S(OFFSET($B$2,$K$1,0):OFFSET($B$2,$L$1,0)).
10. Place in cell O6: =AVERAGE(OFFSET($B$2,$P$1,0):OFFSET($B$2,$Q$1,0)).
11. Place in cell O8: =STDEV.S(OFFSET($B$2,$P$1,0):OFFSET($B$2,$Q$1,0)).
12. Place in cell G3: =AVERAGE(D:D).
13. Place in cell L3: =AVERAGE(I:I).
14. Place in cell Q3: =AVERAGE(N:N).
15. Implement 3 *Data Tables*: =TABLE(,E3) | =TABLE(,J3) | =TABLE(,O3).
16. In G35: =AVERAGE(G3:G33). In L35: =AVERAGE(L3:L33). In Q35: =AVERAGE(Q3:Q33).
17. Place in cells G36, L36, and Q36: =INDEX($B:$B,COUNTA($B:$B)).
18. Place in cell G37: =IF(G35>(G36+E8*0.01),"buy",IF(G35<(G36-E8*0.01),"sell","-")).
19. Place in cell L37: =IF(L35>(L36+J8*0.01),"buy",IF(L35<(L36-J8*0.01),"sell","-")).
20. Place in cell Q37: =IF(Q35>(Q36+O8*0.01),"buy",IF(Q35<(Q36-O8*0.01),"sell","-")).
21. As to be expected, results may vary, but most of the time we get *sell* signals based on a past performance of 30 and 25 days back, but a *buy* signal for only 20 days back.

	A	B	C	D	E	F	G	H	I	J	K	L	M	N	O	P	Q
1	Date	Value		last	30	0	30		last	25	5	30		last	20	10	30
2	1/6/2016	10.0000															
3	1/7/2016	10.1191		100x next value		30x100	9.8624		100x next value		30x100	9.8208		100x next value		30x100	9.8230
4	1/8/2016	9.8428		9.6635			9.8005		9.7809			9.7751		9.6324			9.8398
5	1/9/2016	9.7680		9.9658	mean		9.8532		9.7999	mean		9.7891		9.9665	mean		9.8167
6	1/12/2016	9.7327		9.7702	9.8277		9.8495		9.6788	9.8147		9.7949		9.8466	9.8451		9.8414
7	1/13/2016	9.5452		10.0389	SD		9.8355		9.6996	SD		9.8232		10.3654	SD		9.8241
8	1/14/2016	9.8715		9.8033	0.2085		9.8081		9.8267	0.2169		9.7767		10.1633	0.2254		9.8528
34				10.0290					10.0498					10.0993			
35				9.5765		mean of means	9.8256		9.9031		mean of means	9.8135		9.4134		mean of means	9.8448
36				9.7199		last value	9.8300		9.5078		last value	9.8300		9.6995		last value	9.8300
37				9.8032		buy or sell	sell		9.4601		buy or sell	sell		9.9878		buy or sell	buy
38				9.7662					9.8752					9.6722			
39				9.9802					10.2481					10.1958			
40				9.6434					9.4434					9.3666			

Chapter 104: S&P500 Performance

What the simulation does

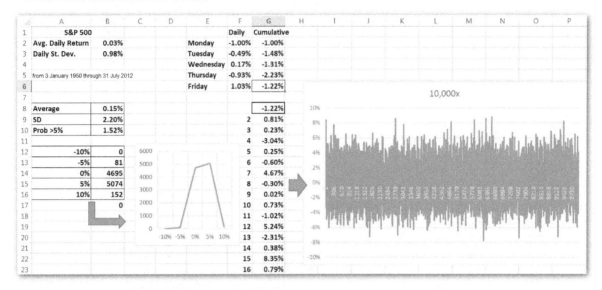

Based on S&P500 data from 1950 to 2012, the simulation uses an average daily return value (in cell B2) and a daily standard deviation value (in cell B3) for past S&P500 performance. This information is used to calculate what the percentage would be at the end of a week (in cell G6).

Then we repeat this volatile calculation some 10,000 times. There is going to be quite some volatility as the chart to the right shows, but because we have a reasonable sample size now, we can find a more reliable average and SD through the array of 10,000 values, as cells B8:B10 show. This may give us a bit more certainty in the midst of uncertainties.

What you need to know

	A	B	C	D	E	F	G
1	S&P 500					Daily	Cumulative
2	Avg. Daily Return	0.0003			Monday	=NORMINV(RAND(),$B$2,$B$3)	=F2
3	Daily St. Dev.	0.0098			Tuesday	=NORMINV(RAND(),$B$2,$B$3)	=(F3+1)*(G2+1)-1
4					Wednesday	=NORMINV(RAND(),$B$2,$B$3)	=(F4+1)*(G3+1)-1
5	from 3 January 1950 throu				Thursday	=NORMINV(RAND(),$B$2,$B$3)	=(F5+1)*(G4+1)-1
6					Friday	=NORMINV(RAND(),$B$2,$B$3)	=(F6+1)*(G5+1)-1
7							

The historical values in column B are used in column F with a NORMINV Excel function.

In cell G6, we calculate the cumulative end-of-week result: *(daily % + 1) * (previous cumulative % + 1) – 1*.

After 10,000 runs, the frequencies of the results are calculated in cells A12:B16, and in the chart next to them.

What you need to do

1. Place in range F2:F6: =NORMINV(RAND(),$B$2,$B$3).
2. Place in cell G2: =F2.
3. Place in cells G3:G6 =(F3+1)*(G2+1)-1.
4. Cell G8 is linked to G6.
5. Cell F9 has either the number 2 in it or a formula: =ROW(A2) which you can then copy down to E10009 or so.
6. Select range F8:G10009 for a *Data Table* with only column input to any empty cell outside the range.
7. Place in cell B8: =AVERAGE(G8:G10009).
8. Place in cell B9: =STDEV(G8:G10009), or use STDEV.S.
9. Place in cell B10: =COUNTIF(G8:G10009,">0.05")/10000. Do not forget the double quotes for criteria when you type the formula.
10. Place in cells B12:B17: =FREQUENCY(G8:G10009,A12:A16). Use *Ctrl Shift Enter*.
11. Recalculating for 10,000 runs and populating the chart may take some time depending on your machine's speed.
12. As always, results may (or should) vary, but less and less so!

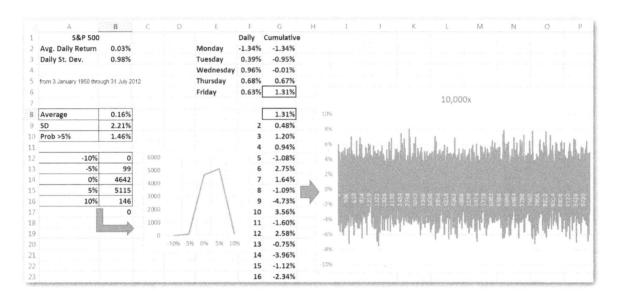

Chapter 105: Stock Market Analysis

What the simulation does

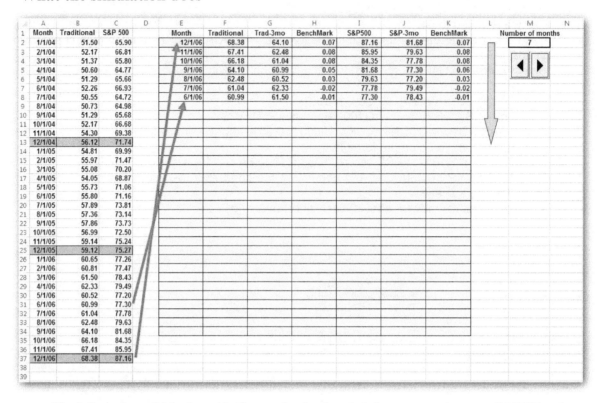

The left section of this sheet (A:C) contains hard-coded data, comparing past S&P500 values (C) with the past values of a traditional portfolio (B).

The right section analyses this information "backwards," from the most recent month on top (in this case 12/1/06) down to the previous month (11/1/06) and much further back in time, if needed. The overview "grows" back in time if you copy its first row down as far as you want to go back in history. The spinbutton control to the right regulates how many months you want to go back in time.

In addition, when new records are added at the bottom of the left section, the first row in the right section will automatically update the history from the most recent data down.

What you need to know

The only new function is COUNTA. The COUNTA function works like COUNT, but it also counts cells with text in them, such as the headers above each column.

As said before, the function INDEX is a more sophisticated version of VLOOKUP. It looks in a table at a certain row position and a certain column position. It uses this syntax: *INDEX(table, row#, col#)*. Whereas VLOOKUP works only with column numbers, INDEX also uses row numbers, which is very important when we want to look at a record that is located, for instance, 3 or 12 rows above another record (like in columns G and J).

This time we use the function ROW again, but for a different reason—to make the month go down: *row# – ROW(A1)+1*. Each time we copy that formula one row farther down, the formula subtracts one more row: *– ROW(A2)*, then *– ROW(A3)*, and so forth.

What you need to do

1. Place a spinbutton control below cell M2: Min 2 | Max 33 | SmallChange 1 | LinkedCell M2.
2. Place in cell E2: =IF(ROW(A1)<=$M$2,INDEX($A:$C,COUNTA($A:$A)-ROW(A1)+1,1),"").
   This formula finds the bottom date in column A.
3. Place in cell F2 a formula to find the corresponding value in column B:
   =IF(ROW(A1)<=$M$2,INDEX($A:$C,COUNTA($A:$A)-ROW(B1)+1,2),"").
4. Place in cell G2 a formula for a value 3 rows up from the previous one:
   =IF(ROW(A1)<=$M$2,INDEX($A:$C,COUNTA($A:$A)-ROW(C1)+1-3,2),"").
5. Place in cell H2: =IF(ROW(A1)<=$M$2,F2/G2-1,"") .
6. Place in cell I2 a formula to find the matching value in column C:
   =IF(ROW(A1)<=$M$2,INDEX($A:$C,COUNTA($A:$A)-ROW(A1)+1,3),"").
7. Place in cell J2 a formula for a value 3 rows up from the previous one:
   =IF(ROW(A1)<=$M$2,INDEX($A:$C,COUNTA($A:$A)-ROW(A1)+1-3,3),"").
8. Place in cell K2: =IF(ROW(A1)<=$M$2,I2/J2-1,"").
9. Copy the cell range E2:K2 as far down as you want to go back in history (e.g. to cell K34).
10. Use the spinbutton control to regulate how many records you want to backtrack.
11. Add new records at the end of the table in columns A:C, and notice how the table to the right nicely updates the history and its analysis.

	A	B	C		E	F	G	H	I	J	K		M
1	Month	Traditional	S&P 500		Month	Traditional	Trad-3mo	BenchMark	S&P500	S&P-3mo	BenchMark		Number of months
2	1/1/04	51.50	65.90		1/1/07	69.35	66.18	0.05	88.37	84.35	0.05		14
3	2/1/04	52.17	66.81		12/1/06	68.38	64.10	0.07	87.16	81.68	0.07		
4	3/1/04	51.37	65.80		11/1/06	67.41	62.48	0.08	85.95	79.63	0.08		
5	4/1/04	50.60	64.77		10/1/06	66.18	61.04	0.08	84.35	77.78	0.08		
6	5/1/04	51.29	65.66		9/1/06	64.10	60.99	0.05	81.68	77.30	0.06		
7	6/1/04	52.26	66.93		8/1/06	62.48	60.52	0.03	79.63	77.20	0.03		
8	7/1/04	50.55	64.72		7/1/06	61.04	62.33	-0.02	77.78	79.49	-0.02		
9	8/1/04	50.73	64.98		6/1/06	60.99	61.50	-0.01	77.30	78.43	-0.01		
10	9/1/04	51.29	65.68		5/1/06	60.52	60.81	0.00	77.20	77.47	0.00		
11	10/1/04	52.17	66.68		4/1/06	62.33	60.65	0.03	79.49	77.26	0.03		
12	11/1/04	54.30	69.38		3/1/06	61.50	59.12	0.04	78.43	75.27	0.04		
13	12/1/04	56.12	71.74		2/1/06	60.81	59.14	0.03	77.47	75.24	0.03		
14	1/1/05	54.81	69.99		1/1/06	60.65	56.99	0.06	77.26	72.50	0.07		
15	2/1/05	55.97	71.47		12/1/05	59.12	57.86	0.02	75.27	73.73	0.02		
16	3/1/05	55.08	70.20										
17	4/1/05	54.05	68.87										
18	5/1/05	55.73	71.06										
19	6/1/05	55.80	71.16										
20	7/1/05	57.89	73.81										
21	8/1/05	57.36	73.14										
22	9/1/05	57.86	73.73										
23	10/1/05	56.99	72.50										
24	11/1/05	59.14	75.24										
25	12/1/05	59.12	75.27										
26	1/1/06	60.65	77.26										
27	2/1/06	60.81	77.47										
28	3/1/06	61.50	78.43										
29	4/1/06	62.33	79.49										
30	5/1/06	60.52	77.20										
31	6/1/06	60.99	77.30										
32	7/1/06	61.04	77.78										
33	8/1/06	62.48	79.63										
34	9/1/06	64.10	81.68										
35	10/1/06	66.18	84.35										
36	11/1/06	67.41	85.95										
37	12/1/06	68.38	87.16										
38	1/1/07	69.35	88.37										

Chapter 106: Employee Stock Options

What the simulation does

	A	B	C	D	E	F	G	H	I	J	K	L	M	N	O	P	Q	R
1	Current stock price	$30.00		Year 0	Year 1	Year 2	Year 3	Year 4		intrinsic	present		$ 8.56	10%	20%	30%	40%	volatility
2	Price of option	$30.00		1.0000	0.5000	0.2500	0.1250	0.0625		value	value		2%	$ 3.70	$ 5.59	$ 8.23	$10.89	
3													3%	$ 4.43	$ 6.30	$ 8.56	$11.22	
4								$96.44		$66.44	$3.69		4%	$ 5.13	$ 6.99	$ 8.88	$11.54	
5	Expected option life	4					$72.02						5%	$ 5.79	$ 7.66	$ 9.24	$11.84	
6	Volatility	30%						$51.93		$21.93	$1.22		risk-free rate					
7	Risk-free rate	3%					$53.79											
8	Dividend yield	0%						$51.93		$21.93	$1.22							
9							$38.78											
10	Fair option value	$ 8.56						$27.96		$ -	$0.00							
11						$40.17												
12								$51.93		$21.93	$1.22							
13							$38.78											
14								$27.96		$ -	$0.00							
15						$28.96												
16								$27.96		$ -	$0.00							
17							$20.88											
18								$15.06		$ -	$0.00							
19				$30.00														
20								$51.93		$21.93	$1.22							
21							$38.78											
22								$27.96		$ -	$0.00							
23						$28.96												
24								$27.96		$ -	$0.00							
25							$20.88											
26								$15.06		$ -	$0.00							
27					$21.63													
28								$27.96		$ -	$0.00							
29							$20.88											
30								$15.06		$ -	$0.00							
31						$15.60												
32								$15.06		$ -	$0.00							
33							$11.24											
34								$8.11		$ -	$0.00							

Companies must determine and report the fair value of stock options they use to compensate employees. But because employee stock options cannot be traded publicly, their fair value is not readily available and must be estimated using option-pricing models. One could do this by building a lattice model that makes the necessary calculations in Excel.

To calculate the fair value of issued employee stock options, we develop a stock-price tree. At each node, there is either an upward movement in price or a downward movement in price. After 4 years, there are 16 nodes. In year 1, the probability of reaching 1 of the 2 nodes is 0.5 (E2), in year 2, the probability of reaching 1 of the 4 nodes is 0.25 (F2), etc. The end nodes depend on the nodes in the previous years.

How much the price goes up or down depends on the variables in the left top corner. The stock price increases by the risk-free rate, 3% (B7); is unaffected by the assumed 0% expected dividend yield (B8); and then either increases or decreases by 30% due to the expected volatility (B6).

What you need to know

Assume that at the grant date (which is year 0) the stock price is $30 (cell B1 and D19). The model assumes also that stock prices will increase at the risk-free interest rate minus the expected dividend yield, and then either *plus* or *minus* the price volatility for the stock.

In column J, we calculate the intrinsic value of each end node. In column K, we calculate the present value with the function PV as follows: *–PV(risk-free rate in B7, option life in B4, , intrinsic value in column J * probability in H2)*.

Remember, in annuity functions, cash you pay out is represented by a negative number, but cash you receive is a positive number. Therefore, we use the negative version of PV (or PV*-1).

The "fair option value" is the sum total of all possible present values in column K—either positive or 0. Based on this value, we use a *Data Table* to see the effect of different volatilities and risk-free rates.

What you need to do

1. Place in cells E2:H2: =D2/2.
2. Place in cell D19: =B1.
3. Place in cell E11: =$D$19*(1+$B$7-$B$8)*(1+$B$6). Copy this formula to all *positive* nodes (the ones upward).
4. In cell E27: =$D$19*(1+$B$7-$B$8)*(1-$B$6). Copy to all *negative* nodes (the ones downward). Notice the negative sign in the last argument.
5. In cells J4: =IF(H4>$B$2,H4-$B$2,0). Copy this to every other cell down.
6. In cells K4: =-PV ($B$7,4,,J4*$H$2). Copy this to every other cell down.
7. In cell B10: =SUM(K4:K34). This is the "fair option value."
8. Place in cell M1 a link to cell B10: =B10. This is going to be the origin of a *Data Table*.
9. Select Range M1:Q5 and start a *Data Table* with the volatility (B6) as row input and the risk-free rate (B7) as column input: =TABLE(B6,B7).
10. Conditional Formatting highlights the current situation in the *Data Table* with the following formula: =N2=$M$1.
11. Changing any variables in column B should update the situation (except for the expected option life in B5, which would require much more work).

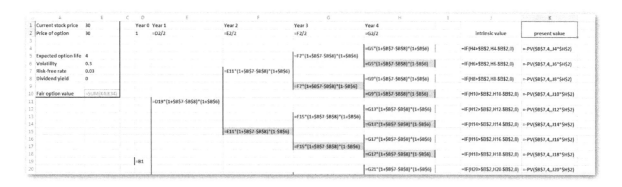

Chapter 107: Stock Volatility

What the simulation does

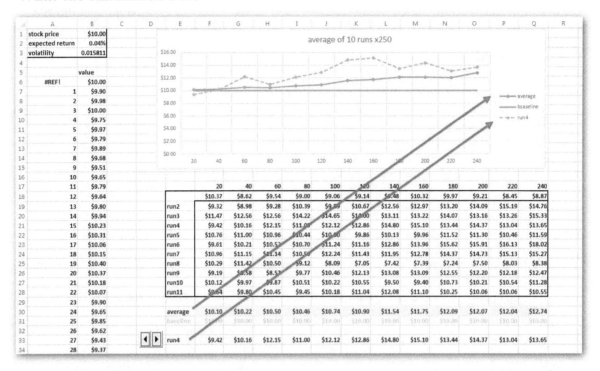

There is much uncertainty on the stock market. The simulation uses the information entered in the left top corner. The expected return in cell B3 is based on history: an expected return of 10% divided by 250 trading days per year. The volatility in cell B4 is also based on past performance: an annualized volatility of 25% divided by the square root of trading days per year.

The simulation plots in column B the changes in stock value up to a maximum of 250 trading days. To harness our uncertainty a little better, the simulation runs at least 250 iterations (B6:B255) and then repeats these another 10 times (E18:Q28) in order to beat volatility. This is to ensure that we have a better statistical chance of getting sufficient outliers (extreme values) to make the variance analysis more meaningful.

What you need to know

The main formulas are in column B (see to the left).

In row 18, we use VLOOKUP to find the return values in column B after 20 days, 40 days, up to 240 days. The average of each column in the *Data Table* is calculated in row 30 (plotted in the chart). In row 31, we mark the baseline of the original stock price (B1), which is also plotted in the chart as a straight line.

In addition, the simulation also allows you to select the results of one specific run from the *Data Table* and plots this in the chart (---) as well. Usually the corresponding curve in the chart is more fickle than the mean of all 10 runs.

What you need to do

1. Place in cell B2: =10%/250 (or replace 10% with a reference to a cell where you can enter that percentage).
2. Place in cell B3: =25%/SQRT(250) (or reference 25% in some cell).
3. Place in cell B6 a link to cell B1.
4. Place in the cell range B7:B255 the following formula based on volatility: =B6+B6*($B$2+$B$3*NORMINV(RAND(),0,1)).
5. In range F18:Q18 we find values after each additional 20 trading days: =VLOOKUP(F17,$A$6:$B$255,2,FALSE).
6. Select range E18:Q28 for a *Data Table* with only column input from any empty cell outside the range.
7. Row 30 calculates the averages after each 20-days period.
8. That range has also conditional formatting: =F$30>$B$1.
9. Row 31 below the *Data Table* creates a baseline for the chart: =$B$1.
10. Place a spinbutton control next to cell E33: Min 2 | Max 11 | LinkedCell D33.
11. Place in cell E33: ="run"&D33. This determines which one of the 11 runs to display in F33:Q33, which is also plotted in the chart.
12. Place in cells F33:Q33: =INDEX($E$19:$Q$28,MATCH($E33,$E$19:$E$28,0),0).
13. Since there is still an enormous uncertainty in these "predictions," you may want to go for many, many more runs to capture some rare extreme values. But as to be expected, results keep varying!
14. The average curve is usually partly above the baseline. It is very unusual that it is located below the base line (like the first case below). The curve for one specific run (run4: ---), on the other hand, could be almost anywhere.

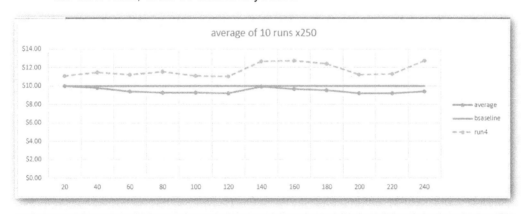

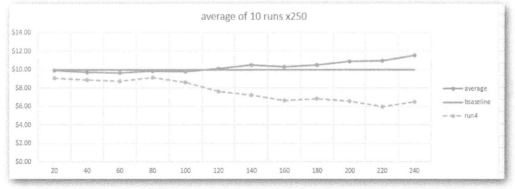

Chapter 108: Net Present Value

What the simulation does

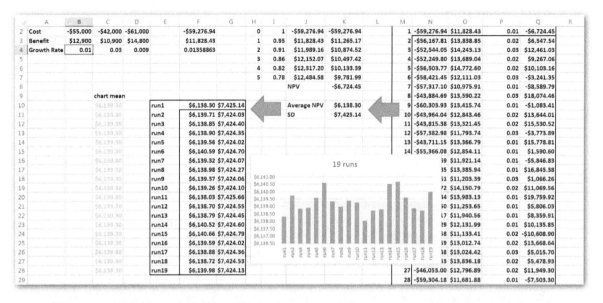

When you have three scenarios (likely, best, worst) for your costs, benefits, and growth rate (in A1:D4), you probably want a random outcome between the extremes of best and worst. Then ultimately you want to calculate the net present value (NPV) of your cash flows (in cell K10).

Here is some terminology. Having projected a company's free cash flow for the next five years, you want to figure out what these cash flows are worth today. That means coming up with an appropriate discount rate which you can use to calculate the net present value (NPV) of the cash flows. A discount rate of 5% is used in column I (see screen shot at the bottom of this page).

The most widely used method of discounting is exponential discounting, which values future cash flows as "how much money would have to be invested currently, at a given rate of return, to yield the cash flow in the future."

After running your 5 year projection (H1:K8), the simulation repeats this with some 10,000 repeats in M:Q. Then it calculates the average NPV and its standard deviation in cell K10 and K11 for all the values in column Q.

The calculation of average and SD in K10 and K11 is then repeated 19 more times in columns F:G. The results are plotted in the chart.

What you need to know

F	G	H	I	J	K
Randomly		Year	Disc. 5%	FV	PV
=RAND()*(B2-D2)+D2		0	=1/1.05^H2	=F2	=I2*J2
=RAND()*(B3-D3)+D3		1	=1/1.05^H3	=F3	=I3*J3
=RAND()*(B4-D4)+D4		2	=1/1.05^H4	=J3*(1+$F$4)	=I4*J4
		3	=1/1.05^H5	=J4*(1+$F$4)	=I5*J5
		4	=1/1.05^H6	=J5*(1+$F$4)	=I6*J6
		5	=1/1.05^H7	=J6*(1+$F$4)	=I7*J7
				NPV	=SUM(K2:K7)

What you need to do

1. Place in cells F2:F4: =RAND()*(D2-C2)+C2.
2. Place in cell I2:I7: =1/1.05^H2.
3. Cell J2: =F2. Cell J3: =F3. Cell J4: =J3*(1+$F$4) to J7.
4. Place in cell K2:K7: =I2*J2.
5. Place in cell K8: =SUM(K2:K7).
6. In N2: =F2. In O2: =F3. In P2: =F4. In Q2: =K8 (not F5).
7. Select range M2:Q10001 for a *Data Table* with only column input for any empty cell outside the range.
8. Place in cell K10: =AVERAGE(Q2:Q10001).
9. Place in cell K11: =STDEV(Q2:Q10001) (or STDEV.S).
10. Place in cells F10:G10: =TRANSPOSE(K10:K11). Don't forget *Ctrl Shift Enter*.
11. Select cells E10:G28 for a *Data Table*: =TABLE(,H10).
12. Place in cells C10:C28: =AVERAGE($F$10:$F$28). This creates in the column chart the average line as an Area chart element.
13. The calculations are extensive, so the simulation may need its time. Don't forget to hit *F9* twice (!) to get new results.
14. Notice below how the 19 runs vary, including their average base-lines.

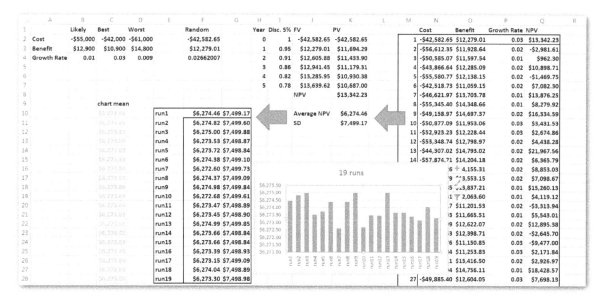

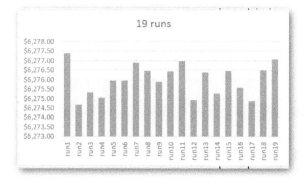

Chapter 109: Asian Options

What the simulation does

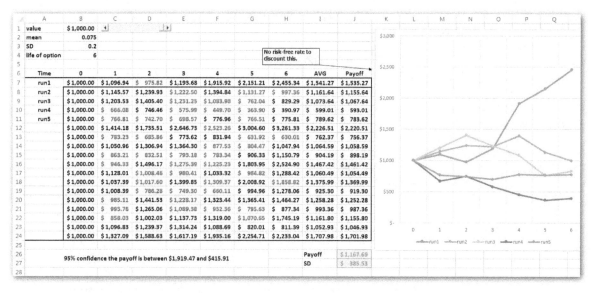

This simulation concerns an Asian option, which is valued by determining the average underlying price over a period of time. Simply put, an option contract is an agreement between two people that gives one the right to buy or sell a stock at some future date for some preset price. To price an Asian option by its mean, we need to know, at least to some degree, the path that the stock will take as time progresses.

An Asian option (or "average value option") is a special type of option contract. The payoff is determined by the average underlying price over some pre-set period of time. This is different from the usual European and American options which are valued at the expiration of the contract.

One advantage of Asian options is that these reduce the risk of market manipulation. Another advantage is the relatively low cost of Asian options. Because of the averaging feature, Asian options reduce the volatility inherent in the option; therefore, Asian options are typically cheaper than European or American options.

What you need to know

To simplify things, we will track the stock over 5 years in yearly increments (C7:H7). To derive the average value in I7, we multiply the initial stock price (column B) by the first randomly generated log-normal number (with the functions EXP and NORMINV in C7:H7) to obtain a value for year 1 (I won't go into further explanations). The result must be multiplied by the second randomly generated number (column C), and so on.

To make the predictions a bit more reliable, we repeat this some 18 times. This is done with a *Data Table*. Rows 27 and 28 report what the payoff amount would be with 95% confidence. The graph only shows the first 5 runs of the *Data Table*.

A scrollbar control can change the option's value.

The function DOLLAR converts a number to *text* with a *currency* format.

What you need to do

1. Place a scrollbar control next to cell B1: Min 10 | Max 1000 | SmallChange 10 | LargeChange 100 | LinkedCell B1.
2. Place in cell B7: =$B$1.
3. Place in cells C7:H7: =B7*EXP (NORMINV (RAND (), $B$2-0.5*$B$3^2, $B$3)).
4. Place in cell I7: =AVERAGE(B7:H7).
5. Place in cell J7: =MAX (0,I7-$B$4).
6. Select range A7:J24 and start a *Data Table* with no row input and any empty cell (e.g. cell A5) as a column input: =TABLE(,A5).
7. Place in cell J18: =AVERAGE(J7:J16).
8. Place in cell J19: =STDEV (J7:J16).
9. Place in the merged cells A26:G27: ="95% confidence the payoff is between " & DOLLAR(J26+1.95*J27,2) & " and " & DOLLAR(J26-1.95*J27,2).
10. The range C7:H24 has conditional formatting: =C7<B7.
11. At each new series of runs (*F9*), the results for runs 1-5 can vary widely (see below). That is why we would need many more runs to get a narrower range of more reliable results.

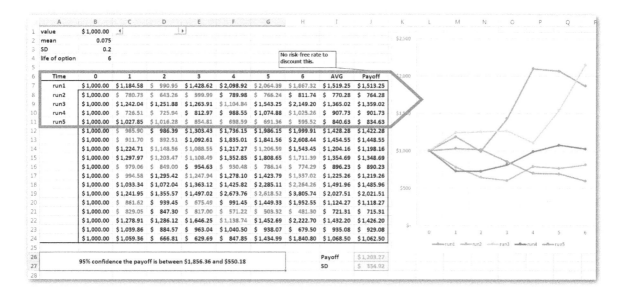

Chapter 110: Black-Scholes Model

What the simulation does

	A	B	C	D	E	F	G	H	I
1		price today	exercise price	duration (yrs)	volatility	risk-free rate (yr)	d1	d2	
2		50.00	50.00	0.25	20.0%	5.0%	0.1750	0.0750	
3							N(d1)	N(d2)	
4							0.5695	0.5299	
5							Call	$ 2.31	
6							Put	$ 1.69	
7									
8		$ 2.31	Call		$ 1.69	Put			
9		10%	$ 1.33		10%	$ 0.71			
10		15%	$ 1.82		15%	$ 1.20			
11		20%	$ 2.31		20%	$ 1.69			
12		25%	$ 2.80		25%	$ 2.18			
13		30%	$ 3.29		30%	$ 2.67			
14		35%	$ 3.78		35%	$ 3.16			
15		40%	$ 4.28		40%	$ 3.66			
16		45%	$ 4.77		45%	$ 4.15			
17		50%	$ 5.26		50%	$ 4.64			
18		volatility			volatility				
19									

The Black-Scholes formula is designed to give the value of an option on a security, such as a stock. It is calculated based on the price of the stock today (cell C2), the exercise price of the option (D2), the duration of the option in years (E2), the volatility of the stock (F2), and the annual risk-free rate (G2). The Black-Scholes model works with some fancy formulas which you can use in Excel to return the Black-Scholes Option value.

What you need to know

Options are divided into two categories: calls and puts. *Calls* increase in value when the underlying security is going up, and they decrease in value when the underlying security declines in price. *Puts* increase in value when the underlying security is going down and decrease in value when it is going up.

A *call* (cell B3) gives you the right to buy a stock from the investor who sold you the call option at a specific price on or before a specified date. For instance, if you bought a 50 October call option, the option would come with terms telling you that you could buy the stock for $50 (the strike price) any time before the third Friday in October (the expiration date). If the stock rises anywhere above $50 before the third Friday in October, you can buy the stock for less than its market value. Or if you do not want to buy the stock yourself or exercise the option, you can sell your option to someone else for a profit. But if the stock never rises above $50, your option won't be worth anything.

A *put* option (cell B4) gives you the right to sell a stock to the investor who sold you the put option at a specific price, on or before a specified date. For instance, if you bought, the option would come with terms telling you that you could sell the stock for $50 (the strike price) any time before the third Friday in October (the expiration date). What this means is, if the stock falls anywhere below $50 before the third Friday in October, you can sell the stock for more than its market value.

To simulate how this works out for different volatility values, we create two what-if tables—one for *calls* given different volatility conditions, and one for *puts* given different volatility values.

What you need to do

	A	B	C	D	E	F	G	H
1		price today	exercise price	duration (yrs)	volatility	risk-free rate (yr)	d1	d2
2		50	50	0.25	0.2	0.05	=(LN(B2/C2)+(F2+(E2^2)/2)*D2)/(E2*SQRT(D2))	=G2-(E2*SQRT(D2))
3							N(d1)	N(d2)
4							=NORMSDIST(G2)	=NORMSDIST(H2)
5							Call	=B2*G4-C2*EXP(-F2*D2)*H4
6							Put	=H5+C2*EXP(-F2*D2)-B2
7								
8		=H5		Call		=H6	Put	
9		0.1	=TABLE(A7,E2)		0.1	=TABLE(D8,E2)		
10		0.15	=TABLE(A7,E2)		0.15	=TABLE(D8,E2)		

1. Place in G2 the calculation for the *d*-factor: =(LN(B2/C2)+(F2+(E2^2)/2)*D2)/(E2*SQRT(D2)).
2. The values for *d1* and *d2* are used to calculate the probabilities that the stock price at expiration will be a certain number of standard deviations above or below the standardized mean (i.e., 0).
3. Place in cell H2: =G2-(E2*SQRT(D2)).
4. Place in G4: =NORMSDIST(G2). The variables N(d1) and N(d2) are probabilities of the stock price being used at a certain price relative to where it is now.
5. Place in H4: =NORMSDIST(H2).
6. Place in H5: =C2*H4-D2*EXP(-G2*E2)*I4.
7. Place in H6: =H5+C2*EXP(-F2*D2)-B2.
8. Place in B8 a link to H5, and in E8 a link to H6.
9. Start a *Data Table* from cell B8: =TABLE(A7,E2).
10. Start a *Data Table* from cell E8: =TABLE(D8,E2).
11. Both tables have conditional formatting to flag the data used in row 2: =B9=$E$2 for the first *Data Table*, and =E9=$E$2 for the second *Data Table*.
12. To make the simulation more dynamic, manually change data in cells B2:F2, or add scrollbar controls.

B	C	D	E	F	G	H
price today	exercise price	duration (yrs)	volatility	risk-free rate (yr)	d1	d2
50.00	50.00	0.50	25.0%	5.0%	0.2298	0.0530
					N(d1)	N(d2)
					0.5909	0.5211
					Call	$ 4.13
					Put	$ 2.90

price today	exercise price	duration (yrs)	volatility	risk-free rate (yr)	d1	d2
50.00	50.00	0.75	30.0%	5.0%	0.2742	0.0144
					N(d1)	N(d2)
					0.6081	0.5058
					Call	$ 6.05
					Put	$ 4.21

Chapter 111: Value at Risk (VaR)

What the simulation does

	A	B	C	D	E	F	G	H	I
1	Portfolio Value	$25,000.00							
2	Average return	0.152							
3	SD	0.135							
4	Confidence	99%							
5									
6	Min. return	-0.16		$4,051.42	0.14	0.15	0.16	0.17	avg. return
7	New value	$20,948.58		0.120	$3,479.04	$3,229.04	$2,979.04	$2,729.04	
8	Daily VaR	$4,051.42		0.125	$3,769.84	$3,519.84	$3,269.84	$3,019.84	
9				0.130	$4,060.63	$3,810.63	$3,560.63	$3,310.63	
10				0.135	$4,351.42	$4,101.42	$3,851.42	$3,601.42	
11				0.140	$4,642.22	$4,392.22	$4,142.22	$3,892.22	
12				0.145	$4,933.01	$4,683.01	$4,433.01	$4,183.01	
13				0.150	$5,223.80	$4,973.80	$4,723.80	$4,473.80	
14				SD					
15									

Value-at-Risk, or *VaR*, is the potential maximum loss in a portfolio (with a certain standard deviation in B3) at a given confidence interval (in B4) over a given period of time (which could be a day, a month, or a year). *Value-at-Risk*, or *VaR*, is a risk measure that answers the question "What is my worst potential loss."

This simulation calculates the minimum expected return with respect to the confidence level chosen—which means, if your confidence level is 99%, then you have 99% confidence that your loss will not be worse than the calculated *VaR*.

Specifically, it is the potential maximum loss in a portfolio (and a certain standard deviation) at a given confidence interval over a given period of time (which could be a day, a month, or a year). So you read the result in cell B8 as follows: 1% of the time this portfolio will lose more than 4K of its value each day.

What you need to know

This calculation is done with the function NORM.INV in B7. However, investments do not always follow a normal distribution; financial markets are known to have non-normal distributions, meaning they have extreme outlier events on a regular basis—far more than normal distribution would predict.

	A	B
1	Portfolio Value	30000
2	Average return	0.152
3	SD	0.135
4	Confidence	0.99
5		
6	Min. return	=NORM.INV(1-B4,B2,B3)
7	New value	=B1*($B$6+1)
8	Daily VaR	=B1-$B$7
9		

The *VaR* is for a single time period (say, one trading day). To convert that value to a longer range, simply multiply the *VaR* by the square root of the number of single periods within the longer period. Say, you calculated the *VaR* for one day and want it for a month, use the number of trading days in a month, say 22, and multiply your *VaR* with $\sqrt{22}$.

VaR is not your worst case loss but your minimum expected loss 1% of the time—so not your maximum expected loss.

What you need to do

1. Place a scrollbar control next to cell B1: Min 1000 | Max 30000 | SmallChange 500 | LargeChange 1000 | LinkedCell B1.
2. Place in cell B6: =NORM.INV(1-B4,B2,B3). This is your minimum expected return at a 99% confidence level (cell B4).
3. Place in cell B7: =B1*($B$6+1). This would be the new value of the portfolio.
4. Place in cell B8: =B1-$B$7. This is the *Value-at-Risk* per day at a 99% confidence level.
5. To see the *VaR* results for different average return values and different SDs, we use a *Data Table*.
6. Place in cell D6 a link to cell B8.
7. Select range D6:H13 and start a *Data Table*: =TABLE(B2,B3).
8. If you want to change the results for one day into a *VaR* value for a month with 22 trading days: =D7*SQRT(22).
9. Obviously, you can change the margin variables in the *Data Table* at any time and watch their impact.
10. To mark the cell in the Data Table that comes closest to cell B8, use conditional formatting:
    =E7=INDEX($E$7:$H$13,MATCH($B$3,$D$7:$D$13,1),MATCH(ROUND($B$2,2),$E$6:$H$6,1))
11. For a smaller portfolio (see below), the *VaR* is also smaller, of course.

	A	B	C	D	E	F	G	H	I
1	Portfolio Value	$15,000.00							
2	Average return	0.152							
3	SD	0.135							
4	Confidence	99%							
5									
6	Min. return	-0.16		$2,430.85	0.14	0.15	0.16	0.17	avg. return
7	New value	$12,569.15		0.120	$2,087.43	$1,937.43	$1,787.43	$1,637.43	
8	Daily VaR	$2,430.85		0.125	$2,261.90	$2,111.90	$1,961.90	$1,811.90	
9				0.130	$2,436.38	$2,286.38	$2,136.38	$1,986.38	
10				0.135	$2,610.85	$2,460.85	$2,310.85	$2,160.85	
11				0.140	$2,785.33	$2,635.33	$2,485.33	$2,335.33	
12				0.145	$2,959.81	$2,809.81	$2,659.81	$2,509.81	
13				0.150	$3,134.28	$2,984.28	$2,834.28	$2,684.28	
14				SD					
15									

Chapter 112: Historical Value at Risk

What the simulation does

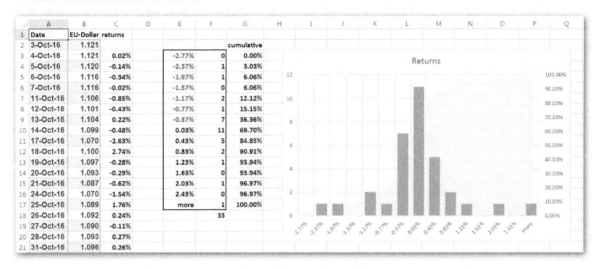

Based on historical records of the performance of a certain commodity, we can answer questions like these: (1) How bad can prices get when they really get bad? (2) What is the most that you can lose on a really bad day due to price changes? (3) What is the worst that can happen when the market hits free fall?

Conceptually *Value-at-Risk* (*VaR*) represents the projected level of losses traders need to protect themselves against, and it is used as a proxy for the amount of capital required to support such losses.

What you need to know

In this simulation[9] we used records of the USD-EUR exchange history which takes the daily exchange rate series and calculates the daily returns. Each return is calculated by the application of *LN(P1/P0)* where LN is the natural log function in Excel, *P1* is the new exchange rate, *P0* is the old exchange rate. This is approximately equal to the daily % price change in the underlying exchange rate.

The chart plots frequencies (column F) on the *left* vertical axis of a column chart, and cumulative percentages (column G) on the *right* vertical axis as an area chart. The horizontal axis has the percentages of returns (column E).

Typically *VaR* is expressed in dollar terms. However since here we only had percentile returns to work with we have expressed it in percentage terms.

To put things together, there is only a 3.03% chance (G4) that you will see a worst case loss of over -2.37% on any given trading day if you *bought* Euros, and a 3.03% chance that you will see loss of over 2.43% if you have *sold* Euros. Since the returns are calculated on a daily basis, your answer applies to one given trading day. But, of course, the historical records need to be up-to-date.

---

[9] My special thanks for part of this simulation goes to Jawwad Farid.

What you need to do

1. Columns A and B contain historical data.
2. Place in cells C3(!):C35 (depending on the number of records): =LN(B3/B2).
3. Place in cells F3:F17 at once: =FREQUENCY(C3:C35,E3:E16). Use *Ctrl Shift Enter*.
4. Place in cell F18: =SUM(F3:F17). This reflects the total number of records.
5. Place in cells G3:G17: =SUM($F$3:F3)/$F$18.

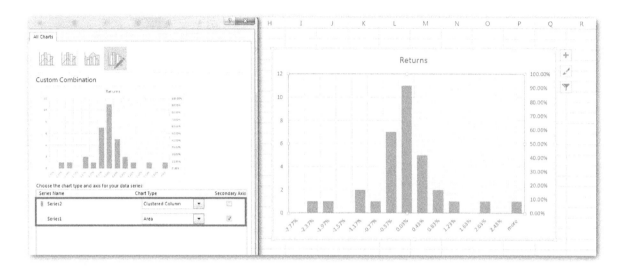

Chapter 113: Combined Value at Risk

What the simulation does

	A	B	C	D	E	F	G	H
1	two portfolios	X	Y	combined				
2	% of portfolio invested	50%	50%	100%				
3	Expected annual return	15%	7%	11.00%				
4	Portfolio SD	16.59%	9.83%	9.00%				
5	Portfolio correlation	15.43%						
6								
7		X	Y				95% percentile	99% percentile
8		-6.90%	18.11%		z-value		1.64	2.33
9		3.29%	-7.82%		portfolio value		1,000,000	1,000,000
10		24.72%	23.36%		VaR yearly	1	-148,103.50	-209,465.66
11		29.78%	4.69%		VaR weekly	52	-20,538.27	-29,047.67
12		-13.60%	-6.76%		VaR daily	252	-9,329.65	-13,195.10
13		40.47%	7.00%					
14		19.08%	23.92%				5% of the time, the portfolio will lose at least 9K	1% of the time, the portfolio will lose at least 13K
15		1.93%	2.27%					
16		0.65%	-2.40%					
17		-11.46%	17.31%					

In this simulation[10] the portfolio is a package composed of portfolio X and portfolio Y—with a certain ratio between them (B2:C2), which can be regulated with a scrollbar control. Each portfolio has its own expected annual return (B3:C3) and its own standard deviation (B4:C4). There is a certain correlation between the two performances (B5). All these values are based on the historical records in B8:B37 (for portfolio X) and in C8:C37 (for portfolio Y).

The value of the combined portfolios is located in G9 and H9. A scrollbar control can regulate this amount of investment. Based on this information, the simulation can determine the *value-at-risk* (on a yearly, weekly, and daily basis) at a 95% level (G10:G12) and at a 99% level (H10:H12).

What you need to know

The simulation limits itself to a two-asset portfolio, for the calculations become extremely complex for a highly diversified portfolio.

The formula we use here for *VaR* is the variance-covariance method of finding *VaR*: *[Expected Weighted Return of the Portfolio - (z-score of the confidence interval * standard deviation of the portfolio)] * portfolio value*.

Usually, a timeframe is expressed in years. But if it's being measured otherwise (i.e., by weeks or days), then we divide the expected return by the interval and the standard deviation by the square root of the interval. For example, if the timeframe is weekly, the respective inputs would be adjusted to *(expected return ÷ 52)* and *(portfolio standard deviation ÷ √52)*. If daily, use 252 and √252, respectively.

For the use of function NORM.S.INV, see Chapter 23.

---

[10] My special thanks for this simulation goes to Investopedia.

What you need to do

	A	B	C	D	E	F
1	two portfolios	X	Y	combined		
2	% of portfolio invested	=E2/10	=100%-B2	=SUM(B2:C2)	5	
3	Expected annual return	0.15	0.07	=(B2*B3)+(C2*C3)		
4	Portfolio SD	=STDEV.S(B8:B37)	=STDEV.S(C8:C37)	=((B2^2)*(B3^2)+(C2^2)*(C3^2)+(2*B5*B2*C2*B4*C4))^0.5		
5	Portfolio correlation	=CORREL(B8:B37,C8:C37)				
6						

1. Place a scrollbar control next to cell D2: Min 1 | Max 9 | SmallChange 1 | LinkedCell E2.
2. Place a scrollbar control next to cell H9: Min 100 | Max 10000 | SmallChange 100 | LargeChange 1000 | LinkedCell I9.
3. Place in cell B2: =E2/10.
4. Place in cell C2: =100%-B2.
5. Place in cell D3: =(B2*B3)+(C2*C3).
6. Place in cell D4: =((B2^2)*(B3^2)+(C2^2)*(C3^2)+(2*B5*B2*C2*B4*C4))^0.5.
7. Place in cell B5: =CORREL(B8:B37,C8:C37). (Or use PEARSON).
8. The rest of columns B and C is filled with record data.
9. Place in cell G8: =NORM.S.INV(0.95).
10. Place in cell H8: =NORM.S.INV(0.99).
11. Place in cell G9:H9: =100*$I$9.
12. Place in cells G10:G12: =$D$3/$F10-($G$8*$D$4/SQRT($F10))*$G9.
13. Place in cells H10:H12: =$D$3/$F10-($H$8*$D$4/SQRT($F10))*$H9.

			95% percentile		99% percentile
6					
7			95% percentile		99% percentile
8	z-value		=NORM.S.INV(0.95)		=NORM.S.INV(0.99)
9	portfolio value		=100*I9		=100*I9
10	VaR yearly	1	=$D$3/$F10-($G$8*$D$4/SQRT($F10))*$G9		=$D$3/$F10-($H$8*$D$4/SQRT($F10))*$H9
11	VaR weekly	52	=$D$3/$F11-($G$8*$D$4/SQRT(F11))*$G9		=$D$3/$F11-($H$8*$D$4/SQRT($F11))*$H9
12	VaR daily	252	=$D$3/$F12-($G$8*$D$4/SQRT(F12))*$G9		=$D$3/$F12-($H$8*$D$4/SQRT($F12))*$H9

	A	B	C	D	E	F	G	H	I	J	K	L
1	two portfolios	X	Y	combined								
2	% of portfolio invested	80%	20%	100%								
3	Expected annual return	15%	7%	13.40%								
4	Portfolio SD	16.59%	9.83%	12.41%								
5	Portfolio correlation	15.43%										
6												
7		X	Y				95% percentile	99% percentile				
8		-6.90%	18.11%		z-value		1.64	2.33				
9		3.29%	-7.82%		portfolio value		500,000	500,000				
10		24.72%	23.36%		VaR yearly	1	-102,062.60	-144,349.14				
11		29.78%	4.69%		VaR weekly	52	-14,153.55	-20,017.64				
12		-13.60%	-6.76%		VaR daily	252	-6,429.35	-9,093.15				
13		40.47%	7.00%									
14		19.08%	23.92%									
15		1.93%	2.27%									

Chapter 114: Stock Price Movements

What the simulation does

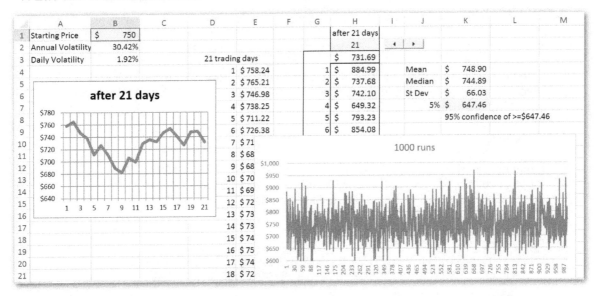

This simulation[11] makes a prognosis of what a certain stock price (B1) is going to do in the next trading days, up to 21 days. The number of days forecast can be regulated with a spinbutton control next to cell H2.

Since there is much volatility involved (B3), we need to incorporate this factor in the prognosis for each trading day (column E). So the end-result after *n* trading days will vary widely. To harness this volatility, we repeat the process of column E some 1,000 times in column H.

The simulation tells us with 95% confidence that the stock price after *n* trading days will be at least what is shown in cell K7.

What you need to know

The left chart plots the changes in stock price during the period of days determined by cell H2. This is just for 1 run. The right chart shows the volatility in outcome for 1,000 repeated runs.

To regulate changes in the number of trading days, the simulation uses the OFFSET function, which offsets cell E4 (3 columns to the left of cell H3: -3) with the number of rows selected in cell H2. This also determines that column F runs the stock price after that specific number of trading days. To make sure that column E and its chart display only that number of days, we use an IF function that activates the NA function beyond that specific number.

---

[11] My special thanks for part of this simulation goes to Matt Macarty.

What you need to do

1. Place a spinbutton control next to cell H2: Min 1 | Max 21 | SmallChange 1 | LinkedCell H2.
2. To convert an annual volatility into a daily volatility, place in cell B3: =B2/SQRT(252).
3. Place in cell E4: =(1+NORMINV(RAND(),0,$B$3))*B1.
4. Place in cells E5:E24: =IF(D5<=$H$2,(1+NORMINV(RAND(),0,$B$3))*E4,NA()).
5. Place in cell H1: ="after " & H2 & " days".
6. Place in cell H3: =OFFSET(H3,H2,-3). This is the last entry after *n* trading days (H2).
7. Select G3:H1003 and implement a *Data Table*: =TABLE(,I2).
8. Place in cell K4: =AVERAGE(H4:H1003).
9. Place in cell K5: =MEDIAN(H4:H1003). Since mean and median are very close, there is hardly any skewness involved.
10. Place in cell K6: =STDEV.S(H4:H1003).
11. Place in cell K7: =PERCENTILE.EXC($H$4:$H$1003,J7).
12. Place in cell K8: ="95% confidence of >=" & DOLLAR(K7).
13. Place in the title of the left chart a formula: =$H$1.
14. The situation after 15 trading days could be as shown below.

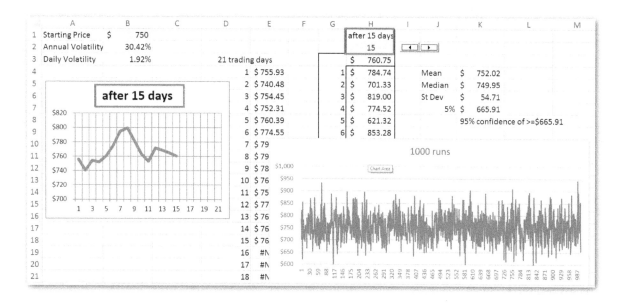

VIII. MISCELLANEA

Chapter 115: Numbering Records

What the simulation does

	A	B	C	D	E	F	G	H	I	J	K	L	M	N	O	P
1		▲	4		▲	00001		▲	5		▲	1		▲	1	
2		▼	5		▼	00002		▼	10		▼	2		▼	1	
3			6			00003			15			3			1	
4			7			00004			20			4			1	
5			8			00005			25			5			1	
6			9			00006			30			1			2	
7			10			00007			35			2			2	
8			11			00008			40			3			2	
9			12			00009			45			4			2	
10			13			00010			50			5			2	
11			14			00011			55			1			3	
12			15			00012			60			2			3	
13			16			00013			65			3			3	
14			17			00014			70			4			3	
15			18			00015			75			5			3	
16			19			00016			80			1			4	
17			20			00017			85			2			4	
18			21			00018			90			3			4	
19			22			00019			95			4			4	
20			23			00020			100			5			4	
21			24			00021			105			1			5	
22			25			00022			110			2			5	
23			26			00023			115			3			5	
24			27			00024			120			4			5	
25			28			00025			125			5			5	
26			29			00026			130			1			6	

This sheet allows you to number your records in a customized way.

Column C numbers consecutively, but starting at a specific number.

Column F numbers consecutively but uses a specific number of leading zeros.

Column I numbers with multiples of a specific number in a row.

Column L numbers up to a specific number and then starts at 1 again. This applies to situations where we have 5 workdays, 7 weekdays, 12 months, dozens, and decades.

Column O repeats consecutive numbers a multiple times—for example, the same number for the same week or so.

Each column has a spinbutton control to change settings.

What you need to know

The Excel functions used here are ROW, TEXT, REPT, MOD, and QUOTIENT.

TEXT converts a number to text, so we don't lose the leading zeros, but it has a 2nd argument where you can set the format. In this case, we use REPT to determine how many 0's we want.

MOD has 2 arguments: MOD(number, divisor). It returns the remainder after number is divided by divisor.

QUOTIENT returns the integer portion of a division; its 1st argument holds the numerator, the 2nd argument the divisor. (See also Chapter 67.)

What you need to do

1. Place a spinbutton control over cell B1: Min 1 | Max 100 | | LinkedCell B1.
2. Place a spinbutton control over cell E1: Min 1 | Max 5 | | LinkedCell E1.
3. Place a spinbutton control over cell H1: Min 2 | Max 10 | | LinkedCell H1.
4. Place a spinbutton control over cell K1: Min 2 | Max 10 | | LinkedCell K1.
5. Place a spinbutton control over cell N1: Min 2 | Max 10 | | LinkedCell N1.
6. Place in cells C1:C100: =ROW()-1+$B$1.
7. Place in cells F1:F100: =TEXT(ROW(),REPT(0,$E$1)).
8. Place in cells I1:I100: =$H$1*ROW().
9. Place in cells L1:L100: =MOD(ROW()-1,$K$1)+1.
10. Place in cells O1:O100: =QUOTIENT(ROW()-1,$N$1)+1.
11. Obviously, these numbers change for each record when you sort records. To prevent that from happening, use these steps: Copy | Paste Special | Values.

	A	B	C	D	E	F	G	H	I	J	K	L	M	N	O	P
1		▲	10		▲	001		▲	10		▲	1		▲	1	
2		▼	11		▼	002		▼	20		▼	2		▼	1	
3			12			003			30			3			1	
4			13			004			40			4			2	
5			14			005			50			5			2	
6			15			006			60			6			2	
7			16			007			70			7			3	
8			17			008			80			1			3	
9			18			009			90			2			3	
10			19			010			100			3			4	
11			20			011			110			4			4	
12			21			012			120			5			4	
13			22			013			130			6			5	
14			23			014			140			7			5	
15			24			015			150			1			5	
16			25			016			160			2			6	
17			26			017			170			3			6	
18			27			018			180			4			6	
19			28			019			190			5			7	
20			29			020			200			6			7	
21			30			021			210			7			7	
22			31			022			220			1			8	
23			32			023			230			2			8	
24			33			024			240			3			8	
25			34			025			250			4			9	
26			35			026			260			5			9	

Chapter 116: Cracking a Password

What the simulation does

	A	B	C	D	E
1	hzoi				
2	evaw		Password:	pass	
3	luql				
4	meia		Combinations:	456,976	
5	vnuu				
6	qcaj				
7	zowd		Count:	0	
8	yruo		Found in cell:	No match	
9	vxzo				
10	uzzt				
11	dbny			count	in cell
12	nras			0	No match
13	jqut			0	No match
14	yuha			0	No match
15	aryl			0	No match
16	ybuu			1	A32010
17	xixg			0	No match
18	vazj		F9	1	A61106
19	rvom			0	No match
20	bqnf			0	No match
21	ovvr			0	No match
22	saot			0	No match
23	jcrw			0	No match
24	gukh			0	No match
25	njwh			0	No match
26	bkbw				
27	qrag				

This is not a real password cracker, of course—that would at least require sophisticated VBA code. But we can still mimic part of the process. Let us assume that the password is "pass." This is a 4-letter word, so if we only use the characters a-z (no capitals), then we would still have 26^4 possible combinations—which amounts to 456,976 (D4).

Since Excel 2003 has only 65,536 rows, we will limit ourselves to that number of rows in column A. This means of course that we may not hit the right combination in one run. That's why we repeat this process some 13 times with a *Data Table*. We report in which cell the match was found or not found. The screenshot above had no match in the 1st run, but 2 in the other runs.

What you need to know

There is a function called CHAR which returns the character that comes with a certain *asci* number. The numbers 97 through 122 represent the characters a through z. (To find out what the *asci* number of a certain key is, you could use the function CODE; for instance, CODE("a") would give you the number 97.)

Now we should be able to generate random numbers between 97 and 122 by using either RANDBETWEEN(97,122) or ROUND(RAND()*(122-97)+97,0) four times in column A. In addition, we need the ampersand operator (&) which hooks characters together—four in a row, this time. Instead you could use the function CONCATENATE.

To determine in which cell the match was found, we use the functions IFERROR, ADDRESS. and MATCH. The function ADDRESS has a syntax with 5 arguments: ADDRESS(row_num,column_num,[abs_num],[a1],[sheet_text]). The 3rd argument, if set to 4, returns a relative cell address (e.g. A1 instead of $A$1; see Appendix).

What you need to do

1. The cells A1:A65536 hold the following heavily nested formula: =CHAR(RANDBETWEEN(97,122))&CHAR(RANDBETWEEN(97,122))&CHAR(RANDBETWEEN(97,122))&CHAR(RANDBETWEEN(97,122)).
2. Cell D7 counts the number of matches: =COUNTIF(A:A,D2).
3. Cell D8 finds the relative cell address of the first match, if there is one: =IFERROR(ADDRESS(MATCH(D2,A:A,0),1,4),"No match").
4. Place in cells D12:E12 at once: =TRANSPOSE(D7:D8). Don't forget *Ctrl Shift Enter*.
5. Select range C12E25 and implement a *Data Table*: =TABLE(,B11).
6. You may want to try other passwords, but to reduce calculation time, cell D2 has been set to 4 characters with validation: Text length | equal to | 4.
7. Often no match will be found in the 1st run, but perhaps in other runs (see below).

	count	in cell
	0	No match
	1	A11666
	0	No match
	0	No match
	0	No match
	0	No match
F9	1	A39686
	1	A44037
	1	A4659
	0	No match
	0	No match
	0	No match
	0	No match
	0	No match

Chapter 117: Area Code Finder

What the simulation does

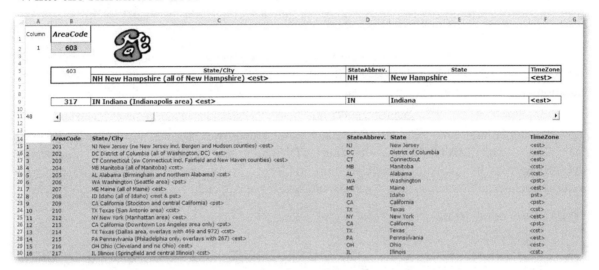

This sheet has much more on it than you might think at first sight. It has a listing of some 270 area codes with information about the state, city, and time zone. Those rows, starting in row 14, could be made hidden, but I decided to make their font white instead, so they are visible in the formula bar when you select one of their cells.

Typing a certain area code in B2 shows additional information about that particular area code in row 6, retrieved from the listing $B$11:$F$278. This could have been done with the function VLOOKUP, but I chose to use Excel's *Data Table* tool instead.

In addition, row 11 has a scroll bar that allows you to scroll through all the records and it then displays one particular record in row 9.

What you need to know

All D-functions in Excel, such as DSUM, are ideal for databases if you want to use a filter (see Chapter 86). One of those D-functions is DGET. It searches in a database for a specific field under certain conditions as specified in a filter.

In our case, DGET is used in cell B5, at the origin of a *Data Table*. The function DGET has a syntax with 3 arguments: DGET(database,field,criteria). The filter used by DGET is located in B1:B2, and must include the label or header of the field corresponding to the database headers.

In row 9 we use VLOOKUP to find a record that starts with the number shown in cell A11. The number in A11 is regulated by a scrollbar control just below it.

What you need to do

1. Place a scrollbar control in row 11: Min 1 | Max 267 | SmallChange 1 | LargeChange 10 | LinkedCell A11.
2. The rows 11:281 contain manually entered or copied records.
3. Place in cell B5: =DGET ($B$11:$F$278,A2,$B$1:$B$2). This filters for the column number placed in cell A2. The 1st argument refers to the range that holds the listing of area code information. The 3rd argument refers to a filter (in this case, located in B1:B2).
4. Select B5:F6 and implement a *Data Table* (see Appendix) with A2 for the row input and A5 for the column input: =TABLE(A2,A5).
5. Cell B2 also has a custom validation that prevents area code entries that are wrong: =ISERROR (B5)=FALSE. This validation will only work when calculation is set to *automatic*.
6. The formulas in cells B9:F9 find the record with the number shown in A11: =VLOOKUP ($A$11,$A$15:$F$281,COLUMN(B1),0).
7. Changing the area code in cell B2 should bring up a new area code record.
8. Perhaps you want to lock and protect certain cells from being manually changed (see Appendix for how to do this).

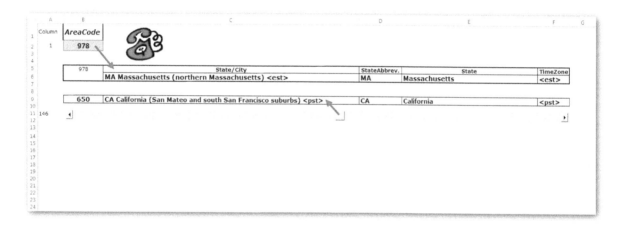

Chapter 118: Data Management

What the simulation does

	A	B	C	D	E	F	G	H	I	J	K	L	M	N
1	Patient	DOB	Systolic BP			List1	sorted/unique		List2	sorted/no-blanks		List3/dyn.	sorted/unique	
2	Bush	05/05/76	120			Reagan	Bush		Reagan	Bush		Bush	Bush	
3	Carter	12/10/45	139			Nixon	Carter		Nixon	Carter		Carter	Carter	
4	Clinton	09/06/82	160			Kennedy	Clinton		Kennedy	Clinton		Clinton	Clinton	
5	Eisenhower	07/05/77	148			Johnson	Eisenhower		Johnson	Eisenhower		Eisenhower	Eisenhower	
6	Ford	06/06/55	167			Johnson	Ford			Ford		Ford	Ford	
7	Johnson	05/05/65	145			Ford	Johnson		Ford	Johnson		Johnson	Johnson	
8	Clinton	09/06/82	155			Ford	Kennedy			Kennedy		Clinton	Kennedy	
9	Kennedy	01/11/47	137			Eisenhower	Nixon		Eisenhower	Nixon		Kennedy	Nixon	
10	Eisenhower	07/05/77	170			Eisenhower	Reagan			Reagan		Eisenhower	Reagan	
11	Ford	06/06/55	164			Clinton			Clinton			Ford	Roosevelt	
12	Johnson	05/05/65	152			Clinton						Johnson	Truman	
13	Nixon	11/08/54	155			Carter			Carter			Nixon		
14	Reagan	08/06/61	137			Bush			Bush			Reagan		
15												Truman		
16	SBP Avg. Top 5		163.2									Roosevelt		
17														
18		SBP	SBP	SBP	SBP	SBP								
19	Ford	167	164	-	-	-								

Here are some powerful single-cell array formulas that may help you manage your data better. The one in cell C16 finds the average of the top five values above it. The ones in row 19 find various systolic blood pressure (SBP) readings for one particular patient.

The three tables to the right sort a listing of patients in three different ways. The first one sorts them without duplicates (in column G). The second one sorts them without blanks (in column J). The third one does the same as the first one, but the list (in column M) is dynamic, made for future growth.

What you need to know

All the formulas used here are *single*-cell-array formulas. Array formulas can be fully customized and allow you to do almost anything you want—but the syntax can get pretty complicated. Be aware that you can always test your trials by using the *F9* key in the formula bar after selecting a part of the formula. But don't forget to end your testing with the *Esc* key, otherwise the selected part will be replaced by values.

There are also some new functions. The function LARGE returns the kth largest value in a data set. Take, for instance, the formula =AVERAGE(LARGE(C2:C14,{1,2,3,4,5})). Testing the LARGE part of the array formula with *F9* in the formula bar would give you the following outcome: {170,167,164,160,155}—which are indeed the top 5 largest values in range C2:C14.

We also use *Range Names* again. The range F2:F14, for example, can be given the name *List1*—which actually stands for $F$2:$F$14. You can assign this name as follows: Formulas | Name Manager | New | Name: *List1* | Refers to: $F$2:$F$14.

What you need to do

1. Calculate in C16 the average of the "top five" SBPs: =AVERAGE(LARGE (C2:C14,{1,2,3,4,5})). Don't forget *Ctrl Shift Enter.*
2. Instead of {1,2,3,4,5} you could also have used ROW(1:5) in this case. Again, you can always use the *F9* key to test the formula piece by piece.
3. In row 19 we display all the readings found for the patient chosen in A19. In B19 =IFERROR(INDEX($A$1:$C$14,SMALL(IF($A$19=$A$1:$A$14,ROW($A$1:$A$14),""),COLUMN(A1)),3),"-"). Don't forget *Ctrl Shift Enter* for this *single*-cell array formula.
4. Now copy B19 to the right to F19 (or even farther if you expect more results for some patients).
5. Use the *Name Manager* to assign two range names: *List1* for F2:F14; *List2* for I2:I14.
6. The third list has in column M a dynamic list that grows automatically when new names get added at the bottom. We do this as follows: Formulas | Name Manager | New | Name: *List3* | Refers to: =OFFSET ($L$2,0,0,COUNTA($L:$L)-1).
7. Instead of using OFFSET, you could also have used the function INDEX as follows: =$L$2:INDEX($L:$L,COUNTA($L:$L),0).
8. Now we are ready to implement the three array formulas.
9. Place a single-cell array formula in G2 (with *Ctrl Shift Enter*) and then copy downwards: =IFERROR(INDEX (List1,MATCH (0,COUNTIF (List1,"<"&List1)-SUM(COUNTIF(List1,$G$1:G1)),0)),"").
10. Test each part with *F9*. The first COUNTIF function, for instance, yields this: {12;11;10;8;8;6;6;4;4;2;2;1;0}.
11. Place a single-cell array formula in J2 (with *Ctrl Shift Enter*) and then copy downwards: =IFERROR(INDEX (List2,MATCH (0,IF(ISBLANK (List2),"",COUNTIF (List2,"<"&List2))-SUM(COUNTIF(List2,$J$1:J1)),0)),"").
12. Copy the M2 single-cell area formula downwards as far as you want to go: =IFERROR(INDEX (List3,MATCH (0,COUNTIF (List3,"<"&List3)-SUM(COUNTIF(List3,$M$1:M1)),0)),"").
13. If you change something in column F or in column I, the column to its right updates.
14. If you add new names to column L, column M should update as well (see below).

	A	B	C	D	E	F	G	H	I	J	K	L	M	N
1	Patient	DOB	Systolic BP			List1	sorted/unique		List2	sorted/no blanks		List3/dyn.	sorted/unique	
2	Bush	05/05/76	120			Reagan	Bush		Reagan	Bush		Bush	Bush	
3	Carter	12/10/45	139			Nixon	Bush W.		Nixon	Carter		Carter	Carter	
4	Clinton	09/06/82	160			Kennedy	Carter		Kennedy	Clinton		Clinton	Clinton	
5	Eisenhower	07/05/77	148			Johnson	Clinton		Johnson	Eisenhower		Eisenhower	Eisenhower	
6	Ford	06/06/55	167			Johnson	Eisenhower			Ford		Ford	Ford	
7	Johnson	05/05/65	145			Ford	Ford		Ford	Johnson		Johnson	Johnson	
8	Clinton	09/06/82	155			Ford	Johnson			Kennedy		Clinton	Kennedy	
9	Kennedy	01/11/47	137			Eisenhower	Kennedy		Eisenhower	Nixon		Kennedy	Nixon	
10	Eisenhower	07/05/77	170			Eisenhower	Nixon			Reagan		Eisenhower	Obama	
11	Ford	06/06/55	164			Clinton	Reagan		Clinton	Truman		Ford	Reagan	
12	Johnson	05/05/65	152			Bush W.			Truman			Johnson	Roosevelt	
13	Nixon	11/08/54	155			Carter			Carter			Nixon	Truman	
14	Reagan	08/06/61	137			Bush			Bush			Reagan	Trump	
15												Truman		
16	SBP Avg. Top 5		163.2									Roosevelt		
17												Obama		
18		SBP	SBP	SBP	SBP	SBP						Trump		
19	Ford	167	164	-	-	-								

Chapter 119: Chart Snapshots

What the simulation does

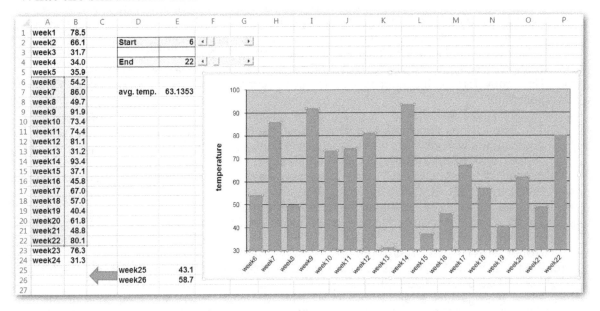

This simulation uses a chart that automatically updates when users add more rows to the columns A and B. It also allows users to determine which "snapshot" to take of the data by regulating in which row of the data to start and where to end in plotting the chart. Notice in the screenshot shown above how the chart only displays the rows 6 (E2) through row 22 (E4).

This kind of work is done by using dynamic *Range Names*, They are dynamic in the sense that they automatically detect how far to go down in columns A and B. These *Range Names* are also used in the chart itself making the chart automatically expand when the data range expands.

What you need to know

- First, we create a *Name* that refers to a dynamic range. This can be done with the OFFSET function or the INDEX function:
    - The syntax of the OFFSET function is OFFSET(start,row-offset,col-offset,#rows,#cols). The range A1:A10, for instance, would be =OFFSET(A1,0,0,10). Usually the number 10 here would be replaced with a COUNT function or so. The 5th argument (#cols) is typically not used.
    - The syntax of the INDEX function is INDEX(array,row#,col#). The range A1:A10, for instance, would be =A1:INDEX(A:A,10). Usually the number 10 here would be replaced with a COUNT function or so.

- Because the simulation also allows users to determine where to start the range, OFFSET may be the wiser option.

- Second, to have a graph work with dynamic *Range Names*, you use the SERIES function for each series of values in the chart, which has the syntax SERIES(*label,categories,values,order*). Usually the second and third argument are replaced with a dynamic *name*, so when the named range becomes shorter or longer, the graph adjusts to that changed range. This functions only works for series of values in charts.

What you need to do

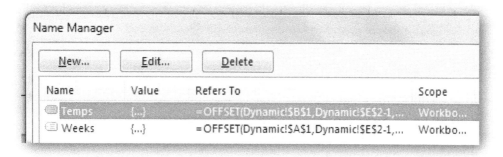

1. Create two new Range Names: *Weeks* and *Temps*.
2. The formula for *Weeks* is: =OFFSET($A$1,$E$2-1,0,$E$4-$E$2+1).
3. The formula for *Temps* is: =OFFSET($B$1,$E$2-1,0,$E$4-$E$2+1).
4. Excel usually adds a sheet name to the references automatically.
5. Place a scrollbar control next to cell E2: Min 1 | Max 100 | LinkedCell F2.
6. Place a scrollbar control next to cell E4: Min 1 | Max 100 | LinkedCell F4.
7. Place in cell E2: =IF(F2>E4,1,F2).
8. Place in cell E4: =IF(F4>COUNTA(B:B),COUNTA(B:B),F4).
9. Place in cell E7: =AVERAGE(Temps).
10. Now use the new dynamic names in the SERIES function by selecting a series of values so that the formula bar shows the SERIES function.
11. Highlight A2:A24 in the formula bar and replace it with the Range Name *Weeks*, but be careful that you do not touch or replace the sheet names in the formula bar.
12. Highlight B2:B24 in the formula bar and replace it with the Range Name *Temps*, but be careful again that you do not touch or replace the sheet names in the formula bar.
13. Now press *Enter*, and the sheet references are automatically replaced by book references because these *Range Names* function at the book level.
14. The end result is the following long winding SERIES formula in the formula bar: =SERIES(,'119-ChartSnapshots.xlsx'!Weeks,'119-ChartSnapshots.xlsx'!Temps,1).
15. When you enter new data at the bottom of columns A:B or move cells D25-E26 into the columns, you will see that the chart nicely updates after you change cell E4 also (see below).

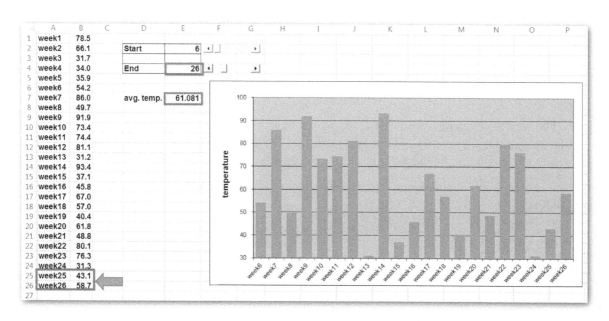

Chapter 120: Sizing Bins for Frequencies

What you need to know

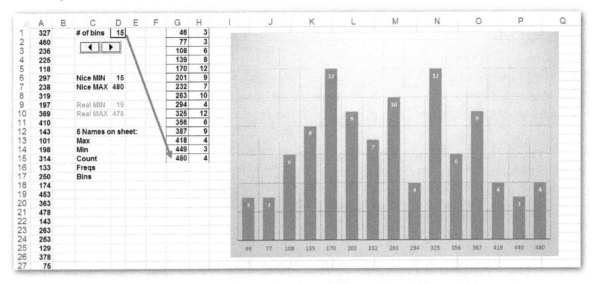

In this simulation, 100 values in column A are counted in a frequency table in columns G:H. The number of bins in the frequency table is regulated by a spinbutton that controls the value in cell D1. Obviously, the bin size has to be adjusted depending on the number of bins chosen in D1.

What the simulation does

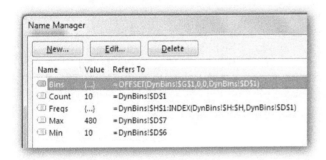

All calculations are done by using *Range Names*—two of which are dynamic with OFFSET or INDEX (see to the left).

The "real" minimum and maximum in D9 and D10 are not ideal for bin-sizing, so we use a better approach in D6 and D7 by using the MOD function. The MOD function returns the remainder after a number is divided by a divisor.

The formula in the bins range (column G) that creates the bins would be calculated this way: $=Min+(ROW(A1))*(ROUND((Max-Min)/(Count),0))$.

The bins column runs from G1:G40, so we have room for a total of 40 bins. Something similar holds for the frequency column, running from H1:H40. The bins that are not being used are hidden with a white font by means of conditional formatting.

The user of this simulation only has to decide on the number of bins, and the simulation does all the rest.

What you need to do

1. Place a spinbutton below cell D1: Min 5 | Max 40 | SmallChange 5 | LinkedCell D1.
2. Place in cell D6: =MIN(A:A)-MOD(MIN(A:A),Count).
3. Place in cell D7: =MAX(A:A)+Count-MOD(MAX(A:A),Count).
4. Create the Range Names *Max* (D7), *Min* (D6), and *Count* (D1).
5. The dynamic formula for *Bins* could be: =OFFSET($G$1,0,0,$D$1).
6. The dynamic formula for *Freqs* could be: =$H$1:INDEX($H:$H,$D$1).
7. Place in cells G1:G40: =Min+(ROW(A1))*(ROUND((Max-Min)/(Count),0)).
8. Place in cells H1:H40: =FREQUENCY(A:A,G:G). Don't forget *Ctrl Shift Enter*.
9. Select G1:H4 and implement conditional formatting with a formula: =ROW()>$D$1. Set the format to a white font color.
10. Replace ranges in the SERIES function of the chart with their new *Range Names* (see in the previous chapter how to do this).

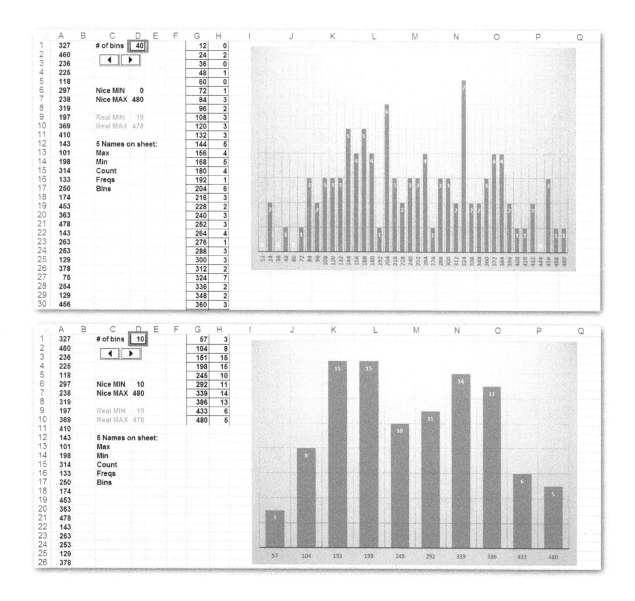

Chapter 121: Chart Markers

What the simulation does

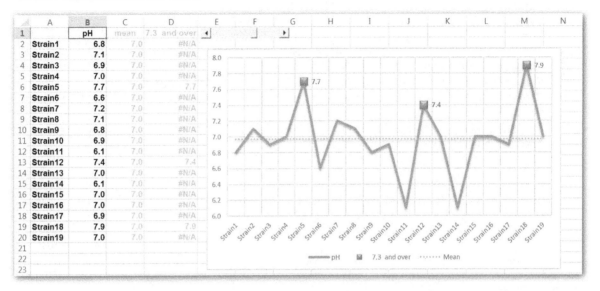

Columns A and B contain the data for this simulation: the pH value for certain strains of bacteria, or whatever. Column C contains the mean of all pH values for the baseline in the chart.

With the scrollbar control, the user can regulate which values in column B to mark in the chart as interesting, relevant, or significant—in the above case, all pH values >=7.3 (column D).

What you need to know

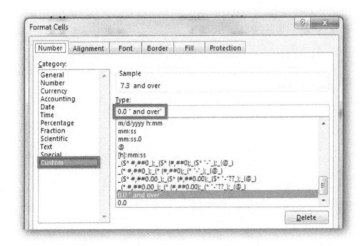

There is not much new in this sheet. We use the function NA again in the formulas of column D. The advantage of NA is that it does not show up in a chart. So when we add the data of column D as a new series of values to the chart, we will not see the "missing" values. Make sure its chart type is a line with markers.

To make sure that cell D1 has a real value in it—and not a line of text—we assign the following custom format to the cell: *0.0 " and over"* (see to the left).

What you need to do

1. Place a scrollbar control next to cell B1: Min 60 | Max 80 | SmallChange 1 | LinkedCell E1.
2. Place in cells C2:C20: =AVERAGE($B$2:$B$20).
3. Place in cell B1: =E1/10.
4. Do the formatting of cell D1 as described on the previous page, so the user can just type a number in this cell.
5. Place in cells D2:D20: =IF(B2>=$D$1,B2,NA()).
6. If you want to hide the "background" calculations of columns C and D, move the chart over them so the simulation seems more seamless.
7. If you want the columns A:B to be expandable, you need dynamic *Range Names* again.

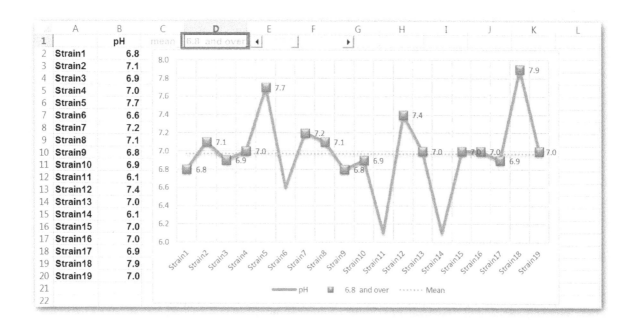

Chapter 122: Scrolling Charts

What the simulation does

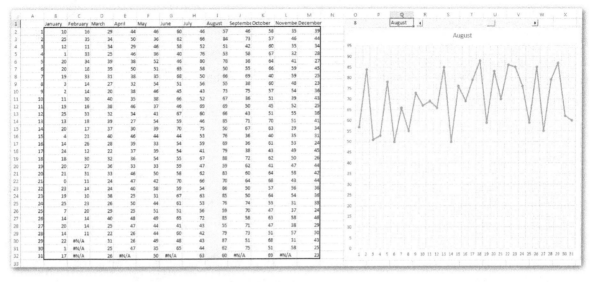

The scrollbar control above the chart to the right allows the user to scroll through each individual month in the database A1:M22. The chart shows only the temperatures or numbers of from one particular month.

Scrolling the control to the right shows the data of another month. The month that is displayed in the chart is also highlighted in the database.

What you need to know

Most of the work is done with the INDEX function.

The line chart is hooked up to column P for the horizontal axis and to column Q for the vertical axis. Column P holds the days of the month from 1 to 31.

Column Q looks up the corresponding values for the specific month that was chosen in cell O1 through the scrollbar control.

O	P	Q
10		=INDEX($B$1:$M$32,ROW(),$O$1)
	1	=INDEX($B$1:$M$32,ROW(),$O$1)
	2	=INDEX($B$1:$M$32,ROW(),$O$1)
	3	=INDEX($B$1:$M$32,ROW(),$O$1)

What you need to do

1. Make sure in the database that missing days at the end of the month have =NA() in them so they don't show up in the line chart (see rows 30 to 32).
2. Place a scrollbar control next to cell Q1: Min 1 | Max 12 | SmallChange 1 | LinkedCell O1.
3. Place in cells P2(!):P32: =A1.
4. Place in cells Q1(!):Q32: =INDEX($B$1:$M$32,ROW(),$O$1).
5. Select range B1:M32 and apply conditional formatting: =B$1=$Q$1.
6. Scrolling to another month changes the curve in the chart as well as the highlighted month in the database. That's all there is to it.

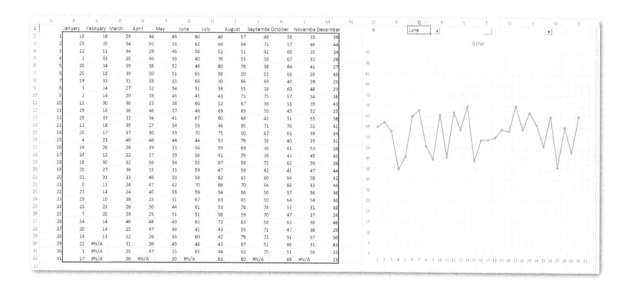

Chapter 123: Graph Manipulation

What the simulation does

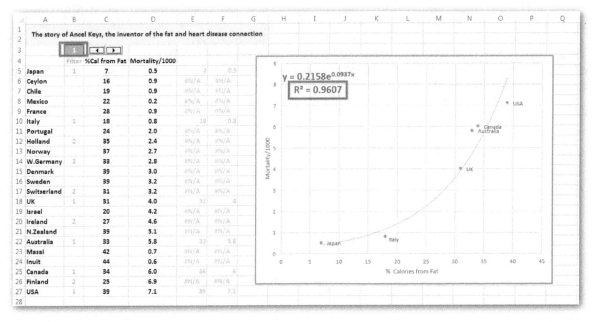

On this sheet we filter the data we would like to be plotted in a graph. The graph plots historical data used by Ancel Keys, who "invented" the fat and heart disease connection around 1956. He selected from the table to the left a series of countries that were "in line" with his hypothesis: heart disease and mortality are strongly correlated with a high consumption of fat in a daily diet. The regression line in the XY or scatter chart is certainly exponential, combined with a high R-squared value (0.96), which makes the curve a nice fit.

What you need to know

His story sounds great until we realize that his selection of countries was very biased. Had he used all the data available to him at the time (1956), he would have gotten a curve that does *not* show a strong correlation between his two variables (R-squared has plummeted from 0.96 to 0.14, as you can see to the left).

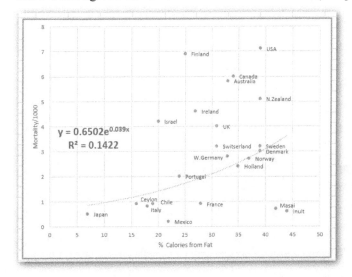

Sometimes it can be very legitimate to leave extreme values out—so-called outliers (more on those in Simulation 32). In this case, however, it is hard to call the ignored data outliers.

Nowadays, we know Ancel Keys did not only use biased data, but also forgot to factor in the existence of other variables—the consumption of sugar, for instance. These are called confounding factors or hidden variables.

To switch from one graph to the other, the simulation uses a filter (regulated by cell B3 and the numbers below it). In this case there are 3 filter settings (0, 1, and 2). The "real secret" behind this filter, however, is hidden in the columns E and F behind the graph.

What you need to do

1. Place a spinbutton control next to cell B3: Min 0 | Max 2 | LinkedCell B3.
2. The filter numbers were manually assigned in cells B5:B27.
3. Place in cells E5:E27: =IF($B$3=0,C5,IF($B$3=B5,C5,NA())).
4. Place in cells F5:F27: =IF($B$3=0,D5,IF($B$3=B5,D5,NA())).
5. The XY-chart is hooked up to the columns E and F.
6. The Data Labels are customized to the range A5:A27 (see below).
7. Filter 1 shows Ancel Keys' selection; filter 0 shows *all* the data available. Had you chosen filter 2 (see below), you would have actually found a very strong *negative* relationship (R-squared is high again, 0.96)—but once more a spurious relationship.

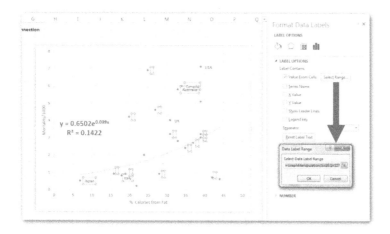

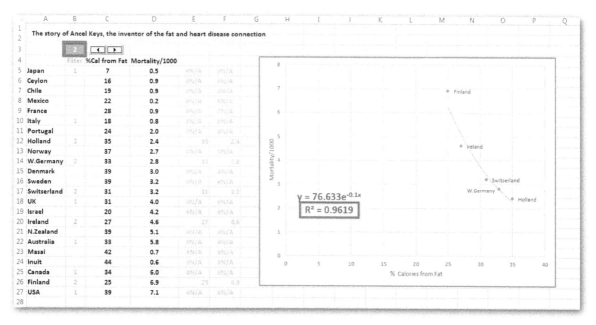

Chapter 124: Creating Gradients

What the simulation does

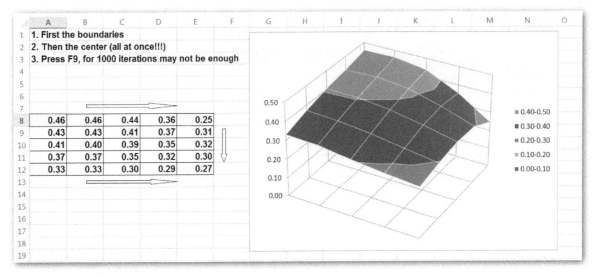

This simulation creates gradients between the four corner cells of range A8:E12. At each run the four corner cells change randomly (between 0 and 1). All the other cells have to be adjusted so they form a smooth gradient with gradual transitions.

Gradients are very common in life: a gradient of temperatures, a gradient of altitudes, a gradient of pressure, a gradient of concentrations, a gradient of colors, a gradient of allele frequencies in a population, and the list goes on and on.

What you need to know

The "trick" to achieve this is using the AVERAGE function, but in such a way that the formula refers to two neighboring cells on both sides plus itself—for instance, in cell B8: =AVERAGE(A8:C8). Since the formula in such cells uses a reference to itself, it causes circular reference. Excel does not allow this, unless you temporarily turn *Iteration* on.

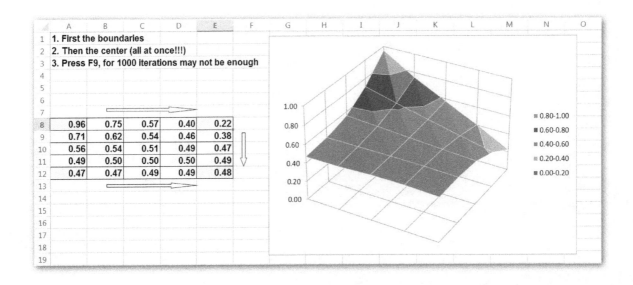

What you need to do

1. Make sure iteration is ON and set to at least 1,000 iterations (for a larger matrix this may not even be enough).
2. Place in the 4 corner cells (A8, E8, A12, and E12): =RAND().
3. Place in cell B8: =AVERAGE(A8:C8). Copy to C8 and D8.
4. Place in cell E9: =AVERAGE(E8:E10). Copy to E10 + E11.
5. Place in cell B12: =AVERAGE(A12:C12). Copy to the cells C12 and D12.
6. Place in cell A9: =AVERAGE(A8:A10). Copy to A10 + A11.
7. Finally the center part. Place in cell B9: =AVERAGE(A8:C10).
8. Copy this formula down to cell B11, and then to the right to cell D11.
9. The end result may look like one of the graphs below.
10. At any time can you create a new gradient pattern with the key *F9*.

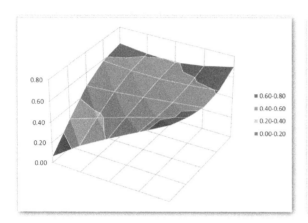 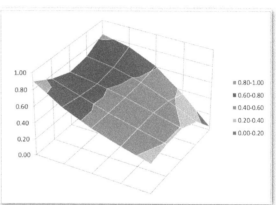

Chapter 125: Summarizing in Steps

What the simulation does

	A	B	C	D	E	F	G	H	I
1									◄ ►
2	Rep	Jun	May	Apr	Mar	Feb	Jan		avg up to May
3	Brown	$5,832.29	$6,366.06	$7,999.65	$8,900.03	$9,800.40	$10,700.78		$ 6,099.18
4	Burke	$7,896.66	$5,071.97	$6,351.08	$4,894.32	$3,437.57	$1,980.81		$ 6,484.32
5	Caruso	$4,792.26	$2,737.44	$3,906.50	$2,926.31	$1,946.11	$965.92		$ 3,764.85
6	Ellis	$4,225.47	$4,470.05	$5,214.88	$5,626.21	$6,037.54	$6,448.87		$ 4,347.76
7	Jones	$2,734.27	$1,004.35	$2,076.51	$3,010.00	$3,943.49	$4,876.98		$ 1,869.31
8	Kelly	$3,471.40	$5,604.34	$6,702.20	$8,490.11	$10,278.03	$12,065.94		$ 4,537.87
9	Mendez	$8,165.21	$4,712.48	$8,399.51	$7,326.70	$6,253.90	$5,181.09		$ 6,438.85
10	Ming	$9,855.32	$10,900.76	$11,591.51	$12,518.72	$13,445.93	$14,373.13		$ 10,378.04
11	Minsky	$6,709.16	$3,832.42	$5,469.10	$4,096.83	$2,724.56	$1,352.29		$ 5,270.79
12	O'Brian	$5,805.85	$8,046.09	$3,986.78	$4,127.18	$4,267.57	$4,407.97		$ 6,925.97
13	Plante	$921.69	$1,807.83	$3,737.72	$4,971.78	$6,205.84	$7,439.89		$ 1,364.76
14	Roberts	$6,248.52	$10,627.81	$10,263.96	$13,062.20	$15,860.45	$18,658.69		$ 8,438.17
15	Russell	$5,832.29	$6,366.06	$5,999.65	$6,233.36	$6,467.07	$6,700.78		$ 6,099.18
16	Stein	$5,416.06	$6,104.31	$7,735.34	$8,737.85	$9,740.36	$10,742.87		$ 5,760.18
17	Young	$11,999.83	$10,157.44	$9,528.97	$8,091.22	$6,653.47	$5,215.72		$ 11,078.64
18									
19	select								
20	Plante	$921.69	$1,807.83	$3,737.72	$4,971.78	$6,205.84	$7,439.89		
21									

This simulation summarizes average sales by different Sales Reps from June back to January by stepping one month back or forth, regulated by a spinbutton control in cell I1.

It also displays the entire record for a specific sales representative in row 20. That record is highlighted in the database as well—row 13 in the case shown above.

What you need to know

There isn't much new on this sheet. Column I calculates the average of a repeatedly changing range. This can be done with the function OFFSET or INDEX. On the sheet shown above we chose INDEX to do the job.

In row 20 we used an array formula: INDEX with a nested MATCH function. INDEX can display multiple cells in a row if you set the last argument to 0 (the column position). In addition, the best month for sales is highlighted with conditional formatting (in this case January).

The alternating pattern in the database—so as to make records easier to read—is accomplished with the function MOD in conditional formatting.

If you want to check the accuracy of the outcome, select a certain range of cells (e.g. B2:E2) and watch the status bar for the average (see below):

	A	B	C	D	E	F	G	H	I
1									◄ ►
2	Rep	Jun	May	Apr	Mar	Feb	Jan		avg up to Mar
3	Brown	$5,832.29	$6,366.06	$7,999.65	$8,900.03	$9,800.40	$10,700.78		$ 7,274.51
19	select								
20	Minsky	$6,709.16	$3,832.42	$5,469.10	$4,096.83	$2,724.56	$1,352.29		
21									

AVERAGE: $7,274.51   COUNT: 4   MIN: $5,832.29   MAX: $8,900.03   SUM: $29,098.03

What you need to do

G	H	I
		1 ◀ ▶
Jan		="avg up to " & INDEX(B2:G2,,I1,1)
10700.78		=AVERAGE(B3:INDEX(B3:G3,,$I$1,1))
1980.8		=AVERAGE(B4:INDEX(B4:G4,,$I$1,1))

1. Place a spinbutton control over cell I1: Min 1 | Max 6 | LinkedCell I1.
2. Place in cell I2: ="avg up to " & INDEX(B2:G2,,I1,1).
3. Place in cells I3:I17: =AVERAGE(B3:INDEX(B3:G3,,$I$1,1)).
4. In cell A20, use Data Validation: Data | Data Validation | List | Source: =$A$3:$A$17.
5. Select the cells B20:G20: =INDEX($B$3:$G$17,MATCH($A$20,$A$3:$A$17,0),0). Because this is an *array* formula, you must use *Ctrl Shift Enter*.
6. A regular alternative is: =INDEX($A$3:$G$17,MATCH($A$20,$A$3:$A$17,0),COLUMN(B2)).
7. Select cells B20:G20 for conditional formatting with a formula: =B20=MAX($B$20:$G$20).
8. Select cells A3:G18 for conditional formatting with a formula: =MOD(ROW(A1),2)=1.
9. Select cells A3:G18 for conditional formatting with a formula: =$A3=$A$20.
10. Make sure the last condition (in 9.) kicks in before the previous one (in 8.).

	A	B	C	D	E	F	G	H	I
1									◀ ▶
2	Rep	Jun	May	Apr	Mar	Feb	Jan		avg up to Mar
3	Brown	$5,832.29	$6,366.06	$7,999.65	$8,900.03	$9,800.40	$10,700.78		$ 7,274.51
4	Burke	$7,896.66	$5,071.97	$6,351.08	$4,894.32	$3,437.57	$1,980.81		$ 6,053.51
5	Caruso	$4,792.26	$2,737.44	$3,906.50	$2,926.31	$1,946.11	$965.92		$ 3,590.63
6	Ellis	$4,225.47	$4,470.05	$5,214.88	$5,626.21	$6,037.54	$6,448.87		$ 4,884.15
7	Jones	$2,734.27	$1,004.35	$2,076.51	$3,010.00	$3,943.49	$4,876.98		$ 2,206.28
8	Kelly	$3,471.40	$5,604.34	$6,702.20	$8,490.11	$10,278.03	$12,065.94		$ 6,067.01
9	Mendez	$8,165.21	$4,712.48	$8,399.51	$7,326.70	$6,253.90	$5,181.09		$ 7,150.98
10	Ming	$9,855.32	$10,900.76	$11,591.51	$12,518.72	$13,445.93	$14,373.13		$ 11,216.58
11	Minsky	$6,709.16	$3,832.42	$5,469.10	$4,096.83	$2,724.56	$1,352.29		$ 5,026.88
12	O'Brian	$5,805.85	$8,046.09	$3,986.78	$4,127.18	$4,267.57	$4,407.97		$ 5,491.47
13	Plante	$921.69	$1,807.83	$3,737.72	$4,971.78	$6,205.84	$7,439.89		$ 2,859.75
14	Roberts	$6,248.52	$10,627.81	$10,263.96	$13,062.20	$15,860.45	$18,658.69		$ 10,050.62
15	Russell	$5,832.29	$6,366.06	$5,999.65	$6,233.36	$6,467.07	$6,700.78		$ 6,107.84
16	Stein	$5,416.06	$6,104.31	$7,735.34	$8,737.85	$9,740.36	$10,742.87		$ 6,998.39
17	Young	$11,999.83	$10,157.44	$9,528.97	$8,091.22	$6,653.47	$5,215.72		$ 9,944.37
18									
19	select								
20	Minsky	$6,709.16	$3,832.42	$5,469.10	$4,096.83	$2,724.56	$1,352.29		
21									

Chapter 126: A Monthly Calendar

What the simulation does

	A	B	C	D	E	F
1	Month	October		Sunday, October 01, 2023		
2	Year	2023		Monday, October 02, 2023		
3				Tuesday, October 03, 2023		
4	January	2017		Wednesday, October 04, 2023		
5	February	2018		Thursday, October 05, 2023		
6	March	2019		Friday, October 06, 2023		
7	April	2020		Saturday, October 07, 2023		
8	May	2021		Sunday, October 08, 2023		
9	June	2022		Monday, October 09, 2023		
10	July	2023		Tuesday, October 10, 2023		
11	August	2024		Wednesday, October 11, 2023		
12	September	2025		Thursday, October 12, 2023		
13	October	2026		Friday, October 13, 2023		
14	November	2027		Saturday, October 14, 2023		
15	December	2028		Sunday, October 15, 2023		
16				Monday, October 16, 2023		
17				Tuesday, October 17, 2023		

This sheet displays the calendar of a certain month (B1) in a certain year (B2). These options have Data Validation based on a list of values in A4:A15 and B4:B15.

Column D displays the corresponding calendar by means of the function DATE.

What you need to know

Dates in Excel are different from what you might expect. The way Excel handles dates may need some explanation. Excel stores dates as sequential serial numbers so that they can be used in calculations. By default, Jan 1, 1900 is serial number 1, and January 1, 2008 is serial number 39448 because it is 39447 days after January 1, 1900. This number can also have decimals to indicate the time of the day. So basically 39447 is January 1, 2008 at 12 AM, and 39447.5 is 12 PM on that same day.

You don't want to see the serial numbers, so Excel lets you simply format them in more human-readable date formats. If you want to quickly glimpse at the serial numbers behind dates, you can use *Ctrl~* (the tilde is just below the *Esc* key). Sometimes they pop up automatically on your spreadsheet, so you probably want to change their format to *Date/Time*.

The function DATE (see Chapter 102) has 3 arguments: DATE(year,month,day). The year number can be found in cell B2. The month number requires a bit more time: the month October, for instance, is found in row 10 of the range A4:A15. And the day number is simply 1. Based on this information, DATE returns the serial number of that date as explained above. All you have to do is assigning a nice date format—so you don't get the serial number.

What you need to do

1. Use Data Validation for cell B1: Data | Data Validation | List | Source: =$A$4:$A$15.
2. Use Data Validation for cell B2: Data | Data Validation | List | Source: =$B$4:$B$15.
3. Place in cell D1: =DATE(B2,MATCH(B1,A4:A15,0),1).
4. Place in cells D2:D31 a more complicated formula to also solve February issues: =IFERROR(IF(MONTH(D1+1)=MATCH($B$1,$A$4:$A$15,0),D1+1,""),"").
5. Choose the appropriate date format for column D.
6. To highlight today's date, if available in a particular calendar, apply conditional formatting to D1:D31: =D1=TODAY(). Select a color if it is today's date.
7. To mark off a new week, apply conditional formatting to D1:D31: =WEEKDAY(D1)=1. Use a top border for Sundays (which is weekday 1 by default).
8. Notice that 2020 is a leap year (see below).

	A	B	C	D	E	F	G	H
1	Month	February		Saturday, February 01, 2020				
2	Year	2020		Sunday, February 02, 2020				
3				Monday, February 03, 2020				
4	January	2017		Tuesday, February 04, 2020				
5	February	2018		Wednesday, February 05, 2020				
6	March	2019		Thursday, February 06, 2020				
7	April	2020		Friday, February 07, 2020				
8	May	2021		Saturday, February 08, 2020				
9	June	2022		Sunday, February 09, 2020				
10	July	2023		Monday, February 10, 2020				
11	August	2024		Tuesday, February 11, 2020				
12	September	2025		Wednesday, February 12, 2020				
13	October	2026		Thursday, February 13, 2020				
14	November	2027		Friday, February 14, 2020				
15	December	2028		Saturday, February 15, 2020				
16				Sunday, February 16, 2020				
17				Monday, February 17, 2020				
18				Tuesday, February 18, 2020				
19				Wednesday, February 19, 2020				
20				Thursday, February 20, 2020				
21				Friday, February 21, 2020				
22				Saturday, February 22, 2020				
23				Sunday, February 23, 2020				
24				Monday, February 24, 2020				
25				Tuesday, February 25, 2020				
26				Wednesday, February 26, 2020				
27				Thursday, February 27, 2020				
28				Friday, February 28, 2020				
29				Saturday, February 29, 2020				
30								

Chapter 127: Comparison of Values

What the simulation does

	A	B	C	D	E	F	G	H
1	Date	Patient	Old SBP	New SBP		up by more than	▲	
2	5/5/2006	Bush	120	127		10	▼	
3	5/8/2006	Carter	139	152				
4	5/9/2006	Clinton	160	165		filtermarkedcells		
5	5/10/2006	Eisenhower	148	180		FALSE		
6	5/11/2006	Ford	167	158				
7	5/12/2006	Johnson	145	160		mean of marked cells		
8	5/15/2006	Kennedy	137	142		161.1		
9	5/16/2006	Nixon	155	190				
10	5/17/2006	Reagan	137	125				
11	5/18/2006	Bush	120	141		mean with array formula		
12	5/19/2006	Carter	139	155		161.1		
13	5/22/2006	Clinton	160	155				
14	5/23/2006	Eisenhower	148	160				
15	5/24/2006	Ford	167	141				
16	5/25/2006	Johnson	145	132				
17	5/26/2006	Kennedy	137	139				
18	5/29/2006	Nixon	155	147				
19	5/30/2006	Reagan	137	151				
20								

This sheet allows the user to highlight new systolic blood pressure (SBP) readings (column D) that went *up* by more than a certain value in cell F2, compared to a previous SBP reading in column C. However, users can also select "*down* by more than" in cell F1.

The sheet also calculates the average of the cells marked in column D (in cell F8 or F12).

What you need to know

This is basically all done by conditional formatting, although the formula can get a bit more complicated: =IF(LEFT($F$1,2)="up",($D2-$C2)>$F$2,($C2-$D2)>$F$2). Just make sure you lock cell references properly (see Appendix).

Calculating the average of marked cells in column D is done with the function DAVERAGE in F8, which requires a filter. The filter is located in cells F4:F5, with a filter label in F4 (without spaces) and a computed field in F5 (for more information on computed filter fields, see Chapters 86 and 117).

Calculating the average of marked cells in column D can also be done with a single-cell array formula, which is done in cell F12. However, formulas like this are always harder to come up with on your own. Although you can test them by selecting parts of it in the formula bar and then pressing *F9* for a partial result (followed by *Esc*), they can still be very daunting.

What you need to do

1. Place a spinbutton control next to cell F2: Min 5 | Max 40 | SmallChange 10 | LinkedCell F2.
2. Apply Data Validation to cell F1: Source: up by more than,down by more than.
3. Select cells D2:D19 and implement conditional formatting with the following formula: =IF(LEFT($F$1,2)="up",($D2-$C2)>$F$2,($C2-$D2)>$F$2).
4. Place a computed field in F5: =IF(LEFT($F$1,2)="up",$D2>($C2+$F$2),$C2>($D2+$F$2)).
5. Make sure the label above this field (in F4) has no spaces in it.
6. Place in cell F8: =IFERROR(DAVERAGE(C1:D19,D1,F4:F5),"none marked").
7. Place in cell F12 a single-cell array formula that you must implement with *Ctrl Shift Enter*: =IF(LEFT(F1,2)="up",AVERAGE(IF((D2:D19-C2:C19)>F2,D2:D19)),AVERAGE(IF((C2:C19-D2:D19)>F2,D2:D19))).
8. This simulation becomes even more useful when you have much longer rows of records, but that can best be done with dynamic *Range Names* (see Chapter 118, e.g.).

	A	B	C	D	E	F	G	H
1	Date	Patient	Old SBP	New SBP		down by more than		
2	5/5/2006	Bush	120	127		5		
3	5/8/2006	Carter	139	152				
4	5/9/2006	Clinton	160	165		filtermarkedcells		
5	5/10/2006	Eisenhower	148	180		FALSE		
6	5/11/2006	Ford	167	158				
7	5/12/2006	Johnson	145	160		mean of marked cells		
8	5/15/2006	Kennedy	137	142		140.6		
9	5/16/2006	Nixon	155	190				
10	5/17/2006	Reagan	137	125				
11	5/18/2006	Bush	120	141		mean with array formula		
12	5/19/2006	Carter	139	155		140.6		
13	5/22/2006	Clinton	160	155				
14	5/23/2006	Eisenhower	148	160				
15	5/24/2006	Ford	167	141				
16	5/25/2006	Johnson	145	132				
17	5/26/2006	Kennedy	137	139				
18	5/29/2006	Nixon	155	147				
19	5/30/2006	Reagan	137	151				
20								

Chapter 128: Letter Permutations

What the simulation does

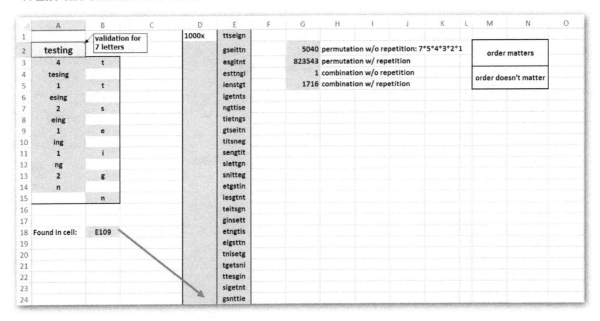

This simulation runs a *Data Table* 1,000 times in columns D:E to re-create a 7-letter word (from cell A2) after it has been randomly broken up into its individual letters (in column B).

Column B breaks up the 7 letters randomly, so the *Data Table* can again reassemble them in a random order which is done in column E.

A 7-letter word can undergo 5,040 permutations without repetition (G2). So during 1,000 runs the original word may not come up during each run. If it does, cell B18 displays in which cell from column E the perfect match is located.

What you need to know

The functions to decompose the 7-letter word, step by step and randomly, are LEN, LEFT, MID, RIGHT, and RANDBETWEEN. The function MID, for instance, has the following syntax: MID(text,start_num,num_chars). So MID returns a specific number of characters from a text string, starting at the position you specify, based on the number of characters you specify.

Locating a match in column E is done with the functions IFERROR, ADDRESS, and MATCH (see Chapter 116).

$$P_{k,n} = \frac{n!}{(n-k)!}$$

$$\frac{P_{k,n}}{k!} = \frac{n!}{k!(n-k)!}$$

Other new functions in this simulation are PERMUT (left), PERMURATIONA, COMBIN (below it), and COMBINA.

All four have a similar syntax: (number,number_chosen). *Number* is the given number of objects (*n*); *number_chosen* is the number of objects in each permutation or combination (*k*). The function name with *A* at the end does the same but allows each object to be chosen more than once (with repetition).

Finally there is the function CONCATENATE. It strings multiple elements together (which could also have been done with ampersands).

What you need to do

1. Control cell A2: Data | Data Validation | Whole Number | Between 7 and 7.
2. Place in cell G2: =PERMUT(LEN($A$2),LEN($A$2)).
3. Place in cell G3: =PERMUTATIONA(LEN($A$2),LEN($A$2)).
4. Place in cell G4: =COMBIN(LEN($A$2),LEN($A$2)).
5. Place in cell G5: =COMBINA(LEN($A$2),LEN($A$2)).
6. Select cells A3, A5, A7, A9, A11, and A13: =RANDBETWEEN(1,LEN(A2)).
7. Select cells B3, B5, B7, B9, B11, B13, and B15: =IF(LEN(A2)=1,A2,MID(A2,A3,1)).
8. Select cells A4, A6, A8, A10, A12, and A14: =LEFT(A2,A3-1) & RIGHT(A2,LEN(A2)-A3).
9. Place in cell E1: =CONCATENATE(B3,B5,B7,B9,B11,B13,B15).
10. Select range D1:D1000 for a *Data Table*: =TABLE(,C1).
11. Place in cell B18: =IFERROR(ADDRESS(MATCH(A2,E:E, 0),5,4),"no match").

	A	B	C	D	E	F	G	H	I	J	K	L	M	N	O
1		validation for 7 letters		1,000x	tgensit										
2	testing				itnsgte		5040	permutation w/o repetition: 7*5*4*3*2*1					order matters		
3	1	t			sgnteit		823543	permutation w/ repetition							
4	esting				stinetg		1	combination w/o repetition					order doesn't matter		
5	6	g			ngsttie		1716	combination w/ repetition							
6	estin				ietgnst										
7	1	e			sgnetit										
8	stin				nsitetg										
9	4	n			tesintg										
10	sti				tnietsg										
11	1	s			tngteis										
12	ti				ingstet										
13	2	i			etnsgti										
14	t				ittegsn										
15		t			ettings										
16					sgetnit										
17					tgtesni										
18	Found in cell:	E631			ntgetsi										
19					ettnsgi										

Chapter 129: Metric Conversion

What the simulation does

	A	B	C	D	E	F	G	H	I	J	K	L	M	N	O	P
1	ft-in	5'2"		feet												
2				inch												
3		↓														
4	feet	5		split feet												
5	ft->m	1.524		and												
6	inches	2		inches												
7	in->m	0.0508														
8																
9		↓														
10	total in m.	1.5748	0 in	1 in	2 in	3 in	4 in	5 in	6 in	7 in	8 in	9 in	10 in	11 in		
11			0 ft	0.0000 m	0.0254 m	0.0508 m	0.0762 m	0.1016 m	0.1270 m	0.1524 m	0.1778 m	0.2032 m	0.2286 m	0.2540 m	0.2794 m	
12			1 ft	0.3048 m	0.3302 m	0.3556 m	0.3810 m	0.4064 m	0.4318 m	0.4572 m	0.4826 m	0.5080 m	0.5334 m	0.5588 m	0.5842 m	
13			2 ft	0.6096 m	0.6350 m	0.6604 m	0.6858 m	0.7112 m	0.7366 m	0.7620 m	0.7874 m	0.8128 m	0.8382 m	0.8636 m	0.8890 m	
14			3 ft	0.9144 m	0.9398 m	0.9652 m	0.9906 m	1.0160 m	1.0414 m	1.0668 m	1.0922 m	1.1176 m	1.1430 m	1.1684 m	1.1938 m	custom
15			4 ft	1.2192 m	1.2446 m	1.2700 m	1.2954 m	1.3208 m	1.3462 m	1.3716 m	1.3970 m	1.4224 m	1.4478 m	1.4732 m	1.4986 m	format
16			5 ft	1.5240 m	1.5494 m	1.5748 m	1.6002 m	1.6256 m	1.6510 m	1.6764 m	1.7018 m	1.7272 m	1.7526 m	1.7780 m	1.8034 m	
17			6 ft	1.8288 m	1.8542 m	1.8796 m	1.9050 m	1.9304 m	1.9558 m	1.9812 m	2.0066 m	2.0320 m	2.0574 m	2.0828 m	2.1082 m	
18			7 ft	2.1336 m	2.1590 m	2.1844 m	2.2098 m	2.2352 m	2.2606 m	2.2860 m	2.3114 m	2.3368 m	2.3622 m	2.3876 m	2.4130 m	
19																
20	back to decimal feet		0.0000 ft	0.0833 ft	0.1667 ft	0.2500 ft	0.3333 ft	0.4167 ft	0.5000 ft	0.5833 ft	0.6667 ft	0.7500 ft	0.8333 ft	0.9167 ft	
21				1.0000 ft	1.0833 ft	1.1667 ft	1.2500 ft	1.3333 ft	1.4167 ft	1.5000 ft	1.5833 ft	1.6667 ft	1.7500 ft	1.8333 ft	1.9167 ft	
22				2.0000 ft	2.0833 ft	2.1667 ft	2.2500 ft	2.3333 ft	2.4167 ft	2.5000 ft	2.5833 ft	2.6667 ft	2.7500 ft	2.8333 ft	2.9167 ft	
23				3.0000 ft	3.0833 ft	3.1667 ft	3.2500 ft	3.3333 ft	3.4167 ft	3.5000 ft	3.5833 ft	3.6667 ft	3.7500 ft	3.8333 ft	3.9167 ft	custom
24				4.0000 ft	4.0833 ft	4.1667 ft	4.2500 ft	4.3333 ft	4.4167 ft	4.5000 ft	4.5833 ft	4.6667 ft	4.7500 ft	4.8333 ft	4.9167 ft	format
25				5.0000 ft	5.0833 ft	5.1667 ft	5.2500 ft	5.3333 ft	5.4167 ft	5.5000 ft	5.5833 ft	5.6667 ft	5.7500 ft	5.8333 ft	5.9167 ft	
26				6.0000 ft	6.0833 ft	6.1667 ft	6.2500 ft	6.3333 ft	6.4167 ft	6.5000 ft	6.5833 ft	6.6667 ft	6.7500 ft	6.8333 ft	6.9167 ft	
27				7.0000 ft	7.0833 ft	7.1667 ft	7.2500 ft	7.3333 ft	7.4167 ft	7.5000 ft	7.5833 ft	7.6667 ft	7.7500 ft	7.8333 ft	7.9167 ft	
28																

The use of measurements in terms of feet and inches is notoriously awkward for scientific purposes. This sheet separates the notation in cell B1 into a feet component (B4) and an inches component (B6), converts them into metric equivalents (B5 and B7), adds them together (B10), shows that converted value in a wider matrix through a *Data Table*, and then converts those values back to feet with a decimal notation.

Two spinbutton controls allow the user to separately change the feet component and the inches component in cell B1. All the other calculations on the sheet will then update accordingly.

What you need to know

There are at least two new functions here. One is FIND. Its syntax is: FIND(find_text, within_text,[start_num]). FIND locates one text string within a second text string, and returns the number of the starting position of the first text string from the first character of the second text string. So FIND("rt", "start") returns 4.

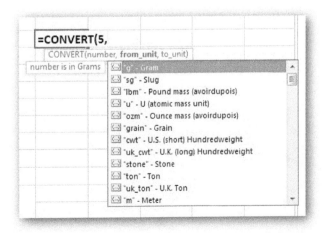

The other new function is CONVERT. Its simple syntax is: CONVERT(number,from_unit,to_unit). It is a very rich and powerful converting function, because it includes an enormous variety of units as you can gaze from the left. This listing pops up whenever you *type* the function in a cell.

What you need to do

	A	B
1	ft-in	=D1 & "'" & D2 & "''"
2		
3		
4	feet	=LEFT(B1,FIND("'",B1)-1)
5	ft->m	=CONVERT(VALUE(B4),"ft","m")
6	inches	=MID(B1,FIND("'",B1)+1, LEN(B1)-LEN(B4)-3)
7	in->m	=CONVERT(VALUE(B6),"in","m")

1. Place a spinbutton control next to cell C1: Min 0 | Max 7 | LinkedCell D1.
2. Place a spinbutton control next to cell C2: Min 0 | Max 11 | LinkedCell D2.
3. Place in cell B1: =D1 & "'" & D2 & "''" (so 1 single quote inside double quotes and 2 single quotes inside double quotes).
4. Place in cell B4: =LEFT(B1,FIND("'",B1)-1).
5. Place in cell B5: =CONVERT(VALUE(B4),"ft","m").
6. Place in cell B6: =MID(B1,FIND("'",B1)+1, LEN(B1)-LEN(B4)-3).
7. Place in cell B7: =CONVERT(VALUE(B6),"in","m").
8. Place in cell B10: =B5+B7.
9. Select cells B10:N18 for a *Data Table*: =TABLE(B6,B4).
10. Select cells C11:N18 for a custom format: R-click | Format Cells | Custom: 0.0000" m".
11. Select cells C11:N18 for conditional formatting: =C11=$B$10.
12. Place in cells C20:N27: =CONVERT(C11,"m","ft").
13. Select cells C20:N27 for a custom format: R-click | Format Cells | Custom: 0.0000" ft".
14. Select cells C20:N27 for conditional formatting: =C20=CONVERT($B$10,"m","ft").
15. Test with the two spinbutton controls whether everything works properly.

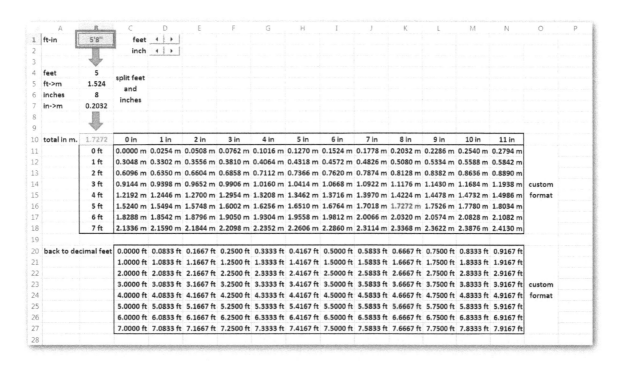

Chapter 130: Probability of Beliefs

What the simulation does

	A	B	C	D	E	F	G	H	I	J	K	L	M	N	O	P	Q	R
1		YES	4															
2		NO	1															
3		out of	100															
4																		
5																		
6	hypo-	probability	number of cases	corrected														
7	thesis	of belief		probability		23%	1	2	3	4	5	6	7	8	9	10	YES	
8	5%	0.1	0.0006	0%		1	15%	18%	21%	23%	27%	31%	34%	36%	37%	38%		
9	15%	0.1	0.0430	0%		2	18%	18%	20%	23%	25%	28%	30%	31%	34%	38%		
10	25%	0.1	0.2930	1%		3	21%	20%	21%	23%	25%	27%	28%	31%	34%	35%		
11	35%	0.1	0.9754	3%		4	23%	23%	23%	24%	26%	26%	29%	31%	31%	33%		
12	45%	0.1	2.2553	7%		5	27%	25%	25%	26%	26%	28%	29%	30%	33%	34%		
13	55%	0.1	4.1178	12%		6	31%	28%	27%	26%	28%	28%	30%	31%	31%	34%		
14	65%	0.1	6.2477	19%		7	34%	30%	28%	29%	29%	30%	29%	32%	33%	33%		
15	75%	0.1	7.9102	23%		8	36%	31%	31%	31%	30%	31%	32%	31%	34%	35%		
16	85%	0.1	7.8301	23%		9	37%	34%	34%	31%	33%	31%	33%	34%	32%	35%		
17	95%	0.1	4.0725	12%		10	38%	38%	35%	33%	34%	34%	33%	35%	35%	33%		
18						NO												
19			33.7456	23%														

Probabilities have everything to do with uncertainty. So far in this book we have been talking about probabilities in terms of *frequencies*. But there is another kind of probability and uncertainty: this one measures the degree to which we *believe* something. To say that there is a 98% probability that Shakespeare wrote Hamlet does not mean that if 100 Shakespeares were born, 98 of them would have written Hamlet. Apparently, this is not an uncertainty about frequencies but an uncertainty about beliefs. The initial probability of a hypothesis can and will be updated in the light of new relevant data.

Let us study what the fraction of a certain disease in the population is based on hypothetical possibilities of 5%, 15%, etc. (column A). We start assuming—a belief—that each possibility has the same probability, 0.1 (column B). Then we find out that, from the first 5 individuals that we studied, 4 (in cell C1) did have the disease, while 1 did not (in C2). Based on these findings, we calculate how often doctors would find 4 out of 5 individuals with the disease in a population of 100 individuals (column C). Then we recalculate in column D the probabilities we had assumed in column B. It turns out that the highest probability is now concentrated around the 75% option. So we believe this is the hypothesis with the highest probability at this point.

What you need to know

Apparently, there are two different views of probability. The so-called frequentist probability is the view in which probability is defined in terms of frequency in outcomes of repeated experiments (column C). The so-called Bayesian probability, on the other hand, is the view in which probability is interpreted as a measure of degree of belief—a belief one has about possible values of a certain feature (column D). In this Simulation, our ultimate goal is the latter approach.

In the table to the right we will find out how various values in cell C1 (from 1 to 10 people *with* the disease)—shown in the top row of the table—and how various values in cell C2 (from 1 to 10 people *without* the disease)—shown in the left column of the table—lead us to different beliefs about the entire population.

What you need to do

	A	B	C	D	E	F	G
1		YES	7				
2		NO	4				
3		out of	100				
4							
5							
6	hypo-thesis	probability of belief	number of cases			=D19	1
7				corrected probability			
8	0.05	0.1	=A8^$C$1*(1-A8)^$C$2*$C$3	=C8/$C$19		1	=TABLE(C1,C2)
9	0.15	0.1	=A9^$C$1*(1-A9)^$C$2*$C$3	=C9/$C$19		2	=TABLE(C1,C2)
10	0.25	0.1	=A10^$C$1*(1-A10)^$C$2*$C$3	=C10/$C$19		3	=TABLE(C1,C2)

1. Cells C1 and C2 have Data Validation for the values 1 to 10.
2. Cell C8 calculates how many out of 100 doctors would find, for example, 7 out of 11 people with the disease: =A8^$C$1*(1-A8)^$C$2*$C$3. Copy the formula downwards to cell C17.
3. Cell C19 sums all these cases: =SUM(C8:C17).
4. Place in cells D8:D17 the new probabilities: =C8/$C$19.
5. Cell D19 locates the highest probability in the previous list: =MAX(D8:D17).
6. With conditional formatting in range D8:D17, we mark the cell with the highest probability: Top/Bottom Rules | Top: 1.
7. Based on this information, we can start a *Data Table* to simulate various values in cells C1 and C2, running from 1 to 10. To do so, select range F7:P17, implement a *Data Table* with C1 as row input and C2 as column input: =TABLE(C1,C2).
8. In range A8:A17, we apply conditional formatting to mark the option that corresponds with the highest value in column D: =ROW ($A1)=MATCH ($D$19,$D$8:$D$17,0).
9. In the *Data Table* range G8:P17, we mark the cell in column 4 (the value of cell C1) and row 2 (the value of cell C2) by using the formula: =AND(ROW (A1)=$C$2,COLUMN(A1)=$C$1).
10. Try changing values in C1 and C2 and watch the outcome (see below).

	A	B	C	D	E	F	G	H	I	J	K	L	M	N	O	P	Q	R
1		YES	7															
2		NO	4															
3		out of	100															
4																		
5																		
6	hypo-thesis	probability of belief	number of cases	corrected probability		29%	1	2	3	4	5	6	7	8	9	10	YES	
7																		
8	5%	0.1	0.0000	0%		1	15%	18%	21%	23%	27%	31%	34%	36%	37%	38%		
9	15%	0.1	0.0001	0%		2	18%	18%	20%	23%	25%	28%	30%	31%	34%	38%		
10	25%	0.1	0.0019	1%		3	21%	20%	21%	23%	25%	27%	28%	31%	34%	35%		
11	35%	0.1	0.0115	5%		4	23%	23%	23%	24%	26%	26%	29%	31%	31%	33%		
12	45%	0.1	0.0342	14%		5	27%	25%	25%	26%	26%	28%	29%	30%	33%	34%		
13	55%	0.1	0.0624	25%		6	31%	28%	27%	26%	28%	28%	30%	31%	31%	34%		
14	65%	0.1	0.0736	29%		7	34%	30%	28%	29%	29%	30%	29%	32%	33%	33%		
15	75%	0.1	0.0521	21%		8	36%	31%	31%	31%	30%	31%	32%	31%	34%	35%		
16	85%	0.1	0.0162	6%		9	37%	34%	34%	31%	33%	31%	33%	34%	32%	35%		
17	95%	0.1	0.0004	0%		10	38%	38%	35%	33%	34%	34%	33%	35%	35%	33%		
18						NO												
19			0.2525	29%														
20																		

IX. APPENDIX

Sheet Navigation

The following keystrokes are some important navigation shortcuts:

- *Ctrl+Home* takes you to the origin of the sheet, which is usually cell A1.
- *Ctrl+Arrow* key jumps between section borders. (A border is an empty row and/or column.)
- *Ctrl+Shift+Arrow* key jumps and selects what is between the section borders.
- *Shift+Arrow* key expands or reduces whatever has been selected.

	A	B	C	D	E	F	G	H	I	J	K
1		1	1			0.69	0.42				
2		2				0.33	0.83				
3		3				0.63	0.70				
4		4				0.50	0.43				
5		5				0.12	0.23				
6		6				0.10	0.90				
7		7				0.86	0.94				
8		8				0.42	0.98				
9		9				0.41	0.77				
10		10				0.56	0.20				
11					SD						
12											
13			Column								
14		0.38	0.38								
15		0.69	0.69								
16		0.50	0.50								
17		0.03	0.03								
18		0.94	0.94								
19		0.11	0.11								
20		0.78	0.78								
21		0.31	0.31								
22		0.30	0.30								
23		0.12	0.12								
24	COUNTIF >.5										
25											

Let's use the figure above to see how these shortcuts work.

- **Starting in A1:** Pressing *Ctrl+Down Arrow* takes you to A24 and then to A1048576. Pressing *Ctrl+Up Arrow* takes you back, with the same stops on the way.

- **Starting in B1:** Repeatedly pressing *Ctrl+Down Arrow* jumps to B10, B14, B23, and finally the end.

- **Starting in B1:** Pressing *Ctrl+Shift+Down Arrow* selects the entire range B1:B10. Pressing *Shift+Down Arrow* once expands the selection with one more cell. Instead pressing *Shift+Up Arrow* shortens the selection by one cell. The *Shift* key keeps all in-between cells included in the selection.

- **Starting in J1:** Typing J24 in the *Name* box just above column A and then pressing *Shift+Enter* selects all cells between J1 and J24 (thanks to the *Shift* key). With the range J1:J24 selected, typing =ROW() in the *formula bar* and then pressing *Ctrl+Enter*, all the selected cells will be filled with this formula (thanks to the *Ctrl* key).

Locking Cell References

Most formulas in Excel contain references to one or more cells. When you copy such formulas to another location, the cell references automatically adjust to their new location. These references are called *relative*—they adjust when moved or copied. Usually that is good news, but sometimes you want certain references to keep referring to the same cell, or at least to the same row or the same column. Such references are called *absolute*—they remain "locked" when moved or copied.

Unlocked, or relative, references look like this, =A1, whereas locked, or absolute, references look like =$A$1 or =A$1 or =$A1. The $-sign locks one part of the reference. It is not really a dollar-sign but a string-sign. You can type that sign by hand, but it is usually much easier and faster to hit the key *F4*. The F4-key is a cycle key—it cycles from A1 to $A$1 to A$1 to $A1 and then starts all over again.

	A	B	C	D	E	F	G	H	I	J	K	L
1	A1	B1										
2	A2	B2			APR	4%	5%	6%	7%			
3					$ 5,000.00	$ 200.00	$ 250.00	$ 300.00	$ 350.00			
4	A1	B1			$10,000.00	$ 400.00	$ 500.00	$ 600.00	$ 700.00			
5	A2	B2			$15,000.00	$ 600.00	$ 750.00	$ 900.00	$1,050.00			
6					$20,000.00	$ 800.00	$1,000.00	$1,200.00	$1,400.00			
7	A1	A1			$25,000.00	$1,000.00	$1,250.00	$1,500.00	$1,750.00			
8	A1	A1			$30,000.00	$1,200.00	$1,500.00	$1,800.00	$2,100.00			
9					$35,000.00	$1,400.00	$1,750.00	$2,100.00	$2,450.00			
10	A1	B1			$40,000.00	$1,600.00	$2,000.00	$2,400.00	$2,800.00			
11	A1	B1			$45,000.00	$1,800.00	$2,250.00	$2,700.00	$3,150.00			
12					$50,000.00	$2,000.00	$2,500.00	$3,000.00	$3,500.00			
13	A1	A1										
14	A2	A2										
15												
16												
17					key F4: Cycles between relative and (partially) absolute cell references							
18												
19	=A1	=B1		=$A$1	=$A$1		=A$1	=B$1		=$A1	=$A1	
20	=A2	=B2		=$A$1	=$A$1		=A$1	=B$1		=$A2	=$A2	
21												
22	A1	B1		A1	A1		A1	B1		A1	A1	
23	A2	B2		A1	A1		A1	B1		A2	A2	

I explained this behavior in the figure above. Cell F4 has the following formula in it: =$E3*F$2. Notice that column E is locked, so it stays that way when we copy the formula to the right, whereas row 3 is unlocked and will change into 4 in the next cell down. Notice also that row 2 is locked, so it keeps referring to row 2 when copied down, whereas column F will change to G when copied to the right (or to E when copied to the left). As a consequence of these "locks," the formula can be copied over the entire range F3:I12.

Sometimes it is nice, handy, or even necessary to see all the formulas on your sheet at once—for instance, to make sure your formulas remained correct after you moved or copied them. If you want to get a formula-view of your sheet, just hit (this is called a tilde, which can be found below the *Esc* key). *Ctrl* ~ is a toggle shortcut, switching back and forth between value-view and formula-view per sheet.

	E	F	G	H	I
	APR	0.04	0.05	0.06	0.07
	5000	=$E3*F$2	=$E3*G$2	=$E3*H$2	=$E3*I$2
	10000	=$E4*F$2	=$E4*G$2	=$E4*H$2	=$E4*I$2
	15000	=$E5*F$2	=$E5*G$2	=$E5*H$2	=$E5*I$2
	20000	=$E6*F$2	=$E6*G$2	=$E6*H$2	=$E6*I$2
	25000	=$E7*F$2	=$E7*G$2	=$E7*H$2	=$E7*I$2
	30000	=$E8*F$2	=$E8*G$2	=$E8*H$2	=$E8*I$2
	35000	=$E9*F$2	=$E9*G$2	=$E9*H$2	=$E9*I$2
	40000	=$E10*F$2	=$E10*G$2	=$E10*H$2	=$E10*I$2
	45000	=$E11*F$2	=$E11*G$2	=$E11*H$2	=$E11*I$2
	50000	=$E12*F$2	=$E12*G$2	=$E12*H$2	=$E12*I$2

Locking cells can also be very important when you work with conditional formatting. Say we have the following situation: We want to compare an old value with a new value by marking the new value if it went up by more than 5, 10, 15, or 20 units. In this case (shown below), the values I used are systolic blood pressure (BSP) units in mmHg.

The amount of units up is chosen in cell G1 on the sheet shown below (see also Chapter 127). After selecting the cells that we want to mark conditionally, D2:D19, we implement conditional formatting with the following formula: =($D2-$C2)>$G$1.

Make sure that the references to columns D and C are locked, but not to their rows. The reference to cell G1 has to be completely locked, as every cell in column D has to "listen" to that one cell G1. If you do not follow these rules, conditional formatting will not work the way you want it to work (see Chapter 127 for a fancier version).

	A	B	C	D	E	F	G	H
1	Date	Patient	Old SBP	New SBP		Up by more than	10	
2	5/5/2006	Bush	120	127			5	
3	5/8/2006	Carter	139	152			10	
4	5/9/2006	Clinton	160	165			15	
5	5/10/2006	Eisenhower	148	180			20	
6	5/11/2006	Ford	167	158				
7	5/12/2006	Johnson	145	160				
8	5/15/2006	Kennedy	137	142				
9	5/16/2006	Nixon	155	190				
10	5/17/2006	Reagan	137	125				
11	5/18/2006	Bush	120	141				
12	5/19/2006	Carter	139	155				
13	5/22/2006	Clinton	160	155				
14	5/23/2006	Eisenhower	148	160				
15	5/24/2006	Ford	167	141				
16	5/25/2006	Johnson	145	132				
17	5/26/2006	Kennedy	137	139				
18	5/29/2006	Nixon	155	147				
19	5/30/2006	Reagan	137	151				
20								

Nested Functions

Nested functions are functions "nested" within other functions. They are quite common in Excel—and in this book—but you may not be familiar with them yet.

If you are a "pro," you probably *type* functions, including nested functions. But if you are new to this, it is probably wise to create your functions by clicking the *fx* button in front of the formula bar. This makes a dialog screen pop up, which gives you usually much more detailed information as to what to do (and besides, it has a *Help* option in the lower left corner).

To show you the technique of creating nested functions, I use an example shown below. It creates a formatted version (in column C) of an unformatted phone number (in column B).

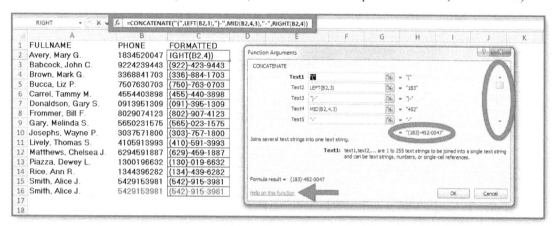

The function to start with is CONCATENATE. This function "strings" a series of components together. It begins with an opening parenthesis in the 1st argument, *Text1*. Click in the 2nd argument, *Text2*, where we want a nested LEFT function.

To do so, while in *Text2*, click on the dropdown box in front of the formula bar (top left in the figure above) and locate the function LEFT. Now the CONCATENATE dialog box gets replaced with the LEFT dialog box. Enter B2 for its 1st argument and 3 for its 2nd argument.

The question is now how we can get back to CONCATENATE in order to finish our work in the main function. We do so—not by clicking OK—but by clicking on CONCATENATE in the formula bar. Notice now how the LEFT function has been nested in the 2nd argument of CONCATENATE.

Click in the 3rd argument, *Text3*, and enter "literally" a closing parenthesis plus a dash: ")-". In the 4th argument, *Text4*, we need a nested MID function with three arguments (B2, 4, 3). Go back to CONCATENATE by clicking on its name in the formula bar and enter a dash in its 5th argument, *Text5* (if you think there are no more arguments available, use its vertical scroll bar to the right). Finally, call the RIGHT function in *Text6*, and set its two arguments to B2 and 4.

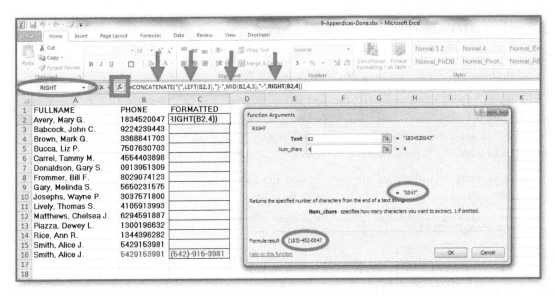

Notice, when you are in a nested argument, how the first formula result (in our picture, "0047") is the result of the nested function (in our case, RIGHT), whereas the final formula result at the bottom of the box (in our case (183)-452-0047) comes from the entire formula.

Once you are finished and you want to check the outcome of a particular nested function, highlight that nested function in the formula bar and hit *F9*. This gives you the result for that particular part of the total function. Do not forget to hit *Esc*, otherwise you would replace that function with a numeric value.

By the way, instead of using CONCATENATE, you could also "hook" the parts that were inside CONCATENATE together by using the ampersand (&)—like this: ="(" & LEFT(B2,3) & ")-" & MID(B2,4,3) & "-" & RIGHT(B2,4).

Data Tables

A *Data Table* is a range of cells that shows how changing one or two variables in your formulas will affect the results of those formulas. A *Data Table* provides a powerful way of calculating multiple results in one operation and a way to view and compare the results of all the different variations together on your worksheet.

	A	B	C	D	E	F	G
1	AMOUNT	$ 5,000.00					
2	APR	4%					
3		$200.00	4%	5%	6%	7%	APR
4		$ 5,000.00	$ 200.00	$ 250.00	$ 300.00	$ 350.00	
5		$10,000.00	$ 400.00	$ 500.00	$ 600.00	$ 700.00	
6		$15,000.00	$ 600.00	$ 750.00	$ 900.00	$1,050.00	
7		$20,000.00	$ 800.00	$1,000.00	$1,200.00	$1,400.00	
8		$25,000.00	$1,000.00	$1,250.00	$1,500.00	$1,750.00	
9		$30,000.00	$1,200.00	$1,500.00	$1,800.00	$2,100.00	
10		$35,000.00	$1,400.00	$1,750.00	$2,100.00	$2,450.00	
11		$40,000.00	$1,600.00	$2,000.00	$2,400.00	$2,800.00	
12		$45,000.00	$1,800.00	$2,250.00	$2,700.00	$3,150.00	
13		$50,000.00	$2,000.00	$2,500.00	$3,000.00	$3,500.00	
14		AMOUNT					

To implement a *Data Table*, you select the entire range, including its point of origin (often with a formula in it, but it may also be empty)—so that is B3:F13 in the example above. Then you go through the following menus: Data | What-If Analysis | *Data Table*. In the dialog box, set the row input to cell B2 and the column input to cell B1.

Once you click OK, Excel replaces all empty cells (in the shaded area) with an array formula like this: {=TABLE(B2,B1)}. Or more in general terms, *{=TABLE(row-input-cell, column-input-cell)}*. Sometimes, one or both of the two arguments are missing. Never *type* the braces—Excel creates them automatically when you hit the *Data Table* button. And do not type the formula!

Why use a *Data Table*? There are several reasons. First, it might be easier to implement one than working with locked and unlocked cell references. Second, no part of the array can inadvertently be deleted or changed, because the array acts as one entire unit. Third, a *Data Table* has much more extra potential, as you can see in many of the simulations we use in this book.

However, there is one drawback. Because there may be many operations involved in a *Data Table*, Excel may run into speed and memory problems. There are two ways to get around the speed issue. Method #1 is to stop automatic recalculation—at least for *Data Tables*. Do the following: File | Options | Options | Formulas | Automatic Except for *Data Tables* (you can even set all calculations to manual). If you ever need to recalculate a *Data Table*, just use *Shift F9*, and that will recalculate only the particular sheet you are on (whereas *F9* alone would recalculate the entire file).

Method #2 is that, after you run a specific what-if analysis, you copy the *Data Table* section—that is, the area between the top row and the left column—and then paste it as values over itself. Move on to the next *Data Table*, run it, and paste values again. Whenever you need to run a pasted table again, quickly re-implement the *Data Table*.

One more limitation: A *Data Table* cannot accommodate more than two variables. So they are at best two-dimensional but never three-dimensional. There are ways to get around this limitation as shown for some simulations in this book.

Simulation Controls

Controls such as spinbuttons and scrollbars are great tools for many kinds of what-if analysis. They quickly reset specific hard-coded values and then show you the impact of such operations.

NOTE: F9 does not recalculate the sheet if you have not clicked on a cell after clicking on a simulation control. So shift the focus from control to sheet!!!

In order to create such controls, you need the *Developer* tab in your menu, which may not be present on your machine. To add it to the ribbon, you do the following, depending on your Excel version. Pre-2010: File | Options | General | Enable the Developer Tab. In 2010 and later: File | Options | Customize Ribbon | in the far right list: ☑ Developer. From now on, the tab can be found in the menu on top.

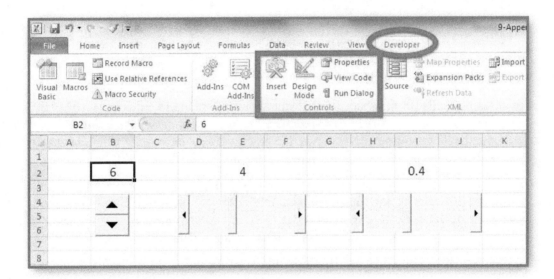

On the above sheet, we placed three controls. You do so by clicking on the *Insert* button and then on one of the options in the *lower* section of the list (Active-X Controls). Draw the control you have chosen on your sheet.

Then click on the *Properties* menu (make sure the control you want to set the properties for is still selected, otherwise select it). Set at least the properties *Min*, *Max*, and *LinkedCell* (that is, the cell where you want the control's value to appear). If you get an error message, just ignore it.

Once you are done, do not forget to click the *Design Mode* button OFF, so you can go back to your sheet!!! Be aware, though, that when you change a control and calculation is not automatic, you need to activate the sheet first before you can hit the "run" keys *Shift F9*.

You probably noticed already that the properties *Min* and *Max* can only hold integers. So if you want to regulate decimals with your control (like in the scroll bar to the far right above), you need an intermediate cell. I happened to choose a *LinkedCell* reference located behind the control (e.g. cell I5). In the cell where you want the decimal number visibly displayed, you need to place a formula like =I5/10 (or I5/100, etc.).

NOTE: It may be wise to protect cells regulated by a control. This is what you do: Select all cells | R-click on any cell | Format Cells | Protection | Unlock. Now you should lock only the specific cells you want to protect. After doing so: Review | Protect Sheet. Only the locked cells are now protected.

Monte Carlo Simulations

Why are they called *Monte Carlo* simulations? The name came up in the 1940s when Los Alamos physicists John von Neumann, Stanislaw Ulam, and Nicholas Metropolis were working on nuclear weapon projects during the Manhattan Project in the Los Alamos National Laboratory. They were unable to solve their problems using conventional, deterministic mathematical methods. Then one of them, Stanisław Ulam, had the idea of using random simulations based on random numbers.

Being secret, the work of von Neumann and Ulam required a code name. Von Neumann chose the name Monte Carlo. The name refers to the Monte Carlo Casino in Monaco where Ulam's uncle often gambled away his money. The Monte Carlo simulations required for the Manhattan Project were severely limited by the computational tools at the time.

But nowadays we have Excel! Monte Carlo simulations are computerized mathematical techniques that allow people to account for risks in quantitative analysis and decision making. Nowadays, the technique is used by professionals in such widely disparate fields as finance, project management, energy, manufacturing, engineering, research and development, insurance, and transportation. Monte Carlo simulation furnishes you as a decision-maker with a range of possible outcomes and the probabilities they will occur for any choice of action.

How do they work? Instead of using a fixed value for input variables, we can model an input variable with a probability distribution and then run the model a number of times and see what impact the randomized variation has on the output. Always run at least 1,000 iterations of Monte Carlo models. This is to ensure that you have a statistical chance of getting sufficient outliers (extreme values) to make the variance analysis meaningful. This is important because as the number of iterations increases, the variance of the average output decreases.

In life most distributions are *normal* in nature indicating that the distribution is bell-shaped around a mean with a known method of describing the variability around this. However, the functions RAND and RANDBETWEEN both have a *uniform* or *equal* distribution—that is, any value between the minimum and maximum values will have the same probability of occurring.

Luckily, we can convert a uniform distribution into a normal distribution with the simple function NORMINV or NORM.INV, which has the following syntax: *=NORM.INV(RAND(), mean, SD)*. For instance, =NORMINV(rand(),100,10) will generate a distribution of random numbers centered on 100 with a spread having a bell shaped curve with a standard deviation of 10. This means that the function will produce a number with a 99.7% probability of being between 70 and 130 and, on average, will have a mean of 100.

This really illustrates how we can tame the uncertainty of the future with ranges and probabilities, but it also shows how impossible it is to be extremely precise. The amazing accomplishment of probability calculus is to put a meaningful numerical value on things we admit we do not know exactly.

Be prepared, though, that a file using several Monte Carlo Simulations with more than 1,000 iterations will save slowly and open slowly because of its numerous calculations. So be patient or change your Excel settings.

X. INDEX

A

ABS 47, 189
Active-X Controls 268
ADDRESS 233
alpha error 42, 46
ampersand (&) 233
Analysis Toolpak 2
ANOVA 38
APR 203
Asian option 218
AVERAGE 175, 249

B

bacterial growth 150
ballistic curve 148
Bayes Theorem 162
Bayesian probability 260
bell curve 34
beta error 46
bi-modal 38
BINOM.INV 36, 54, 188
BINOMDIST 52, 54
Black-Scholes model 220
Boltzmann equation 132
bootstrapping 62
Brownian motion 78

C

CEILING 134
CHAR 18, 233
CHISQ.TEST 66
Chi-squared distribution 66
chromosomes 104
circular reference 8, 248
CODE 18, 233
COMBIN 257
compounding 202
CONCATENATE 233, 265
CONFIDENCE 42
confidence interval 42
confidence level 223
confidence margin 42
confounding factor 246
controls 268
CONVERT 258
CORREL 58
correlated distributions 58
correlation coefficient 58
COUNTA 210
COUNTIF 4
CRITBINOM 54, 188
Ctrl ~ 3, 263
Ctrl Sh Enter 25

D

Data Table 12, 116, 181, 203, 213, 235, 267
DATE 204, 252
dates 252
DAYS 194
degrees of freedom 44
DGET 234
discrete distribution 24
distribution
    binomial 54
    chi-squared 66
    discrete 24
    lognormal 60
    normal 30, 270
    sampling 40
    t-values 44
    uniform 18, 270
DNA sequencing 124
DOLLAR 218
DSUM 172

E

EC50 determination 132
Ehrenfest Urn 80
employee stock 212
epidemic 154
equilibrium 80, 114, 116, 142, 146, 158
evolutionary strategy 158
exchange rate 92
EXP 94
expiration date 221
exponential discounting 216
exponential smoothing 196
extrapolation 130

F

F4-key 263
F9-key 2, 266
fair option value 213

false positives 162
filter 172
FIND 258
fiscal year 182
fitness 118
flocking behavior 28
FLOOR 134
fluctuating APR 202
founder effect 112
FREQUENCY 25, 32
frequency bins 240

G

Galton board 56
game theory 158
Gantt chart 194
GDP growth 178
genetic drift 112
gradients 248
growth rate 180

H

half-life 136
Hardy-Weinberg law 110
Hayes Theorem 162
heterozygote 108, 114, 116
HLOOKUP 160, 176, 177
homeostasis 147
homozygote 108, 116

I

IC50 determination 132
IFERROR 54
INDEX 17, 70, 238
INT 2, 182, 183
integration 100, 102
INTERCEPT 158
interpolation 128
Inter-Quartile Range 64
IPMT 204
ISERROR 54
ISFORMULA 84
ISNUMERIC 199
iteration 8, 29, 148, 166, 249, 270

L

LARGE 62, 236
LEFT 265
LEN 256
linear relationship 130
LinkedCell 268
loan 204
logistic equation 132, 150

logistics 190
LOGNORM.INV 36, 60
lognormal distribution 60
Lotka-Volterra model 152

M

margin of error 51
MATCH 70
matrix elimination 126
MAX 261
MEDIAN 166
Median Absolute Deviation 64
medication 156
Mendelian laws 108
Michaelis-Menten equation 140
MID 256, 265
MINVERSE 126
MMULT 126
MOD 7, 134, 182, 183
molecular clock 122
Monte Carlo simulation 74, 270
MONTH 182, 183
moving averages 196
mutations 122

N

NA 65, 76, 247
Name Manager 237
natural selection 114
navigation 262
nested functions 265
net present value 216
normal distribution 30, 32
NORMDIST 32
NORMINV 32
NOW 17
null-hypothesis 66
numbering 230

O

OFFSET 28, 188, 238
option-pricing 212
OR 3
oscillation 146
outliers 64, 246, 270

P

PEARSON 58
PERCENTILE 92, 96, 164
PERMUT 257
PI function 98
PMT 204
polymorphism 116

INDEX

population pyramid 160
power curve 46
PPMT 204
profit *180*
project delay 194
put option 221
PV function 212

Q

quality control 188
QUOTIENT 134, 230

R

radioactive decay 136, 138
RAND 2, 13, 189, 203, 233
RANDBETWEEN 2, 14, 18, 233
random numbers 69, 233
random sampling 70
random walk 76, 78
Range Name 148, *184*, 236, 238
RANK 70
REPT 68
resource allocation *184*
return on investment 200
RIGHT 265, 266
risk analysis *174*
risk-free 213
ROUND 233
rounding 134
ROUNDUP 182
ROW 17, 177, 237
RSQ 140
R-squared 246, 247

S

sample size 48
sampling 40
    random 70
    unbiased 68
scenarios 176, 177
SERIES 238
sex determination 106
sigmoidal curve 128
sigmoidal equation 132
significant 66, 134
simulation controls 268
SIN 147
SIR model 154
SKEW 60
skewness 38, 60
slope 132
SLOPE 158
SMALL 62

smoothing 196
Solver 132, 140, *184*, 190, 198
solving equations 126
sorting 236
spectrum 144
SQRT 223
standard deviation 40
standard error 40
STDEV 13, 30, 175
stock options 212
stock price 94
stock-price tree 212
strike price 221
Student's t-Test 44
SUMIF 164
SUMPRODUCT 191

T

T.INV.2T 44
test sensitivity 162
test specificity 162
TEXT 230
TODAY 17, 182
traffic 186
TRANSPOSE 75
TREND 128, 130, 151
TRUNC 134
Tukey, John 64
t-value 44
Type I error 46, 52
Type II error 46, 52

U

unbiased sampling 68
uniform distribution 18

V

Value-at-Risk (VaR) 222, 226
VBA 232
VLOOKUP 17, 20, 24

W

weighting 68

Y

YEAR 182, 183

Z

z-value 46, 51

About the Author

Dr. Gerard M. Verschuuren is a human geneticist who also earned a doctorate in the philosophy of science. He studied and worked at universities in Europe and the United States and wrote several biology textbooks in Dutch. During this time, he also used and programmed computer software, including Excel, to simulate scientific problems.

Currently, he is semi-retired and spends most of his time as a writer, speaker, and consultant on the interface of science and computer programming.

His most recent computer-related books/CDs are:

1. From VBA to VSTO (book).
2. Visual Learning Series (CDs).
3. VBScript (CD).
4. Excel 2013 for Scientists (CD).
5. Excel 2013 for Scientists (book).
6. 100 Excel VBA Simulations (book).
7. Excel 2013 VBA (CD).
8. Excel Video Medley (double DVD).

For more info see: http://en.wikipedia.org/wiki/Gerard_Verschuuren

For his YouTube videos on Excel and VBA: http://www.genesispc.com/links.htm#videos

All his books, CDs, and DVD's can be found at http://www.genesispc.com

Part 1: General Techniques

   Chapter 2: The Fill Handle

   Chapter 3: Relative vs. Absolute

   Chapter 4: Range Names

   Chapter 5: Nested Functions

   Part 1 Exercises

Part 2: Data Analysis

   Chapter 7: Subtotals

   Chapter 8: Summary Functions

   Chapter 9: Unique Lists

   Chapter 10: Data Validation

   Chapter 11: Conditional Formatting

   Chapter 12: Filtering Tools

   Chapter 13: Lookups

   Chapter 14: Working with Trends

   Chapter 15: Fixing Numbers

   Chapter 16: Copying Formulas

   Chapter 17: Multi-cell Arrays

   Chapter 18: Single-cell Arrays

   Chapter 19: Date Manipulation

   Chapter 20: Time Manipulation

   Part 2 Exercises

Part 3: Plotting Data

   Chapter 22: A Chart's Data Source

   Chapter 23: Combining Chart Types

   Chapter 24: Graph Locations

Chapter 25: Templates and Defaults
Chapter 26: Axis Scales
Chapter 27: More Axes
Chapter 28: Error Bars
Chapter 29: More Bars
Chapter 30: Line Markers
Chapter 31: Interpolation
Chapter 32: Graph Formulas
Part 3 Exercises

Part 4: Regression and Curve Fitting
Chapter 34: Nonlinear Regression
Chapter 35: Curve Fitting
Chapter 36: Sigmoid Curves
Chapter 37: Predictability
Chapter 38: Correlation
Chapter 39: Multiple Regression
Chapter 40: Reiterations + Matrixes
Chapter 41: Solving Equations
Chapter 42: What-If Controls
Chapter 43: Syntax of Functions
Chapter 44: Worksheet Functions
Part 4 Exercises

Part 5: Statistical Analysis
Chapter 46: Types of Distributions
Chapter 47: Simulating Distributions
Chapter 48: Sampling Techniques
Chapter 49: Test Conditions
Chapter 50: Estimating Means
Chapter 51: Estimating Proportions
Chapter 52: Significant Means
Chapter 53: Significant Proportions
Chapter 54: Significant Frequencies
Chapter 55: Chi-Squared Testing
Chapter 56: Analysis of Variance
Part 5 Exercises

**100 Excel VBA Simulations:
very similar to the ones in this book
but all done with VBA**

http://genesispc.com/tocsimulations100VBA.htm

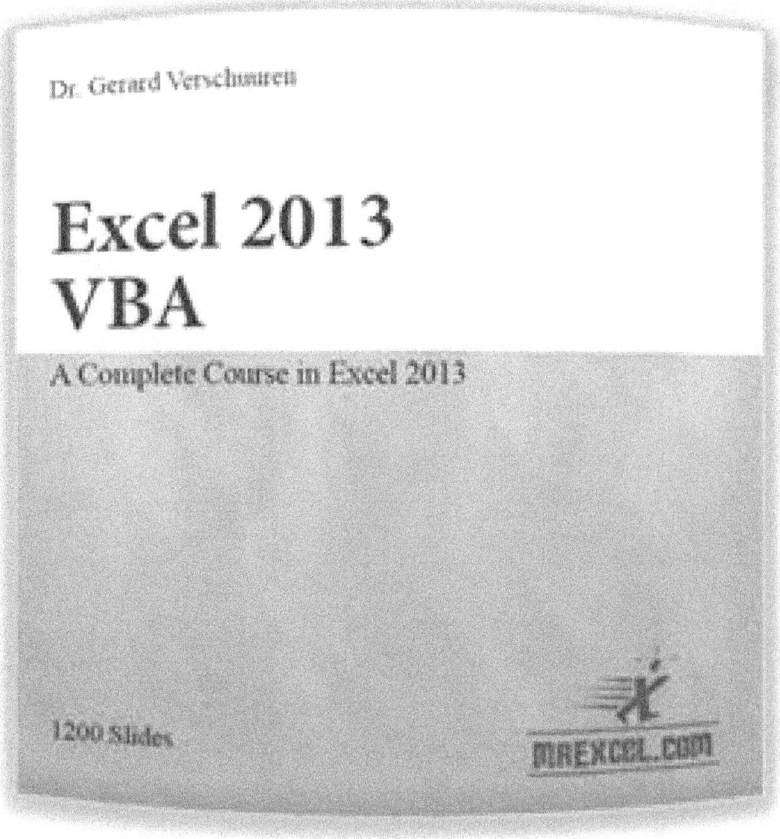

Dr. Gerard Verschuuren

Excel 2013 VBA

A Complete Course in Excel 2013

1200 Slides

MREXCEL.COM

Part 1: Basic Essentials	Part 2: Formulas and Arrays	Part 3: Buttons and Forms
Object Oriented	Dates and Calendars	Importing and Exporting
Recording Macros	The Current-Region	Buttons, Bars, Menus
Branch Statements	WorksheetFunction	Application Events
Interaction	Property Formula	User Forms
Variables (Value Type)	Property FormulaR1C1	Data Entry + Mail Merge
Variables (Object Type)	Custom Functions	Custom Objects (Classes)
Collections	Array Functions	Class Collections
Loop Statements	1D- and 2D-Arrays	Error Handling
Variables as Arguments	Customized Arrays	Distributing VBA code
Pivot Tables and Charts	Variant Arrays	VBA Monitoring VBA

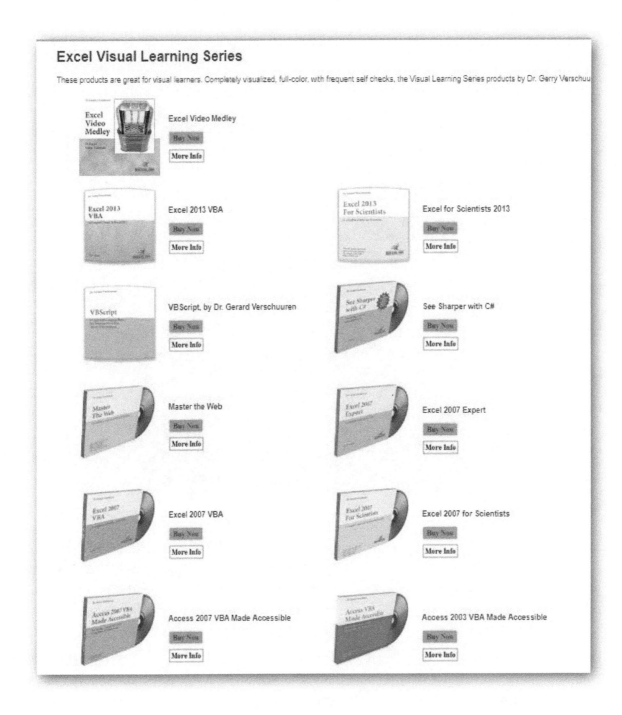

**Explore the Excel Visual Learning Series at
http://www.mrexcel.com/microsoft-office-visual-learning.html.**

All simulations in this book are supported by files that you can download from the following website:
http://www.genesispc.com/download/130XLSimulationsInAction.zip.

CPSIA information can be obtained
at www.ICGtesting.com
Printed in the USA
LVHW062252121118
596923LV00018B/331/P